Learning and Teaching K-8 Mathematics

Janet M. Sharp
Montana State University

Karen Bush Hoiberg
Ames Community School District

PEARSON

Boston • New York • San F
Mexico City • Montreal • Toronto • London
Hong Kong • Singapore • Tokyo • Ca

D1224265

Series Editor: Traci Mueller
Series Editorial Assistant: Janice Hackenberg
Senior Marketing Manager: Krista Groshong
Editorial Production Administrator: Paula Carroll
Editorial Production Service: Omegatype Typography, Inc.
Manufacturing Buyer: Andrew Turso
Composition and Prepress Buyer: Linda Cox
Cover Administrator: Kristina Mose-Libon
Interior Design: Carol Somberg
Electronic Composition and Illustration: Omegatype Typography, Inc.

For related titles and support materials, visit our online catalog at
www.ablongman.com.

Between the time Website information is gathered and published, some sites may
have closed. Also, the transcription of URLs can result in typographical errors.
The publisher would appreciate notification where these errors occur so that
they may be corrected in subsequent editions.

Library of Congress Cataloging-in-Publication Data

Sharp, Janet M.
  Learning and teaching K–8 mathematics / Janet M. Sharp, Karen Bush Hoiberg.
    p.   cm.
  Includes bibliographical references and index.
  ISBN 0-205-38644-X
    1. Mathematics—Study and teaching (Elementary) I. Hoiberg, Karen Bush. II. Title.

 QA135.6.S46 2005
 372.7—dc22

                                                                2004057259

Printed in the United States of America
 10 9 8 7 6 5 4 3 2 1   WEB   09 08 07 06 05 04

Brief Contents

CHAPTER 1 The Basics 1

PART ONE: Geometry and Spatial Thinking

CHAPTER 2 Thinking about the Mathematics of Geometry and Spatial Thinking 18

CHAPTER 3 How We Learn about Geometry and Spatial Thinking 35

CHAPTER 4 Role of the Teacher in Geometry and Spatial Thinking Lessons 56

PART TWO: Whole Numbers and Operation

CHAPTER 5 Thinking about the Mathematics of Number and Operation 76

CHAPTER 6 How We Learn about Number and Operation 92

CHAPTER 7 Role of the Teacher in Number and Operation Lessons 124

PART THREE: Measurement Ideas

CHAPTER 8 Thinking about the Mathematics of Measurement 144

CHAPTER 9 How We Learn about Measurement 156

CHAPTER 10 Role of the Teacher in Measurement Lessons 184

PART FOUR: Rational Numbers and Proportions

CHAPTER 11 Thinking about the Mathematics of Rational Numbers and Proportions 202

CHAPTER 12 How We Learn about Rational Numbers and Proportions 221

CHAPTER 13 Role of the Teacher in Rational Numbers and Proportions Lessons 238

PART FIVE: Data Analysis

CHAPTER 14 Thinking about the Mathematics of Data Analysis 262

CHAPTER 15 How We Learn about Data Analysis 290

CHAPTER 16 Role of the Teacher in Data Analysis Lessons 310

Contents

LIST OF FEATURES   xxi

PREFACE   xxiii

ABOUT THE AUTHORS   xxviii

CHAPTER 1 The Basics   1

Thinking about the Mathematics   2

How We Learn   2

Theories   2
Features   3

Role of the Teacher   3

Algebra Connections   3

Middle School Connections   3

Before We Get Started   4

A Bit about the NCTM and the NCTM Standards   4

TECHNOLOGY CONNECTIONS: **The Basics   5**

Classroom Connections   7

Instruction   7

CLASSROOM CONNECTIONS   Understanding How Children Learn Math   8

Problem Solving   8
The Try it! See it! Teach it! Feature   8
Lesson Plan Components   9

Try it! See it! Teach it!

VideoWorkshop
CD-ROM

Understanding How Children Learn Mathematics   10

CLASSROOM CONNECTIONS   Providing Interactive Instruction   12

Questioning   12

Assessment   13

Curriculum   13

CLASSROOM CONNECTIONS   Using Assessment of Many Forms   14

LET'S REVIEW   15

HOMEWORK   15

SUGGESTED READINGS   15

REFERENCES   15

PART ONE: Geometry and Spatial Thinking

 CHAPTER 2 **Thinking about the Mathematics of Geometry and Spatial Thinking**   18

UNDERSTANDING THE MATHEMATICS: **Mental Ideas versus Physical Models**   18
Pulling Plane Knowledge from Solid Shapes   20
Using Models Effectively   20
Analyzing a Circle   21
A Cylinder or a Circle?   21

CONCENTRATING ON THE CONCEPTS: **Relationships among Shapes**   22
Examples and Nonexamples   22
Rigid Motions   24
Symmetry   25
Practicing Spatial Visualizations   27

   CLASSROOM CONNECTIONS   Finding Symmetry in Nature   28

GRASPING THE PROCEDURES: **How to Build Shapes**   29
Children Describe a Square   29

   MIDDLE SCHOOL CONNECTIONS   The Net of a Solid Shape   32

Drawing a Triangle   32

LET'S REVIEW   34

HOMEWORK   34

SUGGESTED READINGS   34

REFERENCES   34

 CHAPTER 3 **How We Learn about Geometry and Spatial Thinking**   35

UNDERSTANDING RELEVANT LEARNING THEORY: **The van Hiele Theory**   35
Level 0 (Visual)   35
Level 1 (Analysis)   35
Level 2 (Informal Deduction)   37
Level 3 (Formal Deduction)   37
Level 4 (Rigor)   37
Characteristics of the Theory   37
Issues Specific to Spatial Visualization   42

USING RELEVANT PATTERNS: **Extending Pattern Starters   43**

Repeating versus Growing   43
Recognizing Deep Structure   44

USING TEACHING AIDS APPROPRIATELY: **Concrete, Pictorial, Symbolic   45**

Concrete Representations   45
Pictorial Representations   46
Symbolic Representations   46
Concrete Materials versus Level 0 Thinking   46
Concrete Together with Symbolic and Pictorial Together with Symbolic   47

Types of Concrete Materials   47

Cubes   47
Pattern Blocks   47

MIDDLE SCHOOL CONNECTIONS   Manipulatives Are (Not) for Babies   48

Tangrams   48
Assessment and the Use of Materials   48

CULTURAL CONNECTIONS   Creating a Mosaic   49

LITERATURE CONNECTIONS   Developing Mathematical Imagery   53

LET'S REVIEW   54

HOMEWORK   54

SUGGESTED READINGS   54

REFERENCES   54

CHAPTER 4 **Role of the Teacher in Geometry and Spatial Thinking Lessons**   56

ANALYZING ONE OF THE TEACHING MODELS: **Discussion   56**

TECHNOLOGY CONNECTIONS   Using Digital Technologies as Geometry Discussion Platforms   57

HIGHLIGHTS OF A LESSON PLAN COMPONENT:
Creating Good Questions   58

SUGGESTIONS FOR ESTABLISHING DISCOURSE: **The Importance of Knowing the Mathematics   58**

Mrs. Hawthorne's Rhombus Lesson   59
Ms. Steffen's Rectangle Lesson   60
Comparing Quadrilaterals   60

MIDDLE SCHOOL CONNECTIONS   Know the Math Well Enough to Ask Questions   61

The Next Question   61

ASSESSMENT: **Making an Instructional Decision**   **61**

CLASSROOM CONNECTIONS   Using the van Hiele Theory to Guide Instruction   63

CLASSROOM CONNECTIONS   Thinking Carefully about Assessment   63

Try it! See it! Teach it!

Using the van Hiele Theory to Guide Instruction   64

IDEAS FOR STRUCTURING CLASS TIME: **Providing Reflection Time**   **66**
Worthwhile Tasks   66
Reflection   66

ADVICE FOR PROFESSIONAL DEVELOPMENT: **Get to Know the Mathematics in Different Ways**   **66**

ALGEBRA CONNECTIONS   Geometry and Spatial Thinking   67

A Big Idea: Geometric Representations in Algebra   67
Algebraic Ideas to Explore: Symmetry and Rigid Motions   68
Variable as a Functional Role   68
K–8 Algebra Connections: The Concept of Variable   69

LET'S REVIEW   70

HOMEWORK   71

SUGGESTED READINGS   71

REFERENCES   71

Summing Up   **Geometry and Spatial Thinking**   **72**

PART TWO: Whole Numbers and Operation

CHAPTER 5 **Thinking about the Mathematics of Number and Operation** 76

UNDERSTANDING THE MATHEMATICS: **Number and Operation 76**
Number Is an Amount 76
Numerals Are Symbols 76
Numbers Are Ordered 77
Addition 77
Subtraction 77
Multiplication 77
Division 78

CONCENTRATING ON CONCEPTS: **Coordinating Counting, Operation, and Number Sense 79**
Counting 79
Operation 81
Number Sense 81

GRASPING THE PROCEDURES: **Building Algorithms from Concepts 82**
Addition 82
Subtraction 83
Multiplication 84
Division 86

MIDDLE SCHOOL CONNECTIONS Algorithms That Can Be Easily Generalized 88

MIDDLE SCHOOL CONNECTIONS Just Show Me How to Do It 90

LET'S REVIEW 90

HOMEWORK 90

SUGGESTED READINGS 91

REFERENCES 91

CHAPTER 6 **How We Learn about Number and Operation** 92

UNDERSTANDING RELEVANT LEARNING THEORY: **Number Is a Mental Relationship 93**
Number Ideas 93
Level 1 93
Level 2 93
Level 3 93
Knowing Number Words 93
Growth Happens in Chunks 94

Principles of Teaching Number   94
Principle I (Relationships)   94
Principle 2 (Quantification)   94

CLASSROOM CONNECTIONS Finding Number Relationships   95

Try it! See it! Teach it!

Understanding Number Relationships   96

Principle 3 (Social Interaction)   98
Number Sense   98

UNDERSTANDING RELEVANT LEARNING THEORY:
Procedures Build from Solving Problems   99

Addition   99
Classifying Addition Problems   101
Subtraction   102
Classifying Subtraction Strategies   104
Learning Addition and Subtraction   104
Multiplication   105

MIDDLE SCHOOL CONNECTIONS Add the Opposite   106

Division   107

USING RELEVANT PATTERNS: **Skip-Counting Lays a Foundation   107**

Calendar as Context   108
Concrete Representations   109
Number Line   III
Connecting Skip-Counting to Operations   III

USING RELEVANT PATTERNS: **Figurate Numbers   112**

MIDDLE SCHOOL CONNECTIONS Fact Families for Integers   113

CULTURAL CONNECTIONS Numeration Systems and Mexican Subtraction   114

LITERATURE CONNECTIONS Comparing Counting Books to Literary Works   117

USING TEACHING AIDS APPROPRIATELY: **Discrete versus Continuous
Materials   118**

Concrete Representations   118
Pictorial Representations   118

MIDDLE SCHOOL CONNECTIONS Encounters with Integers   119

Types of Concrete Materials   119

Base-Ten Blocks   119
Cuisenaire Rods   120
Chips   120

LET'S REVIEW   121

HOMEWORK   121

SUGGESTED READINGS   122

REFERENCES   122

CHAPTER 7 **Role of the Teacher in Number and Operation Lessons** 124

ANALYZING ONE OF THE TEACHING MODELS: **Concept Attainment** 124
Deductive 125
Inductive 125

HIGHLIGHTS OF A LESSON PLAN COMPONENT: **Match Evaluation with Objective** 125

ASSESSMENT: **Evaluating Achievement (Concepts versus Procedures)** 126

CLASSROOM CONNECTIONS Dealing with Incorrect Comments 126

CLASSROOM CONNECTIONS Orchestrating the Sharing of Strategies 127

SUGGESTIONS FOR ESTABLISHING DISCOURSE: **Listening to Students to Guide Their Thinking** 127

Try it! See it! Teach it!

Orchestrating Sharing Strategies 128

TECHNOLOGY CONNECTIONS Communication Tools 130

IDEAS FOR STRUCTURING CLASS TIME: **Using Daily Routines for Number Knowledge** 131

ADVICE FOR PROFESSIONAL DEVELOPMENT: **Compare across Grade Levels** 131

MIDDLE SCHOOL CONNECTIONS Daily Routines of Middle Graders 132

CLASSROOM CONNECTIONS Reacting to CGI for the First Time 132

ALGEBRA CONNECTIONS Number and Operation 133
A Big Idea: Properties, Formulas, and Equivalence 133
Properties 133
Algebraic Ideas for You to Explore: Patterns 133
Variable as Functional 136
Variable as a Generalization 136
Variable as Standing for an Unknown to be Found 136
K–8 Algebra Connections: Arithmetic to Algebra 137

LET'S REVIEW 137

HOMEWORK 138

SUGGESTED READINGS 138

REFERENCES 139

Summing Up **Whole Numbers and Operation** 140

PART THREE: Measurement Ideas

CHAPTER 8 **Thinking about the Mathematics of Measurement**   144

UNDERSTANDING THE MATHEMATICS: **Geometry and Number**   144
Continuous   145
Standard Unit   145

CONCENTRATING ON THE CONCEPTS: **It Begins with the Idea of "Size"**   147
Nonstandard Units   147
Size, Comparing, and Conservation   148
Size Is Summative   148
Standard Unit   148
Iteration of Units   150
Coverage   150
Tiling   151
Part-Whole   151
Coordinating Concepts   151

CLASSROOM CONNECTIONS Using a Magnified Inch   152

GRASPING THE PROCEDURES: **How to Measure Shapes**   152
The Zero (Origin)   152
Counting Spaces   153
Describing a Part   153
Formulas   154

LET'S REVIEW   154

HOMEWORK   155

SUGGESTED READINGS   155

REFERENCES   155

CHAPTER 9 **How We Learn about Measurement**   156

Understanding Relevant Learning Theory   156
Comparing and Ordering   156
Transitivity   156
Mixing Units   157
Visualizing   158

MIDDLE SCHOOL CONNECTIONS Measurements from the Real World   158

Using van Hiele   159
Using the Geoboard   159
Phases of Learning   159

Phase 1: Inquiry/Information 161
Phase 2: Directed Orientation 162
Phase 3: Explication 162
Phase 4: Free Orientation 162
Phase 5: Integration 163
Ms. Hawthorne Measures a Bus 163
Finding Angle Measure 163
Using Measuring Devices 164

USING RELEVANT PATTERNS: **Formulas, Skip-Counting, and Similarity 166**
Developing General Formulas 166
Using Skip-Counting 166
Generalizing Ratios of Similar Shapes 168

CULTURAL CONNECTIONS Measuring Time and Visualizing Congruence 170

LITERATURE CONNECTIONS Illustrating Cultures and Solving Problems 177

USING TEACHING AIDS APPROPRIATELY: **Measuring Devices and Discrete Manipulatives 177**

CLASSROOM CONNECTIONS Using Literature to Pose Different Problems 178

CLASSROOM CONNECTIONS Using Literature That Already Describes Problems 179

Types of Concrete Materials 179
Square Tiles and Cubes 179
Geoboards 181

LET'S REVIEW 181

HOMEWORK 181

SUGGESTED READINGS 182

REFERENCES 182

CHAPTER 10 **Role of the Teacher in Measurement Lessons** 184

ANALYZING ONE OF THE TEACHING MODELS: **Presentation and Partnered Work 184**

MIDDLE SCHOOL CONNECTIONS Writing Their Own Problems 185

HIGHLIGHTS OF A LESSON PLAN COMPONENT: **Acceleration versus Enrichment in Content Differentiation 185**
Tiered Assignments 186
Compacted Curriculum 186
Modifying Roles 186
Guided Exploration 186

CLASSROOM CONNECTIONS Dealing with High-Ability Students 187

SUGGESTIONS FOR ESTABLISHING DISCOURSE: **Importance of Sharing Thinking** 187

CLASSROOM CONNECTIONS Enriching a Gifted Student's Learning 188

TECHNOLOGY CONNECTIONS Presenting Measurement Projects 190

CLASSROOM CONNECTIONS Sharing a Good Plan for Solving a Problem 191

IDEAS FOR STRUCTURING CLASS TIME: **Student Presentations and Assessment of the Presentation** 191

ADVICE FOR PROFESSIONAL DEVELOPMENT: **Any Activity You Choose Should Match Your District Goals** 191

Try it! See it! Teach it!

Sharing a Good Plan   192

MIDDLE SCHOOL CONNECTIONS Have Fun and Create Wonder 194

ALGEBRA CONNECTIONS Measurement 194

A Big Idea: Making Generalizations about Measurements 194
Algebraic Ideas for You to Explore: The Pythagorean Theorem 194
Variable as a Generalization and an Unknown 196
K–8 Algebra Connections: Relating the Area of a Triangle to Other Shapes 196

LET'S REVIEW 196

HOMEWORK 197

SUGGESTED READINGS 197

REFERENCES 197

Summing Up **Measurement Ideas**   198

PART FOUR: Rational Numbers and Proportions

CHAPTER 11 **Thinking about the Mathematics of Rational Numbers and Proportions** 202

UNDERSTANDING THE MATHEMATICS: **What Exactly Are Rational Numbers?** 202

CONCENTRATING ON THE CONCEPTS: **Connections among Rational Number Genres** 205

Sharing 205
Congruent Parts 205
Equivalent Fractions 206
Contextualized Situations 206
The Whole Unit 207

CLASSROOM CONNECTIONS Illuminating Fraction Concepts 211

GRASPING THE PROCEDURES: **How to Operate and Move between Genres** 212

Whole Number Knowledge 212
Addition and Subtraction 212
Selecting Contexts 213
Multiplication 215
Division 215
Finding Equivalent Fractions 217
Revisiting Procedures 218

LET'S REVIEW 219

HOMEWORK 219

SUGGESTED READINGS 220

REFERENCES 220

CHAPTER 12 **How We Learn about Rational Numbers and Proportions** 221

Understanding Relevant Learning Theory 221

Personal Knowledge 221
Representations and Intuition 222
Technical Symbols 222
Building Knowledge 222
Designing Activities 223
Begin with Contexts 223
Share Strategies 224
Using Tools 225

Building Knowledge   225
Partitioning Whole Units   226
Ms. Hawthorne Shares Cookies   226
Revisiting Ms. Hawthorne   226

USING RELEVANT PATTERNS: **Skip-Counting in Ratio Tables**   228

CULTURAL CONNECTIONS Using and Making Unexpected Ratios   228

USING TEACHING AIDS APPROPRIATELY: **Discrete versus Continuous**   231

Continuous   231
Discrete   232
Role of Context   232

Types of Concrete Materials   232

Fraction Circles 232
Paper Folding   233
Chips   233
Base-Ten Blocks   233
Using Metrics   234

LITERATURE CONNECTIONS Letting Characters Physically Illustrate Proportions   234

LET'S REVIEW   235

HOMEWORK   235

SUGGESTED READINGS   235

REFERENCES   236

CHAPTER 13 **Role of the Teacher in Rational Numbers and Proportions Lessons**   238

ANALYZING ONE OF THE TEACHING MODELS:
Problem Solving (Discovery)   238

Ms. Steffen's Experiment   238
Asking Good Questions   240
Solving Division Problems   241

TECHNOLOGY CONNECTIONS Using Digital Images to Make Mathematics Come Alive   244

MIDDLE SCHOOL CONNECTIONS Problem Solving Can Ground Algorithms   245

ASSESSMENT: **To Monitor Progress toward a Goal**   246

MIDDLE SCHOOL CONNECTIONS Select Homework Thoughtfully   246

CLASSROOM CONNECTIONS Assessing Problem Solutions with a Rubric   247

VideoWorkshop CD-ROM

Try it! See it! Teach it!

Grading Problem Solutions 248

HIGHLIGHTS OF A LESSON PLAN COMPONENT: **Importance of Context (Lesson Setup)** 250

SUGGESTIONS FOR DISCUSSION: **Listening for Benchmark Numbers $(0, \frac{1}{2}, 1)$** 251

IDEAS FOR STRUCTURING CLASS TIME: **To Create Shared, Rich Experiences Using Proportions** 252

MIDDLE SCHOOL CONNECTIONS Appropriate Tasks Build Proportional Thinking 253

ADVICE FOR PROFESSIONAL DEVELOPMENT: **Fraction Scavenger Hunt** 253

ALGEBRA CONNECTIONS Rational Numbers and Proportional Thinking 254

A Big Idea: Proportional Thinking 254
Algebraic Ideas for You to Explore: Proportional Thinking 254
K–8 Algebra Connections: Recognizing General Strategies—The Case of Proportions 254

LET'S REVIEW 255

HOMEWORK 256

SUGGESTED READINGS 257

REFERENCES 257

Summing Up **Rational Numbers and Proportions** 258

PART FIVE: Data Analysis

CHAPTER 14   **Thinking about the Mathematics of Data Analysis**   262

UNDERSTANDING THE MATHEMATICS: **Statistics and Probability**   262

Statistics   262
Sample versus Population   263
General Statements   263
Types of Data   263
Averages   263
Basic Variance   264
Prediction versus Description   264

CLASSROOM CONNECTIONS   Doing Data Analysis with Physical Materials   265

Prediction versus Inference   265

Try it! See it! Teach it!

Making Statistics Physically

266

CONCENTRATING ON THE CONCEPTS:
What Generalizations Really Mean   269

Statistics   269
Data   269
Sample   269
Generalization   269
The Need for Probability   271
Probability   272
Experimental Probability   272
Theoretical Probability   273
Likelihood   273

GRASPING THE PROCEDURES: **Organizing Data and Finding Probabilities**   275

Data Organization   275
Making Picture Representations   275

CLASSROOM CONNECTIONS Teaching Students to Move from Data to Representations of Data   278

Ms. Hawthorne's Weather Data   279

CLASSROOM CONNECTIONS Creating Picture Graphs with Physical Objects   281

Probability   281

Try it! See it! Teach it!

Organizing Messy Data 282

Fairness 284
Expected Value 285
Odds 285

LET'S REVIEW 288

HOMEWORK 288

SUGGESTED READINGS 288

REFERENCES 288

CHAPTER 15 **How We Learn about Data Analysis** 290

UNDERSTANDING RELEVANT LEARNING FRAMEWORKS: **Friel, Curcio, and Bright (Statistics), and Jones, Langrall, Thornton, and Mogill (Probability)** 290
Underlying Facts 290
The Importance of Student-Generated Data 291
Statistics Framework 291
Organizing Concepts 292
Making Interpretations Based on a Sample 293
Probability Framework 293
Recognizing Development through Likelihood 294
Recognizing Development through Randomness 295
Comparing Probabilities 295
Recognizing Development through Sampling 295
Confronting Enigmas 296

CLASSROOM CONNECTIONS Guiding Students' Uses of Vocabulary 296

USING RELEVANT PATTERNS: **Organized Counting (Pascal's Triangle)** 297

CULTURAL CONNECTIONS Organizing Data and Simulating Game Situations 297

LITERATURE CONNECTIONS Using Stories about Chance and Organized Counting 304

USING TEACHING AIDS APPROPRIATELY: **Using Student-Generated Data** 306

Types of Concrete Materials 306
Two-Color Counters 306
Dice 307
Spinners 307

LET'S REVIEW 307

HOMEWORK 308

SUGGESTED READINGS   308

REFERENCES   308

CHAPTER 16 **Role of the Teacher in Data Analysis Lessons**   310

ANALYZING THE TEACHING MODELS: **Presentation, Problem Solving, Partnered Learning, Discussion, and Concept Attainment**   310

TECHNOLOGY CONNECTIONS The Power of the Spreadsheet   311

HIGHLIGHTS OF A LESSON PLAN COMPONENT: **Matching Materials to Objective**   312

Creating the Situation   312
Selecting Supportive Materials   312
Guiding the Data Analysis   313

ASSESSMENT: **To Guide Instructional Decisions**   314

SUGGESTIONS FOR ESTABLISHING DISCOURSE: **Using Student Comments to Analyze Teaching**   314

IDEAS FOR STRUCTURING CLASS TIME: **To Defend Viewpoints**   316

CLASSROOM CONNECTIONS Using Sports to Create Interest   316

MIDDLE SCHOOL CONNECTIONS Wise Consumers of Statistical Knowledge   317

Advice for Professional Development   318

ALGEBRA CONNECTIONS Data Analysis   318

A Big Idea: Using Models to Represent Quantitative Relationships   318
Algebraic Ideas for You to Explore: Linear Regression   318

MIDDLE SCHOOL CONNECTIONS Algebra as Social Justice   320

Algebra in Unusual Places   321
K–8 Algebra Connections: One Grain of Rice   321

LET'S REVIEW   322

HOMEWORK   322

SUGGESTED READINGS   322

REFERENCES   323

Summing Up   **Data Analysis**   324

APPENDIX   ANSWERS TO PART-CLOSING ACTIVITIES   326

INDEX   331

List of *Features*

ACTIVITIES

1.1 Danny Dickson's Problem 7
I.1 Decorative Tiles 17
2.1 Pulling 2-D Ideas from a 3-D Model 19
2.2 Inspiration 23
2.3 The Topological Alphabet! 30
2.4 Building Polyhedra 33
3.1 Proud Goose 40
3.2 Basic Patterns 44
3.3 Square 50
3.4 Your Culture and Mathematics 51
3.5 Building Perspectives 53
4.1 What Could Be the Shape? 62
4.2 Des Cartes 69
4.3 Rigid Motions and Symmetry in Algebra 70
II.1 The Notorious Locker Problem 77
5.1 Thinking about 1 Million 80
5.2 In How Many Ways Can You Score 42 Points? 81
5.3 Picturing Addition 83
5.4 Picturing Subtraction 84
5.5 Picturing Multiplication 87
5.6 Picturing Division 89
6.1 Adding Four Numbers 98
6.2 Symbolizing Someone Else's Thinking 100
6.3 Writing Word Problems 105
6.4 Writing More Word Problems 108
6.5 Describe the Pattern in Each Month 110
6.6 Color in the Numbers of These Patterns 111
6.7 Planning a Volleyball Tournament 113
7.1 Draw in the Next Block Pile 134
III.1 Generalize the Area for a Trapezoid 143
8.1 Tool List 146
8.2 Subdividing a Region 149
9.1 Applying van Hiele 160
9.2 Understanding van Hiele on the Geoboard 161
9.3 Finding Angle Measurements without a Protractor 164
9.4 Finding More Angle Measures 165
9.5 Something More about Triangular Numbers 167
9.6 Making Photocopies 169
9.7 Understanding Hopi Moon Cycles 172
9.8 Louise's Quilt Block 175
9.9 Using Discrete Materials to Measure 180
10.1 Making Triangles 195
IV.1 Teacher Ratios 201
11.1 Inspiration 204
11.2 Tracy's Dog 207
11.3 Get Three in a Row! 208
11.4 Sugar Cookies 214
12.1 The New Park 224
12.2 Cutting Pizzas 227

12.3 Baseball Innings Pitched 230
12.4 Tangrams for Fractions 232
13.1 Division Problems to Consider 242
13.2 Evaluating Contexts 250
13.3 Pulling Taffy 254
V.1 Organizing Data with a Venn Diagram 261
14.1 Taking a Survey of Your Classmates 264
14.2 Probability with a Spinner 268
14.3 Statistics Concepts 270
14.4 Two-Color Counter (Coin) 274
14.5 Organizing Data 276
14.6 Finding the Mean 276
14.7 Using Technology to Organize Data 278
14.8 Calculating with Spinner Games 284
14.9 How to Count Outcomes 286
14.10 Guessing the Second 287
15.1 Building Pascal's Triangle 298
15.2 A Two-Week Almanac 301
15.3 Play the Cheyenne Women's Dice Game 302
15.4 The Weather in Chewandswallow 304
15.5 *One Grain of Rice* Calendar 305
16.1 Selecting Materials for a Lesson 313
16.2 Checking the Syllable Count on Chosen Names 319
16.3 Running a Regression to Find a Line of Fit 321

ALGEBRA CONNECTIONS

Geometry and Spatial Thinking 67
Number and Operation 133
Measurement 194
Rational Numbers and Proportional Thinking 254
Data Analysis 318

CLASSROOM CONNECTIONS

Understanding How Children Learn Math 7
Providing Interactive Instruction 12
Using Assessment of Many Forms 14
Finding Symmetry in Nature 28
Using the van Hiele Theory to Guide Instruction 63
Thinking Carefully about Assessment 63
Finding Number Relationships 95
Dealing with Incorrect Comments 126
Orchestrating the Sharing of Strategies 127
Reacting to CGI for the First Time 132
Using a Magnified Inch 152
Using Literature to Pose Different Problems 178
Using Literature That Already Describes Problems 179
Dealing with High-Ability Students 187
Enriching a Gifted Student's Learning 188
Sharing a Good Plan for Solving a Problem 191
Illuminating Fraction Concepts 211

Assessing Problem Solutions Using a Rubric   247
Doing Data Analysis with Physical Methods   265
Teaching Students to Move from Data to Representations
   of Data   278
Creating Picture Graphs with Physical Objects   281
Guiding Students' Uses of Vocabulary   296
Using Sports to Create Interest   316

CULTURAL CONNECTIONS

Creating a Mosaic   49
Numeration Systems and Mexican Subtraction   114
Measuring Time and Visualizing Congruence   170
Using and Making Unexpected Ratios   228
Organizing Data and Simulating Game Situations   297

LITERATURE CONNECTIONS

Developing Mathematical Imagery   53
Comparing Counting Books to Literary Works   117
Illustrating Cultures and Solving Problems   177
Letting Characters Physically Illustrate Proportions   234
Using Stories about Chance and Organized
   Counting   304

MIDDLE SCHOOL CONNECTIONS

The Net of a Solid Shape   32
Manipulatives Are (Not) for Babies   48
Know the Math Well Enough to Ask Questions   61
Algorithms That Can Be Easily Generalized   88
Just Show Me How to Do It   90
Add the Opposite   106
Fact Families for Integers   113

Encountering with Integers   119
Daily Routines of Middle Graders   132
Measurements from the Real World   158
Writing Their Own Problems   185
Have Fun Along with Them and Create Wonder   194
Problem Solving Can Ground Algorithms   245
Select Homework Thoughtfully   246
Appropriate Tasks Build Proportional Thinking   253
Wise Consumers of Statistical Knowledge   317
Algebra as Social Justice   320

TECHNOLOGY CONNECTIONS

Using Digital Technologies as Geometry Discussion
   Platforms   57
Communication Tools   130
Presenting Measurement Projects   190
Using Digital Images to Make Mathematics Come
   Alive   244
The Power of the Spreadsheet   311

Try it! See it! Teach it!

Understanding How Children Learn Mathematics   10
Using the van Hiele Theory to Guide Instruction   64
Understanding Number Relationships   96
Orchestrating Sharing Strategies   128
Sharing a Good Plan   192
Grading Problem Solutions   248
Making Statistics Physically   266
Organizing Messy Data   282

Preface

In a Nutshell

We have developed a book that institutes an active view of learning and teaching mathematics. We ask future and practicing teachers to complete mathematical activities while studying related learning theories. We believe that the book provides the impetus to discuss and analyze mathematical thinking through the lenses of various learning theories. Analysis is further supported or refuted with children's voices from K–8 classrooms. This is all done for the express purpose of developing abilities to encourage children's mathematical thinking.

There are several good K–8 mathematics methods textbooks on the market today. So why does the market need a new one? After teaching the elementary mathematics methods course for only a few years, I began to recognize the need to stretch my students, both future and practicing teachers, in ways that veered dramatically from presentations in existing books. As I observed my students teaching, I noticed disengaged children. They weren't being asked to wonder about the math, only to regurgitate it. Many children did not appear involved, and no probing questions were being asked. My students seemed to expect children to either read through or listen to a few examples of mathematical ideas, perhaps watch the teacher demonstrate a procedure, and then somehow know the mathematics as a result. It appeared that no matter what happened in methods class, my students still taught as they remembered being taught when they were elementary and high school students. I felt partly responsible.

This emerging revelation coincided with the 1991 release of *Professional Standards for Teaching Mathematics* by the National Council of Teachers of Mathematics (NCTM). With a mixture of concern and determination to change the way I taught my undergraduate course, the *Standards* planted a seed and provided the vision I needed. But it was not until an enlightening experience with coauthor and master teacher Karen Bush Hoiberg that I finally knew what I wanted to do. For two weeks, we copresented a workshop for practicing K–8 mathematics teachers with several other master teachers. At the conclusion of the first day, one of the participating teachers, Ms. Hawthorne, stayed afterward and talked with us. Ms. Hawthorne was delighted: "I have never thought about mathematics the way you are teaching us. New things are coming together for me. I had no idea of the relationship between the formulas for the area of a triangle and rectangle and the formula for the area of a trapezoid. But I'm really worried now. I *know* this is the best way to teach, but I don't think I can do it. I can't learn all the math I need in a two-week workshop." She told us she wished that during her experiences as a college student, she had been asked to actually *do* mathematics that was new and interesting and then think about what she had done in terms of how it should be taught and how children think.

Our book accomplishes the goal of understanding children's thinking in two ways. First, we use mathematics activities to engage readers in metacognition to clarify their knowledge of learning theories. Second, we provide conversations or comments made by K–8 students as illustrations of each presented learning theory. By asking future and practicing teachers to *do* mathematics while looking at theory, the book matches our teaching philosophies and presumably future and practicing teachers' learning needs. This type of pedagogical preparation stretches thinking and helps to rearrange mathematical knowledge. By learning new mathematics along with theory, it becomes possible to tear apart thinking on the way toward understanding the mathematics from the points of view of both student and teacher.

We also believe that teachers need some knowledge of learning theory to make informed teaching decisions in situations with children. Therefore, we have introduced theories for each mathematical content area that seemed to match our teaching experiences. To do this, we had to carefully choose what we would include and what we would exclude. We recognize that there are several theorists for any given area. Our choices resonated with Karen's 20-plus years of experiences in the classroom and Janet's awareness of each theory's acceptance in the mathematics education community.

The Plan of the Book

This text is divided into five content-based parts. Each part begins with a problem that introduces the big ideas of that section. The parts are divided into chapters organized around four general themes: thinking about the mathematics, learning theories, the role of the teacher, and algebraic connections. Chapter 1 introduces the importance of assessment, an idea that is integrated throughout every chapter.

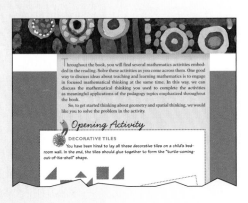

Throughout the book, you will find several mathematics activities embedded in the reading. Solve these activities as you come across them. One good way to discuss ideas about teaching and learning mathematics is to engage in focused mathematical thinking at the same time. In this way, we can discuss the mathematical thinking you used to complete the activities as meaningful applications of the pedagogy topics emphasized throughout the book.

So, to get started thinking about geometry and spatial thinking, we would like you to solve the problem in the box.

Opening Activity

DECORATIVE TILES
You have been hired to lay all these decorative tiles on a child's bedroom wall. In the end, the tiles should glue together to form the "turtle-coming-out-of-its-shell" shape.

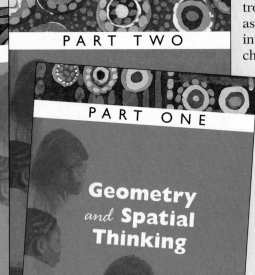

Parts Organized by Content Area

Parts One through Five of the text reflect the five major **NCTM content standards:** number and operations, algebra, geometry, measurement, and data analysis and probability. We begin with geometry first because young learners are better able to make sense of physical geometric objects before understanding number concepts.

Part One	Geometry and Spatial Thinking
Part Two	Whole Numbers and Operation
Part Three	Measurement Ideas
Part Four	Rational Numbers and Proportions
Part Five	Data Analysis

We believe that teachers can foster algebraic thinking in all mathematical areas and across all ages. Therefore, algebra is given special attention, appearing in each of the five parts of the text.

NCTM Principles and Standards for Teaching Mathematics

Not only is the book organized around the major content threads put forth by the **NCTM standards,** but the recurring chapter structure also reflects the process standards of problem solving, reasoning and proof, connections, communication, and representation. Throughout the book, margin icons remind you to note content with specific relevance to the six major **NCTM principles:** assessment, equity, technology, learning, teaching, and curriculum. These icons highlight the connections between the NCTM principles and the content as it appears in each chapter.

Do the Math!

Learning to teach math requires learning math the way you want to teach it. Rather than just including activities for the young learner, several activities are embedded in each chapter for adult learners to pause and complete to ensure that they are grasping the mathematics. When mentioned in running text, the activity is highlighted for quick identification and to signal readers to complete the activity before continuing the text. Completing these activities provides future teachers with invaluable insight into how children think about and learn math, thereby equipping them with the skills to better make sound instructional decisions.

Usable Teaching Ideas for K–8 Students

Coauthor Karen, a practicing, presidential award–winning elementary teacher, provides a multitude of practical applications and real-world examples to give students the opportunity to connect chapter concepts with their own knowledge of teaching in the classroom. We also discuss ways in which you might use teaching aids, such as manipulatives. Throughout this book, we emphasize that manipulatives are a model of mathematics, not a model of students' thinking, and that manipulatives do not in and of themselves teach.

Special Text Features

"Understanding Children's Mathematical Thinking" VideoWorkshop CD-ROM

This technology accompaniment provides you with several short video segments featuring Karen Hoiberg teaching mathematics lessons to young children, ages four to seven, and to her own regular fifth grade classroom.

Video Clip 1 *(time length 5:57)*

Evelyn explains her answer.

Try it! See it! Teach it!

These special two-page sections summarize the context of each video segment and include the student problem featured in the video, as well as authentic student work, author commentary, and questions and observations designed to help you connect the content of each chapter to understanding children's mathematical thinking.

Classroom Connections

In this feature, inserted at various points in each chapter, Karen speaks frankly about how some of the ideas from the chapter connect to actual classroom teaching. Narrative and dialogue examples model the concepts presented, providing immediate applicability to the classroom.

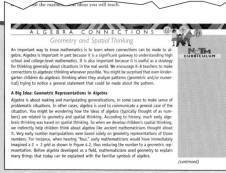

Algebra Connections

The *NCTM Standards* for school mathematics state "a strong foundation in algebra should be in place by the end of eighth grade." As such, we encourage K–8 teachers to make connections to algebraic thinking whenever possible. Special sections devoted to algebra appear at the end of every part, making connections between the big ideas from algebra and how they relate to each of the major content areas.

Middle School Connections

At various points in the text, we delve into the developmental characteristics, complex learning needs, and specific mathematics content unique to middle school students.

Technology Connections

Guest authored by Ann Thompson, a leader in the use of technology in teacher education, these special sections emphasize general approaches to using technology as a tool to focus on improving learners' understanding of mathematics.

Literature Connections

Appearing in each of the "How We Learn About" chapters within each part, this feature provides teachers the means to make critical connections between mathematics and children's literature to aid in lesson planning

Cultural Connections

Also within the "How We Learn About" chapters, we have taken the opportunity to recognize the often overlooked or undervalued impact that various cultures have had on mathematics and the implications for teaching.

Chapter Closing Pedagogy

At the end of the chapter, we provide "Let's Review" summaries, homework problems and activities for students to try outside of class, as well as suggested readings and references.

Acknowledgments

Our first thank you must be given to our husbands, Eric Hoiberg and Tracy Chandler. They sat in the background during phone calls, gave up the computer on Saturdays, and never questioned the "one more thing" we had to discuss. Instead, they listened and were not concerned that the book took the front and center stages of our leisure time. Second, we thank our parents, Jerry and Asta Bush and Wayne and Rosalie Sharp. They were our first, best teachers. Without their expert tutelage during our wonder years and their encouragement and support during the writing of the book, we believe we would not have undertaken the project. Karen thanks her sisters, Bonnie and Jane, both teachers, who listened to and tested ideas with their students. Karen's first students were her sons, Steve, Fred, and Andrew, who helped her to become the teacher she is today.

Other thanks go to Karen's father-in-law, Otto Hoiberg, who provided ongoing encouragement, always asking how the book was coming along, as well as her daughters-in-law Kerry and Carol. Janet's friend and confidant, Sally Beisser, kept Janet's professional life balanced between the book and other work while reminding her to keep Tracy first, no matter the cost.

Our next acknowledgment goes to each other! Whether it was unscheduled visits to Karen's fifth grade class or team-teaching Janet's college students, we supported each others' efforts to make the book as realistic and accessible as possible. Together, we found meaningful ways to challenge all of our students. We also need to acknowledge all of our students, who through the years have provided the impetus for the book in the first place. Special thanks and love go to Karen's very favorite students, better known as her grandchildren, Anna, Paige, Jack, Emma, Sam, and Charlie. In particular, we thank Karen's 2002–2003 class of fifth graders. They appear in the accompanying video and provide the foundation for much of the meaningful dialogue you will find in this book. Thanking children means also thanking their parents, who were excited to have their children involved in the project. Thanks also to a future teacher, Joni Kephart, who read through an early draft and offered a frank, thorough review.

We enormously appreciate Ann Thompson, guest writer for the "Technology Connections" sections. We are grateful for her willingness to provide unparalleled expertise in this area. Finally, we would be remiss if we failed to warmly thank Myrna Whigham, perennial grant-getter for statewide professional development for practicing math and science teachers. She always paired a master teacher with a university professor. She introduced us and paired us as presenters many years ago. Had it not been for her, the thought to write a book might have simply passed through our minds.

Finally, we would like to thank this book's reviewers: Kathleen Chamberlain, Lycoming College; Rainy Cotti, Rhode Island College; Gerald R. Fast, University of Wisconsin–Oshkosh; Elsa Geskus, Kutztown University; Charlene Gonzalez, Baker College; Gae R. Johnson, Northern Arizona University; Kevin LoPresto, University of Texas–Austin; Gretchen McCallister, Northern Arizona University; Jeffrey Wanko, Miami University; and Velma A. Yoder, Messiah College.

Supplements

Instructor's Manual with Test Items

Written by the authors, the Instructor's Manual provides instructors with an explanation about the learning theories selected for each of the five main parts of the text. Each chapter includes teacher notes for implementing the activities from the book along with possible answers for each activity. Some activities naturally have more than one answer. In those cases, the authors provide one sample answer. Also included are brief commentaries about each video clip appearing on the "Understanding Children's Mathematical Thinking" VideoWorkshop CD-ROM. Each chapter is concluded with a listing of the homework problems followed by possible answers for each problem. Each part is concluded with suggestions for additional homework problems and a few sample quizzes with possible answers.

MyLabSchool™

Discover where the classroom comes to life! From video clips of teachers and students interacting to sample lessons, portfolio templates, and standards integration, Allyn & Bacon brings your students the tools they'll need to succeed in the classroom, with content easily integrated into your existing course.

Delivered within CourseCompass, Allyn & Bacon's course management system, this program gives your students powerful insights into how real classrooms work and a rich array of tools that will support them on their journey from their first class to their first classroom.

MyLabSchool is free when packaged with a student access code. Contact your local representative for more details!

About the Authors

Janet M. Sharp is associate professor of mathematics education at Montana State University in Bozeman, where she teaches graduate and undergraduate courses in mathematics and mathematics education. She has won both universitywide and regional awards for excellence in teaching the elementary mathematics methods course. A former middle school teacher, she knows the value of making university courses relevant and practical. She works closely with prospective and practicing teachers to implement strategies that enhance the learning and teaching of K–12 mathematics classrooms.

Karen Bush Hoiberg has taught fifth graders in the Ames, Iowa, community school district for the past 15 years. She has been active in the mathematics education reform efforts, encouraging her students to explore concepts and build meaning around real-world mathematics problems. In 1994 she received the Presidential Award for Excellence in Science and Mathematics Teaching. She has also earned a statewide award for implementing research-based practices in her classroom teaching.

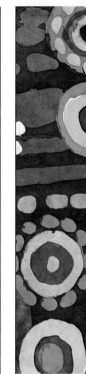

CHAPTER

1

The Basics

We designed this book to provide you with a useful, applicable, mathematics methods textbook. Our hope is that within the pages of this book, you will find information that will help you make sound instructional decisions that create classrooms that are rich environments for mathematics teaching and learning. A good way to think about appropriate teaching decisions is to know about mathematically based learning theories. So our primary goal is to teach you how to apply these kinds of theories in your K–8 mathematics classroom. Of course, we would be foolish to claim that our book is an exhaustive discussion of current theory and research. We would be equally foolish to claim that there is only one way to implement these theoretical ideas. But, we do know you can begin to understand how children learn, by reading about and watching the theories at work. One way we hope to accomplish this goal is with short video clips, where coauthor and practicing teacher Karen Hoiberg allows us glimpses into her classroom after we introduce research and theory about how children learn. A basic theme of all the theories presented is the importance of listening to students explain their thinking about a meaningful task.

We know that learning to teach mathematics in ways that resemble the vision described in this book will require you to relearn mathematics in manners similar to the way you want to teach it. So a secondary goal of this book is for you to learn new mathematics and revisit known concepts in different and exciting ways. You will also analyze your own learning in light of related learning theories and plan instruction in light of various models of teaching. As a result, you will come to know how to make informed decisions about your pedagogical practices. Remember as you work through the activities that they are intended for you, an adult learner. But, as you read about Karen's classroom experiences and watch the video clips, you will likely develop a keen sense of what pieces of an activity would be appropriate for K–8 learners.

In general, we believe no one can prepare you for every conceivable situation you will encounter as you teach students, but we can prepare you with knowledge about how learning occurs and teach you how to make corresponding instructional decisions. We expect that by the end of the book, you will feel competent to implement classroom practice that matches theory. This book is divided into five parts that focus on geometry, whole numbers, measurement, rational numbers, and data analysis. Each part begins with a problem and is then sectioned into three chapters: mathematics, learning theory, and instruction, which includes algebraic connections. As you read each part, you will complete several mathematics activities. In this chapter, we lay the groundwork for assessment, an idea that will also be integrated within each part of the book.

Thinking about the Mathematics

Our journey together will begin with three chapters about geometry. You might be surprised that the geometry chapters precede the number chapters. The reason for that order is related to how young children first begin to make sense of their environments. Numerical relationships do not emerge as early as visual images. In addition, students construct their number sense by using physical, geometric models such as cubes or blocks. As students use geometric models to understand number concepts, it seems likely that they must have first understood and been able to separate the physical and geometric nature of the material from the quantification of the material. The notion of "square" is much more visual than the notion of "four," so children are able to understand "square" fairly early. Why not build the idea of "four" on that existing visual image of a square?

For example, you will learn that at first, young children do not count sides to know that a square is a square. They simply match the whole object to a visual image of square in order to name it accurately. In fact, a square turned 45 degrees is, at first, often not *really* a square to young children. So if a set of four cubes is used to teach "four," it makes sense that students should already be familiar with cubes to minimize the amount of new or confounding information. If students are to make mathematical sense of their worlds, they must first understand the geometric nature of their worlds. In each part of the book, we discuss the mathematics and clarify different concepts and procedures that are part of that mathematical area.

How We Learn

Theories

Teaching well means listening to learners explain their thinking and recognizing the thinking behind those explanations. Familiarity with learning theories helps teachers understand student thinking. Each part of the book includes a chapter that focuses on how students learn. Within those chapters, discussion occurs in the following research-based learning theories.

1. Geometry: van Hiele
2. Number: Kamii *and* Cognitively Guided Instruction
3. Measurement: van Hiele
4. Rational numbers: Kieren, Streefland, and Pothier and Sawada
5. Data/Statistics: Friel, Curcio & Bright (statistics) *and* Jones, Langrall, Thornton, and Mogill (probability)

We anticipate explaining these selected theories as briefly but as thoroughly as possible to maintain the spirit of the theory. We readily admit that each theory is much more intricate than we present and that there are additional theories and specific research projects that illuminate them more fully. We have selected these theories as a beginning for you. Our main goal is to help you make informed teaching decisions based on knowledge about learning at this time. It is our experience that all too often, beginning teachers are not given enough learning theory knowledge to make a reasonable decision about how to deal with a child in a certain situation.

Features

We highlight a few cultural connections to give you the advantage of recognizing the often overlooked or undervalued cultural impact on mathematics. We consider some patterns, and we make literature connections. By studying these topics along with the specific content information, you can synthesize the information and use it to plan lessons. We also discuss ways in which you might use teaching aids, such as manipulatives. Throughout this book, we emphasize that manipulatives are a model of mathematics, not a model of students' thinking, and that manipulatives do not in and of themselves teach.

Role of the Teacher

We rely on and trust in teachers' abilities to make sound instructional decisions because they understand how students learn mathematics and they use that knowledge to make teaching decisions, not just passively plod through the school district's selected textbook. We describe various aspects of teachers' roles, including implementing the various models of teaching, writing lesson plans, guiding discussion, and making assessments. Finally, for practicing teachers, we suggest some ideas for professional development. Preservice teachers should also find the professional development ideas interesting.

Algebra Connections

In each part of the book, we make connections to algebra. Often, algebraic knowledge is needed to understand other material, whether mathematical or otherwise. So algebra is generally recognized as the de facto gateway to many of life's opportunities. Robert Moses (Moses & Cobb, 2001) has even suggested algebra as being so critical to economic success in life, it is a civil right for citizens. He compares it to the civil right to vote, which spawned separate battles waged by and won for both women and African Americans in the twentieth century. In this sense, algebra is an opportunity that opens many doors. That said, you might be wondering what you can do to bring algebra to the forefront of mathematical learning in your classroom, no matter the age of student.

Teachers can foster algebraic thinking in all mathematical areas and across all ages. We believe that you must understand how and when prealgebraic learners, even kindergartners, do prealgebraic tasks. The algebra sections of Chapters 4, 7, 10, 13, and 16 are partitioned into (1) a big idea from algebra, (2) algebraic ideas for you to explore, and (3) some related algebra that K–8 students can know. We will consider several big algebra ideas. These ideas include concepts such as equivalence and properties such as commutativity, roles variables play, and the importance of connecting algebra to arithmetic. We are concerned with exactly what the equal (=) sign means to learners at various stages of thinking. Properties guide our uses of algebra symbols. Different uses of variables require different sorts of thinking. When algebra is connected to arithmetic, important concepts come to light.

Middle School Connections

In various locations in the text, we call out some specific needs of middle school (grades 6, 7, and 8) students. Certainly, all learners have specific and unique individual needs. However, the needs of adolescent learners include complexities related to physical maturation that make their age group worthy of special mention. In addition, the mathematics is also more complex than that in the elementary school.

Before We Get Started

We believe that our integration of ideas into each content area will enable you to better synthesize the material and make connections between and among ideas. You should find that we have painstakingly integrated information, such as learning theory, cultural connections, or algebra, within the confines and relevancy of a given content area. But unlike these kinds of topics, which *should be* immediately tied to a specific content, there are other kinds of topics that we partition away from specific content. First, we want to describe the continuing reform efforts that began in the 1980s with a vision from the National Council of Teachers of Mathematics. Second, we consider three seemingly time-invariant ideas: instruction, assessment, and curriculum.

A Bit about the NCTM and the NCTM Standards

Broadly speaking, "The mission of the National Council of Teachers of Mathematics is to provide the vision and leadership necessary to ensure a mathematics education of the highest quality for all students" (www.nctm.org/about/mission.htm). The NCTM is a national organization that holds as its goals the development and improvement of mathematics education. To that end, the council has set forth six principles that should guide mathematics instruction. Those principles are listed in Table 1.1 along with our ideas about where those principles are addressed in this book. We believe the information in our book provides you with tools you will need to successfully act out the principles of the NCTM (2000).

More generally, the NCTM describes sound classroom experiences in terms of instruction that challenges each student, a curriculum that is complete and coherent, and assessment that runs across multiple modes, including standardized tests, quizzes, observations, performance tasks, and mathematical investigations. The NCTM believes that students develop both concept and procedural knowledge about the mathematics within each component of the curriculum, that the development of that knowledge is tied deeply to appropriate and meaningful instruction, and that this development is maximized when teachers focus on understanding students' mathematical thinking and reasoning. We agree with these ideas and suggest that successful teachers have a sound knowledge of (1) mathematics, (2) how students learn mathematics, and (3) how to guide the learning process in the classroom environment. You will find that these three areas match the organization of the recurrent chapters ("Thinking about the Mathematics," "How We Learn," and "Role of the Teacher") found in each part of the book.

Table 1.1 **NCTM Principles**

NCTM PRINCIPLE	WHERE IT IS IN THIS BOOK
Equity. Excellence in mathematics education requires equity: high expectations and strong support for all students. 	The "Role of the Teacher" chapter appears third in each part. In all chapters, we explain strategies for engaging all students in discourse. However, in Chapter 10, we explicitly discuss content differentiation for students. In addition, "Classroom Connections" features appearing in various locations throughout the text describe Karen's strategies for providing experiences for all of her students.
Curriculum. A curriculum is more than a collection of activities; it must be coherent, focused on important mathematics, and well articulated across the grades. 	The "Thinking about the Mathematics" chapter appears first in each part. We find it important to develop students' knowledge about mathematics in light of their developing knowledge about how children learn. The "Algebra Connections" section appears at the end of the third chapter in each part. This section is a coherent connection to the mathematics content addressed in each part.
Teaching. Effective mathematics teaching requires understanding what students know and need to learn and then challenging and supporting them to learn it well. NCTM TEACHING	In the "How We Learn" chapter, appearing second in each part, we highlight some of the theory regarding how children learn. Within the "Role of the Teacher" chapter, appearing third in each part, we focus on the actual activity in which a teacher must engage for learning to occur in the classroom.
Learning. Students must learn mathematics with understanding, actively building new knowledge from experience and prior knowledge. NCTM LEARNING	The "How We Learn" chapter appears second in each part and describes the processes that children use to develop mathematical knowledge. In the "Thinking about the Mathematics" chapter, appearing first in each part, we include information about conceptual and procedural knowledge and the importance of knowing both.
Assessment. Assessment should support the learning of important mathematics and furnish useful information to both teachers and students. NCTM ASSESSMENT	"Assessment Connections" is a section in the "Role of the Teacher" chapter, appearing in each part. In addition, the "Classroom Connections" sections appearing in various locations throughout, often describe uses of assessment.
Technology. Technology is essential in teaching and learning mathematics; it influences the mathematics that is taught and enhances students' learning. 	"Technology Connections" is a section appearing in various locations in the chapters. These sections describe ways that technology can enhance learning.

Source: NCTM (2000, p. 16).

As you read this book, you should also recognize our efforts to organize the information along content threads. Table 1.2 shows how the structure of this book relates to the NCTM's content standards.

TECHNOLOGY CONNECTIONS:
The Basics

NCTM TECHNOLOGY

In the late 1980s, around the time when the National Council of Teachers of Mathematics (1989) released its original curriculum standards, computer

Table 1.2 **NCTM Content Standards**

NCTM CONTENT STRAND	WHERE IT IS FOUND IN THIS BOOK
Geometry	Part I: Geometry and Spatial Thinking
Number and operation	Part II: Whole Numbers and Operation
	Part IV: Rational Numbers and Proportions
Measurement	Part III: Measurement Ideas
Data analysis and probability	Part V: Data Analysis
Algebra	At the end of the last chapter in each part

companies began to sell microcomputers designed for use in schools. Although both developments had great potential for improving mathematics learning in schools, most educators agree that by 2003, this potential had not begun to be realized. Part of the problem is that the connection between computer-related technology and new teaching approaches to mathematics has not been well defined. In this book, we will work to make this connection explicit for the reader through including a feature entitled "Technology Connections" in each part of the book. These features are guest-authored by Dr. Ann Thompson, a leader in the use of technology in teacher education. She provides numerous examples demonstrating how digital technology capabilities can expand and enhance the approaches suggested in each chapter.

Emphasis will be placed on digital technology applications that relate directly to the theme of teaching mathematics for understanding. Given the dynamic nature of digital technology available for classrooms, emphasis will be placed on types of applications and not on particular packages or products. The "Technology Connections" feature in each part of the book will help readers to consider possibilities for using these applications to more effectively meet the needs of young learners of mathematics. Given the potential power of digital technologies to provide tools for teachers and students to create meaningful mathematics learning environments and experiences and the relative newness of these tools, we have chosen to create these subsections to encourage reader engagement in this topic.

The digital technology applications that are described and discussed in the book will be the type of applications that enable teachers to help students participate actively in mathematics. Simulations featuring rich problem situations, tools that provide students the ability to focus their work on mathematical concepts rather than mathematical details, general-purpose tools that allow students to produce authentic mathematics products and projects, and Internet tools are the four major types of digital tools that will be discussed.

The "Technology Connections" features will emphasize general approaches to using technology as a tool to focus on improving learners' understanding of mathematics. The approaches that are suggested are not recipes for integrating technology into classrooms; approaches are general ideas that relate to learning theory, roles of students, and roles of teachers.

Resources produced by the International Society of Technology in Education (http://iste.org) are highlighted in some chapters. In addition to these resources and the ISTE web site, the ISTE journal *Leading and Learning with Technology* (www.iste.org/LL/31/2/index.cfm) is a valuable resource for mathematics teachers working to use technology to improve student learning.

Classroom Connections

Karen is a coauthor of this textbook and a practicing fifth grade teacher. In each part of the book, we provide "Classroom Connections," in which you glimpse a view into Karen's classroom. In those features, she speaks frankly about how some of the ideas from the chapter connect to her classroom. Her discussion may appear in any section, depending on the nature of her comments. She provides illustrations of, and thoughts about, how the information manifests itself in a real classroom. It is important that the information in this book be clearly applicable for you and your thoughts about teaching mathematics.

Karen credits the NCTM (a leading force in the reform movement for mathematics education that erupted in the 1990s) with playing a part in her professional growth during the course of her career, in which her primary goal now is to teach for understanding. This was a dramatic change in her understanding of and approaches to teaching, and it occurred in the early 1990s. During that time, Karen served on her district's mathematics cabinet, which had the goal of selecting a new math textbook. After studying the material that was available on the market and noticing a slight discrepancy between the books and the NCTM reform efforts, the cabinet delayed selection for a year. During that year, they studied the NCTM standards and wrote their own (new) curriculum, aligning the district scope and sequence. At approximately the same time, most publishers came out with newly revised textbooks, which seemed more in line with the standards. To begin to understand Karen's progress, we ask you first to complete Activity 1.1 before reading the Classroom Connections on the next page. Note that part of Activity 1.1 also suggests you watch the introductory video clip on your CD-ROM so that you can hear about this activity from Karen.

Activity 1.1

DANNY DICKSON'S PROBLEM

Multiply without the aid of a calculator.

23 × 12

_____

_____

_____

_____

_____

_____

Now that you have solved the problem mentally, watch the introductory video clip "Teaching Is a Journey," on your CD-ROM.

Instruction

As Karen described her changing philosophy, you probably recognized that her reform efforts ran across all three components of the instruction process: instruction, assessment, and curriculum. We begin our description of these pieces of teaching with the one that probably has your attention right now: instruction.

Models of Teaching

There are several models of teaching used to plan lessons. We showcase five models (see Table 1.3). As you read the rest of the book, you should think about how the discussion of a given model would have been different if it had been used with different content. We trust that by the end of the book, you will be

CLASSROOM CONNECTIONS

Understanding How Children Learn Math

Many years ago, I was student teaching in fourth grade. One task was to teach two-digit multiplication. Poor Danny Dickson. He simply didn't get it. I showed him and I showed him *how* to do it. I was down on my knees, right at his level. "First you take this number and then. . . ." You get the picture. But Danny didn't. No matter how many times I showed him, he simply did not understand the procedure. Silent tears of frustration dripped from his eyes. I didn't know what to do except show him the same thing over and over again. We were both terribly frustrated. Finally, the light came on—Danny got it! He could do two-digit multiplication.

To this day, I don't know what it was Danny "got." I realize now that I was only showing him a procedure—just the way I had been shown. I have thought about Danny many times over the years. In today's world, I would have done it so differently. Did Danny *understand* two-digit multiplication? Did he know why he was doing this procedure? Probably not. I didn't know any better at that time. I hadn't put the problem into any kind of meaningful context for Danny. According to the NCTM (2000) learning principle, "Students must learn mathematics with understanding, actively building new knowledge from experience and prior knowledge" (p. 11). Simply giving Danny a two-digit multiplication problem meant nothing to him. Giving him a situation that made sense would have helped him, and perhaps we would have avoided the frustration we both felt. I believe that using meaningful contexts can provide connections that help students think about the mathematics.

Today I might say, "Danny, look! We have 23 students in our class. I want you to give each of them 12 pieces of candy. I wonder how many pieces that would be in all." If his eyes glazed over, we could make it a smaller problem. "How many pieces would it be for you and Anna? How many for you, Anna, Jack, and Paige? What if we add Emma?" And so on.

Challenging Danny with a problem such as this would have allowed him to become involved and to build understanding on information he already knew. If a child can't understand what he or she is being asked to do, how can there be mathematical growth? In some ways, I have always been a reformer. I just didn't know it.

I wonder how Danny Dickson would do in my classroom of today?

---

able to make such inferences. For example, we examine the discussion model in Chapter 4 and the problem-solving model in Chapter 13. You might want to think about what might have been different if those roles had been reversed.

Although we separate the five models to examine each more closely, keep in mind that most teachers do not find these models mutually exclusive. One model can be used in conjunction with another model in planning a lesson. For instance, a teacher might use the problem-solving model in conjunction with the partnered learning model or a concept attainment model with the discussion model.

Problem Solving

Table 1.4 **Strategies for Solving Mathematics Problems**

1. Draw a picture or diagram.
2. Find a pattern and predict.
3. Work backward.
4. Make a list or table.
5. Act it out with materials or with a partner.
6. Guess and check.
7. Solve a simpler problem.
8. Use logical reasoning.
9. Write an equation.

Note that the idea of problem solving as a *model of teaching* (i.e., a way to teach something) is different from a *strategy a student might use* (i.e., something students learn) to solve mathematics problems. Problem solving as a model of teaching is the process of engaging students in a task in which the strategy is not prescribed and then using their work on that task to tease out some important mathematical ideas. General problem-solving strategies are ways in which a person might go about solving a problem. Table 1.4 lists some of the strategies for solving a mathematics problem.

The Try it! See it! Teach it! Feature

A problem-solving view of mathematics learning and teaching is rich with interaction and lively discussion. This sort of

Table 1.3 **Five Models of Teaching**

	GENERAL GOAL	WHAT YOU WILL PREPARE	ASSESSMENT
Discussion	For students to ponder "what if" through focused discussion by responding to questions and puzzling situations	*Questions:* Ask questions that elicit thoughtful comments from students. Discussion will be guided by the teacher and be based on student comments that emerge.	Students' discussions are thoughtful and reasonably relate to the object of discussion and in the end, they summarize key points.
Problem solving/ discovery/inquiry	For students to learn by experiencing sustained study of a problematic situation	*Problem Situation(s):* Place students into an interesting and engaging problem situation, for which the students do not have immediate knowledge of a strategy for resolution. Problems often begin with "You are a. . . . You have been put in this situation. . . . What will you do?"	Students use processes that would resolve the situation. Students interpret the situation accurately.
Presentation	For students to acquire, assimilate, and retain informational knowledge or procedural knowledge	*Information:* Provide highly specific information to the student. Usually includes a period of independent study, during which time the student somehow practices using the information.	Students demonstrate correct execution of the procedure or state the fact.
Concept attainment	For students to gain key concept knowledge that is foundational for later material	*Examples and Nonexamples:* Provide the student with a wide variety of specimens that are examples and nonexamples of the concept.	Students identify the classification of a new specimen, articulate a description of the grouping, make generalizations about the group elements, or compare two groups.
Partnered learning (usually in conjunction with another model)	For students to learn by working closely with another person and defending their ideas and results	*Learner's Roles and a Task:* Create group membership. Provide pairs (or triads) of students with a task and the tools to resolve the challenge.	All students in the group will articulate successful completion of the objective.

classroom may seem unfamiliar and difficult to imagine. So we have created a series of video clips on our "Understanding Children's Mathematical Thinking" CD-ROM. These video clips are integrated periodically throughout the text in a feature called Try it! See it! Teach it! The video clips demonstrate the philosophy behind the problem-solving model of teaching and show how Karen's students are actively involved during the problem-solving process. When you interact with the Try it! See it! Teach it! features, you will first *try* the problem that is featured in the video clip. Then, you will *see* how Karen works with learners to engage them in discussion about their solutions. Finally, you will reflect on the lesson and think about how to *teach*. When you watch the first video clip, you will see how the problem solving model for classroom teaching might look.

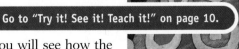

Go to "Try it! See it! Teach it!" on page 10.

Lesson Plan Components

Why do we need to study models of teaching? Teachers build lessons on teaching models. Lessons include an *objective,* a *materials* list, a sense of the *procedures*

Try it! See it! Teach it!

Understanding How Children Learn Mathematics

Step **One**: Try it!

Do the Math . . .

Before watching the video, solve the following problem yourself: Mrs. Bunker's class wonders if one piece of taffy 78 inches long will be enough for the 25 students in her class if they are supposed to get $3\frac{3}{4}$ inches each? What do you think?

A 1944 taffy pull

Step **Two**: See it!

Video Clip 1 *(time length 5:57)*

Evelyn explains her answer.

Watch the Video . . .

Listen to Karen's students solve the taffy pull problem. Be prepared to describe how this approach to teaching is different from her description of how she taught Danny Dickson about two-digit multiplication discussed in the chapter on page 8.

Things to Look for . . .

Appreciate the way the teaching and learning of mathematics has changed, how it now includes more contextualized instruction, and how student discussion is a regular part of the classroom.

Step **Three**: Teach it!

Reflect on Your Own Teaching . . .

1. How did your solution process compare to the students' processes?

_____

_____

_____

2. How does the visualization of a context help you think about $78 \div 3\frac{3}{4}$ and $25 \times 3\frac{3}{4}$?

_____

_____

_____

3. Did you notice that the questions Karen asked during the students' presentations were designed to encourage thoughtful explanations? What other questions might she have asked?

_____

_____

_____

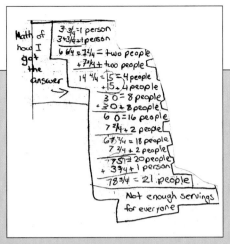

Kody's first attempt. Kody begins with a ratio table to find out how much taffy each child will get.

4. Describe how you would work with students on this problem in your own classroom or a similar problem.

_____

_____

_____

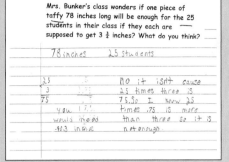

Mrs. Bunker's class wonders if one piece of taffy 78 inches long will be enough for the 25 students in their class if they each are supposed to get $3\frac{3}{4}$ inches? What do you think?

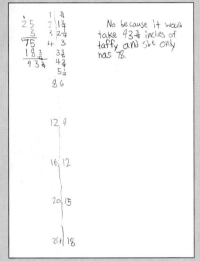

No because it would take $93\frac{3}{4}$ inches of taffy and she only has 78.

Christian's strategy. Christian's approach emphasizes common sense.

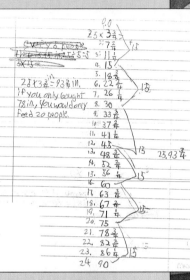

James's strategy. James counts by $3\frac{3}{4}$ until he reaches a whole number.

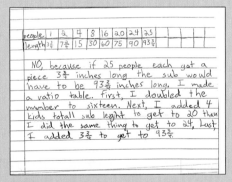

NO, because if 25 people each got a piece $3\frac{3}{4}$ inches long the sub would have to be $93\frac{3}{4}$ inches long. I made a ratio table. first, I doubled the number to sixteen. Next, I added 4 kids totall sub leght to get to 20 than I did the same thing to get to 24, Last I added $3\frac{3}{4}$ to get to $93\frac{3}{4}$.

Kody's second attempt. Kody challenges himself to try a new strategy.

Evelyn's strategy. Evelyn wants to know whether there'll be enough taffy for everyone.

A Comment from Karen

To facilitate learning does not mean standing in front of students to demonstrate one procedure, prescribe some practice of it, and then make an assignment to be corrected the next day. Of course, we want students to learn procedures, but we want the procedure to make sense to them. The procedure must be connected to their experiences, not fragmented or memorized out of context. The procedures should be layered along with concepts. Today my classroom is a busy center where students explore a concept and build meaning. We constantly share strategies, look for patterns and connections, and write in our math journals. One of the most valuable parts of math time is sharing strategies and justifying thinking. It is so exciting to hear a student say, "I used Chris's trick to get this answer."

GO BACK TO PAGE 9

CLASSROOM CONNECTIONS

Providing Interactive Instruction

CURRICULUM

It is important to build all lessons on district or state objectives. Once in a while, I might plan a seemingly wonderful activity, thinking that I'm meeting the objective with a certain problem situation. Sometimes a context doesn't really work for the students, even though I thought it was meaningful. Other times, the mathematics of the activity is obscured by the context. I ask myself, my colleagues, and even my students, "What went wrong? What should I have done differently?" The NCTM (2000) describes the need to select worthwhile mathematical tasks that are "worth the time and attention of students" (p. 15). So I know I have to meet my objectives and select worthwhile tasks.

In my journey as an educator, I have learned that worthwhile tasks often take longer than I might have expected. I have learned to wait on my students as they work through problems. At first, I silently counted to three or four to ensure that I was *waiting* and not *answering* my own questions. This procedure allows students time to arrive at a solution on their own. When a student says, "I don't get it," is it helpful to simply (and quickly) give an answer? Of course not. Instead, I might think for a moment and then ask, "What are you being asked to answer?" or "How can I help you get started?" Waiting to give students time to think and knowing the right type of question to ask is often all that is needed to assist the student in finding a strategy for a given problem. I'm also always listening for whether or not students have met the objective that was the foundation for the problem in the first place. I have to make sure I don't get caught up in the context.

to be completed during the lesson, and a useful *assessment* of the effectiveness of the lesson. In any particular situation, those four elements may look slightly different depending on the teaching model that is used as the lesson foundation and the mathematics content that is studied. Table 1.3 describes the overall goals of each particular model of teaching and lists key components of each of the models.

In planning a lesson, the first order of business is to outline the mathematical *objective* to be achieved. Every component of the lesson grows from that objective, including the *assessment*. Both must match the district's framework. Some teachers like to write the assessment immediately after writing the objective. Then they go back and fill in the *procedures*, based on the characteristics of the model of teaching. Finally, they collect *materials* needed for the lesson.

Questioning

EQUITY

At various points throughout the book, you will read short excerpts from classrooms and analyze students' comments. You might wonder what other questions the teacher might have asked. In those content-specific sections, we give the teachers' specific questions and offer explanations of how and why they chose those questions. But here in Chapter 1, we list several general questions that teachers often ask. In our experience, good questions, "elicit language and challenge each student's thinking" (NCTM, 1991, p. 35). It is also important to work at high thinking levels by asking "students to clarify and justify their ideas orally and in writing" (NCTM, 1991, p. 35).

To elicit justification and reasoning, you might ask these questions:

1. What have you tried that has worked or not worked?
2. How would you explain this in your own words?
3. Tell me what makes this a reasonable solution to the task?
4. You're finished! How did you know you were finished?
5. How do you know your answer is right?
6. How would you explain the answer to a second grade child? (select a younger age than that of the student being questioned)

7. Can you write another problem like this one?
8. Without telling the answer, what could you tell a classmate about how to get started?
9. Explain why you are satisfied with your solution.

To clarify or redirect, you might ask these questions:

10. What have you done so far?
11. What one thing would you like to know that would help you move on?
12. What is a little fuzzy to you at this point?

To check on any students who are working with partners, you might say the following:

13. In your own journal, please write a note to someone at home that explains what you learned in mathematics today.
14. Write what you know about the terms (concepts) written on the board. In your group, divide them up among you, and each of you write about a different one.
15. If someone disagrees with your answer, how would you get someone to go along with it?
16. How would you hope your partner would summarize what you just said?

It should be clear these questions do not have simple yes/no answers. They focus students' thinking and require careful thought, not quick answers. Students' answers will lead you to make judgments about their thinking. When you do that, you are assessing the students' thinking. Assessment, curriculum, and instruction are tightly linked. We explore the issue of assessment next.

Assessment

Throughout this book, two kinds of assessment will be discussed. One kind of assessment is the specific evaluation of the students based on a given lesson plan. In that context, assessment is the opportunity to decide whether or not students met the lesson objective. Usually, this kind of assessment is done regularly for a specific mathematical idea or procedure. Some of you might remember only this kind of assessment measuring how well you completed a particular mathematics assignment, such as the end-of-chapter test.

The other way to think of assessment is more general and might or might not be related to a given specific day's lesson plan. Assessment in this light is thought of as a critical element of the total learning environment. As you study the NCTM (1995) Assessment Standards, you should begin to see that evaluation of student achievement (like the end-of-chapter test) is only one of four reasons a teacher engages in assessment activity. The four reasons are (1) to evaluate achievement (described in the previous paragraph), (2) to monitor student progress, (3) to make an instructional decision, and (4) to evaluate materials being used. With the four reasons to perform an assessment, assessment is much more than an opportunity to record a series of daily scores in a grade book.

Curriculum

The curriculum is generally thought to be what students are expected to learn. In 2000, NCTM updated its 1989 curriculum standards and released a comprehensive document, *The Principles and Standards for School Mathematics*. The new document sets forth several refined mathematical goals for K–12 education with regard to curriculum, instruction, and assessment. As

CLASSROOM CONNECTIONS
Using Assessment of Many Forms

ASSESSMENT

I try to assess my students in a variety of ways. The NCTM Standards describe the importance of using several forms of assessment to glean a more complete and therefore more accurate appraisal of students' thinking. Encouraging students to share their feelings about mathematics is an excellent way to gather important information, which I can use to make instructional decisions. Using evidence from several sources, not just test scores, is another way in which I can show students that I value their opinions and that we are in this together. To illustrate, think about how you would respond to the following writing assignment that I gave to my fifth grade students.

How do you feel about math? How would you describe it as a color? What shape would it be? What would it sound like? Take a few minutes to think about how you feel about math then describe it in terms of a color, shape, and sound.

Nicole is a student in my class. She is very bright and is in our school's gifted program. She regularly volunteers and performs well on daily math work. I had no real concerns about her as a math student until I read her response to the above: "Math makes me feel kind of frustrated because I dread it sometimes. If math were a color it would probably be black because I am not a big fan of math. I always get stuck on a problem or something, or don't get it. If math were a shape it would be a circle, because it reminds me of a black hole. Because every time I get stuck on a problem, it is like I'm in a black hole, just all confused and like my mind is just blank, all black like someone turned off the light bulb in my mind. The sound of math would be foghorns blowing because it's like I am lost in the middle of nowhere. My mind just shuts down, and I am lost."

As I read Nicole's response, I was stunned. The next day, while students were busy working, I asked Nicole to come to sit with me at a table. Before I got out her paper and asked her to tell me about it, I told her that I had been surprised to read it because I considered her to be a strong math student. I told her I was so glad to know how she felt so that I could help her.

She said, "I kind of like math, but sometimes I feel lost."

Although Nicole did well on daily work, it became clear to me that she was having trouble seeing the big picture. Making connections was difficult for her. Nicole knows that she has the reputation of being a gifted student. Having the opportunity to share her true feelings in writing opened doors for both of us. It is critical for a teacher to gather a variety of evidence from students as different forms of assessment. I now know that I need to help Nicole build her confidence in math.

Here is Christian's response: "I think mathematics is a yellowish color. I think that because I like it. It's fun and I learn from it. Mathematics as a shape would probably be a circle because there are no blocks or points in it and it's easy to get through. It would sound soft and light like an angel because you need it to do almost anything."

Does it surprise you to know that I need to challenge Christian every single day? He loves math and constantly wants to be pushed to higher levels.

This assessment provided me with important insights. You might think about what each of those statements indicated I should do for or with these students. In some cases, I needed to know even more about their thinking. I took the opportunity to talk with each of my students. They appreciated the fact that they were allowed to express their true feelings about math. This assignment provided an opportunity for that honest dialogue. It is my role as a teacher to guide them to reach their full potential. This cannot be accomplished without valuing and respecting my students viewpoints.

such, the document guides most states' and districts' curricula development. It also helps to ground discussion at the national level in terms of deciding the specific content mathematics knowledge students should develop. That document is split across four grade bands. Within each grade band, the various mathematical areas of number and operation, geometry, measurement, algebra, and data analysis are afforded their own sections. The curriculum standards for grades K–2, 3–5, and 6–8 are very important for you to read. You can also visit their web site (www.nctm.org) for more information and a list of the specific contents of each standard.

LET'S REVIEW

This chapter was designed to give an overview of the rest of the book's organization. It was also intended to provide general information, such as instruction or curriculum, that can be loosely discussed independently from specific mathematical content such as geometry or data analysis. All of these ideas are revisited in subsequent chapters surrounded by specific content. Our purpose in presenting the information in this chapter is to save time by pointing out basic elements.

HOMEWORK

1. Naturally, teacher questions can be found in all models of teaching. But in which model of teaching do you think you would most likely find the following questions or activities?

    a. You are a city planner and have decided to build a park that is safe for three-, four-, and five-year-olds; has ample room for running paths; and includes a place dedicated to large dogs. What sort of data should you gather to help you make a decision about the location of the park?
    b. A city planner has decided to build a rectangular park in a new neighborhood. How many different types of rectangular parks could she build if she were limited to 1,000 square meters?
    c. Eight different contractors have submitted plans for the new city park. (Six of them are rectangular, and two are not rectangular.) Classify these parks as being acceptable to the city planner, who wants a rectangular park. What are the features that drive those classifications?
    d. Consider one of the contractor's plans for the city park. The contractor worked from the following criteria: The park must be rectangular, fit on 1,000 square meters, have 15% of its space dedicated to running or waking paths, and have 20% of its space dedicated to accommodating large dogs. Draw a plan of the park.

SUGGESTED READINGS

Cognition and Technology Group at Vanderbilt. (1997). *The Jasper Project: Lessons in curriculum, instruction, assessment, and professional development.* Mahwah, NJ: Erlbaum.
The Factory Deluxe. (1998). The Factory Deluxe. [computer software]. Sunburst Communications, Inc.
The Geometer's Sketchpad. (2003). The Geometer's Sketchpad (Version 4.05). [computer software]. Available at: www.keypress.com/sketchpad/.
MicroWorlds. (2000). MicroWorlds Pro. [computer software]. Highgate Springs, VT: Logo Computer Systems, Inc.
Prime Time Math. (2000). Prime Time Math (Version 3.0). [computer software]. Jenkintown, PA: Sheppard Software.

REFERENCES

Moses, R. P., & Cobb, C. E., Jr. (2001). *Radical equations.* Boston, MA: Beacon Press.
National Council of Teachers of Mathematics. (1989). *Curriculum and evaluation standards for school mathematics.* Reston, VA: NCTM.
National Council of Teachers and Mathematics. (1991). *Professional standards for teaching mathematics.* Reston, VA: NCTM.
National Council of Teachers of Mathematics. (2000). *Principles and standards for school mathematics.* Reston, VA: NCTM.

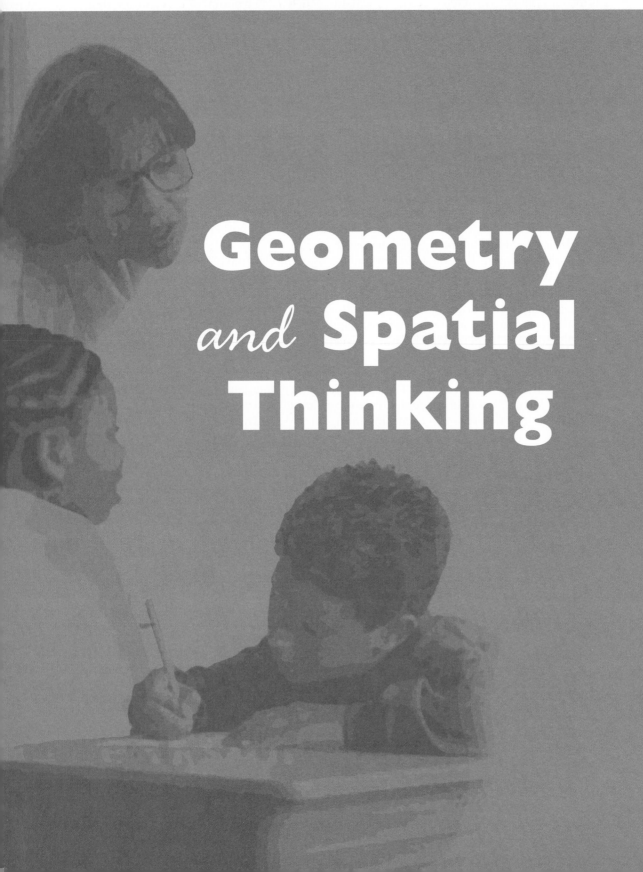

Geometry *and* Spatial Thinking

Throughout the book, you will find several mathematics activities embedded in the reading. Solve these activities as you come across them. One good way to discuss ideas about teaching and learning mathematics is to engage in focused mathematical thinking at the same time. In this way, we can discuss the mathematical thinking you used to complete the activities as meaningful applications of the pedagogy topics emphasized throughout the book.

So, to get started thinking about geometry and spatial thinking, we would like you to solve the problem in the activity.

Opening Activity

DECORATIVE TILES

You have been hired to lay all these decorative tiles on a child's bedroom wall. In the end, the tiles should glue together to form the "turtle-coming-out-of-its-shell" shape.

● What thinking did you use to complete this task? Chances are that you visualized the wall, analyzed your tiles, looked for the right pieces, and then decided whether or not to glue them in place. Your thinking on this problem is called spatial thinking and is a very important component of geometry. You might think geometry is area, perimeter, volume, and those sorts of things. Actually those ideas are different and served in Part III, "Measurement Ideas." For this first part on geometry, we explore shapes, spatial thinking, visualization, rigid motions, and symmetry.

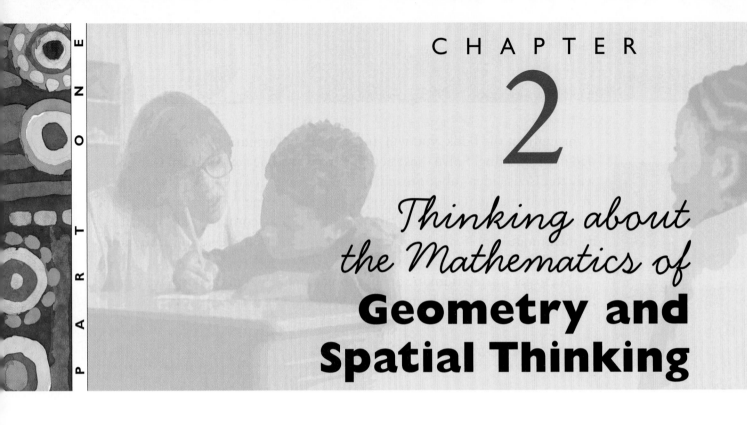

C H A P T E R

2

Thinking about the Mathematics of
Geometry and Spatial Thinking

UNDERSTANDING THE MATHEMATICS:
Mental Ideas versus Physical Models

The building of geometry thinking might begin by working to answer the question: What is the most basic geometric shape? Is it a polygon, a line segment, a point, . . . ? This is followed by creating new, more complex shapes from the basic shape.

If we begin with the idea of a polygon, we can quickly see that it is made up of sides (segments) and vertices (points). So the polygon is unlikely to pass "most basic shape" status. Let's consider the line segment. A line segment is the set of all those points and only those points that lie along a straight path (on a line) between and including two points. Again, a more basic shape is needed. Perhaps the most basic geometric shape is a point. Points do not seem to be made up of anything else. This appears to be a good place to begin.

So we ask, "What are points?" Points are something like locations in space. If we build our thinking from points, we see that as we collect the set of all points that lie in a straight path between two distinct points, we form a segment. Now we can do one of two things. We can extend our collection infinitely and eventually build a line, or we can create a new segment, hook it to our first segment and begin to build a polygon. However, building geometric thinking in this way does not mirror the process that learners follow in developing geometry knowledge.

Instead, children build geometry knowledge by first encountering the whole shape in its three-dimensional or *solid* form and abstracting other geometric ideas (such as *plane* shapes) from it. This means that students must first encounter real, solid shapes, becoming familiar with their physical characteristics. After students know something about the solid shape, they can state consequences about plane shapes, by abstracting them from the solid shape. Spatial thinking like this develops through experiences. Using solid shapes to foster thinking about plane shapes is but one way to promote spatial thinking. Diagrams and picture models of spatial situations are also worthy of analysis. As you complete Activity 2.1, think about how to find plane geometric shapes (e.g., circles, squares, triangles, segments) from faces or edges on the solid shapes.

Activity 2.1

PULLING 2-D IDEAS FROM A 3-D MODEL

You will be issued three solids. Some possible examples of solids are shown:

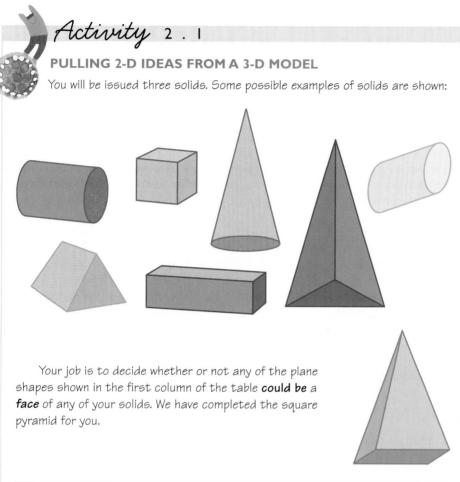

Your job is to decide whether or not any of the plane shapes shown in the first column of the table **could be** a **face** of any of your solids. We have completed the square pyramid for you.

Solid Name	Square Pyramid								
	Yes	No	Yes	No	Yes	No	Yes	No
Circle		x						
Square	x							
Ellipse		x						
Rectangle	x							
Parallelogram	x							
Triangle	x							
Equilateral triangle	x							
Isosceles triangle								

Extension:
Get a truncated solid.
What new shapes can be found on the faces of your solid?

Pulling Plane Knowledge from Solid Shapes

As we accumulate experiences with several solid shapes, we more fully solidify our knowledge of plane shapes. Much of school geometry learning requires students to ponder general plane ideas. A wide range of physical shapes, serving as examples of solid and plane geometric ideas fosters geometry knowledge growth. Ever present in our minds should be the idea that there is a difference between the abstract geometry idea and the physical examples that are used to show someone the idea. Depending on the specific examples with a specific student, those students might form different mental images.

This brings up another important idea. Because there exists a difference between the physical models that we use as examples of geometric ideas and the geometry ideas themselves, each individual child's mental ideas that develop as a result of studying examples will be unique. We can create a classroom in which students and teacher agree on how to classify a certain collection of physical representations (solids or diagrams) of geometric ideas. This classification then serves as the topic of discussion, with all participants working from the same physical models, even though mental images might vary.

Awareness of the difference between the model and the mathematics will influence teaching decisions about geometry. To completely explore the issue "What is a segment?," we must recognize both the beauty of and the limitations of our own personal visualizations. The nature of mathematics is that it lives in each person's individual mental space. Teachers and students must work hard to understand each other's mental visualizations during classroom activities. This fact has many implications for the teaching and learning of mathematics. We attempt to address several of these implications throughout this book. In this chapter, we show you relationships between physical models and mental visualizations described by students.

Using Models Effectively

You might be surprised to learn that very young children can tell the difference between a cylinder, a disk, a sphere, and a circle. There are countless stories of young children using correct terminology and correct language in their work with geometry thinking. ("Educating Hannah," by Cockraft and Marshall, 1999, one of the suggested readings for this chapter, provides an excellent example.) Hannah is a kindergartner who can tell the difference between these ideas and the physical objects that represent them. To explain the difference between a disk and a cylinder, Hannah used the top of a can. She turned the can upside down, pressed the top onto an ink pad, and then stamped it onto a piece of paper. She knew that the stamped figure she saw was a disk. Her teacher referred to this process as *making footprints*. The idea of a footprint gives Hannah a mental image to help her think about the difference between a cylinder and a disk. It also demonstrates pulling a plane shape from a solid shape. Next you might imagine putting a rim of glue around the top of the can's edge, returning to the ink pad (after the glue dries), and stamping it again. This time, the footprint on the page is that outside rim. That footprint represents a circle.

To be sure, *circle* is a mental mathematical idea. No one can ever truly touch a circle, sphere, disk, or cylinder. We touch only physical models of them. There will come a time when the physical model fails while the mathematical idea remains perfect because it is in the human mind. The (mathematical) circle is pure and perfect. But to effectively teach about these mental mathematical ideas, we use physical models.

Analyzing a Circle

What is it that makes a shape a circle? Is it when a basketball player does a 360 degree dunk? Is it when the minute hand goes around the clock? Listen to these fifth grade students explain why a shape is a circle:

> *Min:* A circle has to be perfectly round and has to be the same size all around (like the width). If it is not the same size all around, it is an oval, a stretched out version of a circle. To draw a circle, you just go around in a rotation movement, and there is a circle. [Note that Min has included a nonexample in her explanation.]
>
> *Lydia:* A circle always has to be rounded, have no corners, no straight lines. When you draw a circle, half of it goes to the left and half to the right. There are many things shaped like a circle. [Note that Lydia has included a list of properties and a reference to the real world.]
>
> *Ryan:* A circle is a round, flat shape and sometimes not flat (like a ball) with no crooked lines or edges. [Note Ryan's inclusion of a sphere in his recognition of circular objects.]
>
> *Jamal:* A circle is something completely round, and if you put lines coming out from the middle (center), they should always be the same distance. [Jamal is giving a sophisticated statement that a circle is related to its radius.]

Mathematically, *circle* is defined as all points on a plane, equidistant (a radius) from a given point, which is the center. The circle is only that set of points, not including the center. Knowing this, what would you now ask these students if you could? Why? What would help you to understand their mental images more clearly?

We often show children quarters, plates, jar lids, or CDs as examples of a circle in the physical world. At first, you might recognize that these examples can lead children to a misconception, because a circle is only the set of points along the rim of the circular shape, but no more so than giving the children the general misconception that mathematics is a physical entity in the first place. The learner must distinguish the mathematical properties from the physical properties of the shape. One way to do this is to use physical models as thoroughly as possible and point out all the footprints that could be made. The "circle" things that children encounter are usually physical representations of cylinders. In some instances, we use spheres to represent circles, although we generally find this approach to be slightly more abstract because a footprint is not physically possible without slicing the ball into two parts or without visualizing the front view of it. Explain that the rim of the cylinder is the circle and that when the interior part is included in the footprint, that shape is a disk, not a circle. Technically, it is acceptable to call the disk "circular."

A Cylinder or a Circle?

Consider a penny. Even though it is fairly thick, we might have to pause to recognize that it is a cylinder, not a circle. The top part is a disk. The circle is represented by that set of points on the outer edge of the disk. When we push our spatial thinking, we should be careful to distinguish between the circle and the cylinder, as well as the other plane shapes on the penny cylinder. There are many questions we can ask children that will help them to distinguish between physical models and mathematical ideas. Listen to these fifth graders analyze real-world objects (a hockey puck, a basketball, a quarter, a soup can, a marshmallow, a gumball, a moon, and an oatmeal canister) when asked to categorize where or if there were circles on these objects. They were asked to justify their categorizations.

> **Jamal:** A hockey puck has a circle and a cylinder. If I stamp it like Hannah did, I see the circle on top.
>
> **Lydia:** If I hollow out the quarter, I see now that I could fill it up like a can. At first, I thought it had to be taller to be a cylinder.
>
> **Min:** I don't think a gumball is a circle. Is it? I guess if I look at the top view it looks like a circle.
>
> **Ryan:** The lid on the oatmeal canister has it all! It is a cylinder, and one end can stamp a circle and the other end a filled-in circle. [He means *disk*.]

Any physical circle that humans make will not be mathematically accurate. First, as soon as we make it out of some physical material, we have probably made a physical representation of either a cylinder, doughnut, or sphere. Second, the physical material will affect the perfection of the shape. If we try to cut out a "circle" from a piece of paper, we have (probably) cut out a cylinder, since paper has thickness, albeit small. To convince yourself, look at the pages in this book. If paper had no thickness, how would this book look? Moreover, a circle is merely the collection of points equidistant from a given point. Because the circular piece of paper would include all the points lying within the circle as well as the points that constitute the actual circle, we have created even more problems.

Students sometimes wonder why we need to study shapes, such as circles, since we can apparently never really touch them. Circles are used in many practical areas of life, and we need to understand the mathematics behind how they work. Engineers use mathematical ideas behind circles to calculate stress and strain on dowel-shaped materials used in building structures. A softball pitcher marks off his or her pitching area in the shape of a circle. Geologists use great circles to plot the points of a crystal, which are needed to study the crystalline shape of minerals. Teachers have a variety of physical, real-world situations at their disposal they can use to expose students to the mathematical, mental idea of a circle.

CONCENTRATING ON THE CONCEPTS:
Relationships among Shapes

Concepts are mental relationships between and among ideas. They are visualizations and classifications. Any time learners develop a classification of things, they are developing a concept of it. Anytime learners match things mentally, they are establishing a concept of it. When they pattern or when they order, they create concepts. Completing Activity 2.2 will help you to think about mathematics concepts.

Let's further explore the notion of concept by studying squares. To truly hold an understanding of this concept, one must know how square is related to rectangle and how it is related to rhombus, as well as how it is unrelated to these shapes. An exploration of rhombus and rectangle can lead us to know how these ideas are related to parallelograms, quadrilaterals, and even polygons. In Figure 2.1 (page 24), a hierarchical view of square is presented. In Figure 2.2 (page 25), a set inclusion view of square is presented.

Examples and Nonexamples

Looking at Figure 2.1, you quickly realize that you can see both what a square *is* and what a square *is not*. Figure 2.2 requires an understanding of Venn di-

Activity 2 . 2

INSPIRATION

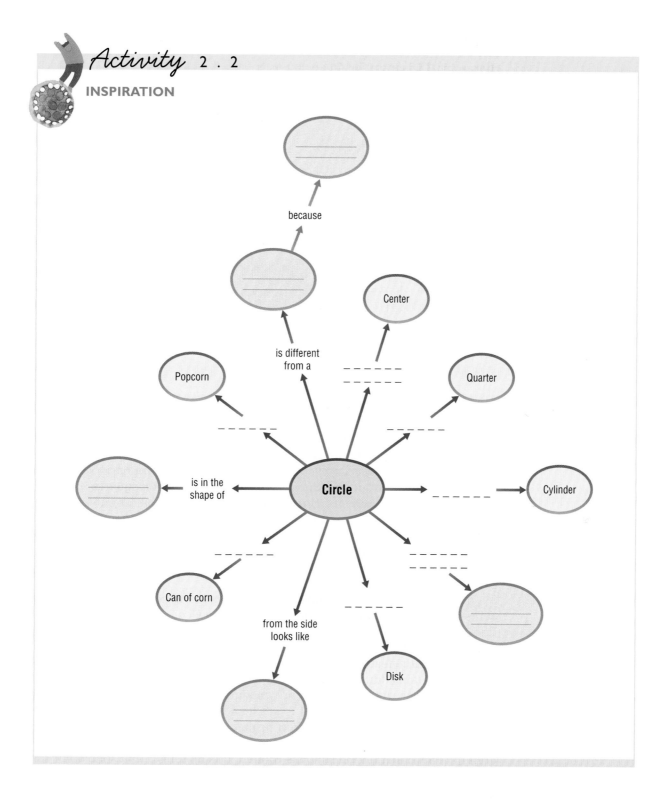

because

is different
from a

Popcorn

Center

Quarter

is in the
shape of

Circle

Cylinder

Can of corn

from the side
looks like

Disk

agrams to determine the relationships between square and not-square. To complete concept development, the learner must encounter nonexamples of the concept in question. Recall Min's statement about a circle. She used her spatial thinking to stretch a circle, making it oblong, and explained what a circle *is not* to better communicate her conceptual thinking. We already know that the learner must see physical examples of squares to abstract a mental image

Figure 2 . 1

Hierarchical Diagram for Quadrilaterals

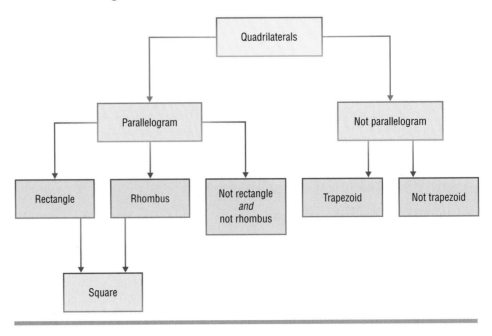

and visualization of a square. We often get so excited to show students examples of squares that we forget the complement. Equal emphasis should be placed on showing students examples of shapes that *are not* squares. Physical nonexamples teach students to rule out mental images that are not squares. If students can do both types of classifying, they have a stronger concept of square because they know what fits and what does not fit. Mental relationships hook concepts together creating new relationships. This is desirable because stronger and more numerous hooks and connections mean stronger concept knowledge.

Figure 2.3 (pages 26–27) shows some examples and non-examples that students need to see when developing concept knowledge of geometric shapes. Each first example is a "best" example. Fuys and Liebov (1997) describe the importance of distinguishing between "best" examples, examples that contain *only* the essential features of the concept, and garden-variety examples, examples that contain additional features such as being rotated, having equal sides, or having congruent angles. You are encouraged to add more examples and nonexamples to these tables and to create a new table so that you can experience selecting a *best* example. You probably noticed that in each table, we included a rotated shape in the example column. It is not uncommon for children to believe that once a shape is rotated, it is no longer that shape. For instance, when very young children see a triangle with the point down, they often say that it is not a triangle. This brings us to two other topics: rigid motions and symmetry.

Rigid Motions

Rigid motions are translations (slides), reflections (flips), and rotations (turns). The mathematical principle behind the rigid motions is that shapes are invari-

Figure 2 . 2

Venn Diagram for Quadrilaterals

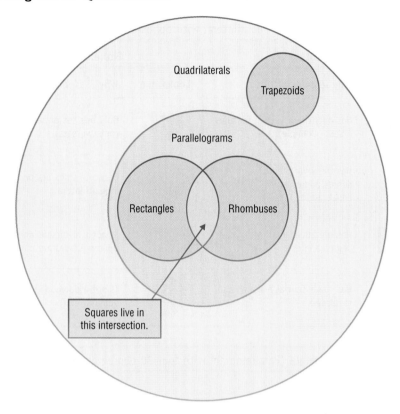

ant under these motions. In other words, if you begin with a square shape and slide it across a table, it remains a square shape. If you take a triangular shape and rotate it around to face someone else, it remains a triangle. Although this might seem obvious to adults, it is not obvious to children. Take the letter **W** and the letter **M**. Children are taught early on that once the **W** rotates one-half turn, it is now the letter **M**. Or the number **5**, once it is reflected across a line, more closely resembles the number **2**. How these rigid motions act differently on geometry shapes (as well as differences in how they act on the surface on which the rigid motion is taking place) is critical for children to grasp spatial thinking.

Symmetry

There are three kinds of symmetry, each of which is related to one of the rigid motions: translational, reflection, and rotational. Translation symmetry is often called "artistic" symmetry. This sort of symmetry occurs when a shape is translated (slid) and copied. Wallpaper is an example of translation symmetry. Reflection symmetry occurs when a shape has a line of symmetry across which it can be folded and the two parts are congruent. Primary school children can cut hearts out of folded construction paper, or fifth graders can check for symmetry in articles of clothing or furniture. Eighth grade students apply various rigid motions to geometric shapes in an effort to validate claims about symmetry. A favorite art activity is to provide students with one-half of a page from

Figure 2 . 3

Examples and Nonexamples for Concept Development

Parallelogram (Quadrilateral with opposite sides parallel)			
Examples		**Nonexamples**	
Looks like	*Why it is important*	**Looks like**	*Why it is important*
	Has only the essential features ("best" example).		Only one set of parallel sides (not two sets).
	Has the added features of 90-degree angles, opposite sides equal, and is rotated.	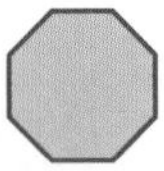	Opposite sides are parallel; not a quadrilateral.
	Has the added feature of 90-degree angles.	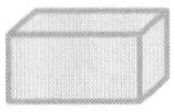	Is not two-dimensional, opposite sides are parallel.
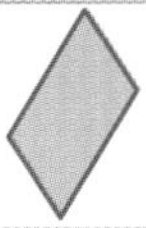	Has the essential features and is rotated.		Is not a polygon (is not a quadrilateral).

Rectangle (Parallelogram with four 90-degree angles)			
Examples		**Nonexamples**	
Looks like	*Why it is important*	**Looks like**	*Why it is important*
	Has only the essential features ("best" example).		Does not have 90-degree angles.
	Has the added features of opposite sides equal; and is rotated.	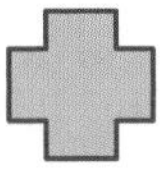	Has 90-degree angles; opposite sides are parallel, but is not a quadrilateral.
	Has the added feature of equal sides.	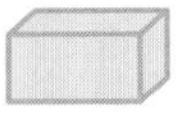	Is not two-dimensional. Has parallelogram faces and 90-degree angles.
	Has the essential features and is rotated.		Is not a polygon (is not a parallelogram).

a magazine and ask them to draw the other half, using symmetry. The third kind of symmetry is rotational symmetry. If a shape can be rotated (other than 360 degrees) and match up exactly with how it looked before the rotation began, then the shape has rotational symmetry. See Figure 2.4 (p. 28) for examples and nonexamples of symmetry. You are encouraged to find several more examples and nonexamples that could have been used in Figure 2.4.

Figure 2 . 3

continued

Triangle (Three-sided polygon)			
Examples		**Nonexamples**	
Looks like	*Why it is important*	**Looks like**	*Why it is important*
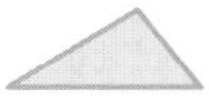	Has only the essential features ("best" example).		Has more than three sides.
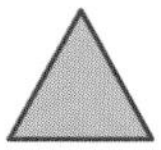	Has the added feature of three equal sides.		Is not simple (is not a polygon).
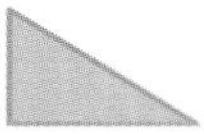	Has the added feature of a 90-degree angle.	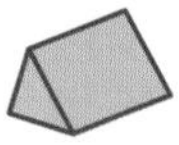	Ends are triangles, but it is not two-dimensional.
	Has the added features of rotated and isosceles.		Is not a polygon.

Triangular Pyramid (or select a kind of pyramid)			
Examples		**Nonexamples**	
Looks like	*Why it is important*	**Looks like**	*Why it is important*
	Has only the essential features ("best" example).		Is truncated.
	Has the added feature of an equilateral triangular base.		Is not _____.
	Has the added feature of _____.		Is not three-dimensional.

Practicing Spatial Visualizations

In the next Classroom Connections you will hear how Karen's students exercised spatial thinking to find mathematical attributes of the leaves they studied. As students mature in their mathematical understanding, the arrangements and the spatial visualizations can and should become more abstract and more

Figure 2 . 4

Examples and Nonexamples for Symmetry

Symmetry				
	Examples		**Nonexamples**	
	Figure	*Why it is important*	**Figure**	*Why it is important*
Rotation (turn)		Clarifies the need to imagine symmetry beyond "line" symmetry.	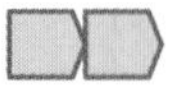	"Looks balanced" but will not rotate into place.
Translation (slide)		Rarely studied (in school mathematics). Demonstrates usefulness of nonsimple figures.	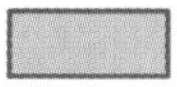	Rectangles often appear to "have it all." It is important to study all of its mathematical properties.
Reflection (line)		Familiar shape, will be heavily used in proof-geometry.		"Looks balanced" but often surprises students that it does not have line symmetry.

CLASSROOM CONNECTIONS

Finding Symmetry in Nature

Planning with colleagues can help to integrate curricular areas. I agree with the NCTM (2000) that "interconnections should be displayed prominently in the curriculum and instructional materials and lessons" (p. 15). When my science colleague asked the fifth graders to bring in leaves for a photosynthesis lesson, I saw an opportunity for a math lesson. I brought in a variety of leaves also. We did several math activities with the leaves before they were needed in science. After students looked at all the leaves, I asked, "What do you notice about the leaves?" We organized them into groups by physical attributes. Depending on the rule, some leaves belonged in more than one group. For example, a leaf could have several tips and be in the category "more than one tip" while also belonging to another group according to its color.

After identifying a large silver maple leaf, I asked the students to imagine what a baby silver maple leaf would look like if a leaf grew in all directions at the same rate. "Would the mature leaf look the same as, or different than, the baby leaf?" We set the leaf on the overhead projector and rolled the projector back and forth to mimic the leaf's change in size from baby to adult. One thing the students noticed immediately was that the overall shape of the leaf did not change. I knew that we would later use graph paper to approximate the area of a silver maple leaf. I wanted to prepare the students for this upcoming measurement lesson by accentuating their spatial visualization skills now. To culminate the lesson, I tore leaves in half and glued one half of each onto a piece of paper. The students visualized and drew the other half. This symmetry lesson builds on students' visualization skills.

NCTM CURRICULUM

general. Activity 2.3 (p. 30) requires you to think carefully about assigning rules or categories to the shapes, which is a form of concept knowledge. You might want to make a few of the objects out of string to get started. But eventually, you should to try to mentally bend the shapes. Pay attention to changes in your spatial thinking skills as a result of this activity.

GRASPING THE PROCEDURES:
How to Build Shapes

As students develop concept knowledge and spatial visualization skills about geometric ideas, sometimes they think about how to draw a shape along with what it is and what it is related to. It is important to help students think about the differences between these ideas and to use them as opportunities to separate concept knowledge from procedural knowledge.

We regularly provide opportunities for students to develop conceptual knowledge about ideas such as circle and square. On the other hand, we also have the responsibility to develop procedural knowledge for these ideas. Procedures are step-by-step directions a learner can follow to accomplish one or more goals of a mathematical task. Procedures can be thought of as specific "how to" descriptions or as general strategies. Knowing procedures well and being able to use them appropriately can greatly simplify mathematical problem solving. Procedures are typically very efficient and can be quickly and easily applied. Compare step-by-step directions for drawing a square to your mental image of a square.

It is important to help students distinguish between a definition that is conceptual (relationship oriented) and a definition that is procedural (how-to oriented). Both definitions are useful types of knowledge, but they represent different kinds of knowledge. Students can memorize how to do a procedure without fully understanding the concept. When conceptual knowledge anchors procedural knowledge, the mathematical knowledge is more connected. It is important to listen to students explain their understandings so that you can decipher their thinking as conceptual or procedural. Thus allow you to ask appropriate follow-up questions.

Children Describe a Square

Listen to these fifth graders give procedural definitions for a square:

Min: You draw a square by making four 90-degree angle lines that are all equal length. [She means segments.] Two of the lines go side to side [She means horizontal.] and are parallel to each other then the other lines go up and down and are parallel too. It's a closed shape.

Ryan: To draw a square, you need four perfectly equal lines [He means segments.] and four corners.

Lydia: Here are the instructions for making a square. You need to remember that all four sides need to be equal. There needs to be four sides and four corners. Those are the instructions for making a square.

Now, listen to a conceptual definition:

Jamal: I know that a square is a quadrilateral with four 90-degree angles and all four of its sides are equal and all sides across from each other are parallel.

Activity 2 . 3

THE TOPOLOGICAL ALPHABET!

Elementary topics from topology can enrich study of geometry. Topological equivalence means that two shapes have the same basic structure. For example, a circle (○) and a square (□) are topologically equivalent because they are both closed curves with no points of intersection. A ○ is not equivalent to an 8 because the 8 has a point of intersection. Imagine the ○ being lifted off the plane and twisted to form the 8. This action is not allowed. That new point of intersection eliminates the possibility of equivalence: ○ ≠ 8.

Basic Structure	A famous problem uses this idea to find equivalent letters of the alphabet. For instance, E and Y are equivalent because they are formed from the same basic structure. Imagine stretching and bending the top and bottom legs of the basic structure around the point of intersection, which acts like a hinge, to create the top and bottom flags on the E.

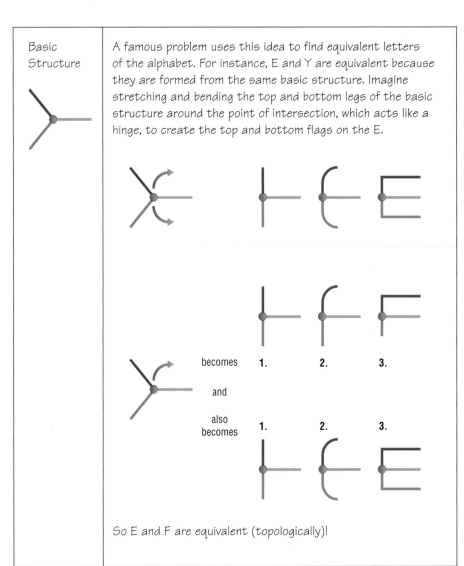

So E and F are equivalent (topologically)!

It helps to think of points of intersection as hinges and segments as malleable rubber.

Use the basic configurations in the table, make letters and numerals.

A B C D E F G H I J K L M N O P Q R
S T U V W X Y Z 0 1 2 3 4 5 6 7 8 9

Basic Structure	The Alphabet Letters	The Numbers
	R R	
	R	

Notice that for some letters like "R," the topological structure depends on how you write the letter.

The Net of a Solid Shape

Just as Hannah, the kindergartner, was able to abstract plane shapes from a solid shape's face by creating footprints, adolescent learners should be encouraged to take that same approach in new directions. The learning should still begin with solid shapes and move to plane shapes. In the middle grades, learners can already abstract all possible plane shapes from a solid object. But a net is formed when a solid shape is peeled apart so that all its faces (or footprints) are drawn on the plane in such a way as to show how the edges of the solid are connected. If that diagram were then cut out of the plane, it could be folded back up and exactly cover the solid. Sometimes we call these "jackets." Adolescent students need experiences in abstracting the net from a solid, which is more complicated than abstracting a single face from a solid because the abstraction includes the joining edges. Once

these nets have been drawn as figures on a plane, many questions can be asked. Is there only one net for a given solid? How many nets are there for a cube? What would have to change on a net to turn a cube's net into a square pyramid's net? As students learn to mentally manipulate nets, they enhance their spatial thinking skills.

After students study nets, the interior of the solid can be studied. Students must learn to visualize the various shapes of cross sections of solids. That is, when a solid is sliced into two parts, what is the shape of the newly created face, the cross section? Our middle school students found it interesting to study the number of cross-sectional shapes they could create by slicing a cube. We used gelatin cubes and string to cut them. Can you slice a cube and create a trapezoid or a nonsquare rectangle cross section?

It is important to note that Ryan and Lydia used the word *corner,* meaning to imply a 90-degree angle. Many students used the word *line* but talked about its length. Through class discussion, we encouraged our students to use the term *segment* instead. They eventually realized that Jamal's statement of "90 degrees" was a more precise statement than "corner." Jamal's definition is different from the other three definitions because he describes square conceptually rather than procedurally. You might want to compare the other students' statements noting procedural steps that could be followed to draw a square.

Drawing a Triangle

Let's try another example. Draw a triangle in the margin. Most of us probably drew a triangle that is a close approximation of an equilateral triangle oriented to set horizontally on one side. People rarely choose to draw a scalene triangle, an isosceles triangle, or a triangle rotated so that a vertex points down. It might be argued that this equilateral triangle is the (1) most easily visualized or (2) most commonly taught procedure. A procedure should include how to draw *any* three-sided shape so that the drawing would not tend toward one particular image. The ability to accomplish this is, of course, enhanced if the concept of triangle is well known. In general, we need to clarify the ways in which a procedure directs students to draw a physical representation of the mental idea, the concept.

Procedures are simply not as obvious in this part as they will be in the next four parts. To clarify, Activity 2.4 provides an opportunity for you to practice building solid shapes. Concentrate on the procedures you used, and try to distinguish between those procedures and the concepts on which your procedures relied. Think about a good way to give a set of step-by-step instructions for building a solid shape.

Activity 2.4

BUILDING POLYHEDRA

1. Build five *different* polyhedra.
2. Determine a name for each polyhedron based on the shape of the base and whether or not it is in the prism or pyramid family.
3. Complete the information in the chart and generalize a pattern about the number of vertices, edges, and faces.

Name	Sketch of Shape	Number of Vertices	Number of Edges	Number of Faces
Triangular pyramid				

LET'S REVIEW

In thinking about the mathematics of geometry, we learned that both concepts and procedures are part of the mathematical knowledge base. Concepts include identifying properties of shapes, being able to compare shapes, and recognizing groupings of shapes, such as being a polygon or not being a polygon. Definitions are conceptual because definitions are relationship statements. For example, *polygons are closed simple plane shapes made only of segments.* Procedures include how to draw or build a shape (plane or solid). Any step-by-step procedure should be accompanied by a demonstration and should have these features: (1) the polygon must be drawn in one plane; (2) the polygon should be composed only of segments (no curves); (3) the polygon's segments should not cross through any other segments (simple); and (4) each of the polygon's segments is connected to adjacent segments at both end points (closed). It is important to see connections between geometric concepts and procedures, as this is demonstrative of deep mathematical knowledge.

HOMEWORK

1. Create a visual image (like the one in Activity 2.2) in which "circle" is the central concept. You must use the following sets of connecting words at least once. Check them off as you use them.

Is	Is not	Is the shape of	Does not look like
Has	Does not have	Looks like	Is the same as

You must use the following concept words in the bubbles. Check them off as you use them.

Ellipse	Rounded	A clock face	Polygon
Cone	Breakfast plate	πr^2	Radius
Center	Disk	Can of corn	

2. a. Draw a four-set Venn diagram. Sometimes it is easier to begin with three sets and then figure out where the fourth set should be drawn.
   b. Label your sets: A. Square shapes, B. Red shapes, C. Smooth shapes, and D. Things found in the kitchen.
   c. Sort and classify the following objects into your four-set Venn diagram.
   d. Explain why the cookie sheet goes where you put it.

Cracker	Baseball diamond	Domino	Trivet
Sneaker	Floor tile	Plate	Brick
Cookie sheet	Your choice	Your choice	Your choice

SUGGESTED READINGS

Carpenter, T. (1986). Conceptual knowledge as a foundation for procedural knowledge. In J. Hiebert (Ed.), *Conceptual and procedural knowledge: The case of mathematics* (pp. 113–132). Hillsdale, NJ: Erlbaum.

REFERENCES

Cockcraft, W. H., & Marshall, J. (1999). Educating Hannah. *Teaching Children Mathematics, 5*(6), 326–329.
Fuys, D., & Liebov, A. K. (1997). Concept learning in geometry. *Teaching Children Mathematics, 3*(5), 248–251.
National Council of Teachers of Mathematics. (2000). *Principles and standards for school mathematics.* Reston, VA: NCTM.

CHAPTER
3

How We Learn about
Geometry and Spatial Thinking

NCTM
LEARNING

UNDERSTANDING RELEVANT LEARNING THEORY: The van Hiele Theory

Van Hiele (1986) outlined a theory of geometric thinking about how students progress and develop sophisticated knowledge about geometry. In 1988, Fuys, Geddes, and Tischler interpreted much of that work. The van Hiele theory is a stage theory, set out in levels (see Table 3.1).

Level 0 (Visual)

The first step for learning about geometry is visualization. At this stage, learners develop a mental photograph of each shape. When confronted with an example, they simply check whether or not a given shape matches their visual image of the shape. When teaching students at this level, teachers need to expose the students to a multitude of good physical examples and nonexamples of the mathematical idea being studied.

Level 1 (Analysis)

The second step for students comes when they begin to notice and talk about the properties of a shape. The students might note that a circle is round, it has no corners, and it has a center. Rather than knowing geometric ideas holistically and visually, the students now start to pick those ideas or shapes apart. To accomplish this, teachers should urge students to recognize and talk about specific parts of an idea or shape. The students then come to include those properties in their knowledge about what the geometric idea or shape either is or is not.

To better compare levels 0 and 1, imagine Niko, a very young child who is considering a square. When asked why it is a square, he says, "That's a square

Table 3.1 **Examples from the First Four Levels of the van Hiele Theory of Learning**

VAN HIELE LEVEL 0 (VISUALIZATION)	
Looks Like	**Sounds Like**
Child selects specified shapes from a set of shapes.	"It looks like a square to me."
Child sorts shapes, matching shapes.	"These are squares (points) and these are not squares (points to shapes)"
Identifies squares from the classroom environment.	"These all look like a baseball diamond."
VAN HIELE LEVEL 1 (ANALYSIS)	
Can reasonably predict a shape's final form after seeing only part of it.	"I see one right angle, it could be a rectangle."
Lists several properties of a square.	"It has four 90-degree angles, four corners, four sides, and no curves—it's symmetric."
Can subdivide a shape into predetermined parts or create a shape from parts.	"These two triangles from the tangram set can be put together to make a square."
VAN HIELE LEVEL 2 (INFORMATION DEDUCTION)	
Recognizes that squares belong in both the rectangle pile and the rhombus pile.	"It has four equal sides, so it's a rhombus. It has right angles, it's a rectangle."
Subdivides a rectangle into two congruent triangles.	"These triangles are congruent because each is half of the same rectangle."
Recognizes that opposite angles in a rectangle are equal because rectangles are parallelograms.	"Since rectangles are parallelograms, these opposite angles should be equal."
VAN HIELE LEVEL 3 (FORMAL DEDUCTION)	
Recognizes that a rectangle can be subdivided into two congruent triangles.	"These two triangles are congruent because of the side-angle-side theorem."
Recognizes that if two circles intersect at two points and these two points are joined together with the centers of the two circles, the resulting figure will be a kite.	"Since they are radii from the same circle, the two adjacent sides within the circle will be congruent. Therefore, together, the four segments will form a kite."

because it looks like a saltine cracker." He is simply matching the object in question with a mental visualization. Later, as he removes himself from a holistic visualization of a square, he might say, "It has to be a square. Look, it's not curved, it has corners, and equal sides." In this case, Niko decides that the shape is a square because it had several properties he associates with a square. His change in thinking becomes particularly important when he encounters a shape that does not match his existing mental visualizations. Once he steps from looking at the entire geometric figure, considering only the whole shape (level 0), to looking at the individual, smaller components of that geometric shape, he has made a leap to level 1.

Level 2 (Informal Deduction)

At this level, students recognize that a shape is whatever it is because being that shape is a consequence of something the child already knows about the shape. Students stop relying on visualization (level 0), a laundry list of properties (level 1), or a multitude of measurements resulting in other empirical evidence (also level 1, discussed more thoroughly in Chapter 9). They use relationships to make a conclusion, create and use definitions easily, and understand the nature of converse statements. They might say, "*If* I have a center point and all the points are 5 centimeters from there, *then* I know I have a circle." This child used an if–then statement, showing consequences for the given situation, making a deduction from the least amount of given information (known as a *premise*). Being able to determine what those consequences are means that the thinking is at the informal deduction level.

Those are the first three levels of van Hiele's theory about how we learn geometry. The K–8 teacher probably needs to focus only on these first three levels and preparing children for the fourth level (level 3), which will be needed to successfully complete high school geometry (Senk, 1989). The K–8 teacher probably should not worry if students do not demonstrate thinking at the fourth and fifth levels. However, you can refer to Table 3.1 to work with that occasional child who demonstrates upper-level thinking.

Level 3 (Formal Deduction)

At this fourth level, the learner is able to make deductions and to support those deductions in a sophisticated and precise manner. This level differs from the informal deduction level in that the learner makes and supports claims on a much more abstract level. This type of geometry is typically associated with high school geometry. Students construct their own formal proofs about their deductions.

Level 4 (Rigor)

This fifth level is typically associated with college-level courses in which students compare different geometries at the proof level. (Consider comparing a proof involving quadrilaterals on the plane to a proof involving quadrilaterals drawn on a sphere.)

The remainder of this book will focus on the first three levels in depth and will refer to them frequently.

Characteristics of the Theory

All learners have to go through each level sequentially for every geometric idea they learn. The levels are not age dependent (Teppo, 1991; Usiskin, 1982). Whether a college student or a kindergartner, the learner must attain each level or the new geometric idea has not really been learned. Without knowing what a shape, figure, or idea looks like (visualization), there will be no chance to look at and study the parts (analysis) and work with it more abstractly (informal deduction). For example, consider the idea of a line segment. First-level (level 0) children would know that a given shape is a line segment when the shape with which they are presented matches their visualization of a line segment. The image of a line segment might conjure up a skid mark, the letter l, or a green bean.

Second-level (level 1) students consider the properties of a line segment. The students notice two endpoints. The segment itself is the shortest distance between the two points. The segment is "straight." The students who consider these (and other) properties to decide whether a shape is a segment are at the analysis stage.

But if students say, "If a figure represents the shortest path between two points, then it is a segment," then they are at van Hiele's third level (level 2). Here students informally deduce that the shape is a segment from the premise that the shape represented the shortest distance between two points. They did not purposely add the statement about the straightness of the path, because they knew that straightness would be a consequence of being a shortest path. This ability to be concerned with necessary and sufficient statements is one clear fact that separates the analysis-level child from the informal deduction–level child.

Table 3.1 used the familiar "looks like," "sounds like" approach to show examples of the van Hiele theory. In Table 3.2, we use one idea (symmetry) to further clarify how a teacher might use the van Hiele theory to help students classify shapes, figures, and designs into categories of symmetric and not symmetric. Knowing about rigid motions helps students to analyze (level 1) why a shape is symmetric. Students can also be taught to categorize shapes and figures according to symmetry just by looking at them (level 0).

Promoting Development. Learners do not just naturally develop in their knowledge owing to physical maturation. Crowley (1987) is very clear about the importance of the teacher in students' development. Only through purposeful instruction will students' geometric reasoning develop. A teacher can use the van Hiele theory to (1) diagnose the child's geometric level and (2) choose targeted follow-up questions. A spatial thinking activity (Activity 3.1, p. 40) will further illustrate this aspect of van Hiele's theory. Like puzzles, tangrams can be used to fill outlines of larger shapes. Use one set of tangrams to build the proud goose, the flying duck, and the attacking crab. While a child is working on such a task, a teacher might ask, "Where does this small triangle go?" After the child explains where to place the piece, asking, "Why do you think it goes there?" will provide a question that can begin diagnosis. Cues about the van Hiele level of the child's thinking will be embedded in the response. One child might say, "It sure looks like it's going to fit." A second child might say, "Well, these edges are the same length so, it seems like it should fit." The third child might give you a variety of reasons, "Well, it's half of this shape, so it must fit."

If we know our students' van Hiele levels, we can think more clearly about what they can do. We can structure activities and formulate questions that are designed to push students to think at the next level. If our students can recognize a circle or disk only visually, we should not expect them to give analysis or informal deductive–type answers. We can structure activities to develop their diverse images about geometric ideas and shapes toward higher levels. We can

Table 3.2 **Example Conversations about Why a Rectangle Has Symmetry**

SHAPE	LEVEL 0	LEVEL 1	LEVEL 2	LEVEL 3
	"It looks balanced."	"When I cut it out and folded it over, all of the sides matched up."	"Since this is a rectangle, opposite sides will match up when I fold it."	"When I join the midpoints of opposite sides with a perpendicular segment, I create two other rectangles that I can prove are congruent. Therefore, the perpendicular line segment is the line of symmetry."
What the teacher notices	To the student the shape just "looks" balanced.	The student is analyzing the shape looking for line symmetry.	The student is making an informal deduction based on properties of rectangles.	The student is looking for a way to prove that the "fold" is the line of symmetry.
Questions that might be asked	Could you point to the balanced parts?	I wonder how you could know that for certain. Can you use tangram pieces?	Where are you going to fold? What makes that the best place to fold it?	What rigid motions would you combine to demonstrate the symmetry?
Questions to further promote thinking	What would a shape look like that wasn't balanced?	I wonder whether all rectangles act like that.	What is special about the rectangle shape that makes this happen?	Can you use any of the triangle congruence theorems here?
Write your own questions:				

You may choose to build a rectangle here using tangram pieces.

ask questions to ensure that images are mathematically correct. Then we can require learners to use those images to consider properties or make deductions. To further clarify these levels, we asked a group of fifth graders to do the following:

1. Draw a square.
2. How did you know what to draw? What makes a square a square? List its attributes or rules.

Activity 3 . 1

PROUD GOOSE

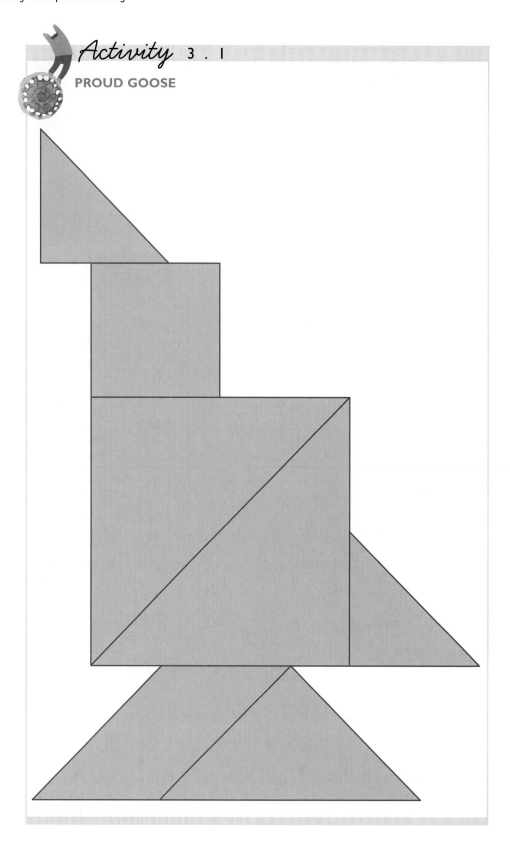

Examples of students' responses to the questions were as follows:

> **Min:** A square has four sides. It has four sides and four corners.
> **Lydia:** I drew a corner first and then kept drawing three more corners with-
> out lifting up my pencil. [van Hiele's second level (level 1)]

FLYING DUCK

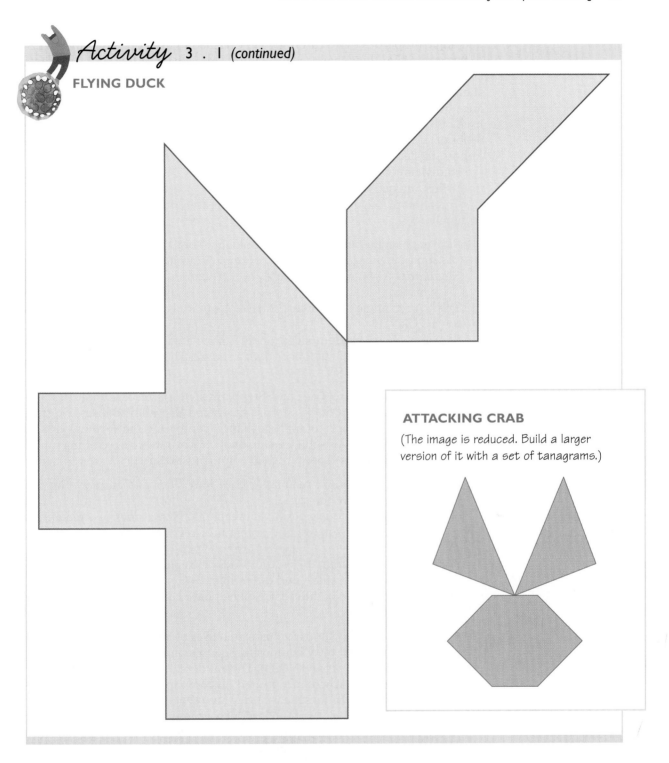

ATTACKING CRAB

(The image is reduced. Build a larger version of it with a set of tanagrams.)

Ryan: I learned in kindergarten that a square has four equal sides, four corners, and is a flattened solid cube.

Jamal: I knew what to draw because of four 90-degree angles and four sides that are all equal. [van Hiele's third level (level 2)]

We found that our students referred to the need for attention to either both sides and angles, just sides, or just angles. We worked to help them deduce informally that statements involving just angles could result in a nonsquare rectangle and that statements involving just sides could result in a rhombus. Through our discussion, they came to understand they needed to consider side and angle properties more carefully. They needed to use both sides and angles to be certain that their shapes were squares. After the discussion, the students charged themselves with adjusting their work by rewriting their rules for a square. Because of the discussion, they knew they had to "get more efficient" and "be more specific," both of which are traits of informal deduction. We had used our knowledge of van Hiele to guide students beyond listing specific properties of squares. Moving past properties and into the realm of deduction is an important step. Often, these deductions are based on some sort of pattern that the students recognize between and among shapes, in the process of engaging in lessons and activities.

To compare, we also asked a group of first graders to define square and rectangle.

> *Akoya:* A square and a rectangle look alike, but they really aren't alike. A square has even lines, and a rectangle is stretched out.
> *Stephanie:* A square looks like a checkerboard and a rectangle looks like a brick.
> *Tyler:* A rectangle is not like a square. A square is a TV, and a rectangle is a VCR.
> *Shera:* A square has four sides. So does a rectangle. But a rectangle's sides have been pulled out longer than a square. The rectangle has two short and two long sides.

You should recognize Tyler and Stephanie's efforts to base their descriptions on how the shapes "look." Yet in Akoya and Shera's responses, we start to see an inkling of efforts to analyze shapes, comparing the various parts of each shape. All four of these children are on their way toward developing sound knowledge about squares. Compare their comments to third graders' comments:

> *Kylie:* Both squares and rectangles have four sides and corners. But the square's sides are the same.
> *T. J.:* Squares have four sides, like a rectangle. Sometimes two rectangles can make up a square, and sometimes rectangles are bigger than a square.
> *Zach:* Squares have four angles, four sides, and equal sides. Rectangles have four angles, four sides, and different sides.
> *Mindi:* Their sides look different. Squares have equal sides, but everything else is the same.

Do you recognize slightly more sophisticated uses of language? Stephanie and Tyler, first graders, were busy comparing squares and rectangles to solid figures in their worlds (bricks and VCRs). They understood the shapes differently from the third graders, who concentrated on comparing the squares and rectangles to one another. In these ways, they are recognizing the importance of analyzing (level 1, van Hiele's second level) the various properties of the shapes. In particular, Mindi and Kyli seem to be appropriately aware that squares are special rectangles, whereas Akoya and Shera, the first graders, erroneously view rectangles as being "stretched" or elongated squares—in other words, special squares.

Issues Specific to Spatial Visualization

As you read through our students' answers, you might notice that students at all ages seemed to use a mixture of solid and plane shapes in their explanations about a square. In general, when students somehow stretch, twist, or modify a shape, they are exercising some of their spatial visualization skills. To become more skilled at manipulating specific shapes mentally, students will need to check their mental manipulation predictions by manipulating corresponding physical objects (Battista, 2002). As students continue with meaningful experiences with physical objects, they refine their mental visualization skills. They become more adept at coordinating and accessing their general mental collections of shapes on the basis of the general class of shapes being referenced. Ryan, who describes a square as a flattened cube, described a cube as a "pushed-up" square. Apparently, he moves fluidly between the plane shape and the solid shape and is comfortable allowing one kind of image to satisfy his description of the other kind of image. We can provide students with opportunities to enhance their spatial visualization skills by asking them to describe their thinking to each other but also by carefully selecting tasks that require them to exert mental manipulation of both solid and plane objects while manipulating the related physical objects.

USING RELEVANT PATTERNS:
Extending Pattern Starters

Children who have experiences with patterning can draw on those experiences to help them make general statements about geometry shapes. In general, mathematics can sometimes be considered the result of having made sense of patterns. When a learner logically considers a pattern and recognizes the pattern in such a way that he or she makes a generalization, then that learner is often said to have engaged in the process of mathematics. Students should be able to describe the general nature of a given pattern, extend a given pattern to any number of terms, and create their own patterns as representative of a situation. As K–8 learners work to describe patterns, they will recognize that we expect them to handle two types of patterns: repeating and growing.

Repeating versus Growing

In geometry, patterns often demonstrate a predictable repetition of shapes. We usually give children a *pattern starter*, which is the first few terms in a pattern. Consider pattern starter A: ▽, ○, □, ▽, ○, □, ▽, ○, □, ... Pattern A is repeating the chunk of ▽, ○, □. Learners should be able to describe what is happening and extend the pattern starter on the basis of shape recognition and identification of repetition of the shapes. In a growing pattern, there is some predictable change that the learner is expected to understand. Consider pattern starter B: ○, □, ○, □, □, ○, □, □, □, ... The learner could recognize that one explanation is the number of □ in each chunk is growing by one, whereas the ○ is serving as a marker that indicates the spot from which the □ is growing.

As learners work to extend given pattern starters, they should be urged to recognize that the last term in a pattern starter is *not* necessarily an ending or a pause between chunks. For instance, consider asking a learner to extend pattern starter C: ○, □, ○, □, ... The learner might believe that this pattern merely repeats the ○, □ chunk when in fact an alternative pattern extension could be pattern B. This also brings up variance in possible pattern extensions that students might suggest when their work is to extend patterns. Because students will be encouraged to open their minds to a variety of extensions to pattern starters, teachers should be ready to hear several solutions.

It is important to accept children where they are and work with them from that point.

Recognizing Deep Structure

Students should come to recognize the deep structure of mathematical patterns. Deep structure is the general, underlying pattern that does not depend on the specific elements in the pattern. In fact, deep structure *is* the mathematical part of a pattern. Consider pattern starter D: ◆, □, ◆, □, ◆, □, ◆, □, . . . ; pattern starter E: ○, □, ○, □, ○, □, ○, □, . . . ; pattern starter F: boy, girl, boy, girl, . . . ; and pattern starter G: left, right, left, right, left, ... The deep structure of these four patterns is identical even though the individual terms that make up the patterns are quite different. We also have begun to depart from strict use of geometric shapes. K–8 learners should engage in activities so that they can identify deep structures of patterns well beyond geometry. But because geometry is so visual, it serves as an easy entry point for pattern explorations. Students can create patterns that are identical to a given pattern, in terms of deep structure, while using or not using geometric shapes. This serves as a springboard to other mathematical areas. In each part of this book, we explore patterns that are relevant to the content of that part.

To encourage children to develop skill with geometric patterning, as well as patterning in general, they must have many experiences describing, extending, and creating patterns. Although an activity such as Activity 3.2 with patterning is a piece of any well-developed mathematics curriculum, patterns can also be considered for use as a general problem-solving tool. When learners recognize the possibility and plausibility of looking for a pattern in order to solve a problem, then they have used patterning as a problem-solving strategy.

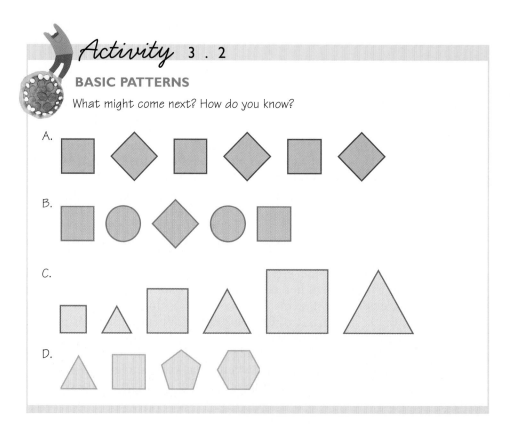

Activity 3 . 2

BASIC PATTERNS

What might come next? How do you know?

A.

B.

C.

D.

USING TEACHING AIDS APPROPRIATELY:
Concrete, Pictorial, Symbolic

Teaching aids are tools, such as manipulatives, that can illuminate certain points and illustrate important mathematical ideas. Manipulatives can be made to model mathematical concepts and can be used to demonstrate procedures. You should recognize that precisely what children are thinking, though, sometimes does not "look" like the manipulative you might have chosen. In a way, that can be a good thing, because the students are building their own abstractions to make sense of the situation. Asking younger children to draw about their thinking is a good way to understand what they are using (or not using) in terms of their ideas about the manipulatives you have chosen. It will also tell you the extent to which the children can represent their own thinking, which will tell you about their levels of abstraction about the mathematics. We do intend that children be able to use more symbolic representations as they progress. However, even older students should be asked to represent their thinking with drawings. Their work can give useful insight into the level of symbolic manipulation with which they are comfortable. For instance, if an adolescent draws a shape that is clearly not rectangular but can use the shape to solve a problem involving rectangles, then he or she is free from the confines of the drawing's need to "look like" the object being studied.

We also want to remind you that manipulatives, in and of themselves, do not teach. Manipulatives can be used to help teachers teach and hence help students to think. Manipulatives give everyone in the room a similar frame of reference. But it is the mathematical questions you ask about the situation being modeled by the manipulatives that teaches. And don't forget that very often, the best representations of students' thinking are their own pictures or drawings. In the end, our goal is to help students to think and to understand as precisely as possible what they are thinking. Teaching tools that we use are representations that might exist in any one of three appearances (concrete, pictorial, or symbolic). Bruner (1966) explains that students might need you to represent the situation using any (or all) of these modes. Our ultimate goal is to ensure that students can work with the most symbolic mode of representation. But Bruner cautions us against assuming that we can simply move through the three modes of representation. "There is no unique sequence for all learners, and the optimum in any particular case will depend upon a variety of factors" (Bruner, 1966, p. 49).

Concrete Representations

At first, learners recognize only the physical elements of the object in question. They might pick up a glass (cylinder) and inspect it. They know if it is smooth. They know if it has any chips. The teacher must prompt the learner's separation from the physical knowledge of the glass to the mathematical circle within the glass. Students do not directly internalize mathematical ideas from the materials through osmosis. The mathematics represented by the object must be enticed *from* the object *for* the student and usually *by* the teacher. In this process, children might be encouraged to trace a fingertip around the smooth circle at the rim of the glass or to make a footprint, as described in Chapter 2. Eventually, students should be made to recognize the match between this circular object and other physical, concrete-level models of a circle, such as a key ring or a bracelet. Students need to hold examples and nonexamples of a circle because the child is forming concept knowledge about "circle." Several different sizes of glasses and other circular and noncircular items should be provided so that the students can connect the physical specimens to the mental notions of "cylinder" and "circle."

Pictorial Representations

Second, collections of photographs and drawings should be presented to and explored by the children. The learners still need to study examples and nonexamples because they are developing concept knowledge but are developing it with representations that are not the real-life object in question. Yakimanskaya (1991) makes clear that there is a tremendous difference in the spatial thinking of a child who is studying a realistic, actual-sized model of something and a child who is studying a pictorial representation of it. One way to connect these ideas is for children to create their own drawings. Other ways include explicitly pointing out various aspects of a pictorial representation. Meaningful drawings enable students to construct mathematical knowledge because learners build their own bridge between the concrete item and a more symbolic representation of it. Children must work hard to develop mental ideas (abstractions) that they can infer from a picture of a glass.

An actual photograph is a more concrete pictorial representation than a drawing, and drawings can be realistic or abstract. All three kinds of pictorial representations should be used as the student begins to get the idea that mathematical information can come from a picture as well as from a physical object. Pictures and drawings of several different circular and noncircular objects should be provided to help construct mental ideas about cylinder, circle, and even sphere. With guided experiences, relationships among all pictures and drawings should develop. Grouping pictures that show something that is circular lays a foundation for the symbolic representation.

Symbolic Representations

Third, it is important to use only symbols and signs that the teacher and students agree to use to communicate the idea of circle. One of those symbols might be the geometric symbol for a circle, which is ⊙A (where A is the center point), or the word *circle*. Either is a symbolic representation of the idea of circle. This journey is necessary. Activities only with concrete materials or only with symbols do not recognize the need to move around representations and to make connections among them. Students must work with a variety of objects that represent circles and be evaluated with materials that match the kind of activity associated with those materials. In particular, spatial thinking that is called up by a symbolic representation is very different from spatial thinking that is used in studying the physical item (Yakimanskaya, 1991). Spatial thinking about a physical item is more like a photograph of it, probably having all of the features of the object itself, whether or not those features are critical to understanding the mathematics of the object. Spatial thinking of a symbolic representation is more abstract and might or might not include "unimportant" features of the actual object.

Concrete Materials versus Level 0 Thinking

We wish to clarify two notes about the three kinds of representation. First, students may be using concrete materials and operating at any of the van Hiele levels of reasoning. It is tempting to assume that concrete materials somehow connect to van Hiele's first level (level 0). However, this is a misuse of the ideas associated with both van Hiele's theory and the nature of abstract reasoning.

It is quite possible that a student makes an informal deduction using concrete solids or uses only visualization reasoning when working with pictorial representations. Interactions with teaching aids depend on levels of abstraction about mathematics. It is important not to confuse interactions with materials as thinking; rather, thinking must be recognized as different from the manipulative. Assuming that a certain representation implies a certain level of abstract thinking is an oversimplification of the thinking and of the learning. Moreover, a student might be comfortable with a symbolic representation of one idea and prefer a concrete representation of a different idea. Neither of these facts is necessarily indicative of the student's van Hiele level of thinking.

Concrete Together with Symbolic and Pictorial Together with Symbolic

Second, students must be guided to connect concrete materials with symbolic representations as well as connecting pictorial representations with symbolic representations before being expected to work exclusively with symbols. If students work with the rim at the top of a physical representation of a cylinder, they should simultaneously see a symbolic version of circle. The teacher might use the word *circle* or the more sophisticated label ○A written on a small card and displayed in full view of the students. See Figure 3.1 for an example.

Figure 3 . 1

Connecting Pictorial Representations with Symbolic Representations

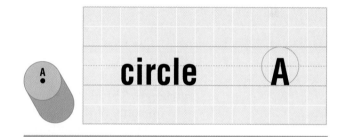

We do eventually want students to communicate exclusively with symbolic representations, so we must support their development of knowledge and facility with representative symbols. However, this desire must be tempered with recognition that in some mathematical situations, a picture *is* the best mode of representation to make a certain point. Here, we are talking about the ability of the student to use symbols exclusively and know if it makes sense to do so. Early lessons should use concrete materials together with symbols, and later lessons should include pictures together with symbols, followed by lessons using symbols only. It is important to plan instruction toward this goal. We must specifically and deliberately sequence and structure activities to make these connections.

 # Types of Concrete Materials

Cubes

Cubes are a fairly generic manipulative that can be used for spatial thinking. The cube is simple, familiar, and easy to handle. Commercial cubes made from wood or plastic have long life, but gelatin cubes or sugar cubes can also be used if your school allows food products in the classroom. Students can be asked to predict where a cube would fit in a building after having been given one particular view. (Activity 3.5 is presented later in this chapter.)

Pattern Blocks

Pattern blocks are a commercial manipulative set of six shapes. The set of shapes includes a hexagon, a square, two sizes of nonsquare rhombi, a trapezoid, and

M I D D L E   S C H O O L   C O N N E C T I O N S

Manipulatives Are (Not) for Babies

All learners need to experience the van Hiele sequence when learning geometry. However, when confronted with the prospect of using manipulatives to make an analysis or informal deduction kinds of statement, many adolescent learners conjure up images of kindergarten and playing with blocks. Feeling that they have grown beyond such use of school time, some adolescent students are reluctant to engage with materials. Be prepared to encourage them. The encouragement should include asking meaningful questions that are unanswerable without the materials. Other strategies include pairing students such that at least one student is likely to be comfortable with the manipulatives. In addition, using concrete materials should not be a one-time-only event. Comfort with the materials will grow from prolonged use. Behavior-related rules (e.g., "Put the materials in the bag when not in use") for using the materials will set important ground rules and inform the student that these materials are not toys but legitimate learning tools.

We take this opportunity to remind you that just because students are in their adolescent years does not mean they are operating at the informal deduction level. For example, when studying parallel lines, students will need to work with a variety of concrete materials that compel analyses (e.g., edges on a box they can measure, front and back cover of a book they can fold, lawn mower tracks they can examine for straightness). Before students can analyze (van Hiele level 1) a figure on paper, they need to analyze physical manifestations of the idea. Manipulating various representations (concrete, pictorial, and symbolic) of the concepts will help to propel meaning into the discussion. After students analyze several representations, informal deductions (van Hiele level 2) about the information can be drawn out.

a triangle. The blocks have been designed to fit together nicely, with many angles on some of the shapes having equal measures. These blocks can be a lot of fun. They are vibrantly colored and lead quickly into interesting pattern building. It is important to monitor the use of these materials (as with any material). They have a somewhat playful air. Be aware of this feature before using them with students of all ages. The first time students use these blocks, it might be necessary to allow them five minutes of play time before engaging the students in a mathematical investigation.

Tangrams

Tangram manipulatives are another tool that can be used to develop students' spatial thinking. They are a seven-piece set of shapes (five triangles in three sizes, one square, and one nonsquare parallelogram). Often, an outline of a figure is given, and students predict where each piece from the set could fit to fill in the outine. Tangrams can be used to demonstrate the results of subdividing a shape or building up a shape, an important component of any spatial thinking curriculum.

Assessment and the Use of Materials

Mathematics is a mental endeavor. If students learn a mathematical idea at the visualization level, by working tasks using concrete materials, then assessment should include concrete materials. If students work and think about the mathematics using concrete materials but the assessment uses pictures, students often do not understand what is needed (or even being asked) because they might not have made those connections yet. They will likely perform poorly on such a mismatched assessment. It is important to distinguish between representations so that assessments inform us about whether or not the students know the mathematical ideas and not just their awareness of representations. Of course, it is acceptable to use manipulatives or pictures on assessments. Imagining that those manipulatives or pictures must be removed for the mathematics to be evaluated discounts the importance of multiple representations. Moreover, it might cause the learner to be embarrassed about using manipulatives or drawing pictures to figure out an answer. Even well-established mathematicians draw pictures to help make sense of a mathematical idea.

CULTURAL CONNECTIONS
Creating a Mosaic

Mathematics was developed by (human) mathematicians. So the content of accepted mathematical ideas is clearly culturally influenced. Often, some children (and some adults) believe that mathematics simply "is" or that there is one math guru somewhere who decides what mathematics "is." On the contrary, mathematics is deeply related to a collective human development and an introduction of this humanistic side of mathematics often interests students in the content. What do we mean by cultural connections to mathematics? Let's begin with a familiar shape. Without question, □ is a square shape. But ways of knowing and thinking about □ or images that one conjures when one thinks about □ are unique to an individual. Even the symbols themselves are culturally influenced through language and recording instruments. Cultural and historical aspects of mathematical ideas can ground exciting and fascinating lessons. Throughout this book, we will include a wide range of general cultural connections to mathematics.

Many general multicultural educators (e.g., Bennett, 1990; Nieto, 1996) believe that students first find meaning in their own cultural backgrounds before being able to successfully celebrate cultures different from their own backgrounds. So it is important to help students explore mathematics in their own backgrounds. Treating mathematical content through cultural eyes should take this into account. So from time to time, we also relate some future teachers' descriptions of their personal backgrounds and the mathematics to which they feel uniquely connected.

In our first example, we travel far away and to a culture situated far back in time to study two specific mathematical ideas: spatial thinking and shape identification. Meet Tan, a construction worker who used spatial thinking to help build an emperor's palace in ancient China.

A Chinese Legend

Once upon a time in ancient China, there lived a very famous emperor, who constructed a beautiful palace. However, his palace was made of perishable materials, so it does not stand today. His palace had a very large room, which the emperor decreed would be decorated with a ceiling mosaic. Mosaics of the time were created with square-shaped bits of pottery and ceramic. The goal was to create a pastoral scene that could be recognized from the floor but when viewed up close would reveal the collection of square shapes used in the creation of the scene.

Several construction workers climbed the scaffolds each day to complete their jobs and appropriately glue tiles into the ceiling mosaic. Scenes from Chinese history sprang to life within the mosaic. As construction neared completion, trees, flowers, and village scenes bustling with human activity graced the palace ceiling.

In Chinese culture at the time, group cohesiveness was very important. Doing one's task to completion was considered paramount. So the way Tan became the most famous of the construction workers worried him at first. Along with his fellow workers, he spent weeks tirelessly gluing tiles and bits of ceramic to the palace ceiling. One day, though, he reached for the next tile he would affix to the ceiling. It slipped from his fingers and fell to the floor. He sighed when he heard it shatter, and he worried about the quiet

NCTM
EQUITY

grumbling he heard from his fellow workers. He decided with grim determination that he would not break any more tiles. At the end of the day, he climbed down his scaffold and inspected the broken tile. It had broken into seven smooth pieces. Something strange caught his eye. In this pile of the tile's rubble, there were five triangle shapes of three different sizes, a small square shape, and a parallelogram shape. "Hmmm," he thought, "It should be easy to reconstruct the square tile that I broke."

After 15 minutes, his fellow workers had gone home and Tan had made a butterfly, a bear, and a turtle, but no square. "Maybe this is not so easy. This is going to take some time." Tan put the pieces into his pocket and headed for home, where he could ponder the shapes after dinner with his children. Tan's family is now credited for having created hundreds of different shapes. One legend reports that he never did figure out the square because he became so engrossed in his artistry and the creation of birds, butterflies, and cats. Construction workers doubled as artisans. And Tan's artistic skill manifested itself

Activity 3 . 3

SQUARE

Build a square with tangrams.

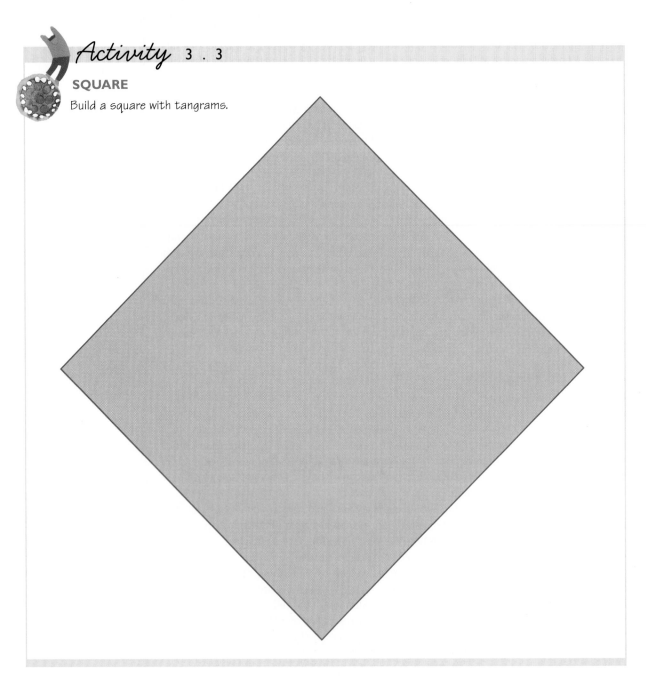

in his endeavor to recreate the square shape. Perhaps you can help him create the square from a set of tangram pieces, as you complete Activity 3.3.

Explore Your Own Culture

After hearing about the tangram legend from China, you might be thinking about your own culture, wondering about the mathematics you could connect. As you complete Activity 3.4, you will explore your own culture and check for opportunities to make geometric connections. When you have developed an awareness of a connection between your own culture and some of the mathematics that is imbedded there, it is more likely that you can synthesize information from a diverse set of cultures into your mathematics lessons. Your ultimate goal is to celebrate the culture *while* teaching the mathematics, thus cementing knowledge more completely for students. Before you write about your cultural mathematics connection, listen to Tammy, a future mathematics teacher, describe some mathematics of her culture.

Activity 3 . 4

YOUR CULTURE AND MATHEMATICS

My Cultural Lesson is about _____ (mathematics.)

Address the following points in a scholarly manner:

1. Give an overview detailing a brief history of yourself or your family. (You might have to ask family members for some facts.) Your goal is to understand the cultural aspects of your history.

2. Outline some uniqueness involved with membership in that culture. Explain some of the mores and codes that members of that culture somehow know because of membership.
   - What does it mean to be a member of your culture? Who can be a member?
   - What is something (such as norms) that members know that outsiders do not know?
   - Give two rules for behavior dictated by this culture.

3. Describe how the culture/heritage description from above is meaningful to you or your family.
   - How do you see this history/culture relating to you?
   - What is it from the culture that is meaningful to you, personally?

4. Your next goal is to celebrate your culture! *Respect* shows there is worth in the culture. *Appreciation* shows you feel positive about your culture. But *Celebration* means you feel festive and excited about your culture. Describe your feelings about your culture.

5. Give other background information necessary to solidify the mathematics. Then explain a mathematical idea related to your culture.

6. Clearly describe the mathematical ideas. Remember, it is *not* that mathematics is different it is that *you somehow know it differently* due to your culture.

Knitting

Knitting was not always a leisure activity as it tends to be thought of today. I am a descendent of a member of the guild system (similar to a blacksmith's guild) that was established in the 1500s in Britain. "Guilds were one of the most important institutions in the Middle Ages" (Rowling, 1968, p. 64). Medieval England was home to as many different sorts of guilds as there were crafts. Bellringers, minstrels, butchers, weavers, candlemakers, and knitters all had their associated guilds. Guilds existed for charitable and business reasons. A guild member who needed support could count on the guild and its members for help. When a guild member died, the guild would often pay for religious ceremonies, and the other guild members would be expected to attend. Guilds also participated in town feasts and celebrations, providing entertaining plays at the community fairs. However, guilds were designed primarily to regulate prices, supervise work, and monitor the quality of the products produced.

Knitting as a craft brims with legends as well as practical—and probably true—stories. Legend has it that the first mermaid to be changed to a human woman donned a shawl she had knitted from the sea foam so that she would not emerge from the water unclothed (Oberle, 2000). Hand-knitted shawls and blankets that are used exclusively for rites of passage ceremonies, such as baptisms, are often handed down from generation to generation. Some knitters believed that if knitting needles were placed into a newborn baby's hands, the child would grow up to be a master knitter and carry on the tradition. To this day, some descendants of the guild give knitting needles to every newborn baby before he or she goes home from the hospital.

Before 1589, all knitting was done by hand and was lucrative for my family. The first knitter in my family was apprenticed to the Knitters' Guild for six years. He spent three years learning fundamentals and three years traveling around the country studying a variety of techniques. However, unfortunate times lay ahead for his descendants, my ancestors, even though they were the knitters who might have made one of those important baptism shawls or placed knitting needles in a baby's hands. In 1589, an English clergyman, William Lee, invented a machine that could knit stockings. This machine would eventually revolutionize (and greatly speed up) knitting. Queen Elizabeth I of England was slow to embrace the machine and refused to grant a patent to Lee. She considered the new invention a threat to many of the hand-knitters in her country; no doubt the Knitters Guild had been in contact with her or her representatives. But in the end, the Knitters' Guild lost out to the machine.

My ancestors were members of the guild and for centuries made their living hand-knitting gloves of silk and gold threads. My ancestors did survive the industrialization for quite some time by using patterns that the machines simply could not reproduce. These patterns were jealously safeguarded by the fishermen and farmer's wives, purchasers of the gloves, in order to preserve their crafts as well.

Although we don't survive by knitting gloves anymore, the techniques and patterns of my family have been passed down through the generations. One way in which my grandmother passes down the heritage is to knit Christmas gloves for all of her grandchildren. The stitches have a very difficult (family) pattern, with two designs fused together. Mathematically, the pattern is a six-piece pattern and begins with a repeating pattern for the first row, like K, K, K, Y, K, K, K, T, which is repeated as many times as necessary for the appropriate width of the final glove. The second row is P, P, P, P, P, P, which is repeated continuously. The third row would be K, K, K, Y, K, K K, T (again), and the fourth row would be P, P, P, P, P, P, repeated. The fifth row is kind of a mirror image of the first row, something like Y, K, K, K, T, K, K, K. The sixth row is P, P, P, P, P, P, which is repeated, again for the duration. Then the whole process gets reversed to create a sort of symmetry in the final project. If you looked down the glove instead of across a row, you would see K, P, K, P, Y, P, Y, P, K, P, K, P, Y, P, Y, P, and so on. Although I am forbidden even to this day to tell the actual pattern, the deep structure of my example matches the deep structure of my family's secret glove pattern. My grandmother is a pretty good mathematician, using spatial thinking, repeated (and growing) patterning, and symmetry. Her ability to reason about the stitches and to predict the placement of the stitches demonstrates her remarkable spatial thinking abilities and at least some of the mathematics in knitting.

LITERATURE CONNECTIONS

Developing Mathematical Imagery

Stories, real or fictional, are often helpful in developing images related to mathematics. For the two cultural ideas discussed earlier, the books *Grandfather Tang's Story* (Tompert & Parker, 1997) and *Knitted by Grandma* (Hearson & Crawford, 2001) are highly recommended to help children develop connected knowledge of the ideas. Including a mathematics lesson in a reading of children's literature is one strategy for connecting the mathematical ideas to a meaningful context. Children's books for spatial thinking could include stories about situations that use both flat objects and solid figures.

A nice example for using cubes to develop spatial thinking is the story *The Fledgling* (Langton, 1980). Georgie is the primary character, and she is learning to fly with her goose prince. (The reader is encouraged to read several children's literature books with an "I want to learn to fly" theme.) While she is flying, Georgie looks down on downtown buildings from above. Her overhead perspective is quite different from the front-door perspective of someone walking down the street that evening. As you complete Activity 3.5, use your spatial thinking to imagine Georgie flying over the buildings.

Another way to introduce those perspectives to children might be to read several variations on one theme, such as the multitude of books about the three pigs and big bad wolf (e.g., *The True Story of the Three Little Pigs* [Scieszka, 1989] and *The Three Little Wolves and the Big Bad Pig* [Trivizas & Oxenbury, 1993]). What do those stories have in common? Each tells a story from a different perspective. Perspective can also be a type of spatial thinking. Earlier, when Georgie saw buildings from a different perspective (aerial view) from that of a person walking down the street (front view), she was looking at the buildings from a different perspective. These books are a good way to talk about the notion of perspective and to relate that information to the ideas of spatial thinking. This alternative approach is an example of how children's literature can be used to base a mathematics lesson.

Activity 3.5

BUILDING PERSPECTIVES

Below are two views (front and right) of the same building. There may be more than one possibility for the overhead view. Identify the maximum number of cubes and minimum number of cubes that would be needed to build this building. Draw the overhead views for each case.

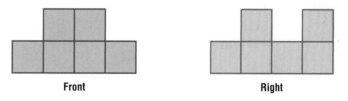

Front   **Right**

maximum   minimum

LET'S REVIEW

To understand how we learn geometry, the van Hiele learning theory (Fuys et al., 1988) suggests that we progress through a series of five stages, the first three of which need to be completed for success in high school geometry. The stages are (0) visualization, (1) analysis, (2) informal deduction, (3) formal deduction, and (4) rigor. Visualization-level learners understand objects solely on the basis of their whole visual appearance. Analysis-level learners are able to compare parts of a shape to other parts of shapes and to compare shapes on the basis of properties. When students make informal deductions, they recognize that some fact about the shape is a result of something they already know to be true about it. Formal deduction–level learners accompany their informal deductions with proof. Rigor-level learners compare geometries at proof level.

Understanding how we learn geometry also requires awareness of how we interact with our environments as we make visualizations or analyses, for example. First, we are curious about solid shapes; second, we learn to abstract plane ideas from the solid shapes. When teachers want to capitalize on this progress, manipulatives can support such learning. When learners interact with manipulatives, it is important to match physical materials with symbolic representations and to match pictorial representations with symbols before requiring students to work with symbols only.

HOMEWORK

1. Think about concrete, pictorial, and symbolic representations in teaching the students how to recognize squares. Explain the factors in your decision to use (a) saltine crackers; (b) plastic, wooden, or paper "crackers"; or (c) a cracker on a worksheet. What will guide your decision?
2. How are a photograph of a quadrilateral, a drawing of a quadrilateral, and a cutout (from paper) of a quadrilateral different from one another? How are they the same as one another?

SUGGESTED READINGS

D'Ambrosio, U. (1990). The history of mathematics and ethnomathematics: How a native culture intervenes in the process of learning science. *Impact of Science on Society, 160,* 369–377.

Giganti, P., & Cittadino, M. J. (1990). The art of tessellation. *Arithmetic Teacher, 37*(7), 6–16.

REFERENCES

Battista, M. T. (2002). Learning in an inquiry-based classroom: Fifth graders' enumeration of cubes in 3D arrays. In J. Sowder & B. Schappelle (Eds.), *Lessons learned from research* (pp. 75–84). Reston, VA: NCTM.

Bennett, C. I. (1990). *Comprehensive multicultural education.* Boston: Allyn & Bacon.

Bruner, J. S. (1966). *Toward a theory of instruction.* New York: W. W. Norton.

Crowley, M. L. (1987). The van Hiele model of the development of geometric thought. In M. M. Lindquist (Ed.), *Learning and Teaching Geometry K–12: 1987 yearbook of the National Council of Teachers of Mathematics* (pp. 1–16). Reston, VA: NCTM.

Fuys, D., Geddes, D., & Tischler, R. (1988). *The van Hiele model of thinking in geometry among adolescents.* Journal for Research in Mathematics Education Monograph 3. Reston, VA: NCTM.

Hearson, R., & Crawford, J. (2001). *Knitted by Grandma.* New York: Dial Books for Young Readers.

Langton, J. (1980). *The fledgling.* New York: Scholastic.

Nieto, S. (1996). *Affirming diversity.* New York: Longman.

Oberle, C. (2000). *Folk shawls.* Loveland, CO: Interweave Press.

Rowling, M. (1968). *Life in medieval times.* New York: Berkley.

Scieszka, J. (1989). *The true story of the 3 little pigs by A. Wolf.* New York: Scholastic.

Senk, S. (1989). Van Hiele levels and achievement in writing geometry proofs. *Journal for Research in Mathematics Education, 20*(3), 309–321.

Teppo, A. (1991). Van Hiele levels of geometric thought revisited. *Mathematics Teacher, 84*(3), 210–221.

Tompert, A., & Parker, R. A. (1997). *Grandfather Tang's story.* Cleveland Heights, OH: Dragonfly Books.

Trivizas, E., & Oxenbury, H. (1993). *The three little wolves and the big bad pig.* New York: Scholastic.

Usiskin, Z. (1982). *Van Hiele levels and achievement in secondary school geometry.* CDASSG Project. (Eric Document Service: ED 220 288).

Van Hiele, P. (1986). *Structure and insight: A theory of mathematics education.* Orlando, FL: Academic Press.

Yakimanskaya, I. S. (1991). *The development of spatial thinking in schoolchildren. Soviet Studies in Mathematics Education, Vol. 3.* Reston, VA: NCTM.

CHAPTER
4

Role of the Teacher in
Geometry and Spatial Thinking Lessons

ANALYZING ONE OF THE TEACHING MODELS:
Discussion

The first model of teaching we highlight is the discussion model. In this model, the teacher creates a lesson plan that uses a variety of questions designed to promote discussion and develop students' knowledge. High expectations ground discussion-based lessons. It is the teacher's belief that through discussion heavily weighted with student comments and involving all students, learning will occur. Usually, teachers mold the discussion around an activity or a problem. This type of lesson asks students to ponder "What if?" or "Imagine" kinds of situations. To successfully use this model, the teacher prepares a nice collection of questions to promote discussion but also support students as they reach toward meaningful discussions. Sometimes teachers have to design questions; other times, they use questions from their textbook or other resources at school. During actual classroom discussions, it is easy for the discourse to meander a bit. Some indirect topical paths are certainly acceptable. So even though teachers prepare discussion questions in advance, teachable moments will often emerge that need to be pursued. Sometimes students know more than is expected; good teachers are not intimidated by this situation—they are elated by it. They continue to ask open-ended questions to help students think about their ideas more carefully. Recognizing the need for unanticipated questions requires listening to the students for more cues. We cannot stress enough the importance of really hearing the students' responses to well-developed questions. In this model of teaching, teachers spend most of their mental energy during the lesson anticipating student responses, listening to students talk, determining what students know, and deducing what they need to know. It is important for the teacher to keep his or her objective in mind and to work hard to marshal discussion toward that goal.

Using Digital Technologies as Geometry Discussion Platforms

Digital technologies provide valuable tools for teachers who are working to create active, learner-centered experiences in geometry. Several available tools provide teachers the opportunity to allow students to experience geometric ideas and build their understandings of these ideas through describing their experiences in individual and classroom discussions. In selecting digital tools, teachers should work to find tools that help to expand the experiential approach to learning geometry advocated throughout this part.

Logo

The Logo programming language, an application that was developed before the introduction of the microcomputer in the classroom in the 1980s, provides an excellent example of a digital tool for the learning of geometry ideas. Seymour Papert at MIT developed Logo in the 1970s. With Logo (Papert, 1980, 1993), Papert strove to create a "mathland" where students could experiment and experience mathematics in much the same way as a student learns French by living in France. Since its inception, Logo has changed faces many times from the original programming languages to Logowriter (Papert, 1986) to MicroWorlds (2000). All versions have provided students with valuable open-ended tools with which to explore and enjoy geometry and mathematics.

The center of the Logo environment is a turtle that learners "drive" around the screen using a set of simple commands. The turtle leaves a track, and thus learners can create visual images on the screen. Very little instruction is needed to begin working with the Logo primitives. In fact, students can explore interesting geometry concepts using just the primitive commands of Forward, Back, Right, and Left. Each of these commands instructs the turtle to move in a particular way, and each requires a numerical input. Thus, FD 50 tells the turtle to move forward 50 units, and RT 60 tells the turtle to turn 60 degrees to the right. The Repeat command instructs the turtle to repeat a sequence of commands a specified number of times. For beginning students, the challenge of constructing a square using the language provides a powerful environment for learning about characteristics of squares. This Logo task can also create the opportunity for discussions on what is and what is not a square. Logo

also provides an effective environment for exploring and discussing characteristics of polygons and circles.

One sixth grade teacher set up an interesting Logo challenge for her students to investigate. Her question for the students was "How many sides does a polygon need for it to become a circle?" Using Logo, students drew multisided polygons that began to look more and more like circles. Their answers to the question created lively discussion and deep understanding of the concept of a circle. Seymour Papert's book *Mindstorms* (1980) provides more information about the Logo approach to mathematics learning and the power of this digital mathematics environment.

The Geometer's Sketchpad

Another example of a software tool that provides geometry experiences for students is the Geometer's Sketchpad (Key Curriculum Press, 1996). It has been enthusiastically received by mathematics educators as a software tool that encourages student exploration, experimentation, and discussion.

The Geometer's Sketchpad allows students to construct a geometric object and then explore its characteristics through manipulating the object. The opportunity to construct and then play with geometric objects provides students the opportunity to analyze the mathematical properties of the object. The web site for The Geometer's Sketchpad, located at www.keypress.com/sketchpad/, provides information and possible lesson plans for the use of the Sketchpad.

One such activity suggested on the web site shows the experimentation and discussion possibilities enabled by the Geometer's Sketchpad. In this activity, students are asked to construct a quadrilateral with equal diagonals: "Project 51: Construct a quadrilateral so that the only property it must have is that its diagonals are the same length as each other. What special kinds of quadrilateral could this shape be?" Using the Geometer's Sketchpad, students can construct and then experiment with their quadrilateral, providing a rich basis for discussion. Sketchpad is used primarily with students in grades 5–12, but working with Geometer's Sketchpad can also be a useful activity for teachers of younger children as these teachers seek deeper understandings of geometric objects and relationships.

HIGHLIGHTS OF A LESSON PLAN COMPONENT:
Creating Good Questions

Creating good questions is much harder than it sounds. Sometimes experienced teachers think of good questions during the lesson, but good teachers do not count on thinking of all desired questions, or even particularly good ones, during the lesson. However, this will become easier with experience in listening to and responding to students' comments and concerns.

What makes a good discussion question? It must (obviously) generate discussion. Yes/no questions alone do not generate good discussion. Compare the question "What is your name?" to the question "Why do you think your parents selected your name?" Which would be a better discussion question? Now imagine an odd shape. Compare the question "What shape is this?" to the questions "How is this different from a square? What if I wanted to stretch it into a square—how would I proceed? How is it different from a rectangle? How is it the same as a circle? What if we made a footprint of this shape—what could I make?" Opening discussion questions can also begin with "Imagine," "Suppose," or "What if": "Imagine that an alien has visited our planet and has found one of those cardboard paper towel rolls. What sorts of mathematical shapes could you show the alien using that object?"

SUGGESTIONS FOR ESTABLISHING DISCOURSE:
The Importance of Knowing the Mathematics

Once we understand the mathematics and how we learn the mathematics, what does it all mean? How do we connect these ideas to teaching? If mathematics is a mental idea, how will we ever know when students know something? Somehow we have to provide a classroom environment in which students are able to effectively communicate their knowledge and their thinking. Discourse includes the types of arguments and ways students have of communicating their thinking about a problem. It also serves as a general description of the kind of atmosphere that is desirable in classrooms where students are encouraged to discuss and reexamine ideas. During discourse, sometimes a physical model helps students communicate, sometimes a picture helps, and sometimes words are all that is needed. Those communication aids are three very different ways students have for expressing what is going on mentally. In using these categories, a student might build a model, draw a formal and specific picture, or tell a story.

These categories are very different from each other, and as teachers, we have to pay attention to students' mathematics descriptions to nurture conversations in our classrooms. Discussions can make students' thinking known to us. Although it can appear difficult to guide discourse that enables these discussions, it is very important. A highly thoughtful teacher whose mind is active listens to students' comments and tries to use those comments to understand what the child knows. While listening to those comments, of course, the teacher has to be thinking about the van Hiele theory and listening for cues that will inform him or her about how best to facilitate the classroom conversation toward knowledge building. What are some strategies for handling the discussion? Putting mathematical ideas in your own words is a luxury you had as a student. Now, as a teacher, you must carefully use the technical mathematical language and push your students toward the technical language while valuing their use of language that is meaningful to them. Students can put mathematics in their own words. We have the task of listening for mathematical accuracy. How do teachers know when to talk and when to be silent, allowing and encouraging the students to talk? We tackle these questions with a description of a first grade classroom discussion. In the next section, Ms. Hawthorne used her knowledge about learning theory, knowledge of mathematics content, and awareness of what it feels like to have participated in such discourse as a learner.

Ms. Hawthorne's Rhombus Lesson

Ms. Hawthorne teaches first graders. Her goal for the children was to visualize (level 0) a rhombus and to recognize the property (level 1) of four congruent sides. (For our discussion, a rhombus is a quadrilateral with four equal sides. The angle measurements do not matter.) Ms. Hawthorne set out a large pile of shapes cut from construction paper and asked the children to find all the shapes with "four equal sides." Several students selected only *squares* from the pile. (Ms. Hawthorne had been careful to cut out some nonsquare rhombi.) Perhaps children had studied squares more often than rhombi, or they might have recognized squares in their daily lives more often; there is no way to know for sure. But somehow, on this day, squares were the visual images that popped into the children's heads when Ms. Hawthorne asked them to find shapes with four equal sides. A square has four equal sides *and* four right angles. So the children were not incorrect. They were just highly selective and limited in their choices for shapes with four equal sides.

Ms. Hawthorne recognized the children's thinking and adjusted her statement. She said, "Can you imagine a *slanty* square?" So the children stretched and tilted their little mental squares. Suddenly, they had a visualization (level 0) of the rhombus that their teacher had intended. The children then successfully collected all nonsquare rhombi from the pile. As Ms. Hawthorne listened to children discuss this task, she grew alarmed because she realized that many children had reversed the relationship between square and rhombus, developing the misconception that rhombi are special squares rather than the other way around.

The classroom scenario demonstrates how a teacher used her mathematics language to modify the children's answers to an activity. While listening to her students, she heard mathematically incorrect statements such as "A rhombus is a slanty square." Ms. Hawthorne recognized that her second question had caused the children to develop a reverse connection between squares and rhombi. She detected her students' descriptions that rhombi were distortions of squares. That description had to be amended. Ms. Hawthorne knew that she had to act or risk her students' conceptual knowledge development. She called on her knowledge of rhombus to counter the children's visual descriptions of rhombus.

She gathered the students back together and showed several nonsquare rhombi shapes and square shapes. She asked, "What do these shapes have in common?" After the children decided that all sides on each shape had equal lengths, Ms. Hawthorne asked what "extra" thing the square shape had. She did not want children to think that when a square was *slanted*, it was a rhombus, she wanted them to know that when a rhombus was *right* (had four 90-degree angles), it was a square! Because she listened to the students' discussions and did not rely solely on their answers (the originally selected piles of shapes), Ms. Hawthorne was able to successfully guide her students' thinking.

We wish to note that Ms. Hawthorne was willing to share her lesson for you to read an example of how children's discussions prompted her to modify instruction. We hope that you do not judge Ms. Hawthorne, as we surely do not. Rather, we offer her experience as an example of how you might manage your class discussions as a way to support student learning.

Ms. Steffen's Rectangle Lesson

Ms. Steffen teaches fifth grade. One day, she asked her students to compare rectangles and squares. Listening to Min, Ms. Steffen recognized a common visualization error that often occurs as students develop knowledge about squares and rectangles. Min said, "Well, I know that a square has four sides and four corners, it's a square when it has four sides and [is] chubby not long. Because if it is long, it is a rectangle." Her response prompted Ms. Steffen to modify her question: "What do rectangles and squares have in common *and how are they different*?" Min noted that both are quadrilaterals and that both have corners. (Children often use the term *corner* interchangeably with 90-degree angle.) She separated them on grounds according to side lengths, though. So Ms. Steffen asked whether squares were special rectangles or rectangles were special squares. Min thought for a long time. Soon Jamal raised his hand and said, "I look at it this way. Anytime I have a quadrilateral with four corners, I have a rectangle already. I don't have to mention the sides." He showed his thinking with pencils on the overhead projector, as shown in Figure 4.1. "Once I mention the sides, then basically either I have a square or I don't have a square. But I always have a rectangle!" This fellow student's demonstration seemed to help Min move forward in her thinking: "Oh! I see now, the chubby part makes the shape a square, and the corners part makes both shapes rectangles."

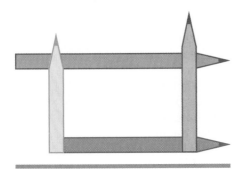

Figure 4 . 1

Jamal shows why four 90-degree angles force opposite sides to be parallel.

We note here that classroom discussion continued among the children. By asking students to compare shapes, Ms. Steffen elicited several important student comments. They included comments about how a quadrilateral with four 90-degree angles automatically had opposite sides parallel. Jamal's earlier definition of square included this requirement. After the class discussion, he modified his definition to say, "I know that a square is a quadrilateral with four 90-degree angles and all four of its sides are equal." Nothing is needed in the definition about opposite sides being parallel or of equal length. In fact, an informal deduction is "*If* a quadrilateral has four right angles, *then* opposite sides will be parallel." We additionally note that we share Min's thinking as a spotlight on how children learn, not as an evaluation of her skills at that time. No grade was entered in a grade book, and no disappointment exists about her original statement. Rather, we celebrate Min's thinking and her efforts to listen to her teachers and classmates as she rearranged her knowledge of rectangle. She provides an example of how class discussions support student learning.

Comparing Quadrilaterals

Figure 2.1 showed the complex relationships between rhombi, rectangles, and squares. Ms. Hawthorne and Ms. Steffen understood the complex relationship and used it to listen for an opportunity to lead students to higher van Hiele levels. Ultimately, students at van Hiele's third level (level 2) should say something like this: "*If* a quadrilateral has four right angles, then it is a rectangle, and *if* the rectangle has four equal sides, *then* it is a square." Because both of these requirements (four right angles and four equal sides) are met, the shape is a square. This informal deduction level statement draws a conclusion based on logical analyses of known premises. (The thinking moves from the previously known to some new statement.) And that final statement is not dependent on either visualizing or on making a comprehensive list of properties. Moreover, the claim uses only that which was needed to draw a conclusion. Clearly, we must (1) know the mathematics to recognize knowledge clues from the children's conversation and (2) be

MIDDLE SCHOOL CONNECTIONS

Know the Math Well Enough to Ask Questions

NCTM TEACHING

Even with prepared questions, on any given day, an adolescent's behavior can appear to be unexpected when compared to that on a different day. Any unexpected behavior should be noted because you need to check for serious causes of that behavior. But you should also be aware that adolescent behavior simply varies. During episodes of unexpected behavior, your attention must remain with the needs of that student as well as those of the other students in the class. Even though the social needs of the student can sometimes appear to overshadow the adolescent's academic thinking, it remains the middle school teacher's goal to foster mathematical thinking.

Middle school teachers must be able to strike a balance between emotionally supporting students and successfully teaching them mathematics. Teachers of adolescents need to know the mathematics well enough to concentrate on the social needs of their students while recognizing the ever-important next mathematical question that needs to be asked. Assessing adolescents' thinking while meeting social needs does not leave a lot of time for remembering the definition of circle or the number of lines of symmetry in a regular octagon. Trying to figure out mathematical content along with a learner has its place, provided that this was the *intention* of the lesson. Trying to remember the mathematics along with the adolescent who is demonstrating unexpected behavior usually results in lost learning opportunities because it is difficult to pose the best question. So we encourage you to continue to build new mathematical knowledge, constantly connecting new and old information, as part of your own lifelong learning process.

able to think about the children's conversation in the frame of van Hiele. Then we can use these two perceptions to analyze the children's thinking and then to frame questions that move the children along the van Hiele levels.

The Next Question

In Chapter 1, we listed some generic questions that teachers can use to facilitate classroom discussion. Some teachers have put questions like these on index cards, poked a hole in the corner of the cards, and set the cards on a key ring. It is then a simple matter to slide the key ring onto a finger and keep it handy for quick reference during the discussion. It is not necessary to develop these questions on your own. Working with coworkers to get suggestions for more questions that have proven successful for them is also a great idea.

ASSESSMENT:
Making an Instructional Decision

NCTM ASSESSMENT

The first step in assessment is to decide the reason to assess. In this chapter, we study assessment as a strategy for making an instructional decision. Recall Ms. Hawthorne's work with students grappling with rhombus. After identifying her mathematical goal of conceptual knowledge of a rhombus, she engaged the assessment process to find where to go next. She entered no grades into a grade book, and there was no formal judgment of individual students. Ms. Hawthorne recognized that students could visually identify a square as having four equal sides but that they did not visualize a nonsquare rhombus when asked to find shapes with four equal sides. This information told Ms. Hawthorne that her next step was to ask students to adjust their visual images by asking for a slanted square. Her students' answers started to flow in. She assessed again and made an additional observation. Now her students were moving down the path backward, so she adjusted instruction once more and asked students to compare squares to rhombi checking for commonalties. Recognizing those commonalties would entice students toward the second van Hiele level (level 1). When teachers want to assess to make an instructional decision, they can identify children's van Hiele levels in order to decide their next step.

Later in the semester, Ms. Hawthorne wanted to know how to approach her students' study of parallelograms. She noted that the lessons required children to be able to analyze parallelograms at van Hiele's second level (level 1).

Go to "Try it! See it! Teach it!" on page 64.

She developed an activity/assessment tool to help her decide whether the children could analyze shapes for parallelogram properties (see Activity 4.1). After students completed the task, Ms. Hawthorne judged her children's knowledge about parallelograms based on an inference about how the children reacted to her assessment tool. Finally, she determined what to teach next.

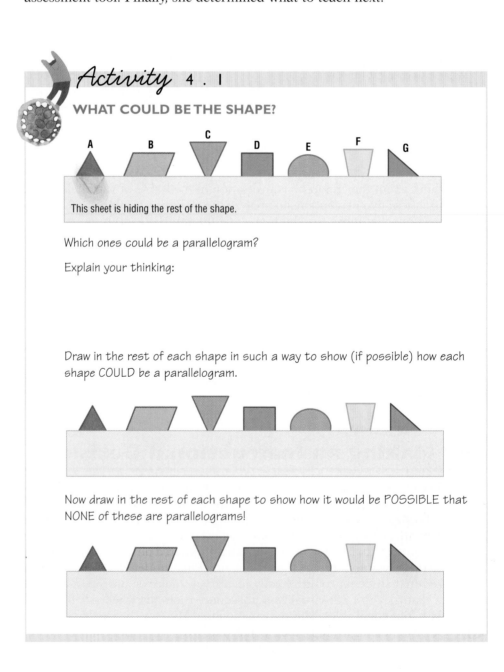

Activity 4.1

WHAT COULD BE THE SHAPE?

This sheet is hiding the rest of the shape.

Which ones could be a parallelogram?

Explain your thinking:

Draw in the rest of each shape in such a way to show (if possible) how each shape COULD be a parallelogram.

Now draw in the rest of each shape to show how it would be POSSIBLE that NONE of these are parallelograms!

Using the van Hiele Theory to Guide Instruction

What could happen as students completed Activity 4.1? There are three basic possibilities. First, the children would not be able to complete the task at all. Second, the children might think none of the shapes could be parallelograms. If either of these two events happened, Ms. Hawthorne would recognize that the next unit should focus on drawing out properties of quadrilaterals. A third possibility would be that the children could do most of the task. Then Ms. Hawthorne might follow up with a unit com-

paring parallelograms to rectangles, because students were operating with properties (analysis) of shapes.

You should additionally note that discussion questions might serve the dual purpose of providing evidence that will guide future lessons. For example, if during a classroom discussion, students uniformly suggest that a given shape is a square because it "looks like one," then the students are at van Hiele's first level (level 0). These statements suggest that that students' next activities might focus on properties of a square.

Thinking Carefully about Assessment

Perhaps the way I have changed the most in my role as a teacher is in regard to assessment. I used to give a test, count the errors, and assign a grade accordingly. I'm quite sure I was testing computation only, with a few story problems thrown in for good measure. I don't remember ever testing whether or not a child could *think*, whether or not he or she could *explain* his or her reasoning, and I certainly never asked a student to *justify* a solution. I did not believe that students could or should talk in class. I did not understand assessment as anything beyond a written test. I used to hand back those written tests and move on to the next chapter, ready or not.

How times have changed! I know now that assessment should improve learning *and* guide instruction. I like the NCTM's (2000) description that assessment should "support the learning of important mathematics and furnish useful information to both teachers and students" (p. 11). An assessment can be done before a unit begins, during a unit, and at the end of a unit. It is ongoing. I know that students should be involved in the learning process, which includes self-assessment. Students should be aware of the expectations for a unit. I need to help my students sow the seeds of learning, help them grow as learners, and watch as they harvest knowledge. I need to create a classroom environment in which students feel safe to express their thinking. I need to foster the sharing of strategies.

Assessment before a unit begins tells me what students know. For example, I might simply have them re-

spond to a question, such as "What do you know about shapes?" They write, and they share their writing with a partner, in small groups, and then as a whole class. I need this information if I am to build the unit on existing knowledge. Assessment during the unit allows me to monitor my students' progress. I might simply say, "Today we discussed the attributes of a square. Please summarize what you learned." I gather the notebooks for a quick check. Reading what they have written gives me the opportunity to reflect on that day's lesson and guide my next day's lesson. Assessment after the unit gives me a summary of their progress and provides all interested people (student, district, parents, etc.) with information about the student's knowledge at that time. I also ask students to describe what *they* think they have learned and what else they would like to know about the topic.

Now I never hand back a paper or notebook with check marks and forget it. We always take time to reflect on our assessment. I write notes or questions by each incorrect answer and give the student a second chance to clarify his or her thinking: "Explain how you knew this," or "You show some really great thinking on this question—try again, you're so close," or "You're on the right track, you made an error that's easy to fix." Writing is difficult for some students. I find it beneficial to talk with them to help them clarify their thoughts and to find out what they are thinking. I record two scores: one for the first test and a second for the corrected test.

Try it! See it! Teach it!

Using the van Hiele Theory to Guide Instruction

Step **One**: Try it!

Do the Math . . .

Before proceeding, refer to page 62 in this chapter and complete Activity 4.1, What Could Be the Shape?

Step **Two**: See it!

Watch the Video . . .

Anna is a second grader, Paige is a first grader, and Jack is four years old. Both girls have studied shapes as you would expect, and Jack can identify a few basic shapes like squares and rectangles. None of these children were part of the rhombus lesson described earlier. You will notice they use the word *diamond* to indicate a rhombus. This terminology is widely used. Later, these children will need to be introduced to correct terminology about parallelograms (e.g., rhombus) and the corresponding relationships to squares and rectangles. In this activity, the children see only parts of shapes and are asked to describe possibilities for the hidden part of each shape.

Things to Watch for . . .

- Recognize student thinking at the different van Hiele levels (see Figure 3.1, page 47)
- Pay particular attention to Karen's questioning techniques. Try to identify the cues in the children's answers that caused Karen to ask the questions she chose to ask.

Video Clip 2 *(time length 6:51)*

Anna and Paige develop their thinking about geometry.

Step Three: Teach it!

Reflect on Your Own Teaching . . .

1. What kinds of things did Anna say that demonstrated the visualization level of van Hiele's theory? The analysis level? The informal deduction level?

_____

_____

_____

2. What kinds of things did Paige say that demonstrates the visualization level of van Hiele's theory? The analysis level? The informal deduction level?

_____

_____

_____

3. What kinds of things did Jack say that demonstrates the visualization level of van Hiele's theory? The analysis level? Did he give any informal deduction–level answers?

_____

_____

_____

4. What questions did Karen ask that were intended to move Paige toward analysis?

_____

_____

_____

A Comment from Karen

You should always be prepared for unexpected answers. When Anna seemed to know about symmetrical shapes, I learned something about her thinking. Her knowledge

prompted me to extend the lesson. I have used a lesson with my fifth graders in which I give them half of a picture from a magazine and ask them to draw the other half, as a way to demonstrate reflective symmetry (see figures). I modified this lesson for Anna and Paige because I wanted to see how much they knew and also to determine their van Hiele levels of thinking. Anna's manipulation of the square to show that it was symmetric strikes me as being at the analysis level,

since she folded. However, her explanation was more of an informal deduction because she told me that the reason for the symmetry was because it was square. She knew that squares had this property; therefore, her square would have the same property. Paige had to fold to see the symmetry. So her thinking is at the analysis level.

GO BACK TO PAGE 62

IDEAS FOR STRUCTURING CLASS TIME:
Providing Reflection Time

You might be wondering how Karen structured her class time to accommodate all the information she discussed above. Karen gives students the opportunity to develop their knowledge by posing worthwhile tasks. Then she embeds questioning in discussion about the task to move her learners along. She knows that it is important to provide the time for her students to reflect as she makes her next instructional decision.

Worthwhile Tasks

The sorts of worthwhile tasks we ask of our students should be consistent with where they are and where we want them to go. Class time might be spent identifying particular objects (visualization) building objects and/or tearing them apart (analysis) or predicting what would happen on the basis of particular aspects of a certain situation (informal deduction). But activities and tasks themselves do not teach. Teaching is not merely a series of activities. Just because students complete an activity does not mean that they learned anything. Thoughtfulness on the part of each student is important. However, this is rarely a quick process, and sometimes the thoughts are fleeting. So we must structure quality time as part of the lesson or immediately after the lesson when students are expected to think carefully about the task. This process is known as reflection. We can understand what knowledge students have built during reflection time by asking questions and listening to students' answers as Karen described earlier.

Reflection

Discussion is an important part of class time, but so is quiet time for private, mental reflection. When teachers provide such time, they demonstrate their valuing of private reflection. Some teachers ask slightly older children to write in journals while teachers write in their own journals. This further demonstrates the fact that taking time to reflect is valued. Younger children can draw pictures or list words they think are related. In any case, children need time to sit back, think, and absorb their thoughts.

Reflection can also be completed in pairs or in small groups. Perhaps the students would be given the charge of using this time to share their thinking. They may discuss some new conclusion they had not found before or compare their visual images. This is a way to nurture thoughtful answers to those ever-important questions. To clarify understanding, Karen sometimes asks partners to decide who is A and who is B. Next she asks person A to explain a concept to person B. After both students have had a chance to clarify and discuss what A has said, she asks B to summarize what A had said. This is one version of partner-pair-share.

ADVICE FOR PROFESSIONAL DEVELOPMENT:
Get to Know the Mathematics in Different Ways

Ms. Hawthorne came to know more about the idea of a rhombus by studying her textbook and by talking with colleagues. The year before she engaged in the lesson described earlier, her district adopted a new mathematics textbook series that included a lesson on rhombus. To her colleagues, she bravely confided she had not heard the word *rhombus* before. Before that year of the new textbook, she recalled having always taught about that particular shape as a "slanty" square, sometimes calling it a diamond. She had not realized that a rhombus's mathematical relationship to square was the reverse (a square is a special kind of rhombus). Her new definition was that a rhombus is a quadrilateral with four equal-length sides.

She admittedly struggled as she prepared for the lesson. She talked with colleagues, and she studied. She had a nagging awareness that teaching rhombus as a "slanty" square might lead to misconceptions, but she had not really identified the source of her misgivings. During the lesson, though, she saw firsthand how children easily built misconceptions in trying to classify shapes. She fell back on her knowledge of van Hiele, recognizing that the children were not building a correct visualization of a rhombus and therefore would have difficulty understanding its properties. Recall that the children thought of modified squares to make rhombi and also placed those shapes in completely different piles. So during the lesson, she asked the children to look at the shapes and compare them for differences and similarities.

After the lesson, she talked about how she anticipated doing the lesson next year, because she better understood the relationship between rhombi and squares. She saw how to classify a shape as a rhombus and to further classify those square shapes within the pile of shapes named *rhombus*. She looked forward to expanding the children's mental images of rhombus, as hers had been expanded. She felt that the lessons went better when she used the accurate mathematics word *rhombus* and when she knew how rhombus and square are related. She said, "You really have to know the mathematics if you want kids to learn the mathematics." This story about Ms. Hawthorne shows how important it is to keep learning the mathematics in new and exciting ways. Do not judge Ms. Hawthorne. Rather, be inspired by her efforts to explore and think deeply about the mathematical ideas you will teach.

ALGEBRA CONNECTIONS $a + b$
Geometry and Spatial Thinking

NCTM CURRICULUM

An important way to know mathematics is to learn where connections can be made to algebra. Algebra is important in part because it is a significant gateway to understanding high school and college-level mathematics. It is also important because it is useful as a strategy for thinking generally about situations in the real world. We encourage K–8 teachers to make connections to algebraic thinking whenever possible. You might be surprised that even kindergarten children do algebraic thinking when they analyze patterns (geometric and/or numerical) trying to notice a general statement that could be made about the pattern.

A Big Idea: Geometric Representations in Algebra

Algebra is about making and manipulating generalizations, in some cases to make sense of problematic situations. In other cases, algebra is used to communicate a general case of the situation. You might be wondering how the ideas of algebra (typically thought of as numbers) are related to geometry and spatial thinking. According to history, much early algebraic thinking was based on spatial thinking. So when we develop children's spatial thinking, we indirectly help children think about algebra like ancient mathematicians thought about it. Very early number manipulations were based solely on geometry representations of those numbers. For instance, when hearing "four," early mathematicians would have immediately imagined a 2 × 2 grid as shown in Figure 4.2, thus reducing the number to a geometric representation. Before algebra developed as a field, mathematicians used geometry to explain many things that today can be explained with the familiar symbols of algebra.

(continued)

ALGEBRA CONNECTIONS (continued)

Figure 4.2

Early Mathematicians' Mental Image of "Four"

Figure 4.3

Early Mathematicians' Mental Image of the Numbers 1, 4, 9, 16

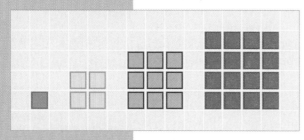

Figure 4.4

Early Mathematicians' Thinking about How to Add Consecutive Odd Integers

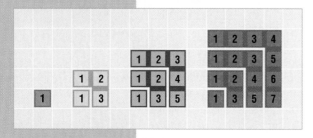

To think about how algebra develops in the K–8 classrooms, we first describe the paths that mathematicians followed as the field of algebra developed through history. As we just noted, in the beginning, mathematicians worked with geometric representations of ideas such as numbers. (By *number*, we mean the amount of objects in a set. We would like to differentiate between the idea of *number* and the representative symbolic *numeral* that mathematicians assigned to symbolize all sets of the same size.) As mathematicians worked with physical models of numbers, they noticed certain things that they could and could not do. They began to notice that some kinds of numbers and shapes always acted a certain way, had a particular characteristic, or were related to another idea. For instance, they generalized the notion that some numbers (1, 4, 9, 16, 25,...) could always be made into a square shape. See Figure 4.3 for an example.

Then, on the basis of such revelations, mathematicians began to make other generalizations. That is, they recognized that in a certain situation, a certain type of result always followed, no matter what number or shape was used. For instance, the square numbers just mentioned are also the sum of consecutive odd integers (1 = 1, 4 = 1 + 3, 9 = 1 + 3 + 5, 16 = 1 + 3 + 5 + 7.) But the visual display of this fact is aesthetically (and mathematically) pleasing (see Figure 4.4). When mathematicians started to understand more about how numbers (and their geometric shape representation) worked, such generalizations often involved lengthy word descriptions. These word descriptions were necessary to describe the spatial image. Eventually, other symbols, such as x^2, came to help in representing generalizations. The symbol x represents an abstraction of the more concrete representation of the length of the side of the square. In the end, mathematicians agreed (socially) to a certain set of rules about symbol usage, and the way the symbols acted, grew from how things worked in arithmetic, which was based on how they had worked when represented geometrically.

The algebraic symbol system that we use today (x, y, x^2, etc.) grew from the basic uses of numbers and a need to communicate about the pure mathematics of how those numbers reacted to situations. Students need to be explicitly taught how to use the symbol system but should also appreciate the related spatial visualizations. Driscoll (1999) notes how important it is to "help smooth the transition to using letter symbols [by giving] students plenty of opportunities to work with visual symbols that are not letter symbols" (p. 122). A more in-depth exploration of this view of algebra will be explored in following chapters.

Algebraic Ideas to Explore: Symmetry and Rigid Motions

In Activity 4.2, you use symmetry and segments to connect a parallelogram shape to an algebraic coordinate grid. In Activity 4.3 (p. 70), you sketch various lines on a coordinate graph and identify the graphs' corresponding equations. These ideas are probably familiar to you from previous algebra studies. You should be prepared to discuss the various levels of van Hiele that you use while you complete the two activities.

Variable as a Functional Role

As you worked on Activity 4.3, you thought about the equation that matched a particular graph, and then you compared that equation with a different equation, which matched a

ALGEBRA CONNECTIONS *(continued)*

similar but different graph. You looked for differences and similarities. For instance, you considered the relationship between the equation $y = 2x$ and the equation $y = 2x + 3$. In that activity, you studied rigid motions and used the idea of variable as being functional. You merely used that variable to explain and communicate your thinking about the translation of the graph of the line. This kind of use of a variable is what Pillay, Willss, and Boulton-Lewis (1998) term *functional* use. The two other ways of looking at variable are thinking of *x* as some sort of *generalization* or as something *standing for an unknown* that you were hoping to find. But here, you thought about the variable differently and in a way requiring deep algebraic thinking. You allowed yourself the luxury of manipulating the variable and using it to make sense of the situation. You did not try to solve for *x*; you did not claim that $2x$ or $2x + 3$ as a general statement about a situation. You manipulated expressions, not worrying about specific values for *x*, beyond recognizing that the *x-y* coordinate grid restricted your domain to the real numbers. In later chapters, we will study other kinds of variables and uses for them.

K–8 Algebra Connections: The Concept of Variable

The concept of variable is an important step in students' development of algebraic thinking. Depending on what sort of algebraic thinking students are doing, their uses of variable vary. One of the algebra standards outlined in all grade bands of the NCTM (2000) principles and standards document suggests that children should "understand patterns, relations, and functions" (p. 37). Just as you analyzed how the graphs and their related equations changed from one visual representation to the next, children as young as kindergarten age can compare patterns. Although they might not use algebraic symbols (variables) to describe their thinking, their thinking is still "functional" and lays the groundwork for using variables in that way. Younger children might be encouraged to describe their age as a pattern in which their age is "more than" or "less than" their siblings. Older students can describe those changes as A + 3 (for a child who is 3 years older than his or her sibling) or B − 2 (for a child who is 2 years younger than his or her sibling). When

NCTM
LEARNING

Activity 4 . 2

DES CARTES

On the grid below, draw any quadrilateral with vertices on grid intersections.

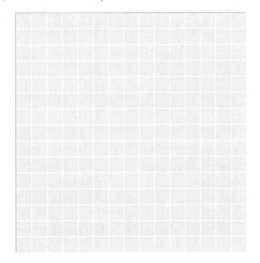

Locate midpoints of each of the four sides of your quadrilateral. Label those midpoints W, X, Y, and Z. Then join those four midpoints with line segments.

What do you see (visual level) about this new midpoint-generated quadrilateral?

Compare your results to the results of one of your classmates.

What prediction might you make about the results for each person in the class?

Calculate the slopes of each of the four sides (WX, XY, YZ, and ZW). Compare these slopes (analysis level). What do you notice?

What general statement might you conjecture about midpoint quadrilaterals? (informal deduction level)

How could you know whether your conjecture holds?

(continued)

Activity 4 . 3

RIGID MOTIONS AND SYMMETRY IN ALGEBRA

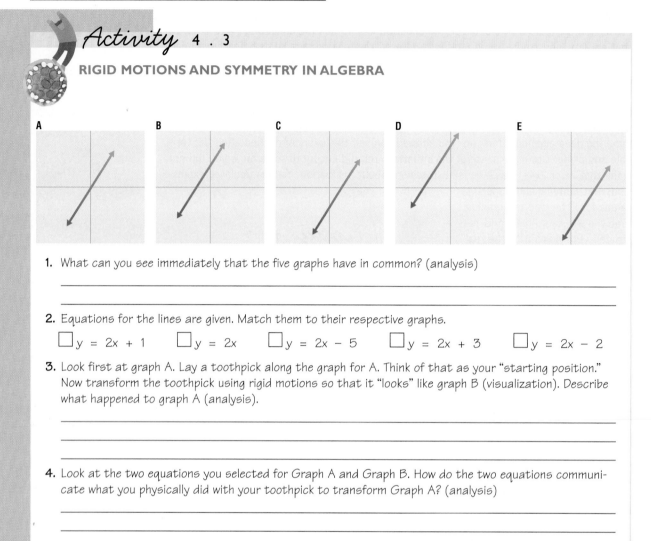

A   B   C   D   E

1. What can you see immediately that the five graphs have in common? (analysis)

_____

_____

2. Equations for the lines are given. Match them to their respective graphs.

☐ $y = 2x + 1$ ☐ $y = 2x$ ☐ $y = 2x - 5$ ☐ $y = 2x + 3$ ☐ $y = 2x - 2$

3. Look first at graph A. Lay a toothpick along the graph for A. Think of that as your "starting position." Now transform the toothpick using rigid motions so that it "looks" like graph B (visualization). Describe what happened to graph A (analysis).

_____

_____

_____

4. Look at the two equations you selected for Graph A and Graph B. How do the two equations communicate what you physically did with your toothpick to transform Graph A? (analysis)

_____

_____

students are encouraged to think about using variables in these ways, they can come to understand that the tool of algebra can help them to communicate and study patterns.

LET'S REVIEW

The role of the teacher in implementing effective geometry and spatial thinking lessons is to listen carefully to learners explain their ways of visualizing the geometric situation. With the van Hiele theory at his or her disposal, a teacher can understand the students' explanations and then create follow-up questions that generate worthwhile discussion. Using a discussion model to build geometry lessons provides a nice forum for learners to explain their thinking and verbally interact with classmates. For this particular chapter, we happened to highlight the discussion model of teaching. We have chosen to concentrate our comments on one kind of model of teaching for each part of the book. Naturally, all the models of teaching are appropriate for geometry and spatial thinking lessons. Earlier, Ms. Hawthorne used a concept attainment lesson format. By the end of the book, we will have studied all five models of teaching as we consider the role of the teacher.

HOMEWORK

1. Go on a geometry walk around your neighborhood, and develop questions that you would ask young children who are learning to identify shapes.
2. Locate a discussion-style lesson on geometry from a current K–8 mathematics textbook. Analyze it in terms of the ideas presented in this chapter.

   a. Is it sequential in terms of the van Heile theory for developing students' spatial thinking?
   b. Does it appropriately develop concept knowledge? (Cite an example of an example, a best example, and a nonexample in the lesson.)
   c. Are the lesson's assessments appropriate in terms of concrete, pictorial, and symbolic?
   d. Does the assessment match the objective of the lesson in terms of concrete, pictorial, and symbolic?
   e. Are models of mathematical ideas differentiated from the mathematical ideas themselves? (For example, does the lesson distinguish between a representation of a square and the mathematical idea of "squareness"?)

3. Read the NCTM standard for geometry for all grades K–8, and select one bullet from each grade band that is about the same mathematical idea. Put that standard in your own words for each grade level, and analyze the standard in the following terms:

   a. Can you identify a sequence according to the van Hiele theory?
   b. Does it appropriately develop concept knowledge?
   c. What sorts of spatial visualization ideas are repeatedly addressed?
   d. Are the representations of geometric ideas differentiated from the mathematical notions of the geometric ideas?

4. Locate a primary (K–2), an intermediate (3–5), and a middle (6–8) textbook from the same publisher, and study the geometry chapters. Do the textbooks appear to follow instruction according to the van Hiele theory? In terms of the van Hiele theory, how are the lessons structured as prescribed by that theory?
5. Locate a series of primary textbooks (K, 1, and 2), and check for evidence of the van Hiele theory's influence on the ordering of the lessons that are designed to develop students' spatial knowledge.

SUGGESTED READINGS

Geddes, D. (1992). *Geometry in the middle grades.* NCTM Addenda Series, Grades 5–8. Reston, VA: NCTM.

REFERENCES

Driscoll, M. (1999). *Fostering algebraic thinking: A guide for teachers grades 6–10.* Portsmouth, NH: Heinemann.

Key Curriculum Press. (1996). Geometers sketchpad. [computer program]. Emeryville, CA: Key Curriculum Press.

MicroWorlds. (2000). MicroWorlds Pro. [computer software]. Highgate Springs, VT: Logo Computer Systems.

National Council of Teachers of Mathematics. (2000). *Principles and standards for school mathematics.* Reston, VA: NCTM.

Papert, S. (1980). *Mindstorms: Children, computers, and powerful ideas.* New York: Basic Books.

Papert, S. (1986). LogoWriter. [computer software]. St. Louis, MO: Media Microworlds.

Papert, S. (1993). *The children's machine: Rethinking schools in the age of the computer.* New York: Basic Books.

Pillay, H., Wilss, L., & Boulton-Lewis, G. (1998). Sequential development of algebra knowledge: A cognitive analysis. *Mathematics Education Research Journal, 10*(2), 87–102.

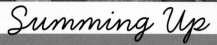

Summing Up

Our approach to help you learn about the geometry and spatial thinking information in Part I has been to actively engage you with the information. As you read about and studied the teaching and learning of geometry ideas, you completed several activities and experienced the information through the eyes of learners like Jamal and Lydia. In keeping with this approach, we believe the best way to summarize and review the information is to provide a culminating activity. It is indeed a difficult enterprise to untangle the complex relationships between teaching and learning. But a good first step is to ask you to think about the information through the eyes of a teacher. In the following activity, we ask you to step back and think like a second grade teacher who is responsible for the following curriculum goal: *The student will be able to correctly identify and communicate at least two differences between plane and solid figures.*

Closing Activity: Summary Lesson

WRITE A GEOMETRY AND SPATIAL THINKING LESSON

This activity is an opportunity for you to put together the information from Part I of the book. You are a second grade teacher who must create a discussion model lesson that will support the following geometry curriculum goal:

The student will be able to correctly identify and communicate at least two differences between plane and solid figures.

Because this is a curriculum requirement, it may take several weeks to achieve. Your task for this activity is to create a single lesson that would fall sometime during those weeks. Remember that your ultimate goal is to help students achieve the more general curriculum goal. But the lesson you create will be completed in one day and serve as only a small support for the more general goal. We guide you through the lesson development task in this activity by asking you to complete the tasks outlined in 1–5.

1. **Think about the Mathematics.** First, think about the prerequisite knowledge in terms of spatial

thinking and the accompanying vocabulary that students would have and need in order to work toward this goal. Second, what is the difference between a concept and a procedure related to this goal? Third, write a focused narrow objective achievable through the discussion model of teaching. Be sure to focus on a small component of the curriculum goal. Fourth, please tell how this lesson will fit into the students' overall experience toward the curriculum goal.

2. **Think about How We Learn.** What are good experiences that foster geometry ideas? Remember how Hannah's teacher approached spatial thinking? Recall the information about selecting teaching aids and create a list of materials you need to gather for the lesson.

3. **Think about the Role of the Teacher.** What does the teacher do before and during a discussion lesson? Recall that the teacher first writes several good discussion questions for the lesson. So take a moment and let your mind visualize several geometry shapes. Think about good "what if"

scenarios or "imagine" scenarios that would engage the students in discussion. List at least four good discussion questions related to your objective.

4. **Think about How the Learning Theory Might Appear during Your Lesson.** Use your knowledge of the van Hiele theory to anticipate student comments and to prepare follow-up questions for each kind of answer.

5. **Finally, Think about Assessment.** How will you know when your students have met your objective? Write an evaluation in which you would engage the students that would indicate to you the objective has or has not been met.

Naturally, there are several correct answers for this activity. It is also true that the lessons you eventually create once you become a teacher will depend on your district's curriculum, and you will have access to a textbook series that should help you write your lessons. Moreover, the lessons you write will take into account the uniqueness of your students during that particular year. We would never suggest that any given lesson is immediately transferable into any second grade classroom. However, we believe that there are correct types of answers for this activity. We can imagine lessons involving building shapes, cutting out shapes, or drawing shapes with a computer program. Sometimes it helps to finish this activity with a partner and then teach it to another pair of students. If you feel you are still having trouble getting started, we have provided you with one possible set of answers for a lesson in the appendix. You may also review that lesson as a check against the lesson you create. You might think through whether your answer would be considered a correct type of answer.

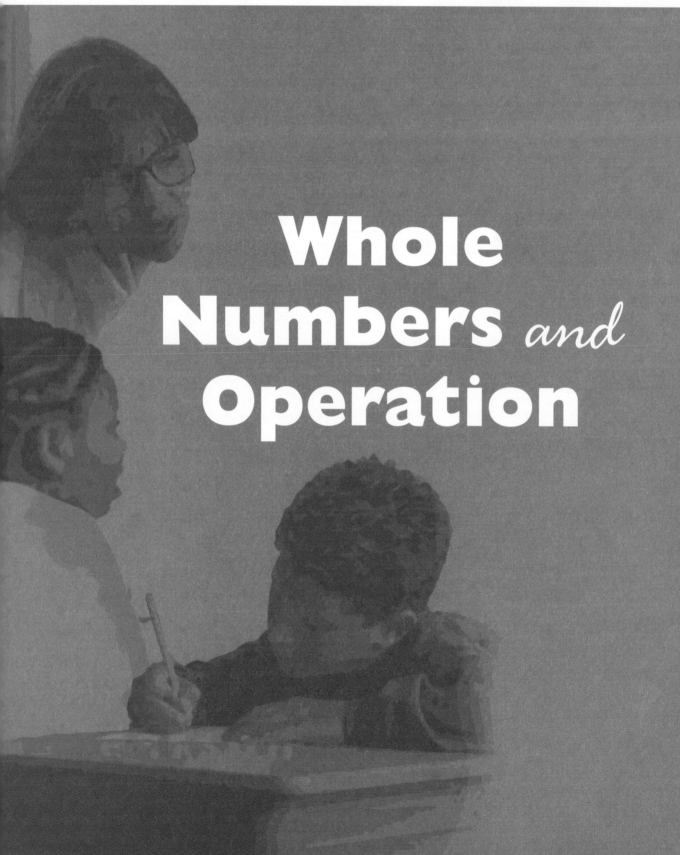

Whole Numbers *and* Operation

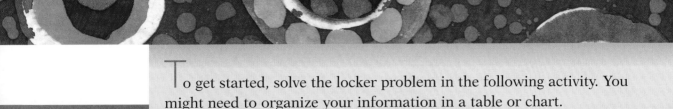

To get started, solve the locker problem in the following activity. You might need to organize your information in a table or chart.

Opening Activity

THE NOTORIOUS LOCKER PROBLEM

100 students lined up in a very long hall with 100 closed lockers. One by one, the students ran through the hall and performed the following ritual:

The first student opened every locker. The second student closed every second locker. The third student changed every third locker. (That is, this student opened it if it was previously closed or closed it if it was previously open.) The fourth student changed every fourth locker, the fifth student changed every fifth locker, and so on until all 100 students had changed their assigned lockers.

| 1 | 2 | 3 | 4 | 5 | 6 | 7 | 8 | 9 | 10 | 11 | 12 | 13 | 14 | 15 | 16 | 17 | 18 | 19 | 20 | 21 | 22 | 23 | 24 | 25 |

You can use this picture to help you keep track of the first 25 lockers. Then use your findings to predict what happens for all 100 lockers. After all students have passed down the hall, which of the 100 lockers are open? What do these lockers have in common? Is there something special about them?

● As you worked this probem, what sorts of number knowledge did you use? You probably relied on multiplication facts to find factors. Your ability to call up factors and operation ideas at will is part of your number sense. The procedures that you executed as you worked with numbers in this problem are some of the ideas in this part of the book.

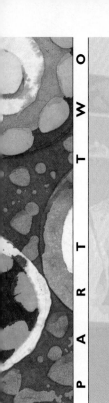

CHAPTER

5

Thinking about the

Mathematics of Number and Operation

UNDERSTANDING THE MATHEMATICS:
Number and Operation

There are several concepts and procedures we need to think about with regard to number and operation. In this chapter, we limit our discussion to how operations interact with whole numbers. (We will revisit operation definitions in the chapters on rational numbers.)

Number Is an Amount

When something can be quantified, it has a number (an amount). You can almost think of amount as a property of a particular set of things (provided that those things can be quantified). Sometimes it is helpful to imagine objects as *having* a number/amount but not *being* a number/amount. For instance, imagine that you are in the park and you pick up five leaves. Can you picture yourself holding the leaves? You might say, "I see five leaves" and thereby impose a mathematical construct on that physical situation. The physical leaves themselves can be thought to be a model of the mathematical amount as a cracker can be a model of a rectangle. The leaves themselves, however, do not have any particular mathematics embedded in them. But you as a human observer of the leaves imposed quantification on the pile of leaves. You recognize that the particular quantification in question is that of "five."

Numerals Are Symbols

Numerals are *symbols* that represent amounts. As a human from a society, you know that there exists a numeral you might use to record the amount of leaves. It is that squiggly mark, 5, that we all agree (socially and conventionally) represents the amount "five."

Numbers Are Ordered

You can impose an order on the leaves in your pile. Can you point to the fourth leaf you picked up? Imagine that this particular leaf is a maple leaf. Physically, maple leaves have nothing to do with being "fourth." It just so happened to be the order of the leaves (as you counted them) at that time. You might also recognize that your pile of leaves has more than someone else's pile of three leaves. In a sense, this is also related to ordering.

Did this seem complicated? We purposely gave such an explanation because it is important to recognize that as adults, we often take all of these structural ideas about number for granted. We learned number at such a young age that it seems to be a natural part of describing a situation. But learning number is complicated. We coordinate ideas of quantification as a general possibility along with our strategies for arriving at specific quantification of "five-ness" or whatever the amount is for that set.

Addition

Addition means joining two (distinct) sets together and then requantifying according to the cardinality (amount of objects) of that new set.

Subtraction

Subtraction usually means breaking a set apart. We can talk about subtraction as the familiar "take-away," in which we begin with a set, remove part of the set, and count what remains. Subtraction can also be used in situations to compare two sets by finding the difference. In *find the difference,* we might show the students two sets—one having seven items and one having four items—and ask students to compare them: Which is bigger? By how much is it bigger? We briefly mention a third kind of situation that is often classified as subtraction: *missing addend.* Here, the size of a set is known to be made up of a smaller set and some unknown set. This idea might look like this: $17 + \square = 32$. Students likely notice that it is written as an addition exercise. As an experienced learner, you recognize that it can be resolved with the subtraction exercise $32 - 17$. Young students often do not see this kind of exercise as a subtraction exercise. They view it as some sort of addition problem.

Multiplication

Multiplication is a complex mathematical idea based on creation of a new set from two other sets. However, unlike addition, in which the new set is a simple union of two other sets, multiplication creates a new *kind* of set. Its elements are ordered pairs. To multiply, first we make several copies of each element in the second set. We stop making copies when we have made as many copies of *each* element of that set as there were elements from the first set. For example, to multiply 3 and 4, first we think about two sets, one with three elements $\{a, b, c\}$ and one with four elements $\{w, x, y, z\}$. Then we make several copies of each element w, x, y, z. How many copies? We make three of each, one for each element a, b, c. In this way, we build the new *kind* of set: $\{(a, w), (b, w), (c, w), (a, x), (b, x), (c, x), (a, y), (b, y), (c, y), (a, z), (b, z), (c, z)\}$.

We describe multiplication in this way because in multiplying, students must learn to coordinate two pieces of numerical information: *How many copies of each element are made? How many elements are there to be copied?* Multiplication merges both conceptual and procedural ideas in a profound way.

Figure 5 . 1

Multiplication as Repeated Addition

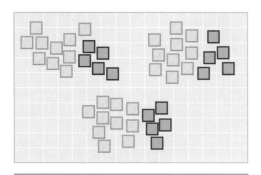

Most textbooks from which you will teach simplify multiplication understanding to *repeated addition*. This definition can be useful to children because multiplication as described above *results in* the need to repeatedly add to efficiently count the elements in the new set. The main *concept* students have to learn is to make copies before they can count the number of copies made. In the *procedure* of repeatedly adding to count the number of copies made, students visualize the act of collecting piles of discrete objects or collecting a series of hops along a continuous number line. For 3 times 15, after making the three copies of each of the 15 elements, we repeatedly add 15 (or hop forward 15) a total of three times, to find out how many elements we now have (see Figures 5.1 and 5.2). Textbooks also describe *arrays* to simplify

Figure 5 . 2

Multiplication as a Line

Figure 5 . 3

Multiplication as an Array and as an Area

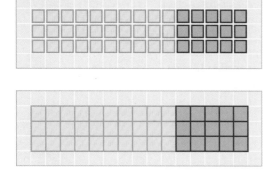

multiplication understanding. Arrays should be thought of differently than repeated addition in that the array is a *model* to help mentally and visually organize the copies in a different way, not a procedure to count the elements in the model. Here we collect all copies of the elements and organize them into stacks to form the discrete sections of a rectangular array. Think of it as a matrix with three rows and 15 items in each row (15 columns) (see Figure 5.3). *Area grids* are the same as arrays in that they are *models* to organize information but are different from an array in that the model is now a continuous rectangle, not a collection of discrete items. Textbooks also include *combination* as a multiplication idea. Here, the notion of repeated addition falls short, but our earlier definition holds. A good context in which to think about combination is to imagine having 15 shirts and three pairs of pants that go together to make several outfits. We need to create ordered pairs of the form (shirt, pants). Ask, "How many outfits could you have by pairing each pair of pants with each shirt?" Each pair of pants could be copied 15 times because each pair of pants can be paired with each shirt. Since we have three pairs of pants, each giving us 15 different outfits, we result with 45 outfits, even though we have only 18 clothing articles. Maintaining the idea of collecting identical copies (in this case, pants) retains the essence of multiplication.

Division

We talk about division in two ways. In *repeated subtraction* (also known as *measurement*), begin with a certain number of items, subtract a specific amount as many times as possible, and ask how many times the subtraction happened.

In 20 ÷ 4, we have 20 − 4 − 4 − 4 − 4 − 4 = 0. Counting the number of subtractions reveals five different times 4 is subtracted from 20. The other definition is *fair sharing* (also known as *partitioning, sharing* or *share equally*). As these names suggest, some items need to be shared equally among a certain number of smaller subsets. For 20 ÷ 4, we have 20 elements to be shared equally across four groupings, and we ask how many are in each group. Five elements are in each grouping. Both cases use 20 ÷ 4, but the action is carried out differently, and the question depended on the kind of division. Listen to these fifth graders describe their definitions of division:

> **Min:** Division is like parting something up equally and counting how many parts.
> **Lydia:** Division is when you split numbers into even groups.
> **Ryan:** Division is when you take some number and another number and try to fit as many of the second number into the first number as possible.
> **Jamal:** Division means to divide things into equal parts. (It is the opposite of multiplication.)

Min, Lydia, and Jamal thought about division as "fair sharing," whereas Ryan gave a "repeated subtraction" description. Jamal went on to tell us that multiplication is the inverse operation for division. It is important to note these students already held an understanding of division, so we did not need to give a context. Had we been teaching them early ideas of division, we would have provided the advantage of a context. What we intend to illustrate here is that once students know about division, they will think of it in their own ways.

CONCENTRATING ON CONCEPTS:

Coordinating Counting, Operation, and Number Sense

Counting

There are three general concepts that underlie the mathematics of number and operations: counting, operation, and number sense. The very idea that we can quantify something with a mathematical construct took a long time for humans to develop. The need to count might seem obvious, but we wish to point out that the underlying concept for number is *being able to* count. *Counting* requires establishment of a *one-to-one correspondence* between two sets. One set is the ordered *words:* {one, two, three, four, five, six, seven, eight, nine, ten, . . .}. Those words must be rotely recited in that order. You probably say them quickly, without thinking about amounts. The other set is the corresponding whole number amounts. When students recite the words and match one word to one item from a collection of items, they are counting. The one-to-one correspondence concept grounds the counting procedure, in which children recite the number words (in order) each and every time an item from the set is touched. After they touch the last item, the words stop, and the last word corresponds to the last item touched. The amount in the set is whatever that last word was. A numeral is sometimes recorded to represent the number of the set.

The number concept also depends on children recognizing the importance of counting each item exactly once and using all number words in the correct order. Sometimes it helps to move each item after touching it, to avoid double-counting or missing items. With a picture, it helps to cross out each item as it is counted. If these concepts are incomplete, then children do not fully understand the mathematical construct of number and cannot correctly execute the counting process.

When we recite a number word and point to the last item in a set, we know that the amount of the number word corresponds to the entire set of items. Children often assign that number word to the last item, sort of "naming" that item with the corresponding number word. If this happens, they do not yet

Activity 5 . 1

THINKING ABOUT 1 MILLION

A. First, take this short quiz to determine your number sense of 1,000,000.

____ 1 There are about 1,000,000 people in your home town. _____

____ 2 There are about 1,000,000 boards in the basketball court floor. _____

____ 3 **You are about 1,000,000 seconds old.** _____

____ 4 **There are about 1,000,000 blades of grass in the football field.** _____

____ 5 There are about 1,000,000 strands of thread in your shirt. _____

____ 6 There are about 1,000,000 plaster bumps on the walls in this room. _____

(You might have to adjust the questions. For instance, if you have carpeting, you could count the carpet loops; if you don't have plaster walls, you could count the ceiling tile holes; etc.)

B. For any statements for which you gave a *False* answer, correct the amount in the space provided on the right.

C. For the statements in **bold**, explain an organized counting procedure to determine whether the answer is true or false.

D. In keeping with the design of the base-10 blocks, what would be the general shape of the 10,000 block, the 100,000 block and the 1,000,000 block? See the following chart:

1,000,000	100,000	10,000	1,000	100	10	1
?	?	?	cube	flat	long	Cube

Along with her students, Joslyn (1990) built the actual-size blocks for 10,000 and 100,000 out of construction paper wrapped around meter sticks. How does creating these items help children to think about large numbers?

E. What would be the shape of the million block? How could we build it with meter sticks? Draw a diagram that someone could use to build a million block. Be certain to label it with helpful units.

F. What would be the shape of the billion block? How could we build it? Draw a diagram that someone could use to build a billion block. Be certain to label it with helpful units.

have the idea that the entire set makes up the amount. In other words, when they say the word *one* and they touch a leaf and push it aside, they might literally name that leaf "one." Then, when they touch the second leaf, they name it "two," and so on until they touch the last leaf and name it "five." They might not recognize that they have five leaves.

However, it is also true that numbers name things. Think of watching a basketball game on channel 5 at 5 o'clock, when you see a basketball player score five points. Suppose the player's jersey has the numeral 5 sewn onto it. Is the fact that the player scored five points related to the fact that her jersey has a 5 on it? Of course not. But it helps us to illustrate the fact that the concept of naming with a number is part of our society and that there is a difference between naming something 5, having five of something, and having the fifth object.

It is true that numbers are related to ordering. Can you remember that the maple leaf was the fourth leaf? When running laps, children know whether they are on their third or fourth lap. They also (usually) know their position in the race. It might be useful to be able to distinguish between the fifth and the seventh row at a baseball game if our seats are in the sixth row. These ideas of *amount, name, and order* need to be very clear to the students as they count and as they use the one-to-one correspondence concept.

Operation

The operation concept is the collection of ideas and relationships among combining, un-combining, separating, partitioning, rearranging, undoing, dividing, and manipulating number amounts. Procedures to operate with numbers are different and will be discussed in the section about procedures.

Number Sense

The last concept we want to talk about is that of number sense. This concept is related to having a sense of the magnitude of a number and flexibility with uses of numbers. Understanding the amount 5 as well as understanding when 5 is a large number and when 5 is a small number are examples of number sense. When children understand that 5 is greater than 3 and can also compare it to 100, they are using number sense. Context will affect the magnitude of a number. Five dogs in a small house is large, while five kittens in a mansion is small. To clarify this idea, let's complete Activity 5.1 to consider a million and a billion.

Number sense is also related to flexibility with operations. Being able to decide to turn 5 into 2 and 3 for one situation and then to turn around and make it 4 and 1 in another situation is representative of number sense. Number sense includes knowing things like the fact that composing 3 together with 2 will give 5 and thinking of 5 as something that can be decomposed into 3 and 2. Recognizing that both of these ideas are the same as 3 + 2 = 5 is related to operation concepts. These things should be thought of differently because they are significantly different. But at the same time, they are also heavily connected. The ability to deal with, understand, and use the ideas behind composing and decomposing *at will* is part of number sense. Complete Activity 5.2 to experience this sort of thinking.

Activity 5 . 2

IN HOW MANY WAYS CAN YOU SCORE 42 POINTS?

CJ scored 42 points in one game.

Determine five different scenarios for the number of each type of basket she might have made to earn 42 points.

GRASPING THE PROCEDURES:
Building Algorithms from Concepts

The execution of an operation is called a procedure. *Algorithms* are the procedures a person prefers to use over and over again for a given operation. You might be surprised to learn that there are several algorithms that could be used with any given operation. Sometimes you even use one algorithm when you execute an operation mentally and a different algorithm when you execute it on paper. Think about 1,002 + 999. How do you do that mentally? How would you write it out on paper?

Addition

Recall that addition is the union of two sets. Let's begin with the example of 4 + 6 to elaborate. One strategy is to take four elements and six elements, put them together, and count them. A slightly more sophisticated strategy would be for students to count onward from one of the numbers. "I have 4," then "5, 6, 7, 8, 9, 10" (keeping track of the next six numbers since they are adding 6). At a more advanced stage, students recognize that it would be efficient to count onward from the larger number. So even though 4 is listed first, they begin with 6 and count onward: "7, 8, 9, 10." Clearly, students use a staggering amount of number sense, such as recognizing that 6 is bigger than 4, to use strategies such as these.

As students become more involved with larger numbers, those strategies quickly become cumbersome and inefficient. To add the values 27 and 65, grouping physical items together to count them or counting onward from 65 would not be terribly efficient. The purpose of an algorithm is to be as efficient as possible. However, it is often helpful to students to have a model for thinking about adding large values. We first consider a continuous model, the empty number line (Klein, Beishuizen, & Treffers, 2002). In this model, students are not anchored onto the line with the placement of zero. They decide where to anchor themselves. Naturally, students would need to have earlier experiences with a number line anchored at 0 before being able to comprehend the number line anchored with a large number. In addition, students would need to be proficient with the counting onward method described earlier. For our example of the empty number line model for 27 + 65, we begin at 65 (the larger number) and then make a plan for moving 27 more spaces. How could you organize that movement? Would you count all 27, or would you move in groups? You might begin with a large hop of 20 spaces past 65, to arrive at 85. Then you are confronted with adding seven more spaces. Do you hop 5 and then 2? Or do you just hop all seven spaces? In either case, of course, you end up at 92. See Figure 5.4.

The algorithm matching this procedure begins with the tens columns. It separates 20 from 7 (number sense) and adds 20 onto 65.

Figure 5 . 4

The Open Number Line for 65 + 27

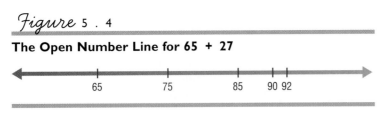

65   75   85 90 92

This algorithm directly matches each process performed on the number line.

```
  65        65        65        65
 +27       +27       +27       +27
           ----      ----      ----
            85        85        85
                     + 7       + 7
                               ----
                                92
```

An alternative written record for this process might begin with 20 and 60 (80) and then use 7 and 5 (12) before putting 80 and 12 together to get 92.

```
   65        65        65        65
  +27       +27       +27       +27
            ___       ___       ___
             80        80        80
                      +12       +12
                      ___       ___
                                 92
```

This algorithm is a slightly different record of the process shown previously.

These algorithms might be unfamiliar to you, since they both begin with the largest place value. It might be more familiar to you to begin with the smallest place value. Perhaps you want to add 7 and 5 first to get 12 but only record 2 of the 12 for now. Then you probably want to save the 10 and add it to 20 and 60. Please do not say, "Okay, add 2 and 6 and put them in the tens place." Students need to call the numbers what they represent. The 2 and 6 are really 20 and 60. Then they are relieved of remembering to "line" things up, since they are dealing with more specific and meaningful representations of the numbers. The procedures should make sense. It helps children to call numbers by what they represent rather than stopping after saying, "That 2 is in the tens place." Children should know that the 2 *is really* 20. As we proceed through this chapter, you will see how stating a numeral's actual number value helps to demystify algorithms.

With regard to the three algorithms discussed here, we need to be clear these are human-developed algorithms and are not the only way to make sense of the procedure. It just so happens that most people in the United States learned the same algorithm that starts with smallest place value, so that is their standard algorithm. Starting with the "ones" is not a *definition* for an operation and is not the only way to add. It does not matter where we start. Addition as a concept puts two sets together, and a person's preferred order for adding the numbers is the algorithm. In the problem 135 + 697, tens could be added first (120), then hundreds (700), then ones (12). No matter where the addition begins, the result will be 120 + 700 + 12 = 832. Work through Activity 5.3 to visualize this kind of algorithm.

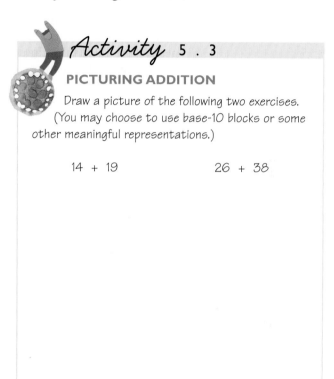

Activity 5.3

PICTURING ADDITION

Draw a picture of the following two exercises. (You may choose to use base-10 blocks or some other meaningful representations.)

14 + 19   26 + 38

Subtraction

To begin thinking about subtraction procedures, let's consider 32 – 17. Many of you are probably familiar with a standard subtraction algorithm that begins with the ones. It is seemingly efficient and clearly uses few lines of paper, something that used to be more important than it is today. Many of us have learned to look at subtraction in the following manner:

This process is probably more familiar to you, if you studied in U.S. schools during your elementary years.

$$
\begin{array}{r} 3\,2 \\ -1\,7 \\ \hline \end{array}
\qquad
\begin{array}{r} {}^2\!3\,{}^1\!2 \\ -1\,7 \\ \hline \end{array}
\qquad
\begin{array}{r} {}^2\!3\,{}^1\!2 \\ -1\,7 \\ \hline 5 \end{array}
\qquad
\begin{array}{r} {}^2\!3\,{}^1\!2 \\ -1\,7 \\ \hline 1\,5 \end{array}
$$

Study this idea using the "take-away" definition in a context. Imagine that you have 32 dollars (in the form of three tens and two ones) in your wallet and you need to purchase 17 dollars' worth of groceries. What do you get out first? How many of you would hand the cashier one of your tens first? You are probably thinking, "Okay, I need 17, let me get 10 of it right off the bat." Then you know you have to think about how to deal with the ones. You look into your wallet and see two tens and two ones remaining. What do you do? You might say to yourself, "I still need to give the cashier seven more ones." The only thing you can do is to hand over one of your tens to the cashier to "break" into 10 ones. When the cashier does that, there are a total of 12 ones (two in your wallet and the 10 the cashier is holding). Then the cashier removes seven ones (from 12), leaving you with five ones. So, 32 – 17 is 15 (1 ten and 5 ones). That process translates to the following symbol representation:

The process might look odd if you have never tried to record this sort of algorithm before. Study it before you complete Activity 5.4.

$$
\begin{array}{r} 3\,2 \\ -1\,7 \\ \hline \end{array}
\qquad
\begin{array}{r} 3\,2 \\ -1\,7 \\ \hline 2\ldots \end{array}
\qquad
\begin{array}{r} 3\,{}^1\!2 \\ -1\,7 \\ \hline \llap{2}\ldots \\ 1\ldots \end{array}
\qquad
\begin{array}{r} 3\,{}^1\!2 \\ -1\,7 \\ \hline \llap{2}\ldots \\ 1\,5 \end{array}
$$

This algorithm uses the idea of breaking and regrouping numbers, a number sense idea we called decomposing and composing and something that Cauley (1988) suggests is related to place-value and borrowing knowledge. This algorithm starts on the left-hand side of the equation (with the largest place value). To execute a process like this requires number sense, to switch smoothly between tens and ones. However, proficiency with an algorithm does not guarantee understanding of the concept (Carpenter, 1986; Cauley, 1988). So it is important to develop procedural knowledge by building on and layering it with conceptual knowledge.

We want you to be familiar with both algorithms for subtraction. When you listen to students explain their thinking, you want to be able to symbolize their thinking in ways that are mathematically appropriate and that match their thinking. Mathematically appropriate means that it will always work. Matching students' thinking means showing concepts of number sense, such as how they choose to break a number and which number they break. Think about what and when you broke numbers as you worked through Activity 5.4.

Multiplication

Let's reconsider 15 × 3. As we recall the Chapter 1 story about Danny Dickson, we realize that Karen would like to have built a

Activity 5.4

PICTURING SUBTRACTION

Draw a picture of the following two exercises. (You may choose to use base-10 blocks or some other meaningful representations.)

26 – 8 (take-away)   52 – 37 (take-away)

Follow up: How would you model 26 – 8 using the comparison definition?

How would you model 26 – 8 for the missing-addend definition?

context for the process. Suppose Danny has three baskets, and he placed 15 apples into each basket. How many apples does Danny have? Danny might recognize that he needs to do several additions, and then we can help him to establish a meaningful procedure. Modeling this situation as three groups of 15 (Figure 5.1), he might see three groups of 10 and three groups of 5. It is easier to develop an algorithm by looking at pieces of the repeated addition. Three groups of 10 is thirty (30), and three groups of 5 is fifteen (15); then 30 and 15 is 45. Compare this process for 15×3 to your favorite algorithm.

Another useful way to model 15×3 is to set out or draw three groups of 15 items in a long row. Organizing the blocks this way rather than in random-looking piles of 15 models the multiplication on a number line and lays a foundation for thinking about multiplication in an array format, which is desirable for larger values. Compare the information in Figure 5.3 to the following well-known multiplication algorithm:

$$\begin{array}{r} 15 \\ \times\ 3 \\ \end{array} \qquad \begin{array}{r} {}^{1}15 \\ \times\ 3 \\ \hline 5 \end{array} \qquad \begin{array}{r} {}^{1}15 \\ \times\ 3 \\ \hline 45 \end{array}$$

> Here, you have first multiplied 5×3, and later you multiply 3×10 (and add one more ten to that value)

Can you match any of the parts of your thinking with the two smaller rectangles in the area picture? You should be able to find the 10×3 rectangle and the 5×3 rectangle in the larger rectangle. Thus, 15×3 is $(10 + 5) \times 3$ or $(10 \times 3) + (5 \times 3)$. Thinking about multiplication in this way can lead to a general algorithm.

We remind you to think of the 1 in the 15 as "ten." When you use the array to multiply, learn to refrain from saying "1 times 3, but write the answer one place over," in order to make sense of the algorithms you study. You really take 10 times 3, which is 30. Thinking of the product as 30, grows from strong concept knowledge. Thinking of the product as "3 written one place over" does not as clearly grow from concept knowledge. Recall from the subtraction discussion how critical it was to think of the 32 as 30 and 2. It might be the case that in the end, the students will develop their own algorithm that says, "1 × 3, moved one place over." But it should come about because they invented that language, not because we imposed it on them. As teachers, we can ask good questions that guide students to make sense of the situation, apply their concepts, and develop a highly useful algorithm.

To further illustrate, we ask you to think about 13×24. You might first think about 13 groups of 24: If this is one group of 24, what would you notice about two groups, three groups, . . . , 13 groups? In answering, you should identify that you will eventually have 13 groups of 20 and 13 groups of 4. This builds on previously discussed information. How did we handle a two-digit number times a one-digit number? Looking at the problem as 13×20 and 13×4 enables us to consider some smaller products, called intermediate products. Thirteen groups of 20 is $200 + 60$. Thirteen groups of 4 is $40 + 12$. Add 200, 60, 40, and 12 to get 312. It might be useful (and less cumbersome) to organize our thinking into a rectangular array so that we can visualize the intermediate products. Figure 5.5 shows a rectangular way to arrange the problem.

You might draw this figure on graph paper. We stacked information into 13 rows of 24. Now we draw the *inside* rectangles: 10 by 20, 10 by 4, 3 by 20, and 3 by 4. Those values correspond to the values multiplied in the algorithm.

Figure 5 . 5

A View of a Large Array

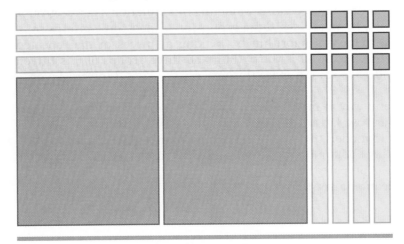

Your symbolic work should show these intermediate products of 200, 60, 40, and 12 and probably should look something like this:

<table>
<tr><td>24
× 13
——
200</td><td>24
× 13
——
200
60</td><td>24
× 13
——
200
60
40</td><td>24
× 13
——
200
60
40
12</td><td>24
× 13
——
200
60
40
12
——
312</td></tr>
</table>

> You might want to try this algorithm on a variety of multiplication exercises.

We must be watchful for students getting steeped in *our* procedures and failing to recognize underlying concepts. By building procedures on concepts (and even moving back and forth between concepts and procedures), students can and will make sense of the procedures and develop their own algorithms for executing procedures. Through Activity 5.5, you can demonstrate proficiency with the intermediate products algorithm.

Division

The first division algorithm that we use is probably familiar. See if you agree with our description of how you might complete the exercise 7)84. We ask, "How many 7s are in 8?" We record a 1 over the 8, write a 7 under the 8, and subtract to get 1 (which is in the tens place). Then we "bring down" the 4 and recognize that we now have 14. Because there are two sevens in 14, we write a 2 over the 4 and write a 14 under the 14, subtract to get zero, and record our answer of 12. This division process uses repeated subtraction. As you inspect your work, you see that you subtract 7 from 8. It is important to relearn well-known arithmetic procedures to recognize the definitions and concepts that your teachers used to help you develop your knowledge.

An analysis of this traditional division algorithm reveals two critical concepts behind the step of checking how many times 7 can be subtracted from 8. First, we need to remember that we *really* want to know how many times 7 can be subtracted from 84. So our process begins by checking how many times 7 can be subtracted from 80. After all, that 8 is not an 8, it represents an 80.

Activity 5 . 5

PICTURING MULTIPLICATION

Use the intermediate product algorithm to symbolically record the steps in the following exercises:

27 • 14   154 • 96   (3x + 5) • (x + 8)

Draw a picture of 27 • 14 if you used base-10 blocks to build it.

Why is it impossible to use the array definition and the commercial base-10 blocks to show 154 • 96?

And we think it's best to call numbers by what they represent, not by their literal digits. So how many times does 7 go into 80? You know that it goes in at least 10 times, since 10 × 7 is 70, which is less than 80. Second, we need to realize that when we recorded "1" earlier and "put it over the 8," we *really* meant that it goes 10 times. This time, go ahead and record the whole 10. Write it on the right side, and record the 70 beneath the 84. Now subtract 70 from 84. You get 14. Now ask, "How many times does 7 go into 14?" Of course, you see that it goes in twice. Record 2 directly below 10, and record 14 below 14. To get your final quotient, add 10 and 2 to get 12. The work should look something like this:

```
 7)84     7)84         7)84            7)84             7)84
        – 70  10      – 70  10        – 70  10         – 70  10    12
                         14              14               14
                                      – 14   2         – 14   2
                                                          0
```

MIDDLE SCHOOL CONNECTIONS

Algorithms That Can Be Easily Generalized

During their middle school years, students need to solidify their number knowledge en route to preparing for learning about algebra. Algebraic thinking can be built up from generalized arithmetic procedures and concepts. The intermediate products algorithm shown above has several benefits to students in prealgebraic mathematics classes. First, there is no "carrying" in this procedure, and there is no direction to "add a zero" to keep track of a place value. Intermediate products come into play because we refer to a number by including the value of its place in the numeral. We did not put in a "place holder." Some middle school learners might be more familiar with a different algorithm for multiplying two two-digit numbers. As they learn to connect the intermediate products algorithm to it, adolescent learners can come to a new understanding of the traditional algorithm. The traditional algorithm involves multiplying individual digits and putting products into the proper "places." We applaud the efficiency of that algorithm, but in our experience, learners rarely fully understand that step. Memorizing steps without making meaning from the words, language, and experiences can result in a memorized algorithm that does not make sense. For 24 × 13, the traditional algorithm multiplies 4 × 3 and records the 2 and carries the 1. What meaning is in the 1 that is carried? If you then multiply 3 × 2, which is 6, and then add that carried 1 and then record it in the tens place, what is the meaning behind that? Clearly, it is efficient to have algorithms memorized, but when procedures grow from students' experiences and are explained and recorded from their drawings and words, connections evolve between memorized procedures and corresponding concepts.

Second, the intermediate products algorithm flows directly into the multiplication of two binomials, an algebraic process that is often learned in late middle school years. For instance, multiplying $(2x + 4)$ and $(x + 3)$ results in the same individual products as multiplying 24 and 13. And in the algebraic situation, no carrying is involved. Hence, the binomial multiplication is more similar to the intermediate products approach than is the typical memorized arithmetic algorithm. When learners connect arithmetic operations to algebraic operations, it is more likely that the operations will make sense.

Do you recognize any advantages of this algorithm? All values are fully written out, not just "in a place." Do you recognize any disadvantages of this algorithm? It could take a lot of paper! To begin thinking in this way, we asked, "How many times can 7 be subtracted from 84?" Even for a child who does not immediately think of subtracting 10 sevens at once (70), it is fine for that child to subtract out 7 at a time. $84 - 7 = 77, 77 - 7 = 70, 70 - 7 = 63$, and so on. It is likely that somewhere along the way, the child will recognize a 7 fact. Perhaps at 63, the child will see that there are 9 sevens. Perhaps it will happen later or even earlier. The quotient is the number of times we subtract 7. It does not matter how many we subtract out at any given time because eventually 7 is subtracted a total of 12 times. But as students deal with this division process, number sense will give rise to opportunities to make some leaps in the subtraction process. Let's further illustrate this procedure with an exercise using larger numbers. Consider the exercise 1554 ÷ 37. Your work might look something like this:

> You might be concerned by how inefficient this algorithm appears. But we find this algorithm particularly useful for children who need a little more time to fully develop their own division algorithms. This algorithm relieves the stress of getting things into the correct "place" and allows students to make sense of the concept of division as repeated subtraction.

```
37)1554    37)1554       37)1554       37)1554       37)1554          37)1554
           - 370   10    - 370   10    - 370   10    - 370   10       - 370   10   42
             1184          1184          1184          1184             1184
                         - 370   10    - 370   10    - 370   10       - 370   10
                           814           814           814              814
                                       - 370   10    - 370   10       - 370   10
                                         444           444              444
                                                     - 370   10       - 370   10
                                                       74               74
                                                                      -  74    2
                                                                        0
```

Some students might recognize that they could have started with subtracting out twenty 37s. Then their first step would be 1554 – 740. That would not affect the final answer. The student would just be dealing with 814 in the first step rather than in the second step. In all cases, the operation concept is repeated subtraction. The record of the algorithm should vary depending on what the individual students see, but the process of checking for 37s to subtract out at a time and recording that information, perhaps in a scaffold, should not vary. Complete Activity 5.6 to practice scaffold division.

As a final point, we briefly discuss how the procedure might look for the operation concept of fair sharing. In our 84 ÷ 7 problem, we ask, "If I put these 84 items into 7 piles, how many would be in each pile?" Begin with 84 items, and begin partitioning items into seven piles. As you deal around once, how many have you distributed at that time?

> ## *Activity* 5.6
>
> ### PICTURING DIVISION
> Use the scaffolding algorithm to symbolically record the steps in the following exercises:
>
> 37)159   37)846

As you continue to deal, you should recognize that the number of times you deal around is also the number of items that would be in each of the seven piles. Think about recording the information.

84 – 7 = 77   One distribution leaves 77 in the dealer's hand.
77 – 7 = 70   Two distributions leave 70 in the dealer's hand.
And so on . . .

A total of 12 distributions will be recorded.

Could the fair sharing definition be used to develop an algorithm? Of course. But the words you, the teacher, use to describe what you are doing will be different. To clarify the importance of this point, consider a context, because a context always helps to identify the operation concept.

1. I have 84 cookies and 7 friends. I want to give all the cookies away, and I want to give each friend the same amount. How many cookies will each friend receive?
2. I have 84 cookies. I need to package them into bags so that there are 7 cookies in each bag. How many bags do I need?

Which context is fair sharing and which is repeated subtraction? Do you recognize that these two problems, each representing 84 ÷ 7, would be acted out significantly differently in students' eyes? By studying several kinds of algorithms, you should recognize the importance of meaningfulness for students to develop a procedure by using concepts. One important strategy is to call numbers what they are rather than memorizing a procedure by stating "where the digits go."

MIDDLE SCHOOL CONNECTIONS

Just Show Me How to Do It

Adolescents experience a plethora of emotions and physiological changes during the middle school years. The patience for and delight in learning new things that might have been more obvious to their fourth and fifth grade teachers can seem to suddenly take a back seat to more personal issues, which are more pressing to the students.

Often, middle school students are acutely concerned with not appearing different in any way from their classmates. They might be reluctant to share their thinking out loud. If students do not immediately volunteer to share, it becomes tempting for the teacher to give in and quickly show the entire class *how to do* a procedure. If we do not require individual students to layer their procedural knowledge on and within their own concept knowledge, they can miss an opportunity to possess connected knowledge replete with nuances about the procedure. Showing the procedure is tempting because we come away with spurious beliefs about students' knowledge, since students appear to know *what* to do. In reality, if students did not build the procedural knowledge themselves, by layering it with conceptual knowledge, they are merely mimicking us, and the information will likely be quickly forgotten.

Furthermore, requiring students to layer procedures with concepts allows middle school teachers to spot conceptual misunderstandings the students might have developed on their way to the middle grades. Adolescent students often feel an urgency to get to their next life situation, whether social time in the hallway or their next class. Learning operation knowledge as a consequence of concept knowledge takes a little more time than being told how to do something. But the difference is *learning* rather than *parroting*. In their middle school years, students are expected to refine their existing knowledge and more fully coordinate it for their own development as well as to prepare for the high school years. Therefore, we must take the time to truly develop the new knowledge and to require students to summarize and synthesize their existing knowledge, layering concepts and procedures as deeply as possible. So when students just want to move on, we have to resist the urge to leave students behind. This might require some out-of-class time, extra conversations with parents about home activities, or temporary groups in class completing separate kinds of tasks. But the reward of knowing the mathematics themselves, rather than just being shown how to do it, is incalculable.

LET'S REVIEW

In thinking about the mathematics of number and operation, we learned that both concepts and procedures are part of this mathematical knowledge base. To think about the mathematics of operations, we found it important to revisit the conceptual meaning of number. In particular, understanding place value is critical to becoming fluid with operations. By using the actual value represented by a digit in a numeral, we could elucidate several algorithms. We learned that understanding the concepts behind the operations helps to ground different procedures. We also learned that recognizing patterns in computation can lead to general procedures.

HOMEWORK

1. Create a "looks like, sounds like" chart for the subtraction fact 8 − 3 = 5. Create the chart for (a) a take-away definition and (b) a comparison definition.
2. Explain the difference between a number line model for multiplication and the array model. Use 8 × 3 = 24 to illustrate your explanation.
3. Create a "looks like, sounds like" chart for the division fact 24 ÷ 4. First use (a) fair-sharing, then use (b) repeated subtraction.

SUBTRACT AS:	TAKE-AWAY		COMPARING	
	Looks Like	Sounds Like	Looks Like	Sounds Like
Story problem (context)				
Using chips				
Modeling on a number line				
A child's drawing for your story problem				

DIVISION AS:	FAIR SHARING		REPEATED SUBTRACTION	
	Looks Like	Sounds Like	Looks Like	Sounds Like
Story problem (context)				
Using chips				
Modeling on a number line				
A child's drawing for your story problem				

SUGGESTED READINGS

Baroody, A. J. (1989). Manipulatives don't come with guarantees. *Arithmetic Teacher, 36*(2), 4–5.

Ron, P. (1998). My family taught me this way. In L. J. Morrow, & M. J. Kenney (Eds.), *The teaching and learning of algorithms in school mathematics: 1998 Yearbook for the National Council of Teachers of Mathematics* (pp. 115–119). Reston, VA: NCTM.

REFERENCES

Carpenter, T. (1986). Conceptual knowledge as a foundation for procedural knowledge. In J. Hiebert (Ed.), *Conceptual and procedural knowledge: The case of mathematics* (pp. 113–132). Hillsdale, NJ: Lawrence Erlbaum.

Cauley, K. M. (1988). Construction of logical knowledge: Study of borrowing in subtraction. *Journal of Educational Psychology, 80*(2), 202–205.

Joslyn, R. E. (1990). Using concrete models to teach large number concepts. *Arithmetic Teacher, 38*(3), 6–9.

Klein, A. S., Beishuizen, M., & Treffers, A. (2002). The empty number line in Dutch second grade. In Judith Sowder & Bonnie Schappelle (Eds.), *Lessons learned from research* (pp. 41–46). Reston, VA: NCTM.

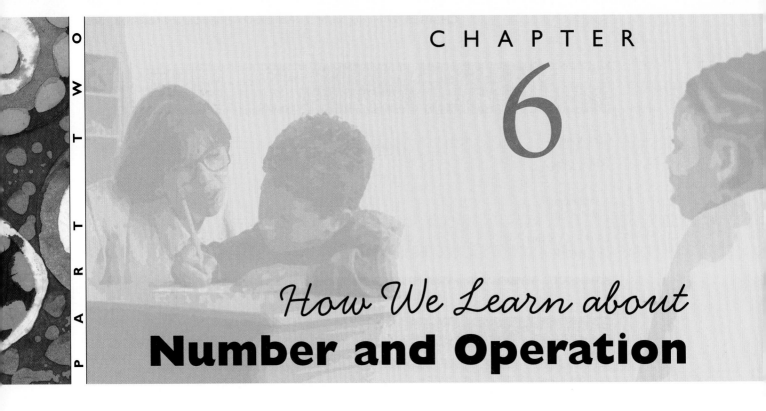

How We Learn about
Number and Operation

P A R T   T W O

In this chapter, we rely on Constance Kamii's work (2000a, 2000b) on understanding children's general development of number, number sense, and operation procedures. Kamii interprets Piaget for mathematics education. Piaget's original work was intended to understand human cognitive development in general. *Number in Preschool and Kindergarten* (Kamii, 2000b) and *Young Children Reinvent Arithmetic* (Kamii, 2000a) are important and go a long way toward interpreting Piaget's theory for teachers.

We also use the work of Carpenter, Fennema, Franke, Levi, and Empson (1999) for understanding specific operations. Their work, known as *cognitively guided instruction* (CGI), includes individual works from these researchers but also extends those works to clarify the way young children interact with arithmetic problems. In general, CGI (Carpenter et al., 1999) found that teachers have a sense of how children develop operation knowledge, but because that pedagogical knowledge may not have been profoundly studied or developed, that knowledge did not overtly appear to impact their instructional decisions.

As you think about the ways in which children build up or tear apart numbers, we want you to use both Kamii's work and CGI work. Both are important for teachers who are building children's number and operation thinking. Therefore, we will give brief overviews, trying at the same time to mesh their works. Our initial effort is by no means exhaustive, and we encourage you to read both independently. Connecting their respective research to teaching decisions will help you to understand how children learn number and to be able to recognize different strategies young children use when they execute operations.

We begin this chapter with some theory about how students learn number relationships. We later discuss how students learn procedures by making sense of how operations can be carried out on the number relationships that the students have already developed. We remind you that there is a difference between the concept of an operation and the procedures for an operation that students use and that both are based on their own reasoning. Procedures are the things we do, and conceptions of operations are the reasons we do the things we do.

UNDERSTANDING RELEVANT LEARNING THEORY: **Number Is a Mental Relationship**

Number Ideas

Children learn number by developing a collection of mental relationships about quantification. The collection is not expanded linearly. It grows nonlinearly and can be refined through a variety of instructional experiences. Although we will describe levels, you should not interpret our ordering of them here as a sequential *instructional* process. According to Kamii, a child can be at one of two levels before being able to understand the number relationship. To help us illustrate these two levels, we would like you to set out two rows of counters, such as colored chips with each row using a different color. In our discussion, we will assume that the two colors of chips are red and blue. Asking children to work with chips is a fairly traditional way for teachers and researchers to understand how the children are thinking about number.

Level 1

At level 1, children assume that any two rows of chips are equal if those rows' first and last chips are roughly lined up. Even if the red row has seven chips and the blue row has 10 chips, children at level 1 base their thinking on the fact that rows begin and end the same distance apart. These children understand the chips spatially and therefore believe that two rows that have the same general length have the same "amount."

Level 2

At level 2, children who look at two rows of chips in which one row goes beyond the other row in one or both directions will conclude that the longer row has "more" elements in it. We are probably all familiar with the idea of conservation (knowing that it does not matter whether a row extends farther out or not—what matters is the number of chips in each row). Given a row of red chips and a row of blue chips, each containing seven chips and spread out so that the blue row extends past the red row, children who cannot conserve will say that those rows do not contain the same amount.

Level 3

At this level, children are able to understand and work with numbers, with no concern about where the rows of chips begin and end. Levels 1 and 2 exist before the child understands these relationships about number. It would be a mistake to assume that children simply move from one level to the next. It is a very complex process and takes many experiences for children to arrive at level 3, since number is constructed individually, by coordinating existing concepts and developing new ones.

Knowing Number Words

In their efforts to develop the idea of amount, children must first know the language of number words (Fuson & Hall, 1983; Fuson, 1983). Children sometimes appear to be counting chips when in fact they are naming chips. For example, if a child who has eight blue chips in front of her counts out loud, "One, two, three, four, five, six, seven, eight," pointing to each chip as she goes along, and then says,

"Eight," we need to ask questions. "How do you know" or "Show me eight" will tell us whether she recognizes that the entire set makes up eight-ness or merely that the last chip is named "eight." Is she thinking, "This is chip 1, this is chip 2, this is chip 3" rather than understanding the mathematical structure of amount? Children often do not really understand that the set makes 8, not the last chip being named "8." By asking, "How is this set 8?" and listening to students explain their thinking, we recognize whether or not they understand the mathematical structure of number. They must understand that the idea of amount is inclusive of all the previously counted chips and not a property of the last chip counted.

Growth Happens in Chunks

Kamii (2000b) notes that number knowledge will take place gradually. She describes increasingly large numbers as being in certain groups or chunks of numbers. The first chunk includes numbers 1 through 7, the second contains 8–15, and the third contains 15–30. A child might understand 6 but not 8 simply because of the sheer magnitude of the number. So we should not deduce that children are thinking incorrectly if they appear to understand 6 but not 8. After 30, children think of these numbers as more than or less than something that is known. Eventually, students do not have to count 75 objects to understand that a set has 75 objects in it, whereas up to 30, it seems that they need to count the objects to understand the magnitude of the set.

Principles of Teaching Number

"How *precisely* the child constructs number is still a mystery just as the child learning of language is still a mystery" (Kamii, 2000b, p. 25). Even in 2000, in *Number in Preschool and Kindergarten*, Kamii indicates that there is still a lot we do not know about how exactly a child constructs knowledge of number. If you are feeling downhearted, do not despair. There are things we can do that indirectly teach number. Kamii proposes three principles of teaching that help us to guide children's learning of number.

Principle 1 (Relationships)

The first principle is the creation of all kinds of relationships. Children should *sort, classify,* and *order* all kinds of objects, events, and actions. Paying particular attention to objects, events, and actions that provide opportunities to quantify situations is especially useful in developing number knowledge. Here the child makes his or her collection of mental relationships between ideas, mathematical or not, and is inventing number knowledge. For example, realizing that every school lunch the day after hamburgers is pizza (whether or not this is accurate) is recognizing a relationship. Basically, the relationships that are developed at this level, among other things, lay the groundwork for recognizing that things *can be* put into number relationships and that things *need to be* put into number relationships.

Principle 2 (Quantification)

The second principle is *quantification* of objects. Children should be encouraged to think about number and quantity of objects in meaningful situations. For instance, when it is time to put away crayons, ask each student to bring four crayons to the basket. To deepen quantification knowledge students should compare sets rather than merely count them (Kamii, 2000b). Ask the student with the most crayons to bring his or her crayons first. Sharing is another useful way to encourage students to compare two sets, even though they might not need to count the elements in them (Pepper & Hunting, 1998). To achieve

Table 6.1 **Principles of Learning to Count**

LEVEL	WHAT CHILDREN DO:	WHAT CHILDREN THINK:
0	Cannot complete the task.	Really does not understand the task the adult has requested.
1	Visually estimates the spatial configuration, trying to copy what the adult has produced.	Builds on spatial thinking, as discussed in Chapter 2. Not yet abstracting the idea of number.
2	Looks back and forth between the adult's chips while setting out their own chips. Might even alternate between pointing chip by chip at the adult's pile of chips while collecting their own pile of chips.	Uses a rudimentary form of a one-to-one correspondence but is not yet counting. Merely matches chip to chip.
3	Reproduces the same number of chips, simply by counting the adult's set and then retrieving the same number of chips for their own set.	Counts.

this task, it is important to use movable objects. Using movable objects puts the children in control of their work. They can command their own way of looking at the objects in question. You might ask one student to hand out crayons, giving three crayons to each child at the table.

We remind you that "relationships do not have an existence in external reality" (Kamii, 2000b, p. 9). So the relationships do not exist *in* the external movable objects. Children must construct the internal mental relationship from their interaction with the external reality—in this case, the movable objects. Pepper & Hunting (1998) suggest that such development may result from the use of larger and larger numbers of objects.

Go to "Try it! See it! Teach it!" on page 96.

Within this complex second principle, four levels of development appear. The levels are outlined in Table 6.1. It helps to use Kamii's (2000b) example to

CLASSROOM CONNECTIONS
Finding Number Relationships

"This [number] relationship exists only in the minds of those who can create it between the objects" (Kamii, 2000b, p. 9). This statement intrigued me. I wanted to know how the number relationship exists in the minds of Anna (seven years old), Paige (six years old), and Jack (four years old). I used two different sets of chips and asked them to tell me about the number of chips. First, I used two rows with four chips, but with one row spread out, taking up more space. Second, I used two rows taking up the same amount of space but with different numbers of chips (three and four). I wanted to learn how the children thought about the number of chips.

Anna mentally counted the chips and said, "They are the same." With that, Anna demonstrates her proficiency with counting, which is level 3.

Paige said, "They are the same." She showed some basic one-to-one matching between rows in her explanation saying, "They match." Even though the two rows did not end in the same place, it was interesting to watch Paige describe this level 2 thinking.

Jack was surprised when one row *looked* longer yet had the same number of chips. He appeared to be moving between levels 1 and 2 of Kamii's second principle. His ability to use a rudimentary form of a one-to-one correspondence, between those early number words and pointing to chips, indicates that he is counting, which is level 3. But still he was swayed by the spatial arrangement of the chips. So I suspect that with a larger number of chips (more than seven), he probably would have functioned mostly at level 1. What do you think?

Try it! See it! Teach it!

Understanding Number Relationships

Step **One**: Try it!

Do the Math...

Have a look at the arrangements shown below. Keep them handy as you watch the video.

First Chip Arrangement

Rearrangement of the Chips

Step **Two**: See it!

Watch the Video...

Anna is seven years old, Paige is six years old, and Jack is four years old. Anna has a good command of counting processes and Jack is just learning about this new concept. All three children are being asked to compare two rows of chips and to decide what they know about the number of chips in each row.

Things to Watch for...

- Recognize that student thinking about number is overpowered by spatial thinking.
- Pay particular attention to Karen's questioning techniques, try and identify the cues in the children's answers that caused Karen to ask the questions she chose to ask.

Video Clip 3 *(time length 6:04)*

Jack is beginning to understand the relationship between number and size.

Step **Three**: Teach it!

Reflect on Your Own Teaching...

1. What kinds of things did Anna say that demonstrate her knowledge of number?

2. What kinds of things did Paige say that demonstrate her knowledge of number?

3. What kinds of things did Jack say that demonstrate his knowledge of number?

4. What would you have liked to ask Jack after he "squished" the chips together?

5. Why did Karen keep asking Jack the same thing over and over again?

_____

_____

6. What do you think Jack wanted to tell Karen about the ends matching? Did he mean that something happened when the ends of each row matched? That is, that the rows began and ended at roughly the same place, representing level 1 thinking? Did he mean that something happened when a coin in each row matched a coin in the other row? That is, was there a one-to-one correspondence between the rows, representing level 2 thinking? Or did he mean that it mattered only if the coins themselves touched (matched)? That is, the pennies in a row needed to be squished together, with no spaces between them. This is also level 2 thinking.

_____

_____

7. Recall how Kamii describes young children's progressions through the levels. At level 1, students think that two rows of chips are equal if they begin and end at roughly the same spot. At level 2, children believe that two rows with the same number of coins somehow unevenly spaced are not actually showing equal amounts. So when Jack talked about matching, was he at level 1 or level 2? Kamii tells us that once children work through levels 1 and 2, they can understand these kinds of tasks by counting. Because he eventually counted, he must have been ready to move to level 3. It appeared that he suddenly understood a new way to complete the task. Wasn't it exciting to watch the look on his face after he counted the two rows of four that were unevenly spaced? What do you guess he thought about his realization that those two rows were made up of an equal number of coins? Do you think he made progress? How did Karen's continual questioning lead him toward a new understanding?

_____

_____

A Comment from Karen

Did you notice how Anna wanted to give me more information? She is clearly well-grounded at the counting level. She wanted to tell me about odd numbers too!

Paige seemed to be roughly at level 2. I wish I had used more than seven coins, to check her progress more carefully. By the way, did you notice that Paige said 4 and 4 is 9? I did not dwell on that at all; I was more interested in the process she used so that I could identify her level of thinking. When Paige said, "This doesn't mean you have more," I knew that she was ignoring the spaces between the chips, so I knew she was beyond level 1. She did some matching but also some counting. It seemed that she was moving between levels 2 and 3.

I wish I knew exactly what Jack wanted to tell me about the ends matching. I continually prompted him to tell me how he knew. Did you notice how many times I asked him, "But *why*?" I wanted to know whether he thought counting would be a good way to see if the rows of coins were equal. Jack was eventually receptive to the idea of counting. He counted three coins just by looking at them, but to count four coins, he had to alternately touch the coins and say his number words. Because he eventually counted, it seems that he is at level 3 for those small amounts, but I suspect he needs several more experiences before he would rely on counting (especially with more than seven coins) as a strategy for deciding the number of coins in the rows.

GO BACK TO PAGE 95

illustrate the four levels of learning that students pass through as they work to understand quantification. The example is this: An adult has shown a child a row of chips and has asked the child to put out the same number of chips. This table describes the child's thought processes within principle 2.

Principle 3 (Social Interaction)

The third principle is *social interaction*. When students exchange ideas with peers, it gives us opportunities to figure out how they are thinking. We can then choose to intervene according to what we detect is going on mentally. As children discuss with one another, they agree or disagree with their peers. As they listen to peers justifying solutions, they make sense of the situation and incorporate their peers' thinking if it makes sense to them. While they explain to one another, we listen for opportunities to guide them.

Kamii does caution that development of number relationships occurs simultaneously with a significant number of other concepts, such as moral and social relationships. Number concepts do not develop in isolation, nor should they be expected to develop in that way. All mathematics should be developed in a connected way with other forms of knowledge. (For a thorough treatment of the ideas of social and moral relationships, the reader is strongly encouraged to review Kamii and DeVries's works (1976, 1980) on Piaget's theory.)

Number Sense

Mental relationships about number include number sense. Connecting number sense ideas of composing, decomposing, and seeing magnitudes of numbers is critical for number sense development. Sowder (1988) nicely describes number sense in the following ways. Number sense includes relationships between and among place-value concepts, ability to work with powers of 10, ability to use number properties, and understanding symbol systems. These relationships can be used to do mental computation (in which the goal is an exact answer, not an estimate) and can grow from experimenting with number properties.

Students rely on number sense to execute mental computation. Rather than practicing paper-and-pencil procedures, whether invented or standard, students must think creatively and flexibly. Before we consider an example of number sense, complete Activity 6.1, in which you are given four numbers to add mentally. You should take care to think about everything you do as you complete the addition and write down *everything* you thought about as you arrived at your answer. Then read through first grader Jake's solution:

Activity 6.1

ADDING FOUR NUMBERS

You will be given an addition exercise to complete mentally. Complete the exercise in your head, using a variety of mental strategies that you have developed throughout your life. As you complete the addition problem, please record everything you think about and exactly how you deal with the numbers.

$$3 + 5 + 9 + 6$$

> *Jake:* First, I took 2 from the 3, to get a 1. I added that 1 to 9, making 10. [He wrote that down.] Then, I took 1 off from the 6, to get a 5. I added that 5 to 10, giving me 15. [He wrote that down.] Then I added in the last 5, for 20. [Again, he recorded this accomplishment.] Now, I go back and pick up the 2 and the 1 took off earlier, for 3. I add 3 to 20 to get 23.

Jake solidified some of his number sense by doing the mental computation. At the same time, you probably recognize that he used a variety of composing and decomposing strategies to complete his computation.

UNDERSTANDING RELEVANT LEARNING THEORY:
Procedures Build from Solving Problems

NCTM TEACHING

When teaching students about computation, we do not begin by showing them how to perform algorithms. Rather, we begin by posing arithmetic exercises, such as the one shown in Activity 6.1, or context problems at the children's appropriate level. By solving problems, children can invent procedures for arriving at their solutions. As students invent procedures that are meaningful to them, they establish mental abstractions about those experiences from their everyday worlds. Through active involvement and exploration, students who are encouraged to openly test hypotheses about procedures for resolving and managing situations that evolve from those problem situations will develop sophisticated knowledge about those procedures. By active involvement, we mean, of course, far more than observable moving around of objects. We mean active *mental* involvement.

Letting procedures for executing computation grow naturally from students' work with problems probably evokes an image of teaching that is slightly different from what you remember. In the United States, "Teachers present definitions of terms and demonstrate procedures for solving specific problems. Students are then asked to memorize the definitions and practice the procedures" (Stigler & Hiebert, 1999, p. 27). It is difficult to teach differently from the way we were taught, but knowing that we can expect students to invent a way of dealing with situations and help them to understand the procedures they completed to deal with those situations is a good start. Rather than being shown the procedures without any ownership of the work (i.e., without making their own sense), it is preferable for students to grapple with situations themselves. Sometimes it is hard to believe, but "by struggling to figure out a way of dealing with problems, children create new relationships (by constructing abstractions). Relationships that a child has created from within are not forgotten like relationships fed from the environment" (Kamii, 2000a, pp. 200–201). Those relationships serve as part of the foundation for students' procedural inventions, which they can invent if they are given the time and opportunity to discuss and defend their thinking. To facilitate this sort of discussion, teachers and students all have to learn to write down verbally communicated information. In Activity 6.2 (p. 100), practice recording someone else's thinking. Be sure to record each step of the process as the person describes it.

With all this talk about concepts and procedures, you might be thinking that because the role of practice is not mentioned, we do not value skills. Of course, to excel at a procedure, a person must practice that procedure. What we are suggesting is that the way the procedure develops in the first place is unique for each child and that our understanding of how students develop this procedure knowledge must be based on students' knowledge of concepts for the procedures to be meaningful. Practice *is* important, and we expect you to require students to practice their procedures. However, what procedure should they practice? We suggest that they practice the procedures they invent.

Addition

In making the move from quantification to addition, it is helpful to pose the addition question in real contexts that literally require children to combine two numbers. For instance, rather than simply asking a child like Paige to add 3 and 4, we instead ask her to consider two baskets of kittens. One basket holds three kittens, and the other holds four kittens. If all of the kittens crawl into

Activity 6 . 2

SYMBOLIZING SOMEONE ELSE'S THINKING

You will give three arithmetic exercises to an adult friend, who will complete the problem mentally. Ask the friend to clarify for you the numbers with which he or she operates. There will be time later, to ask why the person chose to work with those numbers. It is important, first, to capture the sequence of the thinking process before asking the person to explain it.

15 + 29

_____

_____

_____

135 – 68

_____

_____

_____

16 • 24

_____

_____

_____

one basket, how many kittens will be in that basket? Using a context helps children to make their own sense and helps them to develop their own autonomy about the operation of adding 3 and 4.

Kamii (2000a) suggests that appropriate objectives for developing operation knowledge follow a sophisticated sequence. She cautions us that this sequence should not be interpreted as requiring mastery before a child can "move" to the next item in the sequence. We use the familiar "looks like, sounds like" approach in Table 6.2 to sequence these objectives while keeping her caution in mind.

This table also illustrates the quite sensible way in which children construct addition knowledge. When confronted with large numbers, children think back to work with smaller numbers and use any variations of strategies that make sense. In Table 6.2, we use chips to describe examples of how the children's work could look and sound when they communicate their thinking. We want to clarify that the chips themselves are not the same as the children's thinking. It is very important for children to "use paper and pencil, [so] they can externalize their own ideas and use these representations as tools. By contrast, counters have their own physical properties that interfere with children's ideas. This is probably why young children do not choose to use counters to solve word problems" (Kamii, 2000a, p. 26). They often use their own drawings instead. But we believe that the chip illustrations will help *you* to understand what form the children's thinking might take.

Table 6.2 **"Looks Like, Sounds Like" Table for Addition**

NAME	EXAMPLE	LOOKS LIKE:	SOUNDS LIKE:
Counting all elements	4 + 7	Child gets out 4 red chips and 7 blue chips and pushes all of them together.	Child counts the entire set of chips one at a time, starting with no particular chip, "One, two, three, . . . , eleven."
Counting on	4 + 7	Child gets out 4 red chips and 7 blue chips and pushes all the chips together.	Knowing that there are 4 red chips, the child begins counting on with the blue chips saying, "Five, six, . . . , eleven."
Counting on from larger	4 + 7	Child gets out 4 red chips and 7 blue chips and pushes all the chips together.	Knowing that there are 7 blue chips, child begins counting on with blue chips saying, "Eight, nine, ten, eleven."
A number plus 1	4 + 1	Child thinks about the next number in order.	Child says, "Four, five."
A number plus 2	4 + 2	Child skip-counts, beginning at appropriate place in the pattern.	Child says, "Four, six."
Adding addends up to 4	4 + 3	Child can use "a number plus 1" and "a number plus 2" to make sense of these small addends.	Child might first add 1 and then 2 onto 4, saying, "Four, five, . . . , seven."
Adding addends up to 6	4 + 6	Child might remember using dice or some other familiar situation.	Child mentally calculates or recalls situations. All you hear is the child saying, "Ten."
Adding doubles up to 10 + 10	4 + 4	Child might use skip-counting or visualize chips.	Child skip counts, "Four, eight."

Note: Kamii (2000a, p. 77) notes that doubles are an "anchor point" for children's development of addition with other numbers. Children should connect doubling to the earlier idea of a number plus 1. For instance, in solving 7 + 8, children will often think of 7 + 7 and then add 1. Later, they might also think of 8 + 8 and then subtract 1.

Making 10 with 2 numbers	10 as 7 + 3	Children might use 10 two-color chips to show all the ways they can be flipped to show 10.	"I can show 7 yellow and 3 red or 6 yellow and 4 red or 5 yellow and 5 red. . . ."
Partitioning numbers up to 6	6 as 5 + 1	Children might use two-color chips to show all the ways they can be flipped to show these numbers.	"I can show 6 and 0, 5 and 1, 4 and 2, 3 and 3. . . ."

Children develop families of number pairs for numbers, such as 10. Children should be encouraged to mentally group all pairs of values that make any given number. Ten is particularly important because facility with 10 allows children to use number sense to make sense of addition problems with larger addends.

Adding addends larger than 6	7 + 9	Now children will use a variety of strategies that make sense to them, such as doubling 7 and then adding 2.	Child says, "Seven and seven is fourteen . . . sixteen."

Classifying Addition Problems

Through contextual experiences, children recognize classes of problems. CGI research has found that all three of the following problems for 4 + 3 = 7 are classified by children as *join* problems:

1. Paige had 4 kittens in a basket. Three more kittens crawled into the basket. How many kittens were in the basket then?
2. Paige had 4 kittens. Her grandmother gave her some more kittens for her birthday. Then she had 7 kittens. How many kittens did Paige's grandmother give her for her birthday?

3. Paige had some kittens. Her grandmother gave her 3 more kittens for her birthday. Then she had 7 kittens. How many kittens did Paige have before her birthday?

Each problem involves an action in which an amount is increased. Children see the similarity of *joining* in the problems, even though the first one is "addition" and the second and third are "subtraction." Given the close connection that naturally occurs, we move now to discussion of subtraction.

Subtraction

Subtraction is a complicated, multifaceted concept and therefore a difficult process for children to execute. Addition is easier because the process requires them to build things up, and there is really only one way to phrase an addition situation. Subtraction is harder because the process can be written to take part away, to break things apart, to compare two quantities, or even as nearly an addition situation (as you saw above). There are three definitions for subtraction: take-away, find the difference, and missing-addend. But children classify subtraction situations into five different types. Eventually they must come to realize that all five types have the commonality of being subtraction. (See Table 6.3.) To further complicate subtraction, the missing-addend definition, seen as one of two kinds of join problem situations (described earlier) is often not viewed as subtraction by children. It often seems more like addition to them. With appropriate experiences directly modeling the situation, they can eventually connect it to the subtraction process because they eventually recognize commonalties between the problem types, thus further understand relationships among the kinds of subtraction. Analyzing children's subtraction thinking requires a complex understanding of the different classification schemes children may utilize.

As with all operations, children go about learning subtraction by making sense of problems within a context. It is easy to tell which of the subtraction definitions is needed by the way in which the characters in a story problem need to act out the operation. It is useful to make the children the actors in the contexts. So we prepared to quiz Paige a little further. We placed her into a separate context about kittens: "If you had 7 kittens and I gave 5 of them to Anna, how many would you have left?" Paige paused and said, "2."

> *Teacher:* How did you figure that out?
> *Paige:* I used my fingers.
> *Teacher:* How did you use them?
> *Paige:* I counted quietly.
> *Teacher:* Tell me out loud what you did.
> *Paige:* I put up seven fingers and folded down five of them.

Paige used a counting-down strategy to complete this *separate* type problem.

To further understand Paige's thinking about subtraction, we asked her a *compare* type question: "Paige has 7 kittens. Anna has 3 kittens. Who has more kittens and how many more kittens does she have?"

At first, Paige said, "4." But we asked her how she figured it out. She said, "I used my fingers, I counted from 3 to 7 and it was 4." She saw this *compare* problem as one that was amenable to the use of a counting strategy. We asked her to think about how she solved both kitten problems. She thought for a moment and said, "I counted up on one and down on the other. I kept track of the counts." The compare problem was more difficult for her, but we wonder whether Paige might be beginning to make some connections between these two subtraction problem types. Children initially recognize that these prob-

Table 6.3 **CGI's Subtraction Strategies**

NAME	EXAMPLE	LOOKS LIKE:	SOUNDS LIKE:
Direct Modeling Strategies			
Join (change unknown) *joining to*	Anna had 3 candies. Paige gave her some more candies. Now Anna has 7 candies. How many candies did Paige give to Anna?	Child gets out a set of 3 chips. Then child begins to add more chips to the pile until reaching a total of 7 chips.	Child says, "Four, five, six, seven. I added 4 more chips. So, four."
Separate (result unknown) *separating from*	Anna had 7 candies. Paige ate 3 of those candies. How many candies does Anna have now?	Child builds a set of 7 chips and then removes 3 of those chips.	Child recognizes the number of chips remaining (either by counting or possibly some strictly visual recognition, perhaps the chips are arranged in a familiar manner).
Separate (change unknown) *separating to*	Anna had 7 candies. Paige ate some of the candies. Now Anna has 3 candies. How many did Paige eat?	Child builds a set of 7 chips. Child removes chips until 3 remain.	Child recognizes the number of chips removed probably through counting, "One, two, three, four," but possibly through some other recognition.
Compare (difference unknown) *matching*	Anna has 7 candies. Paige has 3 candies. How many more does Anna have than Paige?	Child builds two sets of chips. One set has 7 chips; the other has 3 chips. Child matches a chip from each pile until one pile is empty.	Child notes that the number of matches is the answer, probably through counting, "One, two, three, four," but possibly through some other recognition.
Join (start unknown) *trial and error*	Anna had some candies. Her grandmother gave her 3 more candies. Now Anna has 7 candies. How many did she have before her grandmother gave her some candy?	Child builds a set of some number of chips. Child adds 3 more chips to the pile and counts. Child repeats this process until the count is 7.	
Counting Strategies			
Join (change unknown) *joining to*	Anna had 3 candies. Paige gave her some more candies. Now Anna has 7 candies. How many candies did Paige give to Anna?	Child begins counting forward from 3 until reaching 7. Keeping track of this may be done with fingers.	Child says, "Four, five, six, seven" while keeping track of the number of words recited. The child looks at the track-keeping device (fingers) and notes the number of words recited and says, "Four."
Separate (result unknown) *Counting down*	Anna had 7 candies. Paige ate 3 of those candies. How many candies does Anna have now?	The child begins counting backward from 7 for 3 counts.	Child says, "Six, five, four." The child notes the last word said and says, "Four."
Separate (change unknown) *Counting down to*	Anna had 7 candies. Paige ate some of the candies. Now Anna has 3 candies. How many did Paige eat?	The child begins counting down from 7 to reach 3. This counting may occur with fingers where the fingers are merely a track-keeping device, not a direct model.	Child says, "Six, five, four, three," while keeping track of the number of words recited. The child looks at the track-keeping device (fingers) and notes the number of words recited and says, "Four."

lems are different even though adults know that both situations are subtraction problems.

Next, we asked Jack (age four) about the *compare* situations. He said, "Ten." Are you surprised at Jack's answer? He is making some sense of the problem, but subtraction, especially subtraction of this type, is difficult, as we noted earlier. CGI posits that when children are "building up," they are more comfortable and familiar than when they are "tearing apart." Knowing the different problem types helps teachers to develop meaningful learning experiences.

Classifying Subtraction Strategies

We can essentially group children's subtraction strategies into two categories. In one category, children do the subtraction with a direct model of the action in the situation. In the other category, they complete subtraction with a counting strategy. To use their direct modeling subtraction strategies, children draw pictures or use counters (such as chips) and model the exact activity going on in the context. When young children first consider subtraction problems, they usually begin with direct modeling strategies. In fact, CGI found that even very young children can solve subtraction problems when direct modeling strategies are used. It is later that children use counting strategies.

This discussion might spark your interest in writing good word problems. The importance of understanding the structure of word problems is critical in the development of operation (not just subtraction) knowledge. Posing problems with certain kinds of actions and the order of the numbers in the problem can be an indication of why a student can or cannot do a problem.

When given well-thought-out problems to solve, young children first directly model it using objects, drawings, or fingers. Both CGI and Kamii agree that after many opportunities to solve problems themselves and listening to classmates share their strategies, children will abandon less efficient strategies. While simultaneously developing their uses of more sophisticated strategies, children also build their abstractions about subtraction through solving these kinds of problems. They move from a strategy of acting out to a counting strategy (in which fingers are more of a track-keeping tool) and eventually to using number facts.

As we saw with Anna, Paige, and Jack, children eventually come to depend solely on counting strategies. They often play off of their knowledge about addition to do subtraction. In other words, these subtraction strategies mimic *counting up* and *counting onward* addition strategies they already know. In subtraction, the counting process is revealed in one of three ways. *Counting down* appears when children are confronted with a problem in which the beginning amount and the amount removed are both known. *Counting down to* appears when the child is confronted with a problem in which the beginning amount and the ending amount are both known. As you review Table 6.3, you should note that *separating from* (direct modeling) and *counting down* (counting) strategies are both products from the same *separate* (result known) context or problem. It is the strategy children utilize that is different and that we need to be able to recognize and use to inform us of future teaching decisions. In Activity 6.3, write several word problems based on addition and each of the different types of subtraction.

Learning Addition and Subtraction

Kamii has been involved in extensive research efforts to understand how students learn two-digit addition and subtraction (e.g., Kamii, 1989, 2000a, 2000b; Kamii & Ozaki, 1999; Kato, Kamii, Ozaki, & Nagahiro, 2002). Time and time again, her findings have indicated that when children make their own sense of either of these operations, they universally begin with the tens column. You might be surprised to learn that they do *not* begin with ones. You might need

Activity 6 . 3

WRITING WORD PROBLEMS

Write a word problem that would be interesting and understandable by K–2 children and that would require them to solve the exercises:

6 + 9 = 15 (Addition—Join)

_____

_____

8 – 3 = 5 (Subtraction—(take-away) Separate (result unknown))

_____

_____

10 – 6 = 4 (Subtraction—(take-away) Separate (change unknown))

_____

_____

14 – 8 = 6 (Subtraction—Join (start unknown))

_____

_____

13 – 7 = 6 (Subtraction—Compare (difference unknown))

_____

_____

to look back at the subtraction procedures discussed earlier to remind yourself how this sort of algorithm looks on paper. The quest for teaching addition and subtraction becomes one of exploring teaching implications for this finding. If children "naturally" begin with tens, what does it say about building knowledge on their sense-making if during the course of our instruction, we force them to begin with ones?

Multiplication

Multiplication is complex because students are dealing with two quantities: the *number of copies* to be made of the elements and the *number of elements being copied*. This can complicate multiplication learning and should not be taken lightly. Patterning with blocks and connecting those patterns to skip-counting can lay the foundation for helping children to work with these two numbers. For instance, asking children to skip-count by 3 (number of elements being copied) a total of four times (number of copies) helps to connect the skip-counting pattern to the idea of multiplication. Creating a color pattern with groups of three blocks in each of four colors (red, blue, green, and yellow) can also help children to keep the number of copies (three blocks) separate from the number of elements being copied (four colors). Think about how BBBGGGRRRYYY is helpful in guiding children to understand the role of the two numbers in the multiplication statement 3 × 4.

MIDDLE SCHOOL CONNECTIONS

Add the Opposite

You will find that many middle school textbooks introduce integer subtraction by building from the take-away definition of subtraction. Naturally, building on existing knowledge is the approach we *want* to take. Caution should be exercised in teaching about integer operations so that students do not inadvertently internalize thoughts that mathematical ideas have somehow changed. As you already learned, the usual ways of thinking about subtraction are take-away, find-the-difference, or missing-addend in the elementary grades. All three have merits in working with integers, and each way of subtracting can be modeled. We have met with good success with including contextual problems using the missing addend definition and the find-the-difference definition. For example, consider Jenna, an avid hiker. She is standing at a location 2 miles away from Winterlake (let's call her location ⁻2), and her best friend is standing 4 miles past Winterlake (let's call her location ⁺4.) How far does Jenna need to hike to catch up to her friend? The basic question is ⁻2 + ☐ = ⁺4 and is solved by the equation ⁺4 − ⁻2. As simple as addition might appear to most middle school students, subtraction exercises like this pose a distinct dilemma. We have found that adolescents are receptive to using the missing-addend definition with a number line as a way to think about subtracting integers.

On the other hand, the find-the-difference definition using discrete sets closely demonstrates the add-the-opposite definition. This way of working with integers is important in future algebra learning. To begin to think about this process, let's start with a context: On a scale of −10 to 10, students are ranked according to their performance on a gymnastics exercise. Pete scored 7 points on the last demonstration, and Jon scored ⁻4 points. How many more points did Pete score than Jon? Think about the difference between ⁺7 than ⁻4 using two discrete sets of objects (representing the two values being subtracted) in the following figure. Adolescent learners should already know the process of comparing two sets to find the difference: "Match equal items, one from each set, until the second set (against which the comparison is being made) is emptied."

One of our seventh graders, Fatima, noticed right away that she could not complete the operation because the elements in the two sets were not equivalent (green = negative and blue = positive). She suggested adjusting the first set, adding in a carefully conceived zero, to manage the problem, as shown in the following figure. She could then match equivalent elements. The net result is ⁺7 + ⁺4.

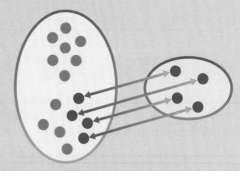

After studying several more examples, our students generalized the problem such that it always reduced to "add the opposite of the amount in the second set," which soon became "add the opposite." Using contexts is particularly important in dealing with integers, precisely because integers are usually a new concept to adolescent learners, even though operation knowledge should be well understood. We also built instruction on their existing whole number knowledge, showing subtraction with comparison and the set model. We suggest that you think about how the find-the-difference definition would play out in a continuous model, such as a number line. Seeing a general pattern to the operation can sometimes feel overwhelming to students. It is important to guide students who are learning to build on their existing knowledge while at the same time encouraging them to make leaps toward new knowledge.

It is equally important to pay close attention to ordering of the numbers in connection to the picture or blocks. Commutativity tells us that 3 × 4 is the same as 4 × 3. This is not necessarily clear to children at first. In one case, we begin with three elements and make four copies; in the other case, we use four elements and make three copies. So if 3 × 4 is three items repeated four times, be certain that when modeling a different problem, such as 5 × 2, you have five items repeated two times (not two items repeated five times). Children pay attention to details, even though *our* advanced knowledge indicates that the detail doesn't really matter. It matters to children when they are first learning the idea.

Earlier, we indicated that skip-counting was related to doubling, an important addition idea. Doubling is also related to multiplication. After students can double, we can help them to connect doubling to efficiently count their copies of sets created for multiplication. When confronted with 7 × 3, some students use doubling knowledge (7 + 7 = 14) and addition knowledge (add 7 more) to arrive at 21. Other students use skip-counting (7, 14, 21 or 3, 6, 9, 12, 15, 18, 21) to arrive at 21. Both skills represent number sense because students are composing numbers at will to find a solution.

Listen to first grader Stephanie explain her thinking about Ms. Hawthorne's question "How many feet would 3 tigers have?" She thought and said, "12." When asked how she figured that out, she replied, "I knew I had four [feet]. I thought of another tiger and knew it [also] had four feet, so I used my brain and counted 4 to 8 then from 8 to 12." Stephanie is making copies of the tiger and then using her knowledge of skip-counting and doubling to calculate an answer.

Division

Division is typically the last of the four operations to be learned because it builds on knowledge of other operations. Students' understanding of division *procedures* requires greater mental effort than that which is required for understanding the *concept* of the operation of division (Slesnick, 1982). We suggest beginning discussion of division with real-world contexts. In presenting problems about division to the students, both operation concepts—fair sharing (partitioning, sharing, or share equally) and repeated subtraction (measurement)—should be used. In Activity 6.4 (p. 108), write word problems for both multiplication and division.

In general, establishing conceptual understanding first results in children inventing highly sophisticated mathematics strategies for all algorithms with whole numbers (Carroll & Porter, 1997). When lessons are planned that tap into students' everyday experiences related to whole number concepts, students can build up those procedures. Students' early procedures are generally represented with their own diagrams about mental reasoning. Because students can develop an overwhelming trust in visual knowledge rather than trusting operational knowledge (Kamii & Clark, 1995), it is important to facilitate connections between informal, pictorial representations and the corresponding procedural knowledge, which eventually must be expressed with mathematical symbols. So it is important to layer concept knowledge with procedural knowledge.

USING RELEVANT PATTERNS:
Skip-Counting Lays a Foundation

Using relevant patterning is probably one of the best and most important ways in which we help students make sense of number. The mathematical ideas required to do number patterning are in effect number sense. Other notions about patterning can aid students' development of operation ideas.

Patterns of skip-counting are critical. Just as children can recite the words "one, two three, . . ." or the alphabet "A, B, C, D, . . . ," they need to be able to recite all kinds of skip-counting as well. Being able to tick off the numbers in

Activity 6.4

WRITING MORE WORD PROBLEMS

Write a word problem that would be interesting and understandable by three to five students for each of the exercises listed below:

4 x 5 (Multiplication—Repeated Addition)

_____
_____
_____

3 x 6 (Multiplication—Rectangular Array)

_____
_____
_____

5 x 8 (Multiplication—Combination)

_____
_____
_____

15 ÷ 3 (Division—Fair Sharing)

_____
_____
_____
_____

15 ÷ 3 (Division—Repeated Subtraction)

_____
_____
_____
_____

skip-counting, such as "2, 4, 6, 8, . . ." or "1, 3, 5, 7, . . ." or "4, 8, 12, 16, . . ." and "10, 20, 30, 40, . . .," aids in the development of number sense and operation. To be successful skip-counters, children need to be involved in many activities.

Calendar as Context

Part of what children need to learn is how to read a calendar and how to understand the concept of time passage. (Because time is an idea related to measurement, it is more completely discussed in the Part III of this book.) For the purposes of this chapter, the calendar's usefulness is dedicated completely to the development of skip-counting skills. The calendar approach establishes a match between elements in the pattern with the numerical days of the month, the natural numbers {1, 2, 3, . . .}. The abstraction you might want to think about is that patterns are basically sequences and, mathematically, a sequence is a relationship between the natural numbers and some other set.

Many K–2 classrooms begin each school day with a 20-minute discussion about the calendar. Beginning with their early school experiences, kindergarten children can study the month of September while simultaneously checking for number patterns. Perhaps the September calendar would have a blue number for every even number and a red number for every odd number. Other ways to distinguish between numbers on the calendar is to use shapes. The next month might build on geometry knowledge by putting the even numbers on a square shape and the odd numbers on a circular shape.

Comparing September and October in this case helps children to extract the mathematics of even and odd numbers. Children are pretty quick to recognize the patterns in the color (red, blue, red, blue) or shape (square, circle, square, circle). But they also start to recognize that the red colors or the circle shapes also land on certain numbers, and they need to be able to describe those numbers. They might predict which number will be blue. Will tomorrow's number be blue or red? They should predict whether it will be on a circle or a square. They should be able to study the calendar's pattern to answer these questions. Throughout the month, children should describe all blue numbers (or all numbers on a square). As students' proficiency with patterning develops, patterns on the calendar should become more challenging. Predictions about patterning lay a foundation for skip-counting and other number sense ideas. Think about the number sense that is required to answer the following questions about February:

1. Yesterday was the 18th. What is today's date?
2. Today is the Tuesday the 19th. What will be the date next Tuesday?
3. Today is Tuesday the 19th. What will be the date tomorrow?
4. Today is Tuesday the 19th. What was the date last Tuesday?
5. Yesterday we used a circle. Today we used a rhombus. What do you think we will use tomorrow?
6. What shape do you think we will use ten days or eight days from today?

Look at the calendars shown in Activity 6.5 (p. 110) and find a way to describe the patterns.

Concrete Representations

Students need to think about properties that make a number even or odd in a variety of ways. Even numbers are much more than just those numbers that follow (or alternate with) odd numbers. Exploring with blocks is a good way to teach students about even numbers. With an even-number set of blocks, each block can find a partner. Students can manipulate blocks to check for pairings. Using blocks and making these kinds of suggestions leads students toward number sense ideas, and they get the idea that numbers can be classified into different kinds of numbers.

Adults know which numbers are even, and young children can understand this concept, but they need help in recognizing that it is an interesting and useful thing to organize numbers into categories. Children need to hear mathematical words that describe such numbers, even though at first, children might know only that for this kind of number, each block has a partner. That's fine. The point here is that children begin to recognize that certain numbers {2, 4, 6, 8, 10, . . .} need to be in memory together with a way of reciting those numbers.

Calendar skip-counting can begin in kindergarten, but older students can learn about larger and more complicated patterns. The daily calendar might take too long to develop or not offer enough room for students to see a

Activity 6 . 5

DESCRIBE THE PATTERN IN EACH MONTH

complicated pattern. After all, there would be at most three numbers that had the characteristic of counting by 10s {10, 20, 30, . . .}. When more advanced students quickly finish number patterns, they might not need to wait and see the entire month to meet a skip-counting objective. A different tool might be needed. More experienced learners can use a 100-chart, as in Activity 6.6, to further develop skip-counting ideas. (This should not to be confused with a 99-chart, which begins with zero and places numbers ending in 9 into the right-hand column.) You could even use a 50-chart or a photocopy of a page from a calendar.

Using these kinds of tools turns a single skip-counting task into a one-day activity rather than a month-long activity. Several patterns can be studied, all in one day. You can then proceed to more complex patterns for the calendar math (such as March or May from Activity 6.5) as soon as the students are ready.

Activity 6 . 6

COLOR IN THE NUMBERS OF THESE PATTERNS

2, 4, 6, 8, 10, 12, . . .

1	2	3	4	5	6	7	8	9	10
11	12	13	14	15	16	17	18	19	20
21	22	23	24	25	26	27	28	29	30
31	32	33	34	35	36	37	38	39	40
41	42	43	44	45	46	47	48	49	50
51	52	53	54	55	56	57	58	59	60
61	62	63	64	65	66	67	68	69	70
71	72	73	74	75	76	77	78	79	80
81	82	83	84	85	86	87	88	89	90
91	92	93	94	95	96	97	98	99	100

3, 6, 9, 12, 15, . . .

1	2	3	4	5	6	7	8	9	10
11	12	13	14	15	16	17	18	19	20
21	22	23	24	25	26	27	28	29	30
31	32	33	34	35	36	37	38	39	40
41	42	43	44	45	46	47	48	49	50
51	52	53	54	55	56	57	58	59	60
61	62	63	64	65	66	67	68	69	70
71	72	73	74	75	76	77	78	79	80
81	82	83	84	85	86	87	88	89	90
91	92	93	94	95	96	97	98	99	100

Describe the visual image.

Number Line

Another tool that many teachers use to help older students visualize skip-counting is the number line. It is not uncommon for teachers to post various number lines around the room with different numbers highlighted depending on the skip-counting task at hand. See Figure 6.1 for an example of using the number line to promote skip-counting.

Figure 6 . 1

The Number Line Together with Skip-Counting

This approach makes the number pattern linear rather than being separated into stacks of 7 as on a calendar or 10 as on a 100-chart. As students develop, they need both kinds of experiences as well as several other patterns of numbers. These activities (calendar, 100-chart, and number line) help students to establish the ability to skip-count. This means that they can recite the words in sing-song fashion and connect those skip-counted words to corresponding amounts.

Connecting Skip-Counting to Operations

We also watch for and capitalize on students' uses of patterning, such as skip-counting, to make sense of operations. Subtracting 17 from 32, one student might skip-count backward by 10s, moving first from 32 to 22 (10) and then recognizing that counting down 7 more from that would result in 15—thus, 32 – 17 = 15. Another student might skip-count up by 5s from 17 (17, 22, 27, 32, . . .) up to 32 and count three skips. Other students might skip-count up by other comfortable amounts. These procedures can lead to symbolic algorithms for students, such as subtracting 10 before subtracting 7.

Skip-counting can manifest itself in a variety of useful formats, and students will use skip-counting when it helps them to make sense of the problem. We recently asked a group of fifth graders to resolve the following problem: "The Boys and Girls' Club was buzzing with activity in the gym. The volleyball nets were up, and as Emily was leaving, Jo was just arriving. Emily and Jo are good friends who are on different teams. 'How come I haven't seen you here before?' asked Emily. 'Coach brings us here every eight days,' Jo said. 'How often do you come here?' Emily explained that her coach brings the girls to the club every three days. How many days will it be until the two girls see each other again at their volleyball practice?" Some of the correct student responses are given below:

> ***Min:*** I just thought about multiplying and knew that they would meet on the 24th day because 3 × 8 is 24 and 8 × 3 is 24.
> ***Lydia:*** I counted by eights until I got to 24, and I stopped then, because I knew that 3 went into 24.
> ***Ryan:*** I just found the least common denominator. I thought to myself, "What do both numbers go into?"
> ***Jamal:*** I made a table because it seemed like that would help. When I saw the two numbers come up the same, I knew the answer was 24.

8	16	**24**	32	40	48	56	64				
3	6	9	12	15	18	21	**24**				

Lydia and Jamal used skip-counting procedures to think about the problem. Min and Ryan relied on knowledge about multiplication. These examples show us how multiplication is related to skip-counting. Making sense of multiplication can often be built directly from patterning skills of skip-counting (Anghileri, 1989). By now, you are probably beginning to sense a strong connection between operations and skip-counting. Making mental relationships that connect these ideas is an example of a concept. Using those relationships develops procedures. In Activity 6.7, use your concept and operation knowledge to try to detect a more complicated pattern and develop a procedure for determining the number of games to be played.

USING RELEVANT PATTERNS:
Figurate Numbers

Considering the following sequence of numbers: 1, 4, 9, 16, 25, . . . You probably recognized the numbers as being a certain *kind* of number. You might remember the locker problem at the beginning of Part II. You probably are not used to skip-counting by these numbers, because the difference between the terms is not constant. We usually skip-count with a constant difference. However, these kinds of numbers are still interesting and warrant further study. There is probably no more useful tool than the visual pattern to help understand how numbers such as these can be classified. Pictures of these numbers make squares, so these numbers are classified as "square."

Activity 6.7

PLANNING A VOLLEYBALL TOURNAMENT

Five different round-robin volleyball tournaments will be held on campus this weekend. (Round-robin tournaments are designed so that each team plays each other team exactly once, without regard for who won or who lost. In other words, no one is eliminated from the tournament.) There are five buildings in which these tournaments will take place. The number of teams in any given building for that building's tournament is noted. Determine how many games will take place in each building.

Four small tournaments will take place in:

Abigail Hall	Bailey Hall	Cobalt Hall	Depot Hall	Eagle Hall
2 teams	3 teams	4 teams	5 teams	6 teams

and the biggest tournament will take place in:

Kid Hall
12 teams

	A	B	C	D	E	...	K
Teams	2	3	4	5	6	...	12
Games	1	3	6			...	...

MIDDLE SCHOOL CONNECTIONS
Fact Families for Integers

When they were younger learners, adolescents typically learned about four-fact families using whole numbers. A whole number fact family is composed of four facts using the same three numbers. For instance, the numbers 3, 4, and 12 form the following fact family: $3 \cdot 4 = 12$, $4 \cdot 3 = 12$, $12 \div 3 = 4$, and $12 \div 4 = 3$. The young learners also experienced several skip-counting strategies, like those in the calendar activity discussed earlier. When adolescent learners encounter integers in the middle grades, making connections to these two pieces of knowledge (fact families and skip-counting) can prove to be beneficial for establishing knowledge about multiplying and dividing integers.

Just as the pattern 3, 6, 9, 12, . . . can be used to guide elementary students toward thinking about $3 \cdot 1$, $3 \cdot 2$, $3 \cdot 3$, $3 \cdot 4$, and so on, counting in the opposite direction, $^-3$, $^-6$, $^-9$, $^-12$, . . . can be used to ground middle school students' thinking about multiplying with negative numbers: $3 \cdot (^-1)$, $3 \cdot (^-2)$, $3 \cdot (^-3)$, $3 \cdot (^-4)$, and so on. The ideas behind fact families can be used to connect this knowledge more deeply. For in-

stance, we used skip counting to help our adolescent learners determine that $5 \cdot (^-4) = ^-20$. Then we used fact families to help them build up the three remaining facts: $(^-4) \cdot 5 = ^-20$, $^-20 \div 5 = ^-4$, and $^-20 \div (^-4) = 5$. Students quickly picked up on this strategy to decide how to multiply a positive value and a negative value.

Next, we prepared our learners to build knowledge toward multiplying two negatives. First, we applied their previously discovered strategy to find the result of the multiplication fact $(^-4) \cdot 3 = ^-12$. Second, we again skip-counted, moving to the right: $^-12$, $^-8$, $^-4$, 0, $^+4$, $^+8$, . . . and associated it with the series of multiplication facts: $(^-4) \cdot 3 = ^-12$, $(^-4) \cdot 2 = ^-8$, $(^-4) \cdot 1 = ^-4$, $(^-4) \cdot 0 = ^-0$, $(^-4) \cdot ^-1 = ^+4$, $(^-4) \cdot ^-2 = ^+8$, ... Students were again quick to pick up on the strategy to decide that multiplying two negative values results in a positive value. We were delighted to see how when our instruction built on students' elementary experiences, they could make connections and apply their thinking into the realm of integer operations.

Figure 6 . 2

Square Numbers and Triangular Numbers

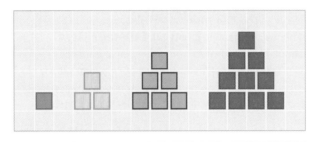

In Figure 6.2, decide how the fifth picture would look in each pattern, and use geometric language to describe them. Then think about how you would describe the *n*th picture.

Are you surprised to learn that the second set of numbers are "triangular"? You might look back to the volleyball problem to see similarities between this pattern and that problem.

CULTURAL CONNECTIONS

Numeration Systems and Mexican Subtraction

Counting and our base-10, place-value system has a long and interesting history. You are encouraged to study other place-value systems, such as the Mayans' 20-place value or Babylonian 60-place value system. For our first example, we visit England slightly before and during the time of Shakespeare. For our second example, we discuss a subtraction algorithm from Mexico.

The Dark Ages of Europe

In about A.D. 1200, Leonardo of Pisa (also known as Fibonacci) wrote the book *Liber Abaci* in an attempt to introduce Europe to an advanced approach to enumeration that he had learned while visiting Africa. Fibonacci recognized that Europe was floundering in a simplistic way of expressing numbers, of counting, and hence of computing by not using place-value strategies. Typical citizens did not "count" their items. Rather, typical citizens had small bags of pebbles for each kind of item that needed to be "counted." In the pebble bag was a certain number of pebbles that was equivalent to the number of items needed for that situation. The only thing citizens knew was that for every item needed, there was one pebble in the bag. The citizens were not concerned with "how many" items, only with having enough items. So to "count" sheep in a field, a shepherd matched each sheep to one pebble from the bag. If there were enough sheep in his herd, there would be no pebbles missing or left over. This process was called counter-casting. It resulted in the correct number of items, though the citizens never even knew how many items they had.

Fibonacci, though, was not satisfied. Because he was very wealthy, he was not constrained by the need to work. He believed that if the commoners were more educated, it would lead to growth in his civilization. So he wrote *Liber Abaci* in an effort to introduce the base-10 system into Europe. The book met resistance. Perhaps you are familiar with the staunch opposition that has stalled efforts in the United States to abandon the use of such units, as yards and Fahrenheit in favor of joining the rest of the world in measuring with the more convenient meters and Celsius. This is much the same kind of resistance that Europe demonstrated when faced with place-value enumeration.

Even after four centuries, Europeans were only beginning to be fully aware of the mathematical abstraction of place-value arithmetic. As late as A.D. 1600, Shakespeare described the character Michael Cassio in "Othello" as, among other things, a *caster-counter*. Shakespeare intended to use the description to make Cassio seem doltish, for if Cassio had only the mental capacity to make a pebble match a sheep, he somehow fell short of actually understanding the concept of number and counting. Shakespeare used this shortcoming to ridicule Cassio, implying that he could not count without the stones; that is,

Cassio did not know the abstraction behind the one-to-one correspondence. The collection of stones was not a "number" to him. Thus, to Shakespeare's keen audiences, eager for sarcasm, Cassio was disparaged. By the 1600s, people were becoming aware of the base-10 system. Although we have oversimplified both mathematics and Shakespeare's great prose, Cassio's situation does illustrate a cultural connection between society and the emerging idea of number as a relationship.

Mexican Subtraction

Consider the subtraction exercise of 62 – 17. Many of you are probably familiar with a standard subtraction algorithm (discussed earlier) that begins with the ones place column and moves left. However, you should be familiar with several algorithms for doing subtraction. Why? It is important for teachers to recognize appropriate algorithms even if they are unfamiliar. For example, we listened recently to a second grader, Luis, explain and symbolize his thinking, and he recorded his process as follows:

Looks Like:

6 2	6 2	6 ^{1}2	6 ^{1}2
–1 7	–1 7	–1 7	–1 7
	5 . . .	5 . . .	5 . . .
		4 . . .	4 5

Sounds Like:
First, I take 10 from 60. That gives me 50. I write down a 5 in the tens place. I try to take 7 from 2 but can't, so I break 1 ten away from the 5 tens and write down 4 in the tens place. I add that 10 to the 2. Now I have 12 and can subtract the 7. The answer is 45.

Does his procedure look different from what you do? His algorithm correctly uses ideas of breaking and regrouping numbers, a number sense idea that we previously called decomposing and composing. First, he subtracts, beginning with the largest place value; next, he breaks 10 from that difference (50) instead of the 60, as you probably expected. Luis symbolized his thinking in a mathematically appropriate way. Luis's way will always work. We wanted him to explain his thinking in his own words and wondered how he learned about this procedure. So we asked him. He shrugged his shoulders and said, "That's how Dad showed me to do it a long time ago." We were interested in Dad's procedure, so we called Luis's father, Antonio, and asked about it. Here is what Antonio said:

My abuelos [grandparents] are first-generation Mexicans. This means that they were born in Mexico and moved to the United States. My father was born in the United States, and my mother was born in Mexico. So, I am a mixed second/third-generation Mexican American. My abuela [grandmother] was the first to arrive from Ciudad Acuña, Coahuila, Mexico, in 1948 as a young girl. She and my abuelo [grandfather] were migrant workers for 33 years, in the cucumber fields of Illinois, Montana, Minnesota, Wisconsin, and Wyoming. They worked from 3:00 A.M. to 8:00 P.M. every day for six months, taking one day off, September 16. I remember living in Montana and Wisconsin. When the field work was complete for six months, we would return to our home in Texas, and I would go to school for six months.

My abuelos have seen much in their lives. But during those six months of school, they always had time to help with my schoolwork, even at 8:00 P.M. I remember having difficulty with subtraction. I asked my abuela for help. She showed me how to subtract going left to right. At first I was confused because my second grade schoolteacher wanted me to subtract right to left beginning with the ones place. I eventually learned both ways but always liked my grandmother's way best. Grandmother told me how in Mexico, children (of her generation, at least) had been taught in school to subtract by beginning on the left (with the largest place value) and moving right. In talking with my abuela, I came to understand that procedures can vary but subtraction is always subtraction. I guess the culture of her community decided that this procedure was most appropriate. That is why I showed the left-to-right subtraction process to Luis. I think it is better and wanted him to be able to choose. I did know, though, to show him both ways so he could make his own decision.

Isn't it exciting to find new ways to complete familiar operations? We hope you become aware of and respectful of ways to subtract that might appear different from the way you learned. There are other ways to subtract, even different from Luis's way. It is most important to know, though, as Antonio pointed out, that the operation remains subtraction. The algorithm builds on the take-away concept of the subtraction operation, and the procedure is the result. As student populations become more diverse, as they will surely continue to become in the future, ways of knowing and doing mathematics will become equally diverse. To understand the myriad of algorithms that are available to your students, it is important not to discount unexpected strategies. Listening to students explain their thinking only enriches the classroom.

Listen to Tammy explain her acquaintance with the numeral system used in Rome before publication of *Liber Abaci*.

Roman Numerals

I was born in Rome, Italy, and lived there for over five years. The Rome I grew up in is very different from ancient Rome. Still, modern people of Rome have spent long hours preserving artifacts and social mores from the ancient Roman Empire, which crumbled toward the end of the fifth century A.D. Several architectural remains of ancient Rome appear in modern Rome, such as the Coliseum, the Pantheon, and many temples. However, people of ancient Rome were interested in culinary delights too. The Romans took great joy in preparing and eating food. Cooking was actually an art form almost on a level with music, entertaining, sculpture, or architecture as we think of them today.

Thousands of years ago, Rome was as busy as it is today. This typically urban environment (for the time) was graced with stately buildings, small shops, and boys' schools. Some homes were ornate, while others were typical apartments. Narrow streets connected the homes, apartments, and shops of the city, as is still true today. In ancient Rome, middle-class people walked, while rich people rode in litters, carried by slaves. It was not uncommon to see soldiers walking though town in full armor or workers hurrying to their next job site. The Forum, of course, hosted famous debates and speeches. The city was alive with festivals, theaters, and games.

Cities like Rome developed over time. Most countries had cities established long before the United States was developed. Sometimes these cities are called *ancient* because they are old in comparison to the United States. But really, *modern* simply means that the buildings are newer than "ancient." In Rome today, some of the older buildings have fallen down and been destroyed. However, over time, Roman cities have grown around these old ruins or fallen-down buildings. In European countries (such as Italy), cities (such as Rome) aged over time, but new parts of the cities were built up. In European culture, instead of destroying the past by taking away ruins, they cherish them and do not disturb them. They often build around them and believe deeply in the reasons for which they were built and the traditions that came from these ancient times.

The narrow street (*via*) where I lived was named Via genovese. I learned to find my way home by learning the ancient Roman numeral system. Many of the modern streets and homes in Rome and in neighboring cities still use the Roman numeral system for their house addresses. As a child, I learned that if a symbol of lesser value is placed before a symbol of greater value, then the total value represented will be smaller. XL in Roman numerals means 50 − 10, or 40. I also knew that if a symbol of lesser value is placed after a symbol of greater value, then the total value represented will be larger. LX in Roman Numerals means 50 + 10, or 60. When a horizontal bar is placed over a symbol, the value is multiplied by 1,000. For example, $\overline{\text{M}}$ means 1,000 × 1,000 = 1,000,000. Finally, the Roman numeral system did not have a symbol for zero.

The number for my home on Via Genovese was MCMXLVIII, which is 1948 in the numeration system we use today. One day, when I was on my way home from the store with my family, we turned onto our street. There was a big fight between members of opposing political parties. A riot had erupted on our street. There were (and still are) a lot of political activist groups in Rome. These protestors would ride, walk, and run through the streets, chanting and displaying banners, protesting against the political parties that were running the government at the time. They did not have much concern for property, especially property of the government. Governments in Italy switched hands easily in the late

1970s and early 1980s. I saw a few changes firsthand when we lived there. One of the cars from a protesting group drove around the corner from the main street too fast and hit the curb of the island in the middle of the street beside our house. This caused the car to careen back the other direction, where it jumped not only the curb at the end of our street but also the short brick wall that separated our street from the sidewalk, knocking down the street sign, a piece of government property.

We were quickly making our way to our home and noticed the dismantled street sign for our street. We picked it up and hurried home. Well, we didn't hurry—not really. The sign was made of marble! It was very heavy. Can you imagine the weight of a marble sign? The next day, we reported the sign and returned it to the city.

I know about Roman numerals from having actually lived in Rome. I learned how to read them. (Of course, I also learned how to read place-value numbers.) It was a unique experience to have grown up understanding that there are several ways to describe a numerical amount—multiplicative (place-value) and additive (Roman numerals).

Think about Tammy's experiences, and look for other ways to connect cultural experiences to the learning and remembering of number ideas.

LITERATURE CONNECTIONS

Comparing Counting Books to Literary Works

There are a number of interesting counting books that can be used with lessons on counting, such as *Over in the Meadow* by Keats (1999), *The M&M's Brand Counting Book* by McGrath (1994), and *10 for Dinner* by Bogart (1989). These books are fun and can give the entire class a common experience with numbers. After reading a story about counting, children can help to write another chapter or even write their own classroom book about counting items, such as crayons. The actors in the story can be brought to life in the classroom, to help with counting processes.

TEACHING

However, you should consult your district curriculum guide to decide whether a given counting book will meet any of your language arts requirements. Sometimes counting books are not classified as literature in the truest sense of the word. Not all of them have typical elements that make up a story, such as plot and character development. Completely integrating mathematics with language arts in a lesson is a complex process, and such a lesson should be based on a piece of literature, not just on reading something. Literature books, such as *Sadako and the Thousand Paper Cranes* (Coerr & Himler, 1977) and *One Grain of Rice* (Demi, 1997), typically meet district curriculum requirements because they contain the necessary elements of a story. The mathematics can be pulled from these realistic stories in a meaningful way because the mathematics is accurate and the experiences and ideas in the story can connect to both language arts and mathematics.

Sadako

Hiroshima-born Sadako is the star of her school's track team. Sadako falls gravely ill with leukemia. But she faces her future with a legend. If a sick person folds 1,000 cranes, the gods will grant a wish, and Sadako wants to be healthy again. This story can be used to help students understand the magnitude of 1,000, a component of number sense.

One Grain of Rice

In this story, a young peasant girl tricks her emperor into giving rice to his citizens. She has strong number sense. She uses the emperor's lack of number sense to save her fellow citizens from hunger. The story of this book can be used to develop the number sequence 2^n and the concept of doubling.

USING TEACHING AIDS APPROPRIATELY:
Discrete versus Continuous Materials

You learned earlier that children need to use discrete (movable) objects to develop number sense. You also saw examples of how children react to materials such as colored chips, and we used base-10 blocks to illustrate the multiplication process. However, before using any kind of concrete materials, students must make sense of the activity and have a need to represent it (Thompson, 1992). Part of that sense-making involves selecting manipulatives on the basis of whether or not discrete or continuous materials are appropriate. Continuous materials are those that cannot be broken apart into singular units. They often represent a length and, as such, represent a different way of numerically visualizing the situation. Kamii (2000b) cautions us to be careful in making this choice, as using continuous material requires students to understand numerical amounts in a measurement sort of way rather than in a set sort of way. Although students need to understand numbers in both ways, we want to be clear that we are building on the existing knowledge, and it is likely that "set" thinking will have come first.

Knowing how children learn helps us to make informed choices about materials used (or not used) with students. Knowing how materials work and how students learn mathematical knowledge enables teachers to determine how materials will affect lessons. Bear in mind that concrete embodiment of concepts can be effective if students see these various notations as reflections of one another (Thompson, 1992). Certainly, discrete concrete materials aid in the teaching of number ideas. But in the end, number is a mental relationship that must exist in the individual child's mind.

Concrete Representations

Physical materials can model the situation and illuminate some of the aspects of the processes of various operations, such as the multiplication process described earlier. However, materials must be used in ways that make sense to students in order to help the operations make sense to them. Asking students to memorize a way to manipulate blocks is no different from asking them to memorize a way to manipulate signs and symbols. Rather, students should develop relationships that are mental abstractions about the mathematics being represented by the physical materials and then develop a corresponding symbolic representation. There is a difference between the physical or symbolic representation and a mathematical abstraction. An abstraction is a mental construction, whereas a representation is an agreed-upon way of communicating that abstraction. Just because a child uses a symbolic form to communicate a mathematical idea does not mean that the child has necessarily abstracted that idea. Just because a child uses concrete materials does *not* mean that the child has *not* abstracted the idea. We have to ask good questions and listen to students explain their thinking to know whether they have abstracted the idea out of the physical models.

Pictorial Representations

Pictorial models would include pictures of discrete objects as well as pictures of continuous situations. One continuous pictorial model worth revisiting is the empty number line. This representation builds on a conceptual foundation of ordered numbers. With the empty number line, students do not require an

MIDDLE SCHOOL CONNECTIONS

Encounters with Integers

Learning to operate with integers can pose a challenge because this kind of number is seemingly different to middle school students. A conceptual basis for negativeness needs to be established. How you choose to focus on the idea of a negative number should take into account the different representations with which adolescents are by now familiar. One strategy is to describe negativeness with a continuous model. The negative of a whole number can be found on the *symmetric* opposed point (with zero at the center) on the number line. In this manner, negativeness is based on a *location* on a continuous number line. You should also encourage students to consider negativeness as a characteristic that a number somehow *has*, as could be demonstrated with a discrete set of objects. The negative of a whole number is shown with the appropriate number of chips, each sporting a negative sign, to indicate that each chip represents a $^-1$. It is clear that both representations ground conceptual understandings, and both must be established for students to operate fluidly with integers.

Of course, contexts can prove helpful. Often, various levels in a tall building, distances gained or lost during an athletic competition, or even things like owing and earning money can prove helpful. On the same day, Jenna borrows $7 from her best friend and finds a $5 bill tucked into her coat pocket. How much money is she worth at the end of the day? This situation can be described arithmetically as $^-7 + {}^+5$. Adding integers

like these using a discrete model seems to be fairly successful for most middle school students. The most important initial understanding, besides finding ways to represent the values, is to recognize that $^+1 + {}^-1 = 0$. Once these two ideas are established, performing addition requires counting the result of joining two sets of objects. For example, $^-7 + {}^+5$ can be represented with the upper part of the figure. The addition is shown with the arrows in the lower part of the figure. To decide on Jenna's overall worth, we count the elements in the upper part. Each pair of one green and one blue chip is the same as zero. The net result is equivalent to $^-2$, represented here by two green chips.

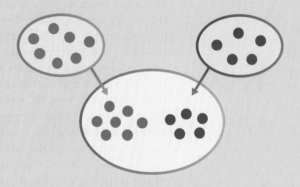

So Jenna is worth $$^-2$ that day. You might make a list of other contexts that would make sense to you and to adolescent learners.

---

anchor of zero; rather, they hop forward or backward from any number of their own choosing. So to add 27 and 19, the student might simply begin at spot 27 and hop forward 19 (or, more likely, the child would hop forward 20 and then hop backward 1). We turn now to the commercial manipulatives that can serve as instructional aids for the development of number and operation sense.

Types of Concrete Materials

Base-Ten Blocks

What follows is an example illustrating both failings of materials and the importance of having children use movable objects to make sets. For this lesson, we wanted to use Base-Ten blocks to help fourth grade students develop number sense for 1,000. In whole class discussion, we attentively compared 10 one-cubes with 1 ten-rod. Next we compared 10 ten-rods with 1 hundred-flat. Satisfied with their answers and their familiarity with the blocks, we gave each child one of the large 1,000 cubes from the set and asked what it was worth. We fully expected them to compare the cube to the 100-flat and decide that it would be 10 of the hundred-flats, thus deducing that the large cube contained 1,000. As expected, our students compared the cube to the 100-flats, but our students surprised us by indicating that this never-before-seen (1,000-cube) block contained 600. What do you think they were thinking about as they made this deduction?

You might note that each face of a 1,000-cube looks like a 100-flat. It looked that way to our students too. The students saw the six faces, each containing 100. So surely the large cube contained 600. Clearly, we had abandoned the idea of movable objects too soon. We had asked the wrong question. We gathered up the materials and handed them back out differently. This time, we gave each pair of students ten of the 100-flats and asked them to tell us how many were present on their desk. One pair of students quickly skip-counted by one hundreds—"100, 200, 300, 400, 500, 600, 700, 800, 900, 1,000"—pointing to each flat as they counted. We asked them to explain to the rest of the class their thinking about this task. As they explained their idea of why their blocks represented 1,000, one other group of students pointed to and stacked their flats into a cube as they counted. We handed them some tape and asked them to physically tape their flats together. They showed their creation to the class. We asked them to discuss with the first group whether or not the amounts were the same. They quickly decided that both the spread-out and stacked sets of blocks showed 1,000. As anticipated, one child suggested that the block we had worked with moments earlier might represent 1,000. We curiously wondered why, since he had formerly been among those students who were certain that the large cube was worth only 600. He laughed and said that the first cube we passed out felt "empty" (indeed, the 1,000-cube that we used is not solid, it is hollow—some 1,000-cubes are solid and heavy). He did not believe that our 1,000-cube felt the way 1,000 little centimeter cubes should have felt (i.e., it did not weigh enough). By the end of this discussion, though, the class was comfortable allowing that hollow cube to represent 1,000, and we were reminded of the importance of using movable objects to develop number sense.

Cuisenaire Rods

These continuous materials are a set of 10 rods that range in (whole-number) lengths from 1 cm to 10 cm. Because this manipulative is continuous, it demonstrates numerical ideas in terms of lengths. When a child places a 2-rod end-to-end with a 7-rod, he or she can compare it to the 9-rod to determine that 2 + 7 = 9. It is up to the teacher to make the determination that students understand the numerical amount as the length of the rod. It is also possible to place enough 1-rods next to a given numerical rod (the one in question) to help students understand that the given rod should be associated with the number of 1-rods set next to it. (Measurement is a difficult subject to master and will be discussed more fully in later chapters.)

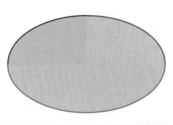

Figure 6 . 3

Part-Part-Whole Model

Chips

These discrete materials are simply circular chips. There are two-color counters (one color on one side, and another color on the other side) and chips that come in sets of different colors (10 blue chips, 10 red chips, etc.). Earlier, we used coins. These discrete objects are useful for demonstrating number because they are handy and easily manipulated by children. Sometimes it useful to provide drawings of operation models on which students can place and manipulate their chips. For instance, teachers can use the part-part-whole model (Figure 6.3), to help students move chips or other discrete materials around on their desks in ways that model both addition and subtraction problems. This couches addition and subtraction problems in a familiar form.

LET'S REVIEW

Two main learning theories explained how we learn about number and operation. Kamii explains principles behind how we help children learn about the notion of number and how they come to understand counting. Three principles guide children's development of number knowledge: (1) making all kinds of relationships, (2) quantifying sets of objects, and (3) socially interacting with peers and teacher. Four levels of awareness of counting come into play when children work toward quantifying sets of objects: (0) Children cannot complete the task; (1) children estimate and copy what they are shown (not abstracting the idea of number); (2) children develop awareness of a one-to-one correspondence and use it in some way; and (3) children count. The ideas necessary to understand how a child is "counting" require awareness that number is a mental relationship. It is not something somehow "in" the objects the child is counting. CGI describes how children use direct modeling or counting strategies to solve word problems for the operations. Both Kamii and CGI explain the importance of allowing children to discuss their thinking about their work because children will abandon old ways of thinking when they become convinced of new ways (from the teacher or fellow students). In addition, personal algorithms can grow directly from meaningful experiences acting out problems, whether through direct modeling or counting.

Several models and/or materials can be used to help children demonstrate the mathematics of the problems. But it is important to distinguish between discrete models, such as chips, and continuous models, such as a number line, that students might choose to use in their work. The part-part-whole model is particularly useful as a background on which children can move discrete materials and that will model both addition and subtraction problems.

HOMEWORK

1. Begin with the fact 6 + 7 = 13. You have five children who think about this fact differently. Describe (using pictures if helpful) the thinking of a child who uses each of the processes listed below. Then put the strategies in order of development.

   a. Counting onward from the first number
   b. Counting
   c. "Making tens"
   d. Counting onward from the larger number
   e. Using doubles

2. Locate a primary mathematics textbook (K–2), and determine whether or not the authors are careful to follow Kamii's findings that number knowledge develops in slices of 1 though 7, 8 through 15, and 16 through 30.
3. Locate textbook for any grade (K–8) and describe whether and how they use the *array* model and/or the *number line* models in the explanations of multiplication.
4. Find five children's or adolescent's (young reader) literature books that could help to ground a lesson on large numbers, such as 1,000,000. Categorize the books according

to the extent to which they have the elements of literature described in this chapter (e.g., *A Million Fish More or Less, How Much is a Million?*, or *Millions and Millions of Cats*).

SUGGESTED READINGS

Joslyn, R. E. (1990). Using concrete models to teach large-number concepts. *Arithmetic Teacher, 38*(3), 6–9.

Kamii, C., Kirkland, L., & Lewis, B. A. (2001). Representations and abstraction in young children's numerical reasoning. In A. A. Cuoco & F. R. Curcio (Eds.), *The roles of representation in school mathematics: 2001 NCTM Yearbook* (pp. 24–34). Reston, VA: NCTM.

Kamii C., Lewis, B., & Livingston, S. J. (1993). Primary arithmetic: Children inventing their own procedures. *Teaching Children Mathematics, 40*(4), 200–203.

Philipp, R. A. (1996). Multicultural mathematics and alternative algorithms. *Teaching Children Mathematics, 3*(3), 128–133.

Ross, R., & Kurtz, R. (1993). Making manipulatives work: A strategy for success. *Arithmetic Teacher, 40*(5), 254–257.

Sowder, J. (1992). Estimation and number sense. In D. Grouws (Ed.), *Handbook of research on mathematics teaching and learning* (pp. 371–389). New York: Macmillan.

REFERENCES

Anghileri, J. (1989). An investigation of young children's understanding of multiplication. *Educational Studies in Mathematics, 20*(4), 367–385.

Bogart, J. E. (1989). *10 for dinner.* New York: Scholastic.

Carpenter, T. P., Fennema, E., Franke, M. L., Levi, L., & Empson, S. B. (1999). *Children's mathematics: Cognitively guided instruction.* Portsmouth, NH: Heinemann.

Carroll, W. M., & Porter, D. (1997). Invented strategies can develop meaningful mathematical procedures. *Teaching Children Mathematics, 3*(7), 370–374.

Coerr, E., & Himler, R. (1977). *Sadako and the thousand paper cranes.* New York: Dell.

Demi (Illustrator). (1997). *One grain of rice: A mathematical folktale.* New York: Scholastic.

Fuson, K. (1988). *Children's counting and concepts of number.* New York: Springer.

Fuson, K. C., & Hall, J. W. (1983). The acquisition of early number word meanings: A conceptual analysis and overview. In H. P. Ginsburg (Ed.), *The development of mathematical thinking* (pp. 49–107). New York: Academic Press.

Kamii, C. (1989). *Double-column addition: A teacher uses Piaget's theory.* [Videotape]. New York: Teachers College Press.

Kamii, C. (2000a). *Young children reinvent arithmetic: Implications of Piaget's theory.* New York: Teachers College Press.

Kamii, C. (2000b). *Number in preschool and kindergarten.* New York: National Association for the Education of Young Children.

Kamii, C., & Clark, F. B. (1995). Equivalent fractions: Their difficulty and educational implications. *Journal of Mathematical Behavior, 14*(4), 365–378.

Kamii, C., & DeVries, R. (1976). *Piaget, children, and number.* Washington, DC: National Association for the Education of Young Children.

Kamii, C., & DeVries, R. (1980). *Group games in early education: Implications of Piaget's theory.* Washington, DC: National Association for the Education of Young Children.

Kamii, C., & Ozaki, K. (1999). Abstraction and represenation in arithmetic: A Piagetian view. *Hiroshima Journal of Mathematics Education, 7*, 1–15.

Kato, Y., Kamii, C., Ozaki K., & Nagahiro, M. (2002). Young children's representations of groups of objects: The relationship between abstraction and representation. *Journal for Research in Mathematics Education, 33*(1), 30–45.

Keats, E. J. (1999). *Over in the meadow.* New York: Puffin.

McGrath, B. B. (1994). *The M&M's brand counting book.* Boston: Charlesbridge.

Pepper, C., & Hunting, R. P. (1998). Preschooler's counting and sharing. *Journal for Research in Mathematics Education, 29*(2), 164–183.

Slesnick, T. (1982). Algorithmic skill vs. conceptual understanding. *Educational Studies in Mathematics, 13*(2), 143–154.

Sowder, J. (1988). Mental computation and number comparison: Their roles in the development of number sense and computation estimation. In J. Hiebert & M. Behr (Eds.), *Number concepts and operation in the middle grades* (pp. 182–197). Hillsdale, NJ: Lawrence Erlbaum; Reston, VA: NCTM.

Stigler, J. W., & Hiebert, J. (1999). *The teaching gap.* New York: Free Press.

Thompson, P. (1992). Notations, conventions, and constraints: Contributions to effective uses of concrete materials in elementary mathematics. *Journal for Research in Mathematics Education, 23*(2), 123–147.

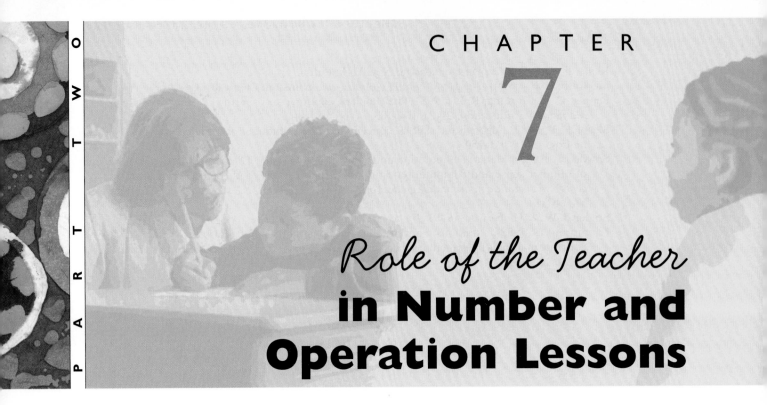

CHAPTER
7

Role of the Teacher
in Number and Operation Lessons

NCTM TEACHING

ANALYZING ONE OF THE TEACHING MODELS:
Concept Attainment

In general, concept attainment lesson plans can take one of two forms. They can be deductive or inductive. In both cases, concept attainment lesson plans include activities that require students to work with *best* examples, *other* examples, and *non*examples. Best examples show only essential features of the concept, other examples have extra features, and nonexamples show students critical attributes that are not to be included in the general idea. Activities that are especially useful for children to develop concept knowledge are those in which students manipulate the three kinds of examples in ways that allow them to apply mathematical structures to sets of examples. Mathematical structures include the ability to recognize and extend patterns using the examples, to compare and contrast examples, to notice complementary characteristics between two or more examples, and to sort and classify examples into several kinds of groupings.

Patterning enables children to become aware of similarities within a sequence and predict (by applying that similarity) future terms in the sequence. Comparing and contrasting lays the foundation for children to describe ideas that may depend on things like size and order. Noticing complementary characteristics allows students to create collections of matched objects or ideas that go together. Sorting and classifying encourages learners to compartmentalize as well as join pieces of information in flexible ways. All four of these kinds of activities allow children to develop, make, and use some sort of generalization, which is a conceptual kind of knowledge. So these four mathematical structures are useful ways to think about good activities for concept-attainment lesson plans. And all three kinds of examples are needed to fully engage students in either deductive or inductive thinking about the mathematical structures.

Deductive

A deductive lesson plan provides students with a general statement or principle and asks them to find examples and nonexamples of the statement. Ability to produce correct examples and nonexamples is evidence of knowledge of the concept. For instance, students might go on a scavenger hunt in the building or classroom hunting for things in sets of four. Their directions should include requirements for finding a few sets that are not a 4. The specimens that students produce should be supported with reasoning, so you are certain that they have not resorted to guessing.

Inductive

An inductive lesson plan is one that presents a series of specimens that are examples, best examples, and nonexamples of the concept. During the lesson, students categorize specimens into yes and no piles. From those groupings, students give a general statement, which is the concept. For instance, in considering the concept of 4, it is important to show students some sets that are not 4, such as A or +. These nonexamples enable students to rule out sets that are not 4. As with the deductive lesson style, students should be required to describe their reasoning for their groupings.

HIGHLIGHTS OF A LESSON PLAN COMPONENT:
Match Evaluation with Objective

Matching evaluation to objective is critical in any lesson plan. Whether the teacher is walking around the room interacting with students or evaluating their written work, it is crucial to make evaluation match the concept objective. Some how you have to decide whether students demonstrated knowledge of the concept. Procedures are simpler to observe because students can execute an observable procedure for you. However, execution of a procedure should not be taken to imply that students understand the concept.

Carpenter (1986) talks in earnest about difficulties in evaluating students' conceptual knowledge. We explained earlier that as students develop number sense, they become more flexible in their choices about operations and procedures. The ability to develop and then select from several options is certainly linked to strong conceptual number sense. But Carpenter (1986) suggests caution in assuming anything about students' concept knowledge on the basis of procedural demonstrations. We know that students can learn procedures by rote, without making connections to concept knowledge. However, we also know that students understand and use procedures better when they build their procedures on concept knowledge. So there must be some sort of a relationship between concept knowledge and the degree of flexibility with procedural knowledge that we can evaluate. For instance, we know that there is a layering effect: When students build procedural knowledge on concept knowledge, they develop more robust knowledge about operations which is a concept. As relationships among operations are formed, students again become more flexible in their demonstration of procedures. So in that sense, it is tempting to assume that because students use procedures well, they must know the underlying concepts. But making an inference about students' conceptual knowledge on the basis of their ability to execute procedures is unwise. "Learning procedures does not, however, ensure that the related conceptual knowledge has been acquired" (Carpenter, 1986, p. 129). Asking "Why?" and asking students to compare two different algorithms for the same operation are good ways to gather some evidence of conceptual understanding. Answers to queries like these will help you determine whether students are actually building their procedures from concepts. In any lesson plan, it is important to connect evaluation to objectives, but it seems to be particularly important in concept attainment lesson plans, since the temptation is to observe a procedure.

NCTM
ASSESSMENT

ASSESSMENT:
Evaluating Achievement (Concepts versus Procedures)

The first step in any assessment process is to decide the reason for engaging in assessment. In this chapter, we study assessment to evaluate *student achievement*. We engage in this assessment when we want to know how well students learned the mathematics (whether you or someone else taught it). So we plan an action that enables evaluation of students' knowledge. This may be done with oral questioning and written tests, with the goal of assessment as an evaluation of student achievement. This is different from gathering information to make an instructional decision, as we described in Chapter 4. The results of this assessment will likely be reflected in students' grading-period evaluations. It will also likely be of interest to parents, administrators, and the community in general. One way to evaluate students' conceptual knowledge is to ask them

CLASSROOM CONNECTIONS
Dealing with Incorrect Comments

Have you ever wanted to raise your hand in class but were afraid to say what you were thinking because you weren't quite sure whether you were right or you were not sure how others would react to your response? I do all I can to create a safe atmosphere in my classroom. My students need to feel comfortable so that they can take risks and so that I can hear their conceptual and procedural thinking. They need to respond to classroom discussions and not worry about what classmates will think. Creating such an environment is crucial for sharing strategies. The NCTM (2000) teaching principle describes supportive classroom environments as those in which students "make conjectures, experiment with various approaches to solving problems, construct mathematical arguments and respond to others' arguments" (p. 18).

In creating a supportive environment, I try to facilitate classroom conversations in which each student's response is valued. Of course, not all responses are cor-

NCTM
EQUITY

NCTM
TEACHING

rect. But all responses are valuable in that either the student is reorganizing his or her thinking, another student is reflecting and reorganizing the first student's thinking, or both. Suppose a student shares an idea or strategy that is way off target. How can I show the student that I value his or her response without making the student feel insecure? Here are a few suggestions:

"Thank you for sharing that, Jamal. I hadn't thought of that. Would you write that down for me? I want to check on something before I comment. I'll let you know when I've found it."

(Walk over to the student's desk.) "Can you show me on paper what you are thinking?"

"Hold onto that thought, Emma. I'll get back to you." (Then sit with Emma at a later time and look things over.)

After listening to others, a student might change his or her thinking. "Has anyone made changes in their strategy after listening to others? Could you explain what made you change your thinking?"

CLASSROOM CONNECTIONS

Orchestrating the Sharing of Strategies

An important part of daily math is for students to share their strategies. It is important to find ways to value each student's comments. As with any topic, a variety of real-life contexts in which students can base their comments and thinking is helpful. Consider the V-pattern (see the figure in the video clip insert), which is like a problem found in the textbooks from which I teach (*Mathematics in Context*, 1998). This problem is wrapped around the context of how geese fly north and south for the winter. The geese always appear to be in a V-pattern. One goose is in front (at the lead), and then the rest of the geese follow in pairs, one trailing off on each side of the leader. How could you find the total number of geese in any particular set of flying geese?

Alyssa was among the students who described her thinking during the class discussion. She said, "In each picture, the number of geese on each tail is the same and also tells me which set of geese. See in the fifth picture, there are five geese on each tail. So I just double that number, 10. Then I add one more for the leader, 11." Chris described the same situation, but

used a formula! He knew that the *x* meant which V-pattern he was studying.

Later in the year, when studying a similar problem, Andrew explained his strategy by saying, "I used Chris's trick." I encouraged him to use Chris's trick because it is important to value each student's thinking, no matter the level of thinking. Tanner could also use Chris's strategy, but could he actually use the formula? Is a symbolic formula always expected? Is it always possible? Several students in class knew that Chris's trick could be stated as a formula (N • 2 + 1), while others insisted on referring to the strategy as Chris's trick.

Accepting students at their individual levels of understanding runs counter to the belief that all students have to embrace *one* method of figuring out a problem and then be tested on that strategy. Asking *volunteer* students to record their responses on construction paper, post them around the room, and explain their conceptual and procedural thinking is a good way to set the stage for class discussion. Through repeated exposure to a variety of justified strategies, students just might find a "Chris's trick" to call their own.

to explain their mathematical thinking about a problem situation. One way to evaluate students' procedural knowledge is to observe their computational efforts.

Go to "Try it! See it! Teach it!" on page 128.

SUGGESTIONS FOR ESTABLISHING DISCOURSE:
Listening to Students to Guide Their Thinking

Our responsibility is to provide students with opportunities to work with various problems. Here the teacher acts as an observer who must learn about the thinking of students in order to use that information to find ways to guide their thinking toward new ideas. You learned earlier that Carpenter and colleagues (1999) developed CGI around experiences with understanding how children's thinking developed. The example of "problem types" is not the totality of their work. Rather, this component of CGI is related to the philosophy that children must be allowed and encouraged to build a strong foundation in mathematics through the process of making sense of the mathematics they are learning. "Children come to school with a great deal of informal or intuitive knowledge that can serve as the basis for developing understanding of the mathematics of the primary school curriculum. Further, students can construct solutions to a variety of problems without formal or direct instruction" (Carpenter et al., 1999, p. 4). The teacher who listens carefully to students' interaction

Try it! See it! Teach it!

Orchestrating Sharing Strategies

Step **One**: Try it!

Do the Math...

Geese fly north for the summer and south for the winter. When they fly, they always appear to be in a V pattern. One goose is in front (at the lead), and the rest of the geese follow in pairs, one trailing off on each side of the leader. How could you find the total number of geese in any particular set of flying geese? Draw the pattern for the 13th pattern of geese. Before watching the video, you should be able to extend and describe the pattern. Understanding the problem helps you understand the conversation in the video. Please have your solution ready before watching the video.

Step **Two**: See it!

Watch the Video...

Karen is working with her fifth graders, who are trying to solve the geese problem.

Things to Watch for...

- Recognize how Karen nurtures sharing of strategies among her students.
- Watch for a moment when a child abandons an idea or uses a classmate's idea when it makes sense to him or her.
- Pay particular attention to Karen's questioning techniques. Listen for the cues in the children's answers that cause Karen to frame her questions.

Video Clip 4 *(time length 4:19)*

Karen checks a student's work.

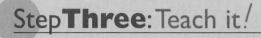

Step **Three**: Teach it!

Reflect on Your Own Teaching . . .

1. What kinds of things did Alyssa say that made you think she learned something new?

    _____

    _____

2. What kinds of things did Chris say that demonsrate his knowledge about patterning?

    _____

    _____

3. What role does patterning have in number knowledge development? Algebraic development?

    _____

    _____

4. What did the table do to help move the thinking forward?

    _____

    _____

A Comment from Karen

I ask the students, "Isn't it amazing that all of these strategies could lead to the correct answer? Let's start with Jennifer. Jennifer, can you explain your strategy? Can anyone repeat what Jennifer said? I like the way you explained that, Alyssa, what made you decide to . . . Wow, Tanner! I'm not sure I would have thought of that! Can you explain when you changed your thinking?"

Alyssa was among the students who described their thinking during the class discussion. She said, "In each picture, the number of geese on each tail is the same and also tells me which set of geese. See in the fifth picture, there are 5 geese on each tail. So I just double that number, 10. Then I add 1 more for the leader, 11." Chris described the same situation, but used a formula! He knew that the x meant which V pattern he was studying.

I always post solutions around the room to further display the different strategies. "As you look around, do you see one that might be more efficient than the one you used today? Would anyone like to have one of these strategies explained again?" Then, I ask students to try another problem similar to the one we just did to see if they can use a strategy that is different from the one already used. Imagine my delight when someone tells me they used "Chris's trick" to solve a different problem.

GO BACK TO PAGE 127

TECHNOLOGY CONNECTIONS

Communication Tools

Developments in digital technology have opened up new possibilities for teachers working to apply the principles suggested in Chapter 6. For learners from kindergarten through high school, digital tools can help to make number experiences authentic and motivating. Two technology connections that can enhance the teaching of numbers in the classroom are the word processor and the handheld computer (PDA). Both tools will help students to communicate ideas about number to a variety of audiences.

Word processors provide an easy and comfortable way for students to write about their mathematics reasoning and strategies, and in using the word processor, students will create files that they can easily share with their peers. Students who are solving the same problem can describe their methods and share them with each other and/or the entire class. Using handheld computers, students can send their strategies to their classmates and ask for feedback on their approaches. In general, digital technologies provide simple means for making students' mathematical thinking more public, both for their peers and for their parents and teachers.

The Center for Highly Interactive Computing in Education (Hi-CE) (www.hice.org) at the University of Michigan and the University of North Texas has created free communication software for handheld classroom computers. Freewrite, a simple word-processing program, and Sketchy, an animation and drawing program, are two software tools that are especially useful to mathematics teachers (Center for Highly Interactive Computing in Education, 2003). Both Freewrite and Sketchy are free, downloadable programs that are available from Hi-CE's web site. Led by Dr. Elliot Soloway, Hi-CE has worked to develop tools to help teachers create active, learner-centered, and inquiry-based environments in their classrooms. Educators and researchers from Hi-CE make powerful arguments for the use of handheld devices in classrooms. Dr. Soloway asserts that for the price of an expensive pair of tennis shoes, students can have 24-hour access to powerful technology capabilities.

Whether or not students use handheld computers, word processors and the Internet provide powerful opportunities for students to record and share their mathematical thinking and strategies. Mathematics teachers are using Internet capabilities to enable their students to "talk math" with students and adults. Current projects range from middle school students in London solving problems with students in South Dakota to second grade students sharing their mathematical thinking with senior citizens. Some colleges of education are now pairing future teachers with K–8 classroom learners, providing the opportunity for these prospective teachers to better understand the mathematical thinking of individual students. Through these collaborative projects, K–8 learners have the opportunity to obtain feedback on their strategies as future teachers have the opportunity to experience and understand these strategies. In general, teachers are increasingly taking advantage of existing technologies to help students go public with their mathematics.

with problems is given insight into and awareness of the thinking of each student.

As we listen to students, it is often tempting to intervene immediately if conversations give us the impression that they are struggling or confused. In fact, when Stigler and Hiebert (1999) compared American teachers to both German and Japanese teachers, they found ample evidence of this aspect of U.S. classroom culture. But if instead we learn to listen carefully to the students' struggles, we might interpret that struggle as a sign of thinking. Silence might mean that the question is past the students' levels of development, or it might mean that students are busy thinking. Quickly interrupting silence, giving correct answers, or calling out incorrect answers results in a socialization that classroom environments are not places where students are expected to take time to develop their own autonomy about whether or not their thinking is accurate. They learn to wait on the inevitable intervention in the classroom conversation that will indicate how their thinking should proceed. Such an intervention should occur only after the teacher listens carefully to the children's words and interprets what is actually going on in a child's head in terms of learning theory. This is not to say that children do not need guidance. Of course they need our guidance—after all, that is what teaching is all about. However, there is room for efforts to change the classroom culture to value quiet thinking.

"If a child suggests a problem such as 4 + 2 is 5, probably the best reaction is to refrain from correcting him and ask instead, '*how did you get 5?*' Children often correct themselves autonomously as they try to explain their reasoning to someone else" (Kamii, 2000, p. 80, italics added). This is an example of constructing knowledge. "According to Piaget, the child acquires knowledge by constructing it from within rather than by internalizing it directly from the environment" (Kamii, 2000, p. 79). By learning to listen to children who are not quickly voicing correct answers, and waiting for a voice from the classroom, we teach students to develop their own autonomy with regard to thinking. They develop their own ideas and abstractions, which is the essence of mathematical thinking.

IDEAS FOR STRUCTURING CLASS TIME:
Using Daily Routines for Number Knowledge

Ideas of number and operation are established in younger grades through several experiences replete with good questioning on the part of the teacher. Involving children in everyday classroom experiences can develop ideas of number. When passing out or dividing up classroom materials, we have wonderful opportunities to quantify in a meaningful way and make number ideas interesting to students. For instance, when children look at collections of things, such as bugs or rocks, we can listen to them explain how many rocks (or bugs) are present. We might ask children to consider the idea of sending one rock home with each child. Would we have all that we need to do this? When we keep records, such as attendance or lunch count, we can ask students to make sense of the numbers being submitted to the office. When we clean up, we can ask students to put three things away. When we listen to students talk about their favorite cartoon or game, we can ask them to vote on likes and dislikes. Voting is a worthwhile way to develop sound number knowledge and also establishes the idea of *more* or *less* in an interesting context. Games that require children to use quantification in order to succeed or even to play the games are also helpful. However, remember to focus the children on the mathematics as they play. Sometimes it is easy to get caught up in the objectives of the game and forget to glean the mathematics objectives from it.

ADVICE FOR PROFESSIONAL DEVELOPMENT:
Compare across Grade Levels

Ask students to complete some computation tasks mentally. Ask them to describe their thinking. Compare results with teachers from different grade levels. How are students viewing mathematics differently? How are they thinking about operations? Do you see CGI's findings in students' work?

Karen is a great example of what the CGI authors already know. Teachers intuitively know a tremendous amount about how children think about

MIDDLE SCHOOL CONNECTIONS

Daily Routines of Middle Graders

Adolescence, associated with physiological changes, is a time when students are extremely self-conscious about their appearance, their actions, and their acceptance by others. On any given day, a student might act very much as you would expect a young adult to act, and then he or she might follow that with a day of childish behavior. Naturally, it appears easier to interact positively with students on the days when they are acting more mature. This behavior feels familiar to us and is behavior to which adolescents aspire. By rewarding appropriate (more mature) behavior, we communicate to the students our preferences for their behavior. However, it is critical that as middle school teachers, we appreciate the diversity of maturation in our classrooms and search for justified opportunities to give positive reinforcement to all students. We must also be careful not to unconsciously bestow all of the positive reinforcement (favors) on students whose behavior seems more adultlike simply because they happen to be maturing earlier. All students want to be accepted. And the later bloomers need to know that you believe

in them at least as much as the students who mature early. That said, it is important to note that students who mature early are also extremely self-conscious about that fact.

Knowing that we value the thinking among these unique individuals as much as we value their appropriate behavior goes a long way toward helping students navigate the difficulties of the middle school years. It is useful to maintain high academic expectations of students to demonstrate our belief in them. Adolescents are savvy individuals and recognize a lowered question as an indication of our assessment of their abilities. Building mathematical activity into the daily classroom lives of middle school students is a good way to build their mathematical thinking and demonstrate your belief that they can solve difficult problems. Using geometry to plan set designs for plays or assemblies, making change at bake sales, and timing races at track meets are good examples of using unique talents of adolescent students. It also proves you believe in them and their mathematical abilities.

CLASSROOM CONNECTIONS

Reacting to CGI for the First Time

NCTM TEACHING

When I read about cognitively guided instruction (Carpenter et al., 1999), I found the philosophy of the authors to be similar to the approach to mathematics learning I was using in my classroom. Through continual training, I am learning more and more about how to guide students' thinking. The information in this book validated my quest to become a better teacher. I made big changes about 10 years ago when my district adopted a standards-based mathematics curriculum. At that time, our district agreed to become involved in a pilot for a National Science Foundation–funded program called *Mathematics in Context* (MiC.) One goal of the MiC program was to ground student learning in realistic situations and then pull the mathematical ideas from those experiences.

It was a tremendous learning experience for me. At the same time, my entire philosophy was verified.

Through meaningful contextual problems, my students would build meaning. Through carefully planned lessons, they would work on problems at their levels of understanding. Then they would listen to classmates share and justify solution strategies. As a teacher, my role was to observe, to listen, and to help my students build on their levels of understanding.

By listening to others, some students might abandon a strategy and use a classmate's "trick." They might become more efficient in their thinking. Other students might not be ready to abandon less efficient strategies. As a teacher, I have learned to respect and value the thinking of each student. We cannot expect all children to think in the same way. However, by providing many problem-solving opportunities, I can help my students to become more efficient in their thinking.

mathematics. But sometimes teachers have not had the luxury of time to put that knowledge together in a coherent way. So their vast knowledge about children's thought processes may not consciously guide instructional decision making.

ALGEBRA CONNECTIONS
Number and Operation

A Big Idea: Properties, Formulas, and Equivalence

Algebra is heavily connected to arithmetic. Making connections in this chapter required a focus on properties, generalizing formulas, and the concept of equivalence. You are encouraged to explore other possibilities for making connections.

Properties

Properties are statements that are true for all members of a certain set of objects. Two examples are the following: (1) Addition between any two whole numbers always results in another whole number, and (2) addition of whole numbers is commutative. *Formulas* are a way to describe a relational situation mathematically. For example, a formula for calculating the cost (C) of 12 oranges is to multiply 12 by the price (P) of one orange, $C = 12*P$. *Equivalence* is a concept that is receiving increased attention because it is an important early step toward algebraic thinking.

In prealgebraic thinking, children see an equal sign ($=$) and assume that it translates to "and the answer is . . ." This can too often lead students to believe that the equal sign is more like an operator rather than a representation of the concept of "is the same as." The difference is subtle and critical at the same time. In the general formula $C = 12*P$, the equal sign is a statement of relationship, not a statement that "the answer is on its way." It is helpful to read, "*C is the same as* 12*P.*" In fact, "is the same as" conjures up a concept, since it is a relationship rather than a request to execute a procedure. Misunderstandings about the concept of equal can cause students to see algebra as completely different from arithmetic. In arithmetic, we ask children to write $3 + 4 = $ ___, and they are expected to *fill in* the answer of 7. But in algebra, we need students to see the relationship between $3 + 4$ as being *the same as* 7. One way to combat this situation is to put students into other situations that call for $3 + 4$ to be *the same as* $5 + 2$, $12 - 5$, or even x. The notion of equivalence is important in developing algebraic thinking.

Algebraic Ideas for You to Explore: Patterns

One context for studying ideas of general formulas and equivalence is describing number patterns and predicting extensions of the patterns. After you work through the numerical patterns in Activity 7.1 (p. 134), you should come to appreciate the role that variables play in developing formulas. You should also recognize that formulas you developed are related to the idea of "is the same as," not "and the answer is. . . ." For example, in pattern A, you see that the formula is $V = 2n$, where V is the value in the pattern and n is the locator number. V, which is at the nth spot in the table, is the same as $2n$. The specific location of a term in the table is accounted for by the formula, since n denotes the location and the goal was to make the generalization, not to find "an answer."

Patterns relate to algebra in several ways. By establishing a relationship between the natural numbers $\{1, 2, 3, . . .\}$ and the elements in the pattern, several algebraic ideas are established. You should see that in linear patterns such as G: 4, 8, 12, 16, . . . , the amount "added to the preceding value" is 4. Another idea results from transferring the pattern to an x-y coordinate graphing representation by creating the implied ordered pairs (1, 4), (2, 8), (3, 12), . . . Plotting those points reveals the slope of the line associated with this pattern if you choose to connect those points. Recall that a line is a continuous entity,

(continued)

Activity 7 . 1

DRAW IN THE NEXT BLOCK PILE

		The number you put into the formula statement to get the value in the pattern.							Recursive Statement	Formula Statement
	1	2	3	4	5	6	13	100	? to previous	Value =
A	2	4	6	8	10	12	26	200	+ 2 to prev.	V = 2n
B	3	6	9	12	15					
C	1	3	5	7	9					
D	3	5	7	9	11					
E	8	10	12	14	16					
F	5	8	11	14	17					
G	4	8	12	16	20					
H	9	12	15	18	21					
I	4	11	18	25	32					
J	1	4	7	10	13					
K	6	11	16	21	26					
L	8	13	18	23	28					
M	1	4	9	16	25					
N	2	5	10	17	26					
P	2	6	12	20	30					
Q	1	3	6	10	15					

<u>A L G E B R A   C O N N E C T I O N S</u> *(continued)*

whereas a pattern is discrete. It is worth noting this difference and thinking back to the similar difference between continuous manipulatives and discrete manipulatives.

Variable as Functional

Now further compare the two representations for the original pattern to similar representations for a new pattern. The algebraic expression for pattern G was *4n,* and the coordinate graph showed several lined up points. When we compare *4n* to the algebraic expression for a new pattern: 5, 9, 13, 17, . . . , we find some interesting results. The graph for the new pattern again showed several aligned points. So in that sense the two graphs were the same. But the two sets of points (for the two patterns) on an *x-y* coordinate system were also different. How were they different? In what other ways were they the same? Comparing two (or more) formulas, in particular, *creating* one formula from another, is using a variable in a functional way as defined by Pillay, Wilss, and Boulton-Lewis (1998). You can see that term by term, the 5, 9, 13, 17 pattern is always 1 more than the 4, 8, 12, 16 pattern. The formula for the new pattern is 1 more than the formula for the original pattern. Thus, the algebraic expression for the new pattern is *4n* + 1.

Notice how your thinking shifted back and forth between the algebraic formula that needed a variable and the numerical computation that did not. When developing pattern formulas, the difference in thinking illustrates one of the differences between algebraic and arithmetic thinking. Solving such problems can lead students to make valuable connections between algebra and arithmetic. By now, you probably realize that in learning algebra, it is insufficient to deal exclusively with algebraic symbols as though they are independent of arithmetic symbols. Students need experiences developing a need for algebraic symbols by expecting them to generalize from numerical situations. Developing algebraic formulas and expressions can provide a foundational understanding of how the two worlds can be connected.

Variable as a Generalization

Making a generalization by creating formulas to describe and predict results of extending patterns in Activity 7.1 represents another way to think about variables. In this case, a variable was used to generalize some sort of relationship between two sets. With the pattern 4, 8, 12, 16, . . . , the variable *n* helped make the generalization *4n*. In this case, *n* represented all possible values for the domain, which was understood to be the set {1, 2, 3, 4, . . .}, whereas the resulting action on *n* resulted in the individual terms in the pattern. Using *n* to stand for *any* number, and at the same time somehow to stand for *all* numbers from a collection of possible values, allows the learner to write a general mathematical statement that describes something about how that set of values is acting. When *n* is used in this way, it is being used as a variable that is a generalization. Describing the relationship in this way also allows us to present some important terminology: *domain* and *range*. This way of thinking about a variable implies that the formula can be applied to any value in the domain. Hence, *4n* is a generalization of the pattern. Using a variable in this way helped us create a general formula. Note that we did not solve for *n* and did not operate on the variable as a functional item.

Variable as Standing for an Unknown to Be Found

If we asked whether or not 90 is in either of the two patterns shown above, how could you find out? You might extend each pattern, skip-counting until you were satisfied about 90's existence in the pattern. However, you also might set your formulas equal to 90 and solve for *n*. If you find *n* to be a whole number, then you would know that 90 is in the pattern *and* you would know the position of 90. When you solve equations, you use a variable to stand for an unknown value that you fully expected to find later. As you compare this idea of a variable to the other two uses of a variable (generalizational and functional), you should recognize a shift in your thinking. You worked to locate the exact

ALGEBRA CONNECTIONS *(continued)*

value that the variable represented. Students need several experiences with all three kinds of thinking associated with using a variable, and they need to explicitly understand when they are using which kind of variable.

K–8 Algebra Connections: Arithmetic to Algebra

Students use all three kinds of variables when they understand, describe, extend, and compare a wide variety of patterns. Students generalize understanding by communicating about patterns in response to guiding questions from their teacher. Soliciting descriptions of the pattern can cause students to be thoughtful as they work to recognize what is happening in the pattern (so that they can ultimately extend it). Perhaps a number pattern is always changing by repeatedly adding 3. In cases like that, students might apply their knowledge of skip-counting, a tremendously valuable tool, to extend the pattern. But asking students to describe or explain their skip-counting with a rule, such as "I always add 3," is another important step toward generalizing. Finally, students should be able to compare two rules to make even stronger generalizations. "Whatever amount I always add is also the amount I skip-count by" is an excellent example of a powerful generalization.

Finally, a connection between arithmetic and algebra can be made clear to students by comparing computation with whole numbers to computation with algebraic symbols. For instance, compare the exercise of multiplying 14 and 23 to the exercise of multiplying $x + 4$ by $2x + 3$. When you think about the intermediate products in 14×23, you can see that you essentially deal with the values 100 (10 • 10), 80 (4 • 20), 30 (3 • 10), and 12 (4 • 3). Similarly, when dealing with $(x + 4) \cdot (2x + 3)$, you use the values x^2 ($x \cdot x$), $8x$ ($4 \cdot 2x$), $3x$ ($3 \cdot x$), and 12 (4 • 3). If you imagine 10 standing for x, the procedural results are identical, and the results are fundamentally equivalent.

K–8 learners do not always view these situations as having anything in common. Lee and Wheeler (1989) found that showing this type of connection did not always serve the instructional role that we would hope in helping students understand algebra. In their study with tenth grade students, algebraic connections to arithmetic were not obvious, and students did not necessarily recognize arithmetic as a useful tool in thinking about algebra. Moreover, and perhaps more disturbingly, they found that some students did not really expect to get the same results with arithmetic as with algebra. For those students, a link between the two worlds has not been forged. It is important to help students connect these worlds while respecting the fact that connecting these worlds is neither straightforward nor simple. Multiple experiences with situations that are similar and ones that seem more disparate are important steps toward making connections.

LET'S REVIEW

The role of the teacher in implementing effective number and operation lessons is to create problem situations for students to solve. These problem situations must allow and encourage students to develop both conceptual and procedural knowledge, as well as to forge connections between these realms of knowledge. As a teacher listens to learners explain their ways of working with the numerical problem situations, he or she should listen carefully for evidence of lucid concept knowledge as well as for misconceptions. With the work of CGI and Kamii at his or her disposal, a teacher can understand the students' ways of categorizing problem types and students' flexibility and automaticity with operations. As students give their explanations, the teacher can evaluate student achievement with number and operation knowledge. The teacher can then plan future lessons, based on students' progress to that point. For this particular chapter, we happened to highlight the concept model of teaching. We consciously chose that model for this part of the book because we believe you might not have thought about the conceptual underpinnings of operations before. Using a concept attainment model for number and operation lessons provides a nice opportunity for learners to demonstrate understanding of concepts that will later prop up procedural demonstrations. Naturally, you will use all the models of teaching when developing lessons for number and operation. We could have as easily chosen to concentrate our comments on a different model of teaching, but by the end of the book, we will have studied all five models of teaching as we consider the role of the teacher.

HOMEWORK

1. Locate a textbook for any grade K–8, and look at the sections on algebra and/or patterning. Check the margin notes (notes to the teacher) in the teacher's edition, and decide whether the teacher's edition guides students toward generalizing patterns using variables and extends those lessons to use the variables as an unknown to be found.
2. Locate a primary mathematics textbook (K–2). Determine whether or not the authors follow CGI's findings that children will interact with subtraction number problems with direct modeling and/or counting. Decide whether the collection of teacher questions (probably in the margins) guides students' thinking according to CGI's findings.
3. A group of fifth grade children studied the following pictures. When they were asked to explain the pattern in general, Samantha said, "*m + n*." What might she have been thinking?

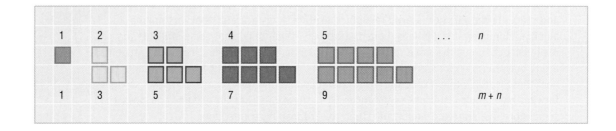

SUGGESTED READINGS

Cotter, J. (2000). Using language and visualization to teach place value. *Teaching Children Mathematics, 7*(2), 108–114.

Ferrini-Mundy, J., Lappan, G., & Phillips, E. (1997). Experiences with patterning. *Teaching Children Mathematics, 3*(6), 282–288.

Harrison, W. B. (1985). How to make a million. *Arithmetic Teacher, 33*(1), 46–47.

Hellwig, S. J., Monroe, E. E., & Jacobs, J. J. (2000). Making informed choices. *Teaching Children Mathematics, 7*(3), 138–143.

Rowan, T., & Bourne, B. (1994). *Thinking like mathematicians* (pp. 17–25). Portsmouth, NH: Heinemann.

Scharton, S. (2004). "I did it my way": Providing opportunities for students to create, explain, and analyze computation procedures. *Teaching Children Mathematics, 10*(5), 278–283.

REFERENCES

Carpenter, T. (1986). Conceptual knowledge as a foundation for procedural knowledge. In J. Hiebert (Ed.), *Conceptual and procedural knowledge: The case of mathematics* (pp. 113–132). Hillsdale, NJ: Lawrence Erlbaum.

Carpenter, T. P., Fennema, E., Franke, M. L., Levi, L., & Empson, S. B. (1999). *Children's mathematics: Cognitively guided instruction.* Portsmouth, NH: Heinemann.

Center for Highly Interactive Computing in Education. (2003). Freewrite [Computer Software]. Retrieved from www.hice.org.

Center for Highly Interactive Computing in Education. (2003). Sketch [Computer Software]. Retrieved from www.hice.org.

Kamii, C. (2000). *Number in preschool and kindergarten.* New York: National Association for the Education of Young Children.

Lee, L., & Wheeler, D. (1989). The arithmetic connection. *Educational Studies in Mathematics, 20,* 41–54.

Mathematics in context: A connected curriculum for grade 5–8 (1998) Chicago, IL: Encyclopedia Britannica.

National Council of Teachers of Mathematics. (2000). *Principles and standards for school mathematics.* Reston, VA: NCTM.

Papert, S. (1980). *Mindstorms: Children, computers and powerful ideas.* New York: Basic Books.

Pillay, H., Wilss, L., & Boulton-Lewis, G. (1998). Sequential development of Algebra knowledge: A cognitive analysis. *Mathematics Education Research Journal, 10*(2), 87–102.

Stigler, J. W., & Hiebert J. (1999). *The teaching gap.* New York: The Free Press.

Now that you have finished reading about how children learn number and operation ideas, it is time to summarize the information from the previous three chapters. We hope you recognize the difference between operation concepts and operation procedures, since our focus in Part II was on concept attainment. Students need to develop number sense with experiences like patterning, problem solving, and completing arithmetic activities as part of their daily routines. In this way, algorithms are made equally meaningful to learners. As usual, we engage you in a closing activity. It is a difficult journey to move away from thinking about school like a student and toward thinking about it like a teacher, but it is a necessary journey. So to elucidate the information in a practical manner, imagine you are a fourth grade teacher who must develop a lesson to help learners meet the curriculum goal: *The student will be able to correctly describe more than two relationships between multiplication and division.*

Closing Activity: Summary Lesson

WRITE A NUMBER AND OPERATION LESSON

This activity is an opportunity for you to put together all the information from Part II of the book. You are a fourth grade teacher who must create a concept-attainment model lesson that will support the following number and operation curriculum goal:

The student will be able to correctly describe more than two relationships between multiplication and division.

Because this is a curriculum requirement, it may take several weeks to achieve. Your task for this activity is to create a single lesson that will fall sometime during those weeks. It might be the first in a series of lessons. Remember that your ultimate goal is to help students achieve the more general curriculum goal. The lesson you create should be designed to be completed in one day and should serve as only a small support for the more general goal. We guide you through a lesson development process, asking you to complete the tasks outlined in 1–5.

1. **Think about the Mathematics.** First, think about the prerequisite knowledge in terms of number and operation and the accompanying vocabulary that students would have and need in order to work toward this goal. Second, what is the difference between a concept and a procedure related to this goal? Third, write a focused narrow objective achievable through the concept-attainment model of teaching. Be sure to focus on a small component of the curriculum goal. Fourth, please tell how this lesson will fit into the students' overall experience toward the curriculum goal.

2. **Think about How We Learn.** What are good experiences that foster number relationships? Remember how we described the relationship between number sense and arithmetic? Recall the information about selecting teaching aids and create a list of materials you need to gather for the lesson.

3. **Think about the Role of the Teacher.** What does the teacher do in a concept-attainment lesson?

Recall that the teacher decides whether the lesson is direct or indirect and then collects specimens to serve as examples or nonexamples. Take a moment to decide what sort of activity you think the students should complete with the examples. List at least six examples and nonexamples related to your objective.

4. Think about **How the Learning Theory Might Appear during Your Lesson.** Use your knowledge of CGI and Kamii to anticipate student comments and to prepare follow-up questions for each kind of answer.

5. Finally, Think about **Assessment.** How will you know when your students have met your objective? Write an evaluation in which you engage the students that indicates to you the objective has or has not been met.

As with the geometry lesson you completed after reading Part I, there are also several correct answers for this lesson about number and operation. We remind you that the lessons you create for your own learners will depend on your district's curriculum and that you will have access to a textbook series that should help you write your lessons. We also know that teachers modify their own lessons from year to year to meet the changing needs of their students. However, we believe that there are correct types of answers for this activity. We can imagine lessons based on skip-counting and reverse-skip-counting as well as lessons involving hopping along a number line. After you finish writing your lesson, you might check your lesson against our sample lesson in the appendix. Again, we remind you that we provided only one possible set of answers for a lesson. We would never wish to imply that our lesson is the only possible lesson, nor that it would meet the needs of every fourth-grader. It is more important to be able to think through your lesson and decide whether it would be considered a correct type of answer.

PART THREE

Measurement
Ideas

Measurement is a combination of number and geometry ideas. You may want to think back to the previous two parts of the book as you complete the activity. Graph paper may prove helpful or you may use cubes or draw other pictures to think visually about the situation.

Opening Activity

GENERALIZE THE AREA FOR A TRAPEZOID

Ayanna inherited 10 trapezoid-shaped pools from her Great Aunt Marie. The pools each require a new cover. To inherit the pools, Ayanna must determine exact sizes of tarps to cover each pool. She decided to look at several examples and find a formula. Then she can quickly use it to find the surface areas of each.

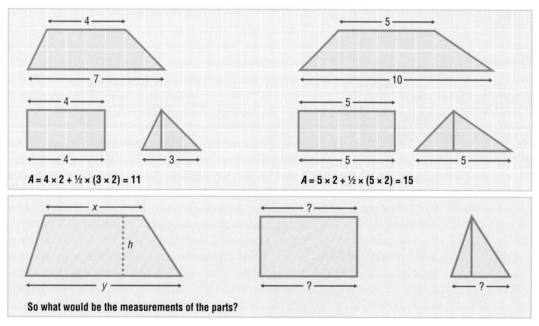

$A = 4 \times 2 + \frac{1}{2} \times (3 \times 2) = 11$

$A = 5 \times 2 + \frac{1}{2} \times (5 \times 2) = 15$

So what would be the measurements of the parts?

What is a formula for finding the area of a trapezoid?

How do you know?

● Refer to your solution to the trapezoid problem and think about how you arrived at your solution. In finding the areas of several trapezoid shapes, we suspect you used a mixture of measuring and counting before you arrived at a formula. Is it difficult to compare and contrast the activities of counting and measuring? They seem too interconnected to separate, but compare your use of counting and measuring to your classmates' uses and you may begin to see important differences. We selected this problem to open Part III because it illustrates the difference between counting and measuring and between learners' thinking, depending on whether they used discrete materials or continuous drawings. In this part of the book, we will emphasize the way teachers must carefully connect activities involving the discrete notions of counting to measurement lessons, a continuous idea.

CHAPTER

8

Thinking about the
Mathematics of
Measurement

N⊂TM
CURRICULUM

UNDERSTANDING THE MATHEMATICS:
Geometry and Number

When you think about measurement, what do you think of? Perhaps you conjure up images of perimeter and area. Those are definitely pieces of measurement, but we ask you in this chapter to dig deeper into the foundation of measurement. Technically, measurement is where geometry and number come together—hence the placement of this chapter. Geometry is a conception of space and number is an assignment of a value to a set of objects that in some way quantifies that set. Taken together, these two ideas result in measurement, a coordination of spatial knowledge and numeric knowledge (e.g., Lehrer et al., 1999; National Research Council, 2001; Reynolds & Wheatley, 1996). For the ancients, geometry literally meant "the science of measuring the land" (Greenberg, 1972, p. 5), but it is important to understand that measurement stands on the shoulders of both geometric space and number. In some ways, it helps to think of measurement as a number that *can be assigned* to a region on the basis of a comparison with another region, which is a standard unit. Sometimes, the region is difficult to visualize. For example, in the case of time (something that we measure), it is difficult to conceptualize time as a "space." So in other ways, it helps to think of measurement as *taking up space* before assigning a number to it.

Measuring includes everything from a kindergartner comparing and ordering simple shapes of different sizes to a sixth grader proving that two given triangles are congruent. Both the kindergartner and the sixth grader are using strategies for completing the measurement process as well as concepts of measurement. In this chapter, we focus on understanding how students construct their respective geometry knowledge and understandings related to measurement. To begin, let's listen to our fifth graders explain what measurement means to them.

Min: A measurement is a certain amount of something. You might see how many pieces fill it up perfectly.

Lydia: Measurement is what you do when you think something doesn't seem like it's going to fit correctly.

Ryan: You need a measurement when you want to know whether something is taller than something else.

Jamal: There are lots of ways to measure something and lots of things to measure with. You measure with a ruler when you want to know how long something is.

All four students recognize that to measure, they have to "do" something to find the size of an object. Ryan is concerned with comparing two objects, and Min wants to count how many pieces fill up her object. Lydia is probably referring to a specific situation from her life when she needed to know whether there was enough space for an object. Jamal is thinking about measurement more generally, providing us with an example: Length requires a ruler.

Continuous

When Min thought about *perfectly* filling her object with pieces, she might have been thinking continuously. Continuousness can be thought of as the idea that a unit "goes from here to there." Awareness of this concept means realizing that a unit has a specific beginning and an ending. That is, the continuous nature of the unit implies not that the unit is a discrete *piece*, but that it is a piece that goes from here to there. In terms of measurement, we are not thinking of the common use of the word *continuous* as something akin to infinity or forever. Nor are we thinking of doing something continuously. The idea of doing something over and over again is the notion of iteration and will be described shortly.

Was Min measuring? Assume that she was thinking about measuring a box by filling it with small cubes. She fit the cubes into the box and found that 24 cubes filled the box *perfectly.* Has she counted, or has she measured? Of course, that depends on how she is thinking about the cubes. When Min assigns a number (supposedly as the measure) to an object, she must be thinking of that number as *an accumulation of space,* not as a collection of discrete objects she has counted. She must have recognized that one cube, itself, has a volume of one unit (that is, it takes up one unit of space from its beginning to its end), and she recognizes that 24 cubes therefore take up a volume of 24 units. When she notices that the box perfectly fits against the end (or face) of the cubes (stacked neatly and tightly into the box) and notes that this implies that the box also has an accumulated volume of 24 units, then she has measured.

Measurement is a complicated concept and process that can be difficult to develop because it requires the coordination of discrete ideas, continuous ideas, number, and geometry.

Standard Unit

Min was also probably thinking about filling up her object with copies of the exact same sized shape. A standard unit is the unit against which the item being measured is compared. The number of standard units used represents the measurement of that item. Activity 8.1 (p. 146) will help you to think about items from the world that are measured. As you complete the activity, be sure to think about the general nature of a standard unit and how it works. In particular, think about the difference between using a standard unit to measure a phenomenon and counting elements in a set (as we did in Chapters 5 and 6). Think

Activity 8.1

TOOL LIST

Complete the chart and add at least three other rows of information. As you discuss these ideas, keep in mind the continuous nature of the standard unit. Think about its beginning and its end and what it means to begin "the next" standard unit immediately after (end-to-end) the preceding standard unit has completed itself.

Idea to be Measured	When Might It Be Needed?	Small Standard Unit Used to Measure It	Tool Used to Keep Track of These Units	Large Standard Unit to Measure It	Tool Used to Keep Track of These Units
Time					
	Running			Kilometer	
	Plant growth	Inch			
			Thermometer		
				Mile	
		Second			Watch
	Reentry into the atmosphere				Protractor

carefully about a standard unit's beginning and end and what it means to begin the next standard unit immediately after (end-to-end) the preceding standard unit. This should feel somewhat different depending on the nature of the standard unit (e.g., a second of time versus an inch of length).

Here, some fifth graders give an account of standard units and when they might be used:

Min: I measured time when cooking. My small unit was seconds on a timer, and my large unit was hours on a clock.

Lydia: I measured time when cooking too! My small unit was seconds on a timer, and my large unit was days on a calendar. (My grandmother does holiday cooking for an entire week.)

Ryan: I measure time when I run. My small unit was seconds (on a timer) when I run yards on the football field, and my large unit was minutes (on a clock) when I run miles.

Jamal: I measured time by thinking about walking my dogs. My small unit was minutes on a watch, and my large unit was hours on a stopwatch.

These students demonstrate the ability to separate the idea of standard unit from the tool used to keep track of that unit. All of them could imagine a context for the different items on the activity sheet. Ryan even described a relationship between shorter distances and smaller units for time. Standard units and ways of keeping track of standard units serve the purpose of coming up with a numerical statement about the region or space in question. The relationship between that region and the number is the idea of a measurement. Your chart contains issues related to concepts and procedures. Measurement, like other areas of mathematics, includes both concepts and procedures. In the next part of this chapter, we discuss some concepts and procedures associated with measurement.

CONCENTRATING ON THE CONCEPTS:
It Begins with the Idea of "Size"

General concepts for this chapter are size, comparison, standard unit, iteration, coverage, tiling, and part-whole. With this many concepts to coordinate, measurement can be difficult to learn. And with so many concepts to develop, it seems like a long time before a procedure for using a ruler is introduced. As in previous chapters, we want to build procedures (such as using a ruler) on strong conceptual knowledge. You will come to appreciate how rulers (and other measuring devices such as protractors, thermometers, and clocks) are designed in such a way that they can be used without full knowledge of the concepts involved. The measuring device can mask one or more concepts within its ease of utility.

But we need students to understand a healthy dose of concepts first. That can present a problem in part because students must use one (or more) of these concepts to understand other concepts. For instance, consider Paige (five years old), who is confronted with the task of measuring a pencil using standard-size paper clips. She sets a row of these paper clips next to the unsharpened pencil. The pencil is exactly six paper clips long. After lining up the paper clips next to the pencil, she counts the paper clips and says, "Six." To understand that a pencil has a *length* of six, requires using the concept of a length of one *nonstandard unit* (the paper clip) to establish the pencil's length of six. But wait, there's more! To measure with six paper clips, Paige had to understand that the standard unit was *iterated*. She must have known the iteration needed to *cover*. She even had to be prepared to think about a *part of a unit* if the pencil had been a little longer or shorter than six paper clips. Full understanding of the concepts behind measuring the linear region (pencil) required coordinating these ideas. But iteration plays a special role. Without understanding that iteration is possible, how could a child iterate the one unit to measure something new? Although the number of concepts a student must coordinate might appear overwhelming, all concepts should be taught together.

Nonstandard Units

Nonstandard units are units other than commercially accepted units such as inches and centimeters. Paper clips and paces are usually good nonstandard units that are familiar to children. The roles of the nonstandard unit are (1) to show students the concept that a uniform unit is needed and (2) to help them understand that because people need to communicate with one another, some widely known unit needs acceptance as a *standard* unit.

Size, Comparing, and Conservation

Three basic premeasurement concepts must be established. First, a child must recognize that things can have size, such as deep, tall, small, short, or long. Second, a child must learn to compare two or more objects to develop the idea that something is deeper, taller, smaller, shorter, or longer than something else. These two understandings should help to solidify the need to find out exactly *how* deep, tall, small, short, or long something may be. Here, Shera, who is six years old, interacts with her teacher, Ms. Hawthorne:

> ***Ms. Hawthorne:*** Think of something that is deep.
> ***Shera:*** Hmmm. My blue cereal bowl is deep.
> ***Ms. Hawthorne:*** Now I want you to think of something that is deeper.
> ***Shera:*** The bowl my mom uses to make salads is deeper.
> ***Ms. Hawthorne:*** How do you know?
> ***Shera:*** Well, all four of us use it. The blue bowl is just for me.
> ***Ms. Hawthorne:*** Can you think of a bowl that is not as deep as your blue cereal bowl?
> ***Shera:*** The cat's food dish. I have to fill it twice each day!

Shera has noticed that some bowls are deeper than others. She is beginning to develop a concept of volume. She is connecting the depth (size) of the bowl with the amount of food that fits in it, even though food is not a standard unit.

   Finally, it is critical that young children use conservation, "recognizing that the length of an object is not altered by a change in its spatial position" (Heibert, 1984, p. 19). Sometimes, children think the length of the pencil or depth of the bowl might change if the object moved into a different position. Would Shera still think that her cereal bowl was deeper than her cat's food bowl if she could look at them only from above?

Size Is Summative

Understanding the concept of "summative" is awareness that the measure of an object is equal to the sum of measures of all parts of the object. This can take two tracks. On one hand, the information can be used to find the measure of a shape by cutting it into pieces. For example, when you solved the opening activity, finding a formula for area of a trapezoid, you realized that you could cut the trapezoid into parts (a triangle and a rectangle). Conceptually, you knew that the sum of the rectangle's area and the triangle's area would be the same as the area of the entire trapezoid. On the other hand, this concept knowledge could have allowed you to put pieces together, building up to a shape that you wanted to measure. In Activity 8.2, you should demonstrate this knowledge.

Standard Unit

The standard unit is *the* unit that everyone agrees will be the one used to communicate the size of an object. The number of these units that is used is the size of the object measured. En route to establishing this standard unit, students must develop the idea that sometimes one standard unit makes more sense than another. Earlier, Ryan knew that to measure shorter distances, he used yards (which he would run in seconds), while he used miles to measure longer distances (which he would run in minutes). The standard unit concept is also related to the idea that each copy of a given standard unit is equal-sized.

   An excellent example for establishing standard units that is often successfully is some variation of the story about a king and his foot (see *How Big*

Activity 8 . 2

SUBDIVIDING A REGION

Use a set of tangrams to complete these tasks.

1. Show that the area of the square piece is the same as the area of the medium triangle piece. Draw a picture or trace around the tangram pieces.
2. Is the square piece the same size as the nonsquare parallelogram? Draw a picture to explain.
3. How can you compare the areas of the medium triangle, square, and nonsquare parallelogram shapes?
4. Explain whether you built up a shape or tore apart a shape to answer question #2.
5. How is your work an example of the concept that size is summative?
6. Is the area of a large shape equal to the sum of the areas of all subregions of the shape? How do you know?

Is a Foot? [Myller & McCrath, 1990]). In this story, the reader encounters a confounding situation related to a kingdom, where lengths are always measured by the king's foot. If the king wants a wagon built, he steps off the length and reports the distance to the wagon maker. If he wants a new bed, he steps off the length and width of it and reports these numbers to the bed maker. The problem occurs when craft makers somehow lose the information from the king (regarding his paces) and opt to step off the numerical distances themselves. Things can become complicated in a hurry if the wagon maker has a smaller foot than the king's! (It helps to model this problem with two students from the class who have noticeably different foot sizes.) Students can help to resolve the situation by finding strategies that include making sure that all of the craft makers use the same basic unit of measurement and what to do when the king is not available to pace off the distances.

Shera, a first grader, explains some of her thinking about length, particularly in this situation in which direct comparisons are not available:

Ms. Hawthorne: Are your shoes very long?
Shera: They are longer than Emma's. (Emma is Shera's little sister.)
Ms. Hawthorne: [Pauses for a moment.]
Shera: And Mom's shoes are longer than mine. [Shera paces off two steps.] Her shoes are that big.
Ms. Hawthorne: Are your Mom's shoes the longest in the family?
Shera: No. Dad's shoes are the longest. [Shera paces off three steps.] His shoes are that big.
Ms. Hawthorne: Are your Dad's shoes longer than your Uncle Fred's shoes?
Shera: That is hard. [Thinks for several seconds.] I think Uncle Fred's shoes would be longer.
Ms. Hawthorne: Tell me how you thought about that.
Shera: Uncle Fred is older, and Uncle Fred is taller!

What idea about standard unit is Shera using? Her own shoe length serves as her standard unit for a while. Once the measurement questions leave her household's family members, she really has to think. No longer is her standard unit (her own shoe length) beneficial to her; she has to think about comparing two objects that she cannot directly stack against one another. She begins to think in other ways. It is critical to ask children to compare things they cannot directly set next to one another.

Iteration of Units

Once students decide on a standard unit, they need to use it repeatedly to determine the size of the object being measured. They learn to use the same unit over and over again. When young children use the standard unit over and over again to say something about the *size* of the thing they are measuring, this iteration lays the foundation for students' coordination of units (Reynolds & Wheatley, 1996). As this concept is more fully developed, students realize the importance of the iterated pieces being of equal size—in other words, being *standard.*

Coverage

Here, students develop appreciation for the importance of having no gaps and no overlaps in the process of measuring. They recognize the importance of coverage to determine the (relative) size of an object. Figure 8.1 shows examples of coverage and iteration.

In coordinating the two ideas of iteration and coverage, discrete notions must diverge from continuous notions. Often, when students begin to iterate in measuring, they are not aware that there can be no space between units. When measuring an unsharpened pencil, some younger children might set three or four paperclips along its length, unconcerned if their paper clips do not touch one another in an end-to-end fashion.

And why should they care? Before children learn to count (discrete) elements in a set, they believe that a row of eight chips spread out has more chips in it than a row of eight (of the same sized) chips scrunched together. Recall that we are cautious to develop the idea of conservation, teaching children that spaces between the objects do *not* matter when it comes to counting discrete objects in a set. So why would we expect them to think that having spaces between the standard units *is* a problem in this new situation? As they transfer their numerical knowledge to the notion of measurement, they might not think that having spaces between their discrete, concrete standard units represents any sort of a concern.

This coverage issue really has much to do with the idea that students must learn to think continuously. We can build on their discrete idea of "more than" by changing it to the continuous idea of "longer than," thus introducing measurement. Instead of lamenting their inability to conserve with discrete pieces when counting, we should instead celebrate the notion that children see one thing as *longer* than the other thing and anticipate

Figure 8 . 1

Iteration versus Coverage

An iteration is a repeated process. Here the rectangular shape is used repeatedly. However, there are gaps and overlaps in the usage. So although the student has iterated, he or she has not tiled (because the shape is not also covered).

A coverage is setting units end-to-end. Here, shapes are set end-to-end, but they are not the same shape, so the students did not iterate with the same standard unit.

When both *iteration* and *coverage* are appropriately developed, students know how to use the same unit to iterate and to cover. These two things together are known as *tiling.*

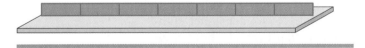

how this will be used later when we teach measurement. We simply have to teach them the corresponding mathematics for the nature of the thinking (discrete or continuous) that is needed for that knowledge (counting or measuring.)

Tiling

When the concepts of iteration and coverage are completely developed, they form a new concept: tiling. Here, students repeatedly trace (iterate) the same standard unit so that the end of each unit is immediately next to the beginning of a new copy of the standard unit (coverage) without gaps or overlaps. The term *end-to-end* might conjure up images of length; however, it is also meant to include the notion of side-to-side, as square tiles might be placed, or stacking cubes up and down, face-to-face, to measure volume. Your image of tiling should include minutes in measuring time. We do not overlap minutes of time; nor is there any space between them. Once one minute has ended, the next has immediately begun. When our students make sense of the general nature of this idea, they understand iterating and coverage.

Part-Whole

Sometimes in measuring, there might be a portion of the object left over after using as many standard units as possible. Students need to understand that even though there is a standard unit, sometimes they might need only part of it. Imagine children measuring their desktops with unsharpened pencils. What will they do when there is some desktop left to measure but that leftover part is less than a whole pencil? (The object sticks out past that last whole pencil, or the last whole pencil extends past the object.) How would they describe the desktop's length? Understanding that the standard unit can be broken into parts is related to the notion of continuousness and that the idea size is summative. It means knowing that the standard unit *can* be broken into parts.

Another option that students sometimes suggest is switching to a different unit. We do want students to understand that they can use a variety of units to measure length (e.g., feet for typical classroom items, centimeters for small things, miles for large things). This does not relieve them of the need to learn about the part-whole nature of the standard unit. Additional caution needs to be taken in following a child's suggestion to switch units: Children are open to the idea of switching between standard units during the process of measuring. That is, they might mix inches with centimeters if this makes the number answer for their measurement more convenient.

Coordinating Concepts

All these concepts have to be coordinated to measure effectively. They cannot be learned independently of one another. We add one other note. You might recall that in Chapter 2, we recommended beginning with solid shapes and abstracting the plane characteristics from them. Here, we recommend building up the idea of measurement from length toward plane (area) and solid (volume) situations. In addition, we recommend making general conceptual connections to other regions to be measured, such as time, temperature, and angles, after students understand the basic measurement concepts with length. Even though time is clearly different from temperature, the same general concepts remain intact and should be more clearly understood and applied in other situations once students can apply them in a first situation—in this case, length. This it not to imply a stage theory of any sort. It is simply meant to imply that

CLASSROOM CONNECTIONS

Using a Magnified Inch

By fifth grade, we study fractions before measurement, since students need to understand the part-whole concept to measure. I like to revisit ideas throughout the year to help cement concept knowledge. So I used an adaptation of the "Magnified Inch" activity from *Family Math* (Stenmark et al., 1986, p. 86) to connect students' fraction thinking to measurement. For my version of this activity, students used an 18-inch length of paper to mark off fractions. We folded once and labeled $\frac{1}{2}$, then folded twice and labeled the fourths, and so on. We used the strip as a giant inch. So often, it seems difficult for students to measure precisely beyond $\frac{1}{4}$ inch. NCTM (2000) talks about how students in grades 3–5 should "begin paying closer attention to the degree of accuracy when measuring and use a wider variety of measurement tools" (p. 171). The magnified inch seemed to help students get between the fourth-inch markings. We pretended that we were giants and used

NcTm
CURRICULUM

our new rulers to measure my desk, the door, the hallway, and so on. With the fractions marked to $\frac{1}{16}$ on the giant's ruler, students easily transferred their thinking to our real rulers.

After measuring with the giant's inch, we used a regular ruler to find answers to the following questions:

1. How many inches long is your pencil?
2. How far is it from your seat to the door?

In which of the above is a label absolutely necessary? When I was a child, I learned that I must always label my answer, no matter how the question was worded. Since then, I have come to believe that sometimes the label is implied. If you answered the first question with "4," I would know that you meant inches because the label is in the question. However, if you answered the second question with "15," I would not be sure which unit of measure you had used. Of course, when in doubt, I suggest to my students they should label.

once a student can measure one kind of region or phenomenon, he or she is better able to quickly develop aptitude for measuring other kinds of situations.

GRASPING THE PROCEDURES:
How to Measure Shapes

Procedures for measuring are literally step-by-step methods for *how to* measure an object. How we measure an object requires effective implementation of the previously mentioned concepts. To effectively measure, we begin with a standard unit (and select a good one), iterate it accurately, take parts of it effectively, and cover with it appropriately. A specific procedure will directly associate these concepts or some collection of these concepts and manifest itself as a step-by-step process and take into account any nuances inherent in the object being measured. Students can memorize how to use a ruler without really understanding the concepts of conservation and transitivity (Hiebert, 1981; Kamii & Long, 2003). We can show them how, but they will not necessarily understand. In this section, we highlight some of the procedural issues that arise when students first learn how to measure.

The Zero (Origin)

Awareness of the zero point is a procedural issue that comes up when students have to figure out how to count the number of units that measure the object. This procedure is twofold: (1) Students recognize that the "zero" indicator on the tool being used to measure should correspond with an "end" of the object being measured, and (2) students eventually recognize that any point can be the "zero" indicator but using a number other than zero requires an adjustment to the number associated with the item being measured. Figure 8.2 shows two different ways to think of the zero point in the process of measuring an eight-inch rectangle. In this figure, paint has been spilled on the first ruler, hiding some of the beginning numbers on the ruler. Helping students to develop a procedure that handles this situation is important.

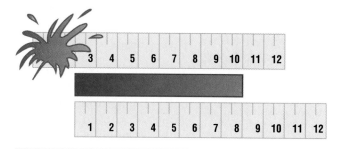

Figure 8 . 2

Deciding on the Zero (Origin)

The zero point directly relates to thinking continuously. When students assign a number (as the measure) to an object, they think of that number as the accumulation of distance, not as a collection of discrete objects that have been counted. They need to understand how to interpret the zero point (origin) as the initial beginning point from which distance is accumulated.

For example, let's consider a Celsius thermometer and a Fahrenheit thermometer. These measuring devices are both tools for measuring temperature, but for each scale, the zero is in a different spot. That is, 0° Celsius is not as cold as 0° Fahrenheit. Yet they are both zero indicators. These devices come with an additional problem: The standard unit is of a different size (Fahrenheit degrees are smaller than Celsius degrees). So here we have two systems designed to measure temperature, but each has its own zero point, and each has a different sized standard unit. Yet the procedure for measuring remains the same.

Counting Spaces

Once students have settled on a zero point, they count *spaces* along the ruler, realizing that the space *itself* has a beginning and an end. They realize that they are not merely citing the *location* of a number when they point to the end. The process of counting needs to be in terms of the accumulation of distance, the length of a hop, the time in a second, or the weight of a pound, and *not* as a location on the measurement tool.

Describing a Part

If students need to measure with only part of a unit, sometimes there is confusion about how to describe that part. Sometimes, young children will not appropriately identify the part. Instead of saying the picture in Figure 8.3 is $7\frac{1}{2}$, students will state it as $8\frac{1}{2}$. Presumably, this is because children can see the 8, and they recognize that they have only a part of 8, but they do not recognize that they don't have a full eight units. This may also be related to students' difficulty with how to say fractions. You will learn in the next part that often, students want to tell you into how many pieces a whole is cut before telling you how many of those pieces they have. For example, when describing $\frac{3}{4}$, young children often want to first indicate that it would take "four" pieces to make a "whole" before telling you how many of those pieces, in this case three, they possess. So they might say, "fourths, three" instead of "three fourths." Describing the part

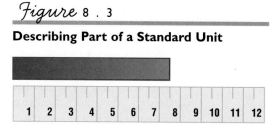

Figure 8 . 3

Describing Part of a Standard Unit

correctly might be related to their efforts to find meaningful ways to correctly report the part of the unit they need. In any event, it is critical that students think about and reason about the situation carefully rather than trying to find a way to use the measuring tool in a nonsensible way (Kamii & Clark, 1997).

Formulas

You might be wondering why we haven't mentioned formulas as part of the procedures section. Formulas do have their place in measurement. At what point should formulas be formally introduced? Formulas may be experienced as part of a lesson even though mastery of the formula is not the primary goal of the lesson. It is important to allow ample time for understanding measurement conceptually before using formulas exclusively. In any given classroom, some students are savvy about formulas, and we want to let those who are ready be exposed to and use formulas. But in general, formulas will need to appear much later because students need to think about formulas in conjunction with the object being measured. When formulas are emphasized too early, students can fail to understand how the formula developed. Students quickly recognize that they can plug numbers into a formula to grind out another number that seems to make the teacher happy, but the students might not really understand the role of the formula. There is really no problem with exposing students to formulas, but in some cases, students will use them without understanding them. It is important not to introduce formulas too early or without a context. Listen to these seventh graders explain the formula for area of a triangle:

> **Fatima:** I use $\frac{1}{2} \cdot b \cdot h$ because it gives me the right answer.
> **Lucretia:** I know the formula is $\frac{1}{2} \cdot b \cdot h$ but I'm not sure why it works.
> **Kaleb:** Sometimes when I forget which formula to use, I see if I can somehow use the rectangle formula (length times width) because I can remember that one. I know triangles are half of rectangles, so I use $\frac{1}{2}(l \cdot w)$.
> **Anthony:** A triangle is half of a parallelogram, so I draw the parallelogram and use $\frac{1}{2}(b \cdot h)$.

Notice how Fatima and Lucretia have memorized the formula using "base" and "height," whereas Kaleb and Anthony are making sense of the situation and building on their understanding of rectangle and parallelogram areas. We would have to question Fatima some more to understand her thinking about the formula. Lucretia, on the other hand, has memorized the formula and can remember it but is bothered by the fact that she does not know why it works. We suspect that Lucretia was not encouraged to make her own sense of the formula, while Kaleb and Anthony have connected their thinking about rectangles or parallelograms to what they know about triangles.

LET'S REVIEW

In thinking about the mathematics of measurement, we learned that concepts and procedures are part of the mathematical knowledge base. The main idea behind measurement is that in measurement, number and geometry concepts come together but must be thought about as a continuous phenomenon. The resulting measurement concepts are size, comparison, standard unit, iteration, coverage, tiling, and part-whole. Measurement instruction can be difficult to break into the smaller concept lessons because measurement requires coordinating all of them together. An important concept is that there is a summative relationship between the sizes of all the parts that make up an object and the size of the whole object. The general procedure for measuring means to (1) select a standard unit, (2) put the unit end to end covering the object being measured, (3) be sure there are no gaps (and no overlaps), and then (4) count the number of units used. In some cases, procedures can be generalized into formulas for specific shapes.

HOMEWORK

1. Describe the contrast between a child's *number* thinking and *measurement* thinking with regard to the importance of space between the counters. That is, describe how in counting, space between units is considered unimportant, but in measuring, the idea of space between units *is* important.
2. Suppose you are an athletic agent-manager for Marion Jones. For a publicity stunt to kick off the next Olympics, she has agreed to sprint 1,000,000 centimeters. Her best races are the 100-meter sprint and the 200-meter sprint. How many 200-meter dashes will she run to complete this charity event? Can she sprint the entire 1,000,000 centimeters all together immediately before the opening ceremonies? Plan a 1,000,000-centimeter route for her.

SUGGESTED READINGS

Lehrer, R., Jaslow, L., & Curtis, C. L. (2003). Developing an understanding of measurement in the elementary grades. In D. H. Clements & G. Bright (Eds.), *Learning and teaching measurement: NCTM 2003 Yearbook* (pp. 100–121). Reston, VA: NCTM.

Young, S. L., & O'Leary, R. (2002). Creating numerical scales for measuring tools. *Teaching Children Mathematics, 8*(7), 400–405.

REFERENCES

Greenberg, M. J. (1972). *Euclidean and non-Euclidean geometries.* San Francisco: W. H. Freeman.

Hiebert, J. (1981). Cognitive development and learning linear measurement. *Journal for Research in Mathematics Education, 12*(3), 197–211.

Hiebert, J. (1984). Why do some children have trouble learning measurement concepts? *Arithmetic Teacher, 31*(7), 19–24.

Kamii, C., & Clark, F. B. (1997). Measurement of length: The need for a better approach to teaching. *School Science and Mathematics, 97*(3), 116–121.

Kamii, C., & Long, K. (2003). The measurement of time: Transitivity, unit iteration, and conservation of speed. In D. H. Clements & G. Bright (Eds.), *Learning and teaching measurement: NCTM 2003 Yearbook* (pp. 169–180). Reston, VA: NCTM.

Lehrer, R., Jacobson, C., Kemeny, V., & Strom, D. (1999). Building on children's intuitions to develop mathematical understanding of space. In E. Fennema & T. A. Romberg (Eds.), *Mathematics classrooms that promote understanding* (pp. 63–87). Mahwah, NJ: Lawrence Erlbaum.

Myller, R., & McCrath, S. (1990). *How big is a foot?* New York: Dell Yearling.

National Council of Teachers of Mathematics. (2000). *Principles and standards for school mathematics.* Reston, VA: NCTM.

National Research Council. (2001). *Adding it up: Helping children learn mathematics.* Kilpatrick, Jeremy, Swafford, Jane, Findell, & Bradford (Eds.). Washington, DC: National Academy Press.

Reynolds, A., & Wheatley, G. H. (1996). Elementary students' construction and coordination of units in an area setting. *Journal for Research in Mathematics Education, 27*(5), 564–581.

Stenmark, J. K., Thompson, V., & Cossey, R. (1986). *Family math.* Berkeley, CA: Lawrence Hall of Science.

How We Learn about
Measurement

Understanding Relevant Learning Theory

In this chapter, we discuss the nature of early experiences and study how the van Hiele theory can help us to develop measurement knowledge. We also focus on ways in which K–8 teachers can make careful use of this information to plan lessons that help students construct their own geometry knowledge.

Comparing and Ordering

Early experiences need to begin with suggesting simple situations as being deep, tall, small, short, long, and so on, as well as directly comparing two (or more) objects. "We can help young children recognize attributes through [our] conversations with them by saying things like 'That's a *deep* hole,' 'Let's put the toys in the *large* box,' or 'That is a *long* piece of rope'" (NCTM, 2000, p. 103). Comments like these help students to focus on important characteristics and notice the idea of size in general. We need students to understand what it means for something to be *long* before we can encourage them to find out exactly *how long*. One important strategy for getting children to step toward comparisons with measuring is to require tasks that obligate students to find out a length of something when a physically direct comparison is impossible (Kamii & Clark, 1997; McClain et al., 1999).

Transitivity

After students see order relationships between pairs of objects and recognize a need to order two objects, they can develop transitivity thinking. Transitivity extends thinking to include the ordering of three (or more) objects. For students to develop knowledge about transitivity, they must be asked pointed questions about comparing objects. Questions might include asking students to compare a baseball to a softball and to a soccer ball and then providing an opportunity for discussion about the relative sizes. Eventually, students should be asked to compare sizes of known objects to sizes of objects that they cannot manipulate. Transitivity is students' ability to first compare two objects, then use only one of those objects in comparison to a third object for the purpose of making a statement about the relationship between this third object and the unused first object. For example, if Ryan is taller than Jamal and Jamal is taller than Min, can we make any statement about Ryan and Min? When we can, we are using transitivity. We do caution that transitivity is not learned simply by being told or shown how to use a ruler. In fact, according to Kamii and colleagues (1997, 2003) for children who do not think in this way, rulers are absolutely useless.

Mixing Units

Before children acquire full measurement knowledge, they often mix units, seemingly unaware of the importance of maintaining the use of one standard unit (e.g., Lehrer et al., 1999; Reynolds & Wheatley, 1996). In the previous chapter we alluded to the fact that sometimes children collect inches together with centimeters if it makes the object being measured coincide with the end of a whole unit. Figure 9.1 illustrates an inappropriate mixing of units. The student who mixed the units might suggest that the length of the board is 16 units. In this case, the student is aware of the idea of coverage (no gaps) but not consciously aware of the need for equal-sized units or perhaps even that the size of the unit matters at all. Iteration is incorporated into the measuring device, so we do not know for certain how the student was thinking about it. She or he is probably aware that the board has a length. When students become aware of how to use different kinds of units for the same object being measured, they are less likely to mix them.

Figure 9 . 1

Mixing Units

We showed a group of fifth graders a huge basketball shoe and said, "We showed this shoe to some other students and asked them how big they thought it would be. We got some interesting answers: '15 or 16,' '34 or 35,' and 'about $\frac{1}{2}$.'" What could they have been thinking about?

> ***Min:*** I think 16 is for U.S.A. and 35 is Europe. I don't know what $\frac{1}{2}$ is.
> ***Lydia:*** Maybe they were thinking about shoe size for the 16, length for the 35 and volume for the $\frac{1}{2}$, since one shoe fits in half of the shoe's box.
> ***Ryan:*** They were thinking about centimeters, inches, and then yards.
> ***Jamal:*** I think they used different sides of the ruler. One side is centimeters, and the other is inches. Maybe they got the $\frac{1}{2}$ wrong, because I can't think what that shoe is half of.

These experienced students recognize that different kinds of units should not be mixed. When they switched between units, they remeasured. This is a sophisticated understanding of the differences in the different kinds of units.

Visualizing

Outhred and Mitchelmore (2000) suggest that visualizing the shape to be measured is a critical first step in learning to measure effectively. That probably goes without saying but points to the importance of using contexts and making a connection to the van Hiele theory of geometry learning. You will recall from Chapter 3 that the first level of thinking, according to the van Hiele theory (Fuys et al., 1988), involves visualizing the object. By this, we mean that students make some sort of mental match between the object and something else they are thinking about. But this time, the way in which the students interact with the object in question (rather than to make statements about the general shape) will be in terms of making statements related to the relative size of (or sizes within) the shape itself. They are busy making comparisons and ordering the shapes visually.

Recall that students mentally compare shapes in their heads when confronted with a new shape, to determine whether or not the new shape is a square. But with the development of transitivity (the cognitive process), students additionally regard the shape in their thoughts with regard to its size. This eventually grows into having a little standard unit in their heads and a visual image of the new shape and of covering the new shape with that unit (using iteration and conservation). Or they might just use that comparison to say, "It's bigger" or "It's smaller." In any event, these comparisons are a foundation of measurement.

MIDDLE SCHOOL CONNECTIONS

Measurements from the Real World

Much of middle school geometry involves spatial thinking about and measuring plane figures.

Adolescent learners are expected to have already experienced the spatial thinking process of abstracting planar figures from solid objects described in Chapter 2. To ground measurement instruction about these kinds of ideas within meaningful tasks, questions first need real-world (solid) relevance. Using mental imagery such as skiing, grocery store aisles, train or subway tracks, and streets on a city block provides realistic examples of parallel lines. What might happen if the subway tracks were not exactly parallel? They would eventually intersect, and a train traveling along those tracks would grind to a halt or fall off the tracks. What can be said about the angles at the point of intersection? Are those angles important? You might remember the property that vertical angles have equal measurements, which occur at these points of intersection.

Other specific examples from the learners' unique worlds, such as hallways in a familiar building or nearby streets that are not parallel, provide grounding for discussions about nonparallel lines cut by a transversal. When nonparallel lines are cut by a transversal, Euclid's fifth postulate becomes more relevant. Euclid described the measurement of the angles on the same side of the transversal as being important indicators of whether or not the two lines being cut are parallel. If the sum of the two angles on the *same side of the transversal* is 180 degrees, then the two lines are parallel. Otherwise, the two lines will intersect. High school geometry flows forward from the ramifications of this postulate. Constructing seemingly parallel lines (such as subway tracks in the real world) with a transversal (such as a cross street) and measuring the newly created angles tells us whether or not those lines are parallel. Just because learners have reached adolescence does not reduce their need for real-world relevance. In fact, during adolescence, learners come upon a "need to affect the outer world" (George et al., 1998, p. 20). Problems like this help to meet that need while simultaneously providing opportunities for learning about measurement.

Using van Hiele

As students are more able to think about relative sizes of shapes, they might say, "Oh, those two shapes look like they are the same size." Do you recognize this as a level 0 answer? By the time students reach van Hiele's second level (level 1), they might say, "It has four 90-degree angles, the angles are the same size, it has four equal sides." Here they have begun adding measurement pieces to their mental information about shapes (in this case a square). They analyze, recognizing measurements as properties of the shape. Then, at that third level (level 2), they begin to use measurement information to make informal deductions about the shape. "Oh, it has four equal-length sides, so it is a rhombus. Because I know one angle on this rhombus is 90 degrees, the other three angles will *have to be* 90 degrees. Aha! It is a square." You should notice three different informal deductions in that series of statements.

As another example, imagine a group of students presented with a rectangle that has been subdivided into two triangles by drawing in a diagonal. What will students know about the measure of the area of the triangle? What about the measure of the sides of the triangle? If they base their answer on appearance, they are thinking at the first level (level 0). If they base their measurement on folding to check for congruence or even measuring to check for congruence, they are thinking at the second level (level 1). And if they make informal deductive statements about the triangle's area being half of the rectangle's area because the two created triangles are congruent (and therefore exactly half of the rectangle). Then they are reasoning at the third level (level 2). We are certain that your experiences with the van Hiele theory of geometric thinking explored in Chapter 3 will have been sufficient for you to fold these measurement components into your understanding of the theory. In Activity 9.1 (p. 160), create a "looks like, sounds like" table for two different situations that are related to measurement. Then in Activity 9.2 (p. 161), continue this exploration with a specific case related to finding the area of a triangle on a geoboard.

Using the Geoboard

The geoboard can be useful in measuring area of polygons. After building a shape, think about how to find the area of the shape. For shapes that contain only 90-degree (or multiples of 90-degrees) vertices, simply cut the shape up into squares and count them. For shapes that have non-90-degree vertices, more creative strategies are needed. It can be helpful to partition angled shapes into right triangles. From these triangles, think about them as being "half" of some rectangle. Then find the area of the angled shape by calculating half of the rectangle's area. Figure 9.2 gives a general overview for finding area on geoboards.

Phases of Learning

Lehrer, Jenkins, and Osana (1998) describe the generally prevailing attitude that the use of the van Hiele's theory for teaching measurement requires recognition that there is much folding back and forth between the levels. For measurement, the levels are not separated by clear lines. With that in mind, we revisit our use of the van Hiele

Figure 9 . 2

An Overview of How to Find Area on Geoboards

Shape with an area of 6 square units.

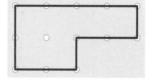

Shape with an area of ½ square unit.

Shape with an area of 1 square unit (It is half of a 2 square unit rectangle.)

Shape with an area of 2 square units. (It can be partitioned into two triangles. Each of the triangles is exactly half of a 2 square unit rectangle.) Sometimes it is helpful to shade in the two triangles with different colors.

Activity 9 . 1

APPLYING VAN HIELE

Figure A: $m \angle 1 + m \angle 3 = 180$

Figure B: WX ∥ YZ, and the pentagon is regular.

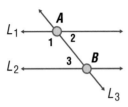

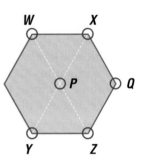

Child Level	Looks Like	Sounds Like
	In Figure A, angle 2 and angle 3 are of equal measure	
0	Stares at the two angles and turns the paper upside down.	"They look the same, even though one is backwards."
1		
2		
	In Figure A, L_1 and L_2 are parallel	
0		
1		
2		"Since angle 1 and angle 3 add up to 180°, I know L_1 and L_2 are parallel, because of a definition of parallel lines."
	In Figure B, triangles WXP and ZYP are congruent.	
0		
1	Cuts out the two triangles and compares them.	
2		
	In Figure B, segment XQ is parallel to WZ.	
0		
1		
2		

When completing "sounds like" answers for level 2, recall that students first make a statement that they believe to be known and then draw a conclusion. For the purposes of your table, remember to decide what known information might be before deciding what a child might conclude.

TEACHING

theory in this chapter and extend it to describe a way to understand how learners develop geometry knowledge associated with measurement. In particular, we study five phases of learning interpreted by Crowley (1987) built on the foundation of the van Hiele theory. These phases can guide the planning of

Activity 9 . 2

UNDERSTANDING VAN HIELE ON THE GEOBOARD

Find the area of triangle *ABC*.

– – – – – – – – – –

Find the area of rectangle *ABCD*.

– – – – – – – – – –

Heavily sketch in and find the areas
of triangles *AEF* and *CGF*.

– – – – – – – – – –

Assume that the two triangles (AEF and CGF) are being viewed and discussed
by three different children, one at each of the first three van Hiele levels.

Each child has declared that the two triangles are congruent (although the van
Hiele level 0 child may not have used that word).

Give an example of reasoning that might be offered by each child for this
congruence.

0 _____

_____

1 _____

_____

2 _____

_____

instruction for measurement. Practicing teachers recognize that using phases
of instruction as a strategy for planning instruction takes a bit of time and that
lesson plans must change from year to year, depending on the unique students
in the class. But the rewards are tremendous. Remember too that these phases
are stated generally and that they are not intended to be completely disjoint,
nor can you associate phase 1 with day 1, phase 2 with day 2, and so on. A single day's lesson might cover all five phases, or the five phases might be spread
out over several days.

Phase 1: Inquiry/Information

This phase is best thought of as a pre-lesson-planning phase, but it begins with
interaction with the learners. So it is not something teachers look up elsewhere.
Teachers ask students what they know, use the van Hiele theory to understand
their answers, then move the rest of the lesson forward from there. Because
students have informal notions of sharing and measuring, these make good
starting points for planning instruction (National Research Council, 2001). To
develop the other phases of the lesson, teachers gently explore each of the basic concepts required for success in the lesson by asking open-ended questions
related to those concepts, such as "Which of these books is bigger?" followed
by "How do you know?" The goal is to find out what the students know and
think about measurement. Asking visual questions and using good vocabulary

get students to notice measurement ideas to be studied, and teachers start to get an idea of how the measurement lessons are probably going to go.

Phase 2: Directed Orientation

At this stage, students get a good idea of where mathematics lessons are heading. The teacher has made or selected activities based on what was discovered in phase 1, making certain that all of the activities capitalize on the learners' knowledge and meet district expectations for that grade level. During this phase, students complete several short, probably one-step, tasks that are carefully sequenced. Students do a lot of *trying things out*. Not all students will be in the same place, and it is critical to the success of these lessons that the teacher knows what his or her students know. It almost sounds as though teachers write their own textbooks doesn't it? It is important to sequence activities so that the unique students in the classroom can gradually develop conceptual understanding. For instance, for the concept of standard unit, a teacher might provide several "funny rulers," some marked off into smaller units than others. Then students would be allowed to select rulers and measure a collection of objects. (See Lehrer et al. [1998] for a similar task.) When the students' measurements do not agree, the next phase comes into play.

Phase 3: Explication

In this phase, students discuss and describe their work. Building concepts on their previous experiences, students learn to describe things the way they want to describe them using their own opinions. Students make the observations; they don't receive lectures from the teacher. Here, the teachers' interactive role in the classroom environment might appear minimal to an outside observer, but it is carefully planned. During this phase, students express their findings and discuss with one another (and the teacher) their thoughts about their findings from those one-step activities. In the case of the funny rulers, students would talk about why their measurements from the previous activity do not agree with one another. Some students might need extra help understanding why there is a problem with having a range of measurements for the same object. The teacher's job is primarily to interject mathematically appropriate language and guide the discussion, offering guidance from time to time.

You might note that phase 2 and phase 3 usually happen concurrently. Teachers' conversations with students, correcting vocabulary, and checking for progress (phase 3) are happening as a result of engagement in the activities selected for phase 2.

Phase 4: Free Orientation

Here, students encounter slightly more complex, multistep tasks either in cooperative groups, pairs, or individually. These in-depth tasks often take open form. The goal is for students to begin to put collections of concepts together or to create and refine their knowledge of a concept by coordinating several of the one-step activities described previously. For instance, students might be asked to compare the measure of two objects that they cannot compare directly (e.g., a bolted-down lunch table and a bulletin board). They determine that they will have to use some sort of intermediate measuring device. They work on solidifying how they think about things like this and find their own ways of resolving the issues.

Pairs of students might be given two different equally spaced rulers and a funny ruler and be asked to design a quilt block for a class quilt. As students work on their quilt blocks, they should begin to see not only that the funny rulers are problematic, but also that if the quilt blocks are to be pieced together, everyone needs to have used the same equally spaced ruler. So they might decide on a classroom measurement device, agreeing to use a tape measure. They are now overtly aware that they are measuring, whereas in phase 2, they might not have been as explicitly aware, especially given the nature of a ruler's cloaked concepts. On agreement to use a classroom-approved measuring device, students are on the precipice of the next phase.

Phase 5: Integration

Now students are ready to make general statements. They can pause for a minute and think about what they are going to do before they do it; they know exactly what they need to get to complete the task. Before whole group sharing of thinking, it is important to structure time into the lesson for students to privately reflect on their work. The teacher can then facilitate classroom discussion so that students know they are to give general statements. They can summarize their thoughts in ways that indicate the development of concepts or the development of connections among concepts.

Ms. Hawthorne Measures a Bus

As an example of these phases of instruction, Ms. Hawthorne shared a measurement lesson that she completed with her first grade children after reading about a similar lesson (Hendry, 1996). She situated her initial lesson within a lesson about going to a zoo, because the class was preparing for a field trip to the local zoo. Before class, Ms. Hawthorne recreated the outline of a bus on the floor with masking tape. The lesson opened with the hasty arrival of Akoya (a classmate) on a mission from the principal, who was trying to reserve a schoolbus. He needed to know the measurement of the bus before reserving the buses. "Well, what do we know about measurement?" Ms. Hawthorne asked. Silence greeted her. Knowing that moments were ticking away did not bother her, for she knew that silence is essential thinking time. Ms. Hawthorne waited. Eventually, a few hands were raised with initial suggestions (phase 1). Tyler shared that he had recently been fitted for a suit (for his brother's wedding) and that he was four feet tall. So Ms. Hawthorne's question became "How many times can Tyler fit in the bus?" (phase 2). They measured how many times Tyler would fit. (He repeatedly lay down inside the bus outline, head to toe.) The children discussed their measurement of 7 and decided to tell the principal (phase 3). At this point, Ms. Hawthorne recognized that the children did not really understand the idea of "feet." They merely understood that Tyler had been measured and had decided to use him because he apparently had some sort of measuring quality. So she redirected them to find a way to communicate the bus's measurement to the principal without sending Tyler to the office (phase 4). Eventually, once again through a period of several carefully planned and sequenced lessons, students decided to use a standard unit, the actual foot-length of Akoya (the original messenger), since the principal apparently knew Akoya. Finally, they measured Akoya's foot using a ruler to understand the actual dimensions (28 feet long) of the real-life bus (phase 5).

Finding Angle Measure

To further illustrate the five phases, we ask you to answer the following questions: What do you know about measuring angles? What does it mean for an angle to be bigger than a different angle? How could you describe the size of an angle? What do you know about the angles in a triangle? We are confident that you visualized angles, thinking about how they might compare to a familiar angle, such as a right angle. We are also confident that you commented about the standard unit of degrees and described how to use a protractor. You should have remembered that a triangle's angle sum is 180 degrees. However, we move now to phase 2 and ask you to complete a small task. We deny you the use of a protractor and ask you to find the measure of each angle of a regular pentagon as described in Activity 9.3.

Activity 9 . 3

FINDING ANGLE MEASUREMENTS WITHOUT A PROTRACTOR

Find the angle measure of each angle in the following pentagon.

You may not use a protractor. If you choose, you may use the pentablock shapes.

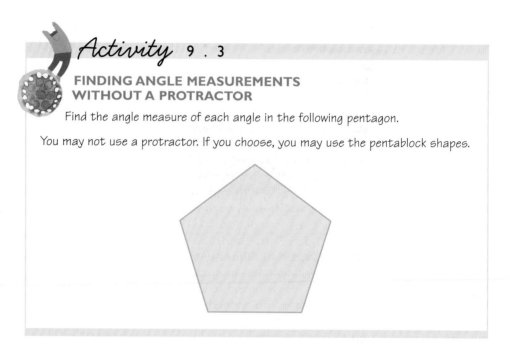

As you discussed your progress and thought about clarifying your vocabulary, we assume that the discussion of the activity you just completed brings us to phase 4. So now we ask you to complete a larger task (Activity 9.4). From a set of pentablocks, find the measure of each angle on each block. Then for phase 5, we will ask you to use the work you completed to search for a general statement you might be able to make about the angle sum of any polygon. Be prepared to discuss your ideas with other members of the class.

You coordinated several concepts as you experienced the five phases of instruction. Were you surprised that you could find the exact measure of each interior angle of the shape without a protractor? We believe that this activity helps you to understand the phases of instruction. Notice how we built the activity on your knowledge about the 180-degree angle sum of triangles and made sure you could handle the task of finding the pentagon's angle measures.

Using Measuring Devices

This activity also serves to help you visualize angle measurement as an accumulation of openness of an angle and clarifies your thinking about the cloaked concepts packed into typical measuring devices. Without the protractor, you still had to think about the idea of one degree (standard unit) of openness immediately after another degree (iteration and coverage), and you had to think about the point of origin. You had to think about these things without the aid of the protractor, which would have made the determination of angle measurement a cinch.

Activity 9 . 4

FINDING MORE ANGLE MEASURES

After finding each angle of the pentagon, find the angle measure of each of the rest of the shapes in the pentablock set. You may not use a protractor. If you choose, you may use the pentablock shapes.

Name each shape according to its number of sides.

Create a general statement about the relationship between the number of sides of a polygon and the angle sum inside the polygon.

Tools that help us measure are measurement devices. The list includes rulers, grids, thermometers, and protractors. Measurement devices embody many concepts of measuring. It is possible to arrive at a correct answer without really understanding the concepts and the procedures associated with that measurement. If used too early, procedures can result in isolated knowledge in the way formulas can become isolated bits of information if the student has not understood the ideas and connected them to other known information. So the phases of instruction can guide us to ensure that students develop the requisite conceptual knowledge before we place a measuring device in their hands.

USING RELEVANT PATTERNS:
Formulas, Skip-Counting, and Similarity

Because measurement is heavily related to number ideas assigning numerical amounts to spaces, this section demonstrates more fully the role that number patterning can play in the learning and teaching of measurement. To explore information related to patterning, we consider three different kinds of relevant patterns and discuss the role each can play in the development of measurement knowledge: (1) using a sequence of numerical measurements to develop a general formula for a class of shapes, (2) using skip-counting in the process of measuring (counting either standard or nonstandard units), and (3) examining patterns in ratios of corresponding parts of similar shapes to make general statements about that class of shapes.

Developing General Formulas

In Chapter 7, you learned how to turn a numerical pattern into a general formula that could be used to determine any term in the pattern on the basis of that term's location in the pattern. You also learned to recognize triangular and square numbers. We generally developed those formulas on the basis of the areas of the shapes of the terms in the pattern. You probably recognize having used concepts and procedures: visualizing the image of the shape, iterating within the shape, using a standard unit, and so on. In Activity 9.5, practice using these ideas to develop a formula for triangular-shaped areas.

Using Skip-Counting

It is common for students to use skip-counting strategies to shorten the process of counting a figure's measure. That is, they move away from literally stacking single, discrete units next to an object that needs to be measured. Here, we peek in on a group of second grade children who are discussing how to count the measure of a classroom window. Before the window-measuring activity and after much debate and work, the children decided to glue paper clips to paper strips (5 paper clips per strip) as their mobile measuring device. They then were charged with the goal of using these clip-strips to measure various objects in the room. Listen to the children explain how they knew the paper clip size of one of their classroom windows (23 clips long) after using their clip-strips:

> *Victoria:* I counted on the clip-strips and counted five clips at a time—five, ten, fifteen, twenty, . . . Then I counted each clip [on her next clip-strip]—one, two, three, ... Twenty-three.
>
> *Sydney:* I knew two strips was 10, so I counted by 10 as long as I could—ten, twenty, ... But the window stuck out past the second strip. I put another strip down and counted one, two, three clips on the strip. Twenty-three.
>
> *Macy:* I counted the strips—five, ten, fifteen, twenty, twenty-five, ... [Macy folded her clip-strip so that it continued up the side of the window frame.] But that was two too many, so I counted back—twenty-four, twenty-three.

SOMETHING MORE ABOUT TRIANGULAR NUMBERS

Study the pattern visually.

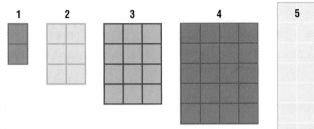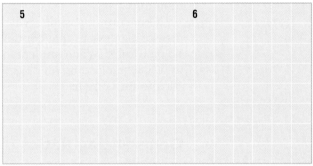

1. On the basis of how the pictures look, describe the pattern according to the shape of each term.
2. Extend the pattern by drawing the fifth and sixth pictures. (Pay attention to area.)
3. Write out the pattern of numerical values that would be associated with the areas of the first five shapes. ____, ____, ____, ____, ____, . . .
4. Extend the pattern numerically for at least four more terms: ____, ____, ____, ____.
5. On the basis of the way the numbers change, describe how the pattern is changing from term to term.
6. Write a general formula for the area of the pattern, using symbolic algebra.
7. Mentally set the original pattern on top of this one (or trace it lightly), term by term, and explain a
   (a) shape relationship between the two patterns
   (b) numerical relationship (in terms of area) between the two patterns
   (c) resulting formula relationship between the two patterns

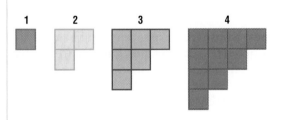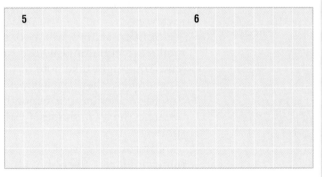

8. Sketch in a parallelogram that makes the three relationships from #7 hold for the following set of triangles.

   A.

Dustin: I counted by fives also, but I got twenty-five. Five, ten, fifteen, twenty, twenty-five.

Note that Dustin did not seem concerned with the fact that the window length was less than the fifth clip-strip. He exhibits an example of early efforts to make sense of measurement but without mental tools related to part-whole thinking.

Skip-counting skills will be useful once students move to continuous measuring devices that contain more than one unit, such as the clip-strip or a 12-inch ruler. When students use rulers, they should be encouraged to count by 12s when finding an object's length in inches, or by 3s when using a yard-stick to measure feet.

Generalizing Ratios of Similar Shapes

As you complete Activity 9.6, think carefully about the relationships that appear between side lengths. Find a relevant pattern from analyzing this collection of shapes.

When you completed the activity, you compared measurements of the sides of the various shapes. You probably recognized that there was a numerical relationship between corresponding sides of shapes when compared to another set of corresponding sides. Are you surprised that although you were sorting and classifying shapes, when you were predicting enlargement values, you were also doing basic trigonometry? You probably noticed that shapes with the same letter designator sort of looked the same, no matter who drew the shape. As you compared your shapes to your colleagues' shapes, can you remember specifically on what parts of each shape you visually focused in order to sort and classify the shapes? Did you make some measurements? Did you eventually draw the conclusion that when the shapes were enlargements of the same original, they had equal ratios of (corresponding) side lengths? As you answer these questions, you might match your answers to van Hiele levels of thinking as a quick review.

Similar shapes are two shapes whose corresponding angle measurements are equal and whose ratios of corresponding side lengths are equivalent. You might take note of the deduction that if two shapes have corresponding angles, then the shapes have the same number of sides. Very often, this idea of equal corresponding angle measure is known as "same shape," because the two shapes (with congruent corresponding angles) "look" the same.

Interestingly, we do not care about the actual lengths of the sides to determine similarity. Even though the *ratio* lengths of pairs of corresponding sides will be equivalent, this does not imply that the side *lengths* themselves are congruent, only that the ratios of side lengths are equivalent. If the additional property of equal corresponding side lengths is present, we then have *congruent* shapes. Therefore, congruence is merely a special case for similarity, with no enlargement (or reduction.)

Did you notice we used three different terms in talking about equivalence? How did we describe two ratios that were "the same"? We used *equivalent.* How did we describe two shapes that were "the same"? *Congruence* is the word to use in talking about two shapes. How should the word *equal* be used? *Equal* is used only in talking about numerical amounts. Recall that measurements are numerical amounts.

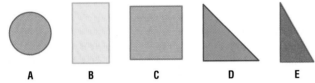

MAKING PHOTOCOPIES

You are one of five new employees at Photocopies Incorporated. Your boss has handed each of you five shapes and has asked you to make a photocopy of each one. He intends to collect them immediately after lunch.

Original shapes

| A | B | C | D | E |

When you are finished making copies, you notice that the photocopying equipment has been permanently set on the "enlarge" setting. However, the display is broken. You do not know exactly how much larger the copied shape is than the original shape. Spin the spinner, and record that value: _____

This is your enlargement factor.

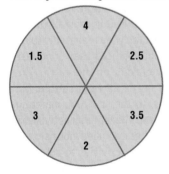

Draw new pictures to show the size of your copies after you photocopied at the enlargement factor. After you are finished, meet with your colleagues and exchange drawings.

1. Find a mathematical strategy for determining your colleague's spinner value.

2. Describe that strategy.

3. Next, measure all three sides of the enlarged shape E that you and your friends made. Fill in the chart.

Name	Base	Height	Slant	Base ÷ Height	Base ÷ Slant	Height ÷ Slant

4. Find a pattern that you could associate with the numbers in the chart.

5. Your boss also used the photocopy machine. His shape E had a height measuring 4.5 inches.
There is a contest: If you can predict the length of his base, you get a raise!

CULTURAL CONNECTIONS

Measuring Time and Visualizing Congruence

In this section, we will describe two cultural connections. First, we discuss the Hopi way of understanding and marking the passage of time. Second, we look at quilting as a way to understand and measure congruence.

The Ancient Hopi Calendar

The Hopi are one of the Pueblo peoples who, for centuries dating well before the time of Columbus, made their home on the mesas in northeastern Arizona in North America. They lived in the community but traveled from their homes to farm their carefully nurtured desert fields. (Past tense is used throughout this description to base the discussion in ancient calendar-watching strategies. This is not meant to imply Hopi culture is not presently vibrant, or that the ceremonies described in this section are in any way defunct.) Successfully growing crops in an inhospitable desert climate severely depended on a balance of moisture. Respecting rain was an integral part of Hopi culture. This aspect of ancient Hopi history and knowledge was one of the mores passed down through oral tradition.

Such storytelling kept history alive during the Soyal celebration. Those who gathered for the sacred stories listened intently as Hopi historians used corporeal words to weave together stories with the spiritual atmosphere. In particular, they repeatedly told the timeless story about Hopi emergence into the Americas and credited their long-lasting existence as a result of having been chosen as the caretakers of the earth. This solemn responsibility that so depended on rainfall impacted nearly all Hopi culture. Cultural activities ranged from the material, planting corn seeds, to the spiritual, maintaining relationships with Katsinas, the spirit beings who guided them. The material activities requested the earth to provide nourishment. The spiritual activities provided nourishment for the earth. Naturally, it was of paramount importance for these activities to coincide with the natural rhythms and seasons of the earth. To further celebrate their role as nurturers of the earth, the Hopi constructed a framework of cultural festivals and celebrations to enfold the hard work of tending the earth. Certain agricultural activities corresponded with certain festivals and celebrations.

Agricultural activities such as planting and cultivating had to be carefully timed, to coincide with the earth's nourishments and needs. "Determination of the last freeze coincident with the vernal equinox is essential to crop survival" (Autrey & Autrey, 1981, p. 96). Planting beans or corn at the right time in the cycle, neither too soon nor too late, was predicated on appropriately forecasting the solar year (winter solstice to winter solstice). Embedding the earth's rhythms in their cultural calendar reminded them of upcoming events. But how did the Hopi elders schedule the community calendar? They matched celebrations and festivals with specific moons, each of which had a specific name (see Table 9.1). As those specific moons appeared, the ancient Hopi knew which ceremony and thus which planting, tending, and harvesting activities had arrived. "Every ceremony is associated with a moon and every moon with a ceremony" (Ellis, 1975, p. 65). In other words, the moons marked time.

There was a Waiting Moon (it is not yet time to plant corn, beans, and squash) and a Planting Moon. The (autumn) Kelmuya season ceremony was always scheduled with the Sparrow-Hawk Moon. In the Kelmuya ceremony, "singing is loud and deep and echoes the drumbeats, which are prayers for long and pleasant life for all mankind, moisture in the form of snow and rain, and a bountiful harvest of nourishing crops" (Secakuku, 1995, p. 6). Kelmuya prepared the Hopi for the next moon, Sacred Moon, which brought the ever-important winter solstice ceremony, Soyal.

Activities of the Soyal ceremony included the storytelling noted earlier. But it was also important because it set in motion the first scheduled event in the yearly cycle of caretaking. During this ceremony, the Hopi persuaded the sun to begin to lengthen and raise

Table 9.1 **Hopi Celebration Calendar**

"The Hopi think of the moons of their calendar as being in a continuous succession which we can best picture as a moving chain encircling a wheel, the upper half of which represents our world and the lower half the underworld" (Ellis, 1975, p. 69).

MOONS	CELEBRATIONS/EVENTS
Sparrow-Hawk Moon (This moon is immediately prior to the moon during which the winter solstice occurs)	• Kelmuya Ceremony • Make new fire • Leads up to winter solstice ceremony
Soyal, winter solstice ceremony when Katsinas appear	
Sacred (or Respected) Moon (Moon during which winter solstice must occur)	• Lengthy winter solstice ceremony • First Katsina appears
Play Moon Joyful Moon	• Gaming and entertainment (Weather is too cold to work outside.) • Social dances are held • Secretly planted beans and corn are brought to heated area for sprouts
Purification Moon	• First initiation period for youths • More katsinas appear to ensure fertility of soil • Preplanting ceremony • Present bean and corn sprouts • Plant more seeds, nurture in heated area • Young children receive Katsina dolls
Whispering Wind Moon	• Plant early corn, so Katsinas will have it for the harvest celebration (much later)
Windbreaks for Small Plants Moon	• Seeds are prepared for planting
Waiting Moon	• Planting of non-corn begins
Planting Moon	• Corn planting begins
Fledgling Raptor Moon (Moon during which summer solstice occurs)	• Planting ceases • Prepare for Niman ceremony
• Niman ceremony, katsinas travel "home" (held shortly after the summer solstice)	
Homedance Moon Moisture Moon	• Rains begin • Snake/Antelope or Flute ceremonies
Big Feast Moon Moon of Plenty	• Smoke meeting of one of the women's societies followed by dancing • Buffalo Dance • Butterfly Dance
Harvest Moon	• Harvest Basket Dance
Corn Husking Moon (If needed—some references do not include this moon.)	• Burden basket is carried

These moon names were compiled from a variety of references: Sekakuku (1995), Wright & Roat (1965), Ellis (1975), James (2000), and the official web site of the Hopi: www.hopi.nsn.us/pages/calendar/Hopi_5.htm.

its path across the sky, slowly relieving the earth of those short, dark, but necessary, winter days (James, 2000). Soyal is also the first time since the preceding summer solstice ceremony that a Katsina returned from the spirit world to walk among the Hopi people. "Katsina dance events combine responsibility with pleasure because of the grave commission to provide moisture for the whole world" (Kealiinohomoku, 1989, p. 58). For ceremonial purposes, selected Hopi people dressed like the spiritual Katsinas to symbolically represent

Activity 9 . 7

UNDERSTANDING HOPI MOON CYCLES

There are three kinds of time measurement we will discuss.

A. **Moon phase.** To run from new moon to (just before) the next new moon requires 29.5 days.

B. **Solar year.** The earth travels around the sun approximately every 365.25 days (winter solstice to winter solstice).

C. **Seasons.** Seasons divide the solar year into four parts, marked by:

Spring equinox ("Light" and "night" are exactly equal in length.)

Summer solstice ("Light" is longest.)

Fall equinox ("Light" and "night" are exactly equal in length.)

Winter solstice ("Night" is longest.)

1. Complete the chart to record the moons and the solar years (use days). Locate the next three winter solstices (in addition to the first one indicated on the chart).

2. Decide when to use the Corn Husking Moon. Ancient farmers generally depended on the winter or summer solstice to determine and plan for upcoming planting seasons. The Hopi year is set by the winter solstice. For purposes of cultural celebrations (related to planting), the winter solstice happens during the Respected Moon.

3. How might this affect the celebrations that typically would accompany the plans for the upcoming growing season?

4. Explain each of the following general concepts of measurement through the eyes of a Hopi celestial body watcher who is responsible for measuring time.

   a. Continuous (beginning to end)
   b. Standard unit
   c. Size (i.e., comparison)
   d. Iteration
   e. Tiling
   f. Part-whole
   g. Origin (where is "zero"?)

Moon	Sparrow-Hawk Moon	Sacred Moon	Play Moon	Purify Moon	Whisper Wind Moon	Windbreaks Moon	Waiting Moon	Planting Moon	Fledgling Raptor Moon	Moisture Moon	Big Feast Moon	Harvest Moon	Corn Husking Moon
Days	29.5	59	88.5	118									Not needed yet

Assume that the first winter solstice happens here, and find three subsequent winter solstices (365.25 days).

Moon	Sparrow-Hawk Moon	Sacred Moon	Play Moon	Purify Moon	Whisper Wind Moon	Windbreaks Moon	Waiting Moon	Planting Moon	Fledgling Raptor Moon	Moisture Moon	Big Feast Moon	Harvest Moon	Corn Husking Moon
Days													

Moon	Sparrow-Hawk Moon	Sacred Moon	Play Moon	Purify Moon	Whisper Wind Moon	Windbreaks Moon	Waiting Moon	Planting Moon	Fledgling Raptor Moon	Moisture Moon	Big Feast Moon	Harvest Moon	Corn Husking Moon
Days													

Moon	Sparrow-Hawk Moon	Sacred Moon	Play Moon	Purify Moon	Whisper Wind Moon	Windbreaks Moon	Waiting Moon	Planting Moon	Fledgling Raptor Moon	Moisture Moon	Big Feast Moon	Harvest Moon	Corn Husking Moon
Days													

the spiritual beings and to perform ritual singing, dancing, and interactions with the people. Just as moons corresponded with ceremonies and agricultural activities fit one or more ceremonies, Katsinas matched with specific ceremonies and dances. So measuring with moons not only had to precisely match the earth's rhythms but also had to match the correct Katsina. Hosting the correct ceremony and thus interaction with the correct Katsinas signaled the correct agricultural activity for successful harvest and tending of the land.

With so much riding on the timing of the Soyal celebration, and with time being measured in moons, it was imperative and a somewhat delicate project to correctly match the moon to the ceremony. At first, it is tempting to think that keeping track of moons and reciting them in order would suffice. However, when the ancient celestial body watchers compared sun movement (solar year) to the moons, they found a small problem. The 365.25 day solar year (winter solstice to winter solstice) is not neatly divisible by the 29.5 day lunar cycle (new moon to new moon.) There is a remainder of around 10 days making a solar year (365.25 days) approximately 10 days longer than 12 iterations (354.9 days) of the moon. Simply counting out 12 moons would have eventually influenced the point in time of moons, like Planting Moon. Within only 3 years, an extra 30 days would occur, which encompassed an entire moon iteration. We can see how quickly tiling the moon unit fell out of synch with the solar year and forced some sort of reconciliation of the part-whole concept. A solar year ends part way through the 13th moon. So, approximately every 4 years, the moons had to be realigned. At that time, a 13th tiling of the moon unit could be fully completed before the height of the sun's path across the skyline alerted the celestial body watchers to conduct Sparrow-Hawk festivities. Think about how this visualization matches the concepts of iteration and coverage. You will learn in Activity 9.7 (pp. 172–173) that adjustments to the calendar were necessary from time to time. You should begin to appreciate the dexterous manner in which the Hopi dealt with the complexities of marking time.

Time is just one of the things we measure. We also measure space. In particular, we are often concerned with situations in which two items take up the same amount of space and tend to be extremely interested in things that take up the same amount of space in exactly the same way: congruence. Anything that needs to be mass-produced probably has some sort of expectation of congruence. Here, you will read about Elizabeth Meyer and how quilting affected the way in which she came to know congruence.

The Scrap Bag

Elizabeth Meyer and her children walked from Pennsylvania to Kansas in 1866 with two other families. They left Pennsylvania to stake a claim in the newly opened Kansas Territory. Elizabeth decided to move because she had lost her husband, Samuel, to wounds he received in the battle of Gettysburg during the Civil War. It seemed like a good idea to move to Kansas, where she could start anew with her children.

One day, while camped at a farm along the trail, Elizabeth traded an Ocean Waves quilt block pattern she had learned in Pennsylvania to the farmer's wife for some much-needed butter. Her quilt block was currency, as important as a silver dollar. It was not uncommon to trade quilt blocks. Quilts played an important role in keeping families warm and in developing friendships. A sense of camaraderie emerged among these pioneering women in the process of moving West. During the journey, Elizabeth and other women with whom she walked worked on quilting projects whenever they could. Quilting was a relief from the difficulties of the walk and provided useful goods. The evening quilting circle was a social event. During these sessions, pioneer women traded recipes, talked of dreams, and comforted one another during times of trial (Stratton, 1981). Elizabeth's daughter Louise and her traveling friends' daughters were molded into pioneer women becoming aware of the mores and codes of this group.

The importance of making congruent quilt blocks cannot be overstated. A typical quilt block is square. Imagine what would happen if that square were measured incorrectly. The quilt would not look *right* in the end, and pioneer women took great pride in designing and stitching appealing quilts. So it was important that girls learned about measurement and congruence. They had to "get an eye" for congruent shapes and be able to measure shapes to ensure congruence. They had to sew straight stitches so that the blocks remained straight even after the quilt blocks themselves were deemed to have been congruent. Incorrectly sewn stitches could pull a quarter inch off a block. If that error was repeated several times (across a row of quilt blocks), the final quilt could be off by several inches on the other side, which is quite noticeable to the eye. The women knew how to visualize the whole quilt after it was stitched.

It was an exciting challenge to them when someone saw a new quilt block but perhaps had not been able to measure it. They might have viewed the whole quilt for only a moment and had to decide where the quilt block was within the larger quilt. (That is, they had to think about how the pieces had been sewn together to make the entire quilt.) It was not unusual to catch glimpses of blocks from other families walking along the trail. Blocks from New Jersey, Connecticut, or Maryland were prized among these Pennsylvania women. Evening sharing sessions were often dedicated to describing those new quilt blocks and trying to decide the measurements within those blocks.

As you complete Activity 9.8, think about Elizabeth's experiences with evening quilting, and consider how her mathematical understanding of congruence was related to those

Activity 9 . 8

LOUISE'S QUILT BLOCK

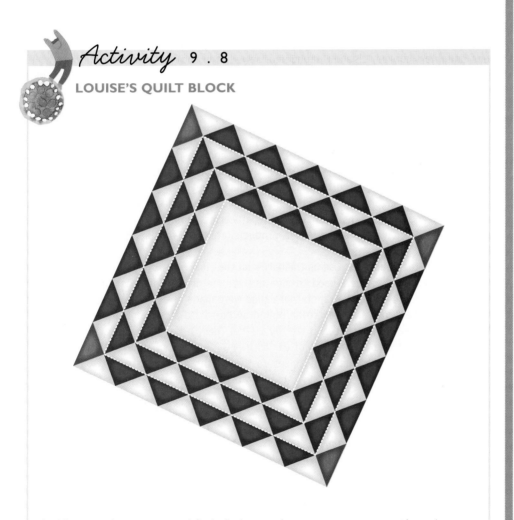

1. Measure the picture, and find all shapes that are congruent to the red corner triangle.
2. Find all congruent shapes within the block as well as sets of shapes that together are congruent. For instance, if you take a blue triangle and a white triangle together, they make a parallelogram. Depending on which ones you join and in what configuration, the parallelogram might even be a square.

cultural experiences. Today, we would use the word *congruence* to describe the shapes in the blocks. What words do you suppose these women used?

Now listen to Brenda DeGeeter explain her new awareness of measurement, after she explored her heritage on a small family farm.

Measuring Bushels

The general notion of farming has changed drastically in the way it has been practiced from the late nineteenth century and now in the twenty-first century. Most farms are quite large, some comprising thousands of acres. Farming practices have changed over time owing to innovations in technology and equipment. Early farmers cultivated with an ox; today, farmers have specially designed equipment for cultivating.

My family is part of a larger culture common to the Midwest: the family farm. My great grandparents established family farms after arriving from Belgium, Luxembourg, and Germany in the mid-1800s. They worked on existing farms while saving enough money to buy their own land. On these farms, the whole family worked together to accomplish what needed to be done. Each family member was responsible for a specific function of the farm. Any one family member's failure to complete his or her tasks resulted in a problem with success of crops and/or livestock. Crops included corn, soybeans, wheat, and oats. Livestock included horses, beef cattle, milk cows, hogs, and chickens. Usually, mothers and daughters cooked, cleaned, laundered, sewed, and took care of small children while fathers and sons tended fields and livestock. Some people might worry that these roles are sexist. But in the culture of farming, they are simply the responsibilities needed to be completed. Rest assured that I drove the tractor and fed the hogs and my brothers peeled potatoes plenty of times!

Most family farms were near small towns so that families could congregate for social needs or expert services such as schooling, church, entertainment, and blacksmithing. Farms of the nineteenth and early twentieth centuries were almost entirely self-sufficient, using many of the products they raised. Leftover products were sold in town for a profit. Sometimes farmers bought products they had chosen not to raise or could not raise, such as staple groceries (flour, sugar, crackers), textiles, or furniture. (Today, of course, most products are sold for profit rather than used personally.)

Farmers (then and now) use mathematics all the time. For example, grain is measured in bushels per acre. Farmers used to measure volume of corn or other grain literally in bushel baskets, which in my grandfather's time were made of galvanized metal. He would throw the baskets into a wagon to be pulled by horses to storage or market. The inside of the wagon measured 3 feet by 3 feet by 10 feet (deep). He knew that when the wagon was full, it would hold 36 bushels of ear corn or 72 bushels of shelled corn. If the last wagon did not get filled, he would measure the depth and calculate the volume of the corn in the wagon. Then he used a proportion to figure bushels in the partially filled wagon. It was important to know the number of bushels because farmers needed to recite their yield to know how much corn they harvested, and they needed to make sure they were paid correctly.

Today farmers have equipment, such as combines, to pick and shell the corn. This is much faster and less labor intensive. Augers transport grain from the combine to the wagon. The elevators in town have large scales to weigh the wagon and corn. The elevators then elevate the corn to a storage unit. Once the wagon is empty, it is reweighed (without the corn) to determine the actual amount of corn sold. So measurement has changed from volume to weight.

As you explore your own culture and listen to your classmates' impassioned descriptions of their backgrounds, you will likely continue your growth in understanding of how to celebrate culture through mathematics lessons.

USING TEACHING AIDS APPROPRIATELY:
Measuring Devices and Discrete Manipulatives

In this section, we distinguish between tools that are real-world artifacts (measuring devices) that students will be expected to use and manipulatives that could be used during the process of developing measurement knowledge. At the risk of redundancy, we again mention the difference between materials that are discrete and those that are continuous. In measurement lessons, this distinction is important because what we have is a moment in time when students need to be conscious and aware of this difference to disconnect discrete materials and connect continuous materials to a continuous idea (measurement). Students can *use* a discrete item to measure, but they must be using the item consciously aware of the idea they are not merely *counting out* discrete items. Rather, they must recognize the discrete item has a measure itself, going *from one end to the other end*.

Students can use measuring devices to measure consciously aware of the continuous nature of measurement. Imagine Dustin, a second grade student who placed a *transparent inch grid* over a region made of seven square inches (see Figure 9.3). Dustin recognized that the region matched with seven small grid sections and said so. Did he really understand? Has he counted the square inches, or has he recognized measurement as the amount of space covered by the object? Is he thinking about seven as a collection of iterated tiles? Movement from discrete counting to recognizing measurement as a continuous entity is a large step. The well-designed grid (or ruler) may have allowed him to arrive at an answer without thinking about the concept of

Figure 9 . 3

Dustin Uses a Transparent Grid to Measure Area

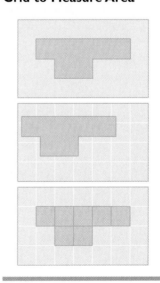

CLASSROOM CONNECTIONS

Using Literature to Pose Different Problems

In *Counting on Frank* (Clement, 1991), a boy is constantly trying to figure things out, such as how long a line he can draw with a pen. The title refers to the boy's dog, Frank. The boy wonders how many Franks would be able to fit into his bedroom. He thinks about his growth compared to that of a tree, figuring that if he grew six feet per year, he would now be 50 feet tall. I showed the book to a group of fifth graders and asked, "Do you think the author was thinking about geometry, algebra, measurement, number sense (adding, etc.), or probability?" My students had not considered this question before. We reread the book to remind them of the stories in the book. Soon Jonathan raised his hand and said, "Measurement."

I posed a new problem: "How many steps would an average fifth grader take to get from the door at one end of our hall to the other?" (My classroom is located near the center of a long hallway.) They thought about it for a few minutes. Listen to my students' responses:

Min: Measure one step. Measure the hallway. Divide the step length into the hallway length.

Ryan: Take the average step and see how many tiles (hallway tiles) it takes, then count the tiles to find out how many steps.

Lydia: Count the number of yards in the hallway, then how many steps in a yard. Multiply.

Jamal: You could measure the hall in feet. Then ask some kid to walk a normal step, then measure how far that one step is. Then see for example if you were a kid and a normal step for you would be about a foot and a half. Then you would see how many of your footsteps it would take in about a 50-foot hallway.

These were all reasonable ideas, and the students wanted to test them. NCTM (2000) talks about how "by sharing strategies, students can compare and evaluate different approaches" (p. 174). So we lined up on both sides of the hallway and looked from one door to the other. After discussion of actual classrooms, space for another corridor, the computer lab, and so on, the students agreed that the hall was about $7\frac{1}{2}$ classrooms long. We came back into our room. I asked how they could use that information and our classroom to discover the answer without actually measuring. Again, Jonathan volunteered: "Well, someone could find out how many steps it would take to walk from one end of our room to the other and multiply that by 7."

Hands were flying up. All agreed that was a great idea, and *all* volunteered to do the walking. Early in the year, I ask each student to write his or her name on a tongue depressor, which I keep in a tin. I drew out the ones for CJ, Tanner, and Michael. After they agreed that it took the average fifth grader 14 steps to walk across our classroom, we figured that it would take about 98 steps to walk the hallway. Again we lined the hallway and quietly counted as the three began their walk from the far end. When they reached our classroom, I asked whether anyone wanted to adjust their answer. Several thought that we were perhaps a little more than halfway, so they lowered the number to 94 steps. It turned out to be 88 steps.

It was a fun problem. As we processed our thinking, we discussed the problem-solving strategy of making a big problem smaller. You might know the strategy as "Solve a simpler problem."

NCTM CURRICULUM

measurement. And you know, there is only one way to find out. We listen carefully to Dustin as he explains his thinking in order to assess what he knows. "I saw the shape take up the same space as the seven squares on the grid." (This figure is also involved in Homework Problem 1.)

As teachers, we need to think cautiously about what Lehrer and colleagues (1998) and McClain and colleagues (1999) called the "transparent" nature of rulers. Rulers have been developed to be the best way to measure length. In the hands of children, this well-designed piece of technology can hide many of the concepts the students should use when they measure. Instead, students can achieve correct answers without being cognizant of the automatic nuances going on within the ruler's design. We can fall under the illusion that our students are measuring with full concept knowledge when they might be doing

CLASSROOM CONNECTIONS

Using Literature That Already Describes Problems

Before I began reading *Spaghetti and Meatballs for All!* (Burns, 1997), I brought an empty desk to the front of the room. I asked the students how many of them could be seated around the desk if each person was entitled to a full side. Of course, the answer was four. I gave each student eight square tiles. I asked how many people could be seated around the eight tiles or tables. "Thirty-two," was the answer given.

This is a wonderful story about Mr. and Mrs. Comfort, who invite many friends and relatives for spaghetti and meatballs. Mrs. Comfort rents eight tables so that their 32 guests can be seated. Of course, not all the guests arrive at the same time, so the tables are constantly being rearranged in one long rectangle to accommodate varying groups. As I read, I had the students keep track of the changes. We kept pushing tiles together to find solutions for the chart.

They had no trouble filling out the chart. When I asked them to predict how many could be seated at 45 tables arranged in a *really* long rectangle, it was not so easy. After a few minutes, Lydia said, "92." When I asked her how she knew, she said, "You just multiply 45 by 2 and add 2." Someone asked where the "add 2" came from. Lydia came up to the board and drew a diagram, saying, "I added two for the people at the end. Two always sit across from each other, then there is one more person at each end." She went on to explain that any number of tables in this arrangement could be known by "$n \times 2 + 2$." Our class had come up with a similar formula (e.g., the geese problem) during an earlier math unit; this book gave us an opportunity to revisit that concept.

Of course, in the end, all of Mr. and Mrs. Comfort's guests are back at the eight original tables set by Mrs. Comfort.

I left the class with the following problem: *All 22 of you are planning to eat together. How could you arrange tables so that you could all sit together?* How would you solve this problem?

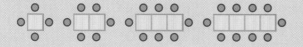

nothing more than identifying a number they notice on the measuring device. The following features of a measuring device can lead to this situation:

It automatically iterates.
It automatically covers.
The whole-parts are already marked off.
It has already been appointed a standard unit.
The zero point is identified.
All units are equal-sized.

Types of Concrete Materials

Square Tiles and Cubes

Discrete manipulatives are typically tiled on a region and then counted to identify the measurement of that region. We have repeatedly noted how critical it is for students to come to understand that they are not counting the (discrete) blocks. Rather, they are using the blocks to measure the (continuous) accumulation of space taken up by the blocks. In other words, students have to coordinate and structure the materials so that they *consciously* measure space of the region in question, not *unintentionally* count the blocks. When children use these materials, we listen carefully to their answers, mindful to hear clues relative to how they are thinking about their numerical answers. We are ever cautious, knowing that discrete teaching aids can seemingly require students to make sense of and measure the space intended but keeping in mind that it is possible to use the materials to obtain the right numerical answer without really measuring.

That said, these materials definitely have useful aspects. They indeed give a visual image of the iterations, of the nature of coverage, and of the general shape of the standard unit. It is important for students to have these visual images for measurement, and these materials can help. Complete Activity 9.9. As you listen to classmates explain differences in thinking between finding perimeter and finding area, pay particular attention to any trends in descriptions of strategies for area and for perimeter.

Activity 9.9

USING DISCRETE MATERIALS TO MEASURE

Use a set of five square tiles. Create as many configurations as possible following these rules:

1. Each configuration uses all five tiles
2. In each configuration, sides must be aligned with one another.
3. Configurations cannot be joined only at a corner.

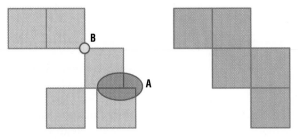

This configuration is illegal. Area A violates #2. Point B violates #3.

This configuration is legal. All of the rules are followed.

Draw a sketch of all legal configurations. Find the perimeter of each configuration and the area of each configuration. Compare these amounts.

Be prepared to explain the difference in thinking between finding the perimeter and finding the area.

In that activity, the area was always 5. Did you count blocks or think about the amount of space a tile took? To find perimeter, a variety of strategies probably emerged. Some people may have mentally walked around or physically pointed to each side of the drawing. As you think about this activity, you should begin to appreciate the difference between walking around and pointing to sides. Which is continuous and which is discrete?

This activity exemplifies how square tiles can make area easy to find, because the coverage concept is cloaked in how nicely they tile (i.e., fit together.) We have a situation in which students can arrive at a correct answer with a manipulative (square tiles), but because the manipulative is discrete and thinking needs to be continuous (because measurement is continuous), that step is a big step. Students cannot necessarily make that step automatically (Othred & Mitchelmore, 2000).

Geoboards

Geoboards are designed to help students build plane shapes quickly and are useful for discussing area. Geoboards are partitioned into unmovable squares, with pegs at each corner. Students can be directed to build shapes with particular areas and to compare the shapes. Caution should be exercised in finding perimeters, because diagonals require the Pythagorean theorem to calculate lengths.

By now, you are probably not surprised to learn that students will not spontaneously model measurement situations using objects in the way that we intend or in ways that actually models measurement. Rather, students will probably use objects as best they can. So it is critical that we demonstrate how we intend the manipulatives to be used (Lehrer & Schauble, 2000). This can be achieved by calling out specific ways in which we use teaching aids.

LET'S REVIEW

To understand how we learn measurement requires forging a connection between how we learn number and how we learn geometry. The van Hiele theory grounded the way we understood the manner in which children interact with physical items from a geometric point of view. Kamii's work described in Chapter 6 provides awareness of the manner in which children impose a numerical quantity on sets of objects from their environments. Both of these theorists cast light on the complexity of how children come to an understanding about size. Because early kinds of knowledge rely on visual awareness, comparing and ordering items by how they look are key first tasks. Eventually, the important notion of transitivity incorporates many of the underlying concepts, but learning experiences must begin with the notion of size (e.g., deeper, taller, smaller, shorter, longer). As children learn to coordinate concepts, they often compare the size of the object in question to the size of a standard unit. It is imperative that children learn to think of the standard unit as going "from here to there" rather than as a discrete element in a set. That is, the difference between continuous and discrete knowledge is illuminated in studying measurement because the process of learning will flow from discrete items, such as square tiles, to pictorial, continuous representation, such as a transparent grid. In the end, students should be able to use typical measuring devices (e.g., rulers) to determine the size of an object.

HOMEWORK

1. Imagine a situation in which two young children are measuring the area of a shape. One child has set a transparent grid on top of the shape, and the other child has set several square tiles on top of the shape. Explain the difference between continuous and discrete by using this context.
2. List some specific questions you could ask to get the second student listed in Problem 1 to move to the idea of accumulation of space, not accumulation of parts.

3. Locate a primary (K–2), an intermediate (3–5), and a middle (6–8) textbook, and study the measurement sections. Do these lessons follow the phases of instruction approach? (Submit photocopies of the lessons.) Cite examples to support your claim.

4. Cut out the given shapes from Activity 9.6. Slide these shapes around on the shapes you and your colleagues drew. What do you notice about the fit of the corresponding angles of your drawn shape to your boss's given shapes?

SUGGESTED READINGS

Aber, L. W. (2001). *Carrie measures up.* (Illustrated by Joy Allen.) New York: The Kane Press.

James, S. E. (2000). Some aspects of the Aztec religion in the Hopi kachina cult. *Journal of the Southwest, 42,* 897–926.

Kidder, F. R., & Lamb, C. E. (1981). Conservation of length: An invariant—a study and a follow up. *Journal for Research in Mathematics Education, 12*(3), 225–230.

Krauskopf, K. B., & Beiser A. (2000). *The physical universe.* Boston: McGraw Hill.

Lehrer, R., Jaslow, L., & Curtis, C. L. (2003). Developing an understanding of measurement in the elementary grades. In D. H. Clements & G. Bright (Eds.), *Learning and teaching measurement: NCTM 2003 yearbook* (pp. 100–121). Reston, VA: NCTM.

Schifter, D. (1996). *What's happening in mathematics class?* New York: Teachers College Press.

Spaulding, N. E., & Namowitz, S. N. (2003). *Earth science.* Evanston, IL: McDougal Littell.

Thompson, L., & Joseph, A. (1944). *The Hopi way.* Chicago: University of Chicago Press.

Young, S. L., & O'Leary, R. (2002). Creating numerical scales for measuring tools. *Teaching Children Mathematics, 8*(7), 400–405.

REFERENCES

Bruchac, J., & London, J. (1992). *Thirteen moons on Turtle's back.* Illustrated by T. Locker. New York: Scholastic.

Burns, M. (1997). *Spaghetti and meatballs for all!: A mathematical story.* (Illustrated by D. Tilley.) New York: Scholastic.

Clement, R. (1991). *Counting on Frank.* Milwaukee, WI: Gareth Stevens.

Crowley, M. L. (1987). The van Hiele model of the development of geometric thought. In M. M. Lindquist (Ed.), *Learning and teaching geometry K–12: 1987 yearbook of the National Council of Teachers of Mathematics* (pp. 1–16). Reston, VA: NCTM.

Ellis, F. H. (1975). Pueblo sun-moon-star calendar. In A. F. Aveni (Ed.), *Archaeoastronomy in Pre-Columbian America* (pp. 59–87). Austin, TX: University of Texas Press.

Fuys, D., Geddes, D., & Tischler, R. (1988). The van Hiele model of thinking in geometry among adolescents. Journal for Research in Mathematics Education Monograph #3. Reston, VA: NCTM.

George, P., Lawrence, G., & Bushnell, D. (1998). *Handbook for middle school teaching.* New York: Longman.

Hendry, A. (1996). Math in the social studies curriculum. In D. Schifter (Ed.), *What's happening in mathematics class?* (pp. 9–13). New York: Teachers College Press.

Hubalek, L. K. (1995). *Trail of thread: A woman's westward journey.* Lindsbor, KS: Butterfield Books.

James, S. E. (2000). Some aspects of the Aztec religion in the Hopi Kachina cult, *Journal of the Southwest, 42*(4), 897–926.

Kamii, C., & Clark, F. B. (1997). Measurement of length: The need for a better approach to teaching. *School Science and Mathematics, 97*(3), 116–121,

Kamii, C., & Long, K. (2003). The measurement of time: Transitivity, unit iteration, and conservation of speed. In D. H. Clements & G. Bright (Eds.), *Learning and teaching measurement: NCTM 2003 yearbook* (pp. 169–180). Reston, VA: NCTM.

Lehrer, R., Jacobson, C., Kemeny, V., & Strom, D. (1999). Building on children's intuitions to develop mathematical understanding of space. In E. Fennema & T. A. Romberg (Eds.), *Mathematics classrooms that promote understanding* (pp. 63–87). Mahwah, NJ: Lawrence Erlbaum.

Lehrer, R., Jenkins, M., & Osana, H. (1998). Longitudinal study of children's reasoning about space and geometry. In R. Lehrer & D. Chazan (Eds.), *Designing learning environments for developing understanding of geometry and space* (pp. 137–168). Mahwah, NJ: Lawrence Erlbaum.

Lehrer, R., & Schauble, L. (2000). Developing model-based reasoning in mathematics and science. *Journal of Applied Developmental Psychology, 21*(1), 39–48.

McClain, K., Cobb, P., Gravemeijer, K., & Estes, B. (1999). Developing Mathematical Reasoning within the Context of Measurement. In L. V. Stiff & F. R. Curcio (Eds.), *Developing mathematical reasoning in grades K–12.* Reston, VA: NCTM.

National Council of Teachers of Mathematics. (2000). *Principles and Standards for School Mathematics.* Reston, VA: NCTM.

National Research Council. (2001). *Adding it up: Helping children learn mathematics.* In Kilpatrick, J., Swafford, J., & Findell, B. (Eds.), *Mathematics Learning Study Committee, Center for Education, Division of Behavioral and Social Sciences and Education.* Washington, DC: National Academy Press.

Outhred, L. M., & Mitchelmore, M. C. (2000). Young children's intuitive understanding of rectangular area measurement. *Journal for Research in Mathematics Education, 31*(2), 144–167.

Reynolds, A., & Wheatley, G. H. (1996). Elementary students' construction and coordination of units in an area setting. *Journal for Research in Mathematics Education, 27*(5), 564–581.

Secakuku, A. H. (1995). *Following the sun and moon: Hopi kachina tradition.* Flagstaff, AZ: Northland.

Stratton, J. L. (1981). *Pioneer women: Voices from the Kansas frontier.* New York: Simon & Schuster.

Waters, F. (1963). *Book of the Hopi.* New York: Penguin Books.

Wright, B., & Roat, E. (1965). *This is a Hopi Kachina.* Flagstaff, AZ: Museum of Northern Arizona.

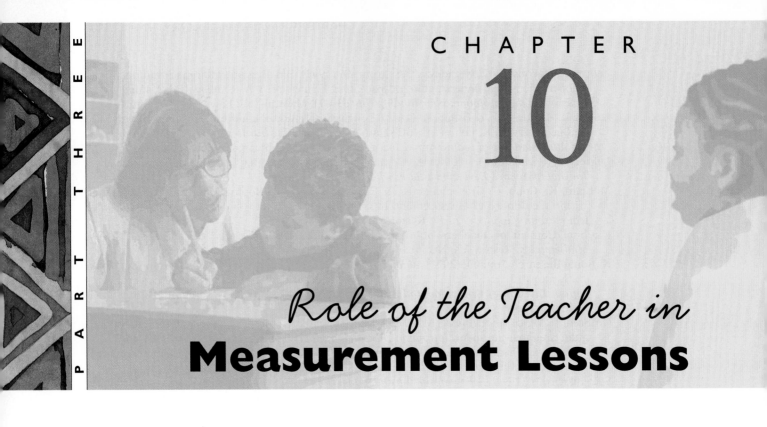

CHAPTER
10

Role of the Teacher in
Measurement Lessons

ANALYZING ONE OF THE TEACHING MODELS:
Presentation and
Partnered Work

You are probably familiar with the presentation lesson plan in which the goal is to acquire, assimilate, and retain informational or procedural knowledge. Here, the teacher provides information to the students and directs students to somehow practice using the information, typically in an independent practice fashion. You have probably already surmised that this type of plan typically follows one or more concept attainment lessons, because procedural and informational knowledge should be layered with concept knowledge. The van Hiele phases of instruction build knowledge on existing informal knowledge before guiding students to use new concepts and procedures. Presentation lessons are opportunities for teachers to demonstrate those skills, give lectures, show examples of procedures, model strategies, give classifications of various bits of information, and outline, magnify, or draw attention to specific information. We like to connect presentation lessons with group discussion and group work.

Sometimes a good way to get students involved in a presentation lesson is to engage them in tasks that are larger than one day's objective. In that way, the presentation lesson is part of a larger set of lessons. The overall task should focus on a learning objective, which should match expectations from your district. Once specific content has been decided, the task can be designed. Sometimes students can help design tasks, drawing ideas from their own interests. As always, though, the teacher keeps the students' readiness level in mind. Tasks may include portions completed independently, portions requiring adult (parent or teacher) help, and still other portions utilizing peers' help.

MIDDLE SCHOOL CONNECTIONS

Writing Their Own Problems

Middle school students arrive having acquired several years of experiences measuring a diverse set of phenomena, finding volume and temperature, using the metric system, measuring both plane and solid shapes, or comparing sizes of shapes (as in similarity). One good way to have students communicate their conceptual understandings about measurement is to ask them to write their own problems. When we read their problems, we garner a rich store of knowledge about what they believe are important aspects of applications using measurement. Did they clearly communicate measurement objectives? Did they include too much information? Did they select appropriate units? Were they aware of the compatibility of units selected? We can use this information to guide our lesson selection and development.

But more than that, adolescents are often excited to solve their classmates' problems. When they hear a real dilemma from a classmate, the motivation to solve the problem is raised. This also communicates to the students that we value their life experiences. As students traverse the terrain of adolescence, they enjoy sharing stories of their own design and knowing that we value their uniqueness. Additionally, in a middle school, we might team with the language arts teacher to coordinate problem-posing assignments to match with certain grammar lessons or to use stories being read in class. In much the way that Karen used *Counting on Frank*, middle school students can put older characters with whom they are familiar into measurement-based problem situations.

HIGHLIGHTS OF A LESSON PLAN COMPONENT:
Acceleration versus Enrichment in Content Differentiation

Walk into any classroom, and you will find a diverse range of knowledge, interest, and excitement. To reach everyone, in addition to using a variety of behavior approaches (such as "standing up and getting the wiggles out"), we have to formulate academic plans that meet many needs. Sometimes we modify instruction for students who simply need extra time or students who have been identified by the school's special education director as needing special consideration. Other times, we modify instruction for students who have physical challenges requiring us to modify our plans. The special education director appreciates help in meeting students' needs. Sometimes you can modify tests and quizzes (assessment); other times, you can modify your entire instructional approach (instruction); still other times, you can modify the mathematics requirements (curriculum) for a student. Special education students should have specific requirements spelled out on their individual education plan (IEP), and you will have access to information in the IEP.

In this chapter, we explore strategies for content differentiation (curriculum-based) for high-ability students. First we keep in mind Tomlinson's (2001) caution that "advanced assignments tend to look more interesting to nearly everyone except the advanced learner, who may perceive it as more work" (p. 14). Enrichment, as a type of content differentiation, is a process that extends lessons laterally to delve into rich, deep knowledge related to the information. Deepening a lesson requires including extending the mathematics. Beisser (1997) summarized much of the literature dealing with content differentiation. We highlight four of her recommendations for varying assignments: (1) create tiered assignments, (2) compact the curriculum, (3) modify students' investigative roles, and (4) allow guided exploration.

In the previous section, we listened as Ms. Hawthorne encouraged first grade students to find some of the dimensions of a school bus. Clearly, this activity was not a test question but added an interesting enrichment to children's measurement experiences. We use this context to give example strategies to provide high-ability students with content differentiated learning.

Tiered Assignments

Tiered assignments provide one avenue for students to accelerate. Tiered assignments permit "varied levels of challenge to ensure the students explore ideas at a level that builds on their acquired knowledge and prompts continued growth" (Beisser, 1997, p. 338). This process extends a lesson upward to more abstract or complicated information. An accelerated lesson moves toward information that might be encountered in subsequent years. An example of this approach might be asking students to design a bus to carry exactly 24 students, one teacher, and a driver. Or students might be asked to determine the number of minivans needed to carry 24 students, one teacher, and a parent (in each) and ultimately to calculate the costs of each.

Compacted Curriculum

A compacted curriculum offers another way to differentiate. This process makes room for an extension of the content. High-ability students need to experience standards and benchmarks of their district's curriculum. However, they can likely accomplish that feat more quickly (or simultaneously). After assessing what advanced learners know, excuse them from that portion of the unit and make plans to spend the freed-up time. This process allows time for lessons to be extended through either acceleration or enrichment. Perhaps these students could tackle the minivan problem instead of designing a new bus.

Modifying Roles

To modify students' investigative roles, students might study information from a different point of view. They should still meet the mathematical objectives, but they may get there by studying the problem differently. If we wanted to design an "Akoya" ruler (see Chapter 9), how would that look? Why is a bus the length it is? Is there a reason those dimensions are preferred by auto designers? What sizes of metal pieces were used and why? How do bus designers actually measure a bus? What other kinds of measurements do they take? Were there any political ramifications for the size of a bus? Thus, students study measurement by looking at bus building through several investigative roles.

Guided Exploration

Guided exploration can take many forms, but in general it is completed independently *by the students* as a way to enhance their study. Perhaps they learn about bus building in the mid-1900s. What kinds and sizes of metal were used in different kinds of buses? How did sizes of larger buses (depending, possibly, on their roles) vary? Why did some companies always use a particular size or design? Do rock stars have specific design concerns related to buses compared to travelers? Perhaps students decide to design a differently sized bus. They might decide to compare relevant measurements of their bus to those of a flying bus that is on a space mission to colonize a planet. They might contrast strategies used to build today's buses with those used to build old-time stagecoaches or other transportation vehicles. Students might even develop

CLASSROOM CONNECTIONS
Dealing with High-Ability Students

"SICK!! . . . GROSS!"
"I'm bored."

These phrases are outlawed in my classroom. During science, we say, "Oh, how interesting!" During math, we say, "I'm finished, do you have something for me to do?" or "I'm finished, may I go to the challenge folder?" or "Now that I'm finished, may I work on my math project?" NCTM (2000) talks about providing equity. Equity means that all students receive education that "is responsive to their prior knowledge, intellectual strengths, and personal interests" (p. 13). As teachers, we all encounter students who fall into the category of extremely bright. What do we do with these students?

I have had many bright students during my career, but three truly gifted ones come to mind. Martin is a high school senior and recently earned a perfect score on the SAT exam. When our local newspaper asked him how he had managed this feat, he humbly answered, "It was mostly luck." I immediately gave him a call not only to congratulate him, but also to remind him, as his former fifth grade teacher, that it was not just luck.

Jayadev will have completed his Ph.D. in mathematics by the time he is 21 years old. He and his family left the United States for a year during Jayadev's sixth grade year. When they returned, he should have been ready to join his peers as a midyear seventh grader at our middle school. Instead, he enrolled as a college freshman.

Luke is a high school sophomore. He was and still is one of those rare well-rounded students. He is an athlete, a musician, popular, and extremely gifted in every academic area.

As I reflect on these boys, I am amazed that none of them was ever bored. Their peers recognized these boys as "smart." There was no jealousy—It was simply a fact. I was well aware of their gifts and knew that they were all far more gifted than I was when it came to math. It is important for a teacher to acknowledge this possibility. It is crucial that we not be intimidated. Rather, we should relish gifted students' brightness, which is exciting for a teacher. At the same time, we must ask ourselves how we can challenge them.

Early in the year, I met with their parents and discussed the mathematical talents of these students. I asked what experiences they had had and asked for input for their fifth grade year. I informed my building principal and our district math consultant. We all agreed that mastering our curriculum would probably be no problem for any of them. How could we best accelerate or enrich these students? All three of these students' parents were aware of our school's ongoing efforts to enrich gifted students' experiences.

I probably own one of the world's largest collections of supplemental mathematics materials. I kept buying them, certain that I would find exactly what was needed to help my gifted students. I found many worthwhile ideas and activities in these materials. I also contacted the mathematics education department at our local university and enlisted the help of interested graduate students. I had lots of materials and a lot of support. But I know that indeed I made the difference, not the materials alone.

speeches for political parties regarding measurement issues for the building and driving of school buses that would arise in the current climate.

SUGGESTIONS FOR ESTABLISHING DISCOURSE:
Importance of Sharing Thinking

How important is it for students to explain why they make the measuring decisions that they make? Recall the phases of instruction and the role student discussion plays in planning lessons. Hearing students share strategies helps in planning future lessons, but it also helps students to think carefully about the information. When students know that they are expected to share their knowledge, they usually double-check their understanding, verify their thinking, and clarify their wording.

CLASSROOM CONNECTIONS

Enriching a Gifted Student's Learning

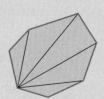

NCTM TEACHING

While Luke was my student, I was enrolled in a graduate geometry education class. Because all of the students in that course were teachers, our assignments included trying out assignments with our students so that we could study van Hiele's theory firsthand. I compacted the curriculum for Luke. While other students worked on regular mathematics assignments that Luke had already mastered, he and I sat at a table, where I showed him *my* geometry homework. He was challenged, and as I watched him work, I used the van Hiele theory to formulate my questions and guide him in his thinking. For example, "What would happen if . . ." or "Can you explain how you knew to do that?"

Then I got another idea. I would modify Luke's investigative role. I asked him to come to my graduate class with me (it was on a Saturday morning). He could become a college student for a day! He was excited, and his parents were pleased for this opportunity.

Luke amazed the teachers and the professor. As we worked on Activity 9.4 (see Chapter 9), Luke first tried to recall a formula he knew for finding the angle sum of a polygon. He showed the formula [$(n - 2) \cdot 180$] to one of the teachers, who expertly asked him how he knew that formula would work. He took another step and tried to verify it (a level 3 effort). Through his efforts to verify his formula, he clarified his thinking processes: "I can cut any polygon into triangles. The number of triangles will always be two less than the number of sides, because the first cut and the last cut will each take care of one extra side. Since each triangle has 180 degrees, the angle sum of the polygon will be 180 times the number of triangles I drew."

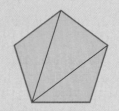

Luke wasn't finished! He gave himself his own tiered assignment: "Or I could find a point inside the polygon and draw out to each vertex, making the same number of triangles as sides. But then I have 360 degrees too much (the angles around the center), so I have to subtract off the 360 degrees. That formula, $n \cdot 180 - 360$, is really just the same as the other formula."

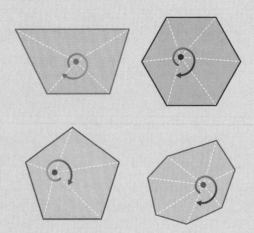

We can't take all students to a college classroom. I was fortunate in this case. But the point is to recognize opportunities to support students' learning. I do not deny opportunities for enrichment to any of my students. It is safe to say that every year I am amazed by the work of all of my students. Clearly, students perform to the level of expectation. As you read about Luke, keep in mind that this discussion addresses the needs of exceptional students—the ones who are smarter than the rest and often smarter than the teacher.

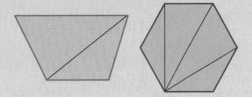

Understanding measurement requires communication. "Discourse builds students' conceptual and procedural knowledge of measurement and gives teachers valuable information for reporting progress and planning next steps" (NCTM, 2000, p. 103). Plain and simple interaction with the teacher and peers is critical. The teacher's reciprocal interactions must be carefully thought out and planned for students to develop the knowledge they need. This seems to play out in phase 3 (explication) of the instructional theory described earlier.

In phase 3, teachers provide guidance during students' discourse and efforts at communication.

It can be helpful to require students to explain their results and procedures to someone else. As in the case with Ms. Hawthorne's class, they had to communicate with the principal. This required recognition of a useful standard unit. If they had no standard unit when they communicated, it would not make sense to the person receiving the information. For another example, if Grandmother Elizabeth told Louise to make a quilt block that fit a certain quilt, Louise would need to know more about the quilt. Communicating about the size of a quilt block, they agreed on the standard unit being used. Louise usually preferred an eight-inch square. Students must come to understand the importance of an agreed-upon standard unit. Moreover, this should be replicated for all measurement concepts. Generally, appropriate and useful communication will not simply pop out of students' mouths in a linear string of sentences. We must listen for reasoning statements to tell us what students are thinking, so we know where to go next.

We asked a group of fifth grade students and a group of kindergarten children to solve a puddle problem (Westley, 1994) the day after a rainstorm that left puddles of water all around the playground. We asked, "How would you measure a puddle?"

Min: I would get a ruler and poke the zero end in the middle of the puddle. I would check where the water hit the ruler. That way, I would know the depth. I think I would probably use inches.

Lydia: I would put a meter stick from the farthest edge of the puddle (puddles are not squares, so you have to measure the longest part) and hold it flat across the top. If it didn't reach, I'd put a stick where it ended, pick up the meter stick, and begin again where the stick was. Hopefully, the puddle isn't bigger than that. Then I would add 100 to where the meter stick lined up with the other edge of the puddle. I would know its length.

Ryan: I would get a tape measure and hold it across the top to see its width. Then I would measure the other way, to see its height. I would multiply those two numbers to get its area. I know that number would be larger than the actual area, but it would be a good estimate.

Jamal: It seems like it might be impossible, since the puddle is an irregular shape. But I could scoop out all the water into a bucket and then pour the water into a graduated cylinder to see how many liters of water there was.

Listening to these fifth graders share their thinking, we know something about their conceptual and procedural knowledge. Min thinks about how to use the zero to check depth, and she thinks inches would be the best unit. Lydia understands iteration and coverage, since she describes what to do if the puddle is longer than a meter stick. Ryan is thinking about finding the surface area of puddle and recognizes that his procedure will result in a larger value. Jamal has doubts about measuring an irregularly shaped object but recognizes that he could measure volume using liters. Now we know more about what to ask next. Should students compare answers? Will they come to terms with the different ways (and reasons) to measure a puddle? Depending on why we need to know its measurement, we could rely on different units. Min would know how tall her rain boots should be. Lydia would know whether she could jump across it. Ryan would know how it compared to a piece of carpeting. Jamal would be able to collect it all in a jar.

We wondered how kindergarten children would think about this problem. What sorts of ideas did they have about measurement in such a unique situation? We were not surprised that most of the children said that they did not know how to measure a puddle. But a few students had some ideas about how to get started.

Beth: You'd just go around it.

Jewells: You'd use a ruler. [We pressed her for how she might do this, and she shrugged her shoulders.]

Amanda: You'd put the ruler next to it. [She demonstrated how she would set the ruler along one side of the puddle. We urged her to tell us what this would mean, and, like Jewells, she shrugged her shoulders.]

Hillary: [Stood up and showed us two things she could compare to the puddle.] The computer screen and the chair seat are both smaller, and the cupboard door is larger.

Clearly, Hillary is working on her transitivity skills, comparing the puddle to other objects that are familiar to her. However, she is not thinking about the need for a standard unit. Although Jewells recognizes something about the usefulness of a ruler, she does not really know how one works. Amanda demonstrates how to use a ruler but is unsure what to do after she sets the ruler next to the puddle. Beth is mostly concerned with navigating past the puddle, presumably because this resolves any dilemma about needing to know its size.

Go to "Try it! See it! Teach it!" on page 192.

TECHNOLOGY CONNECTIONS

Presenting Measurement Projects

NCTM TECHNOLOGY

Measurement topics provide an ideal content for students to present and communicate their mathematical adventures and approaches. Although students can make presentations and communicate approaches without digital technologies, these technologies offer new possibilities for using individual and group presentations as teaching and learning tools.

Digital video cameras and user-friendly editing capabilities now make it possible for students to record and share their approaches to solving measurement problems. The process of constructing and sharing the video can provide students with a strong motivation to clarify, organize, and justify their solution to a problem. For example, students working outdoors on a measurement challenge might share their approach with their peers, parents, or teachers. Videos depicting several groups of students' approaches to solving the same problem can be compared and discussed. A teacher in California carried out this kind of project-based activity in a sixth grade class working on triangles. The teacher asked groups of students to estimate the length of a ladder needed to reach the top of a flagpole, given the height of the flagpole and information about the shadow cast by the pole. Each set of students prepared a video describing their approach and solution to this challenge. Videos contained students' description of the processes as well as a record of the actual process. Student groups presented their videos and discussed similarities and differences in approaches to the challenge. Videos were then shared with sixth grade students in other locations on a project website, and online discussions among the sixth graders developed.

Digital video also provides the opportunity for students to evaluate their own explanations of problem solutions. Given the opportunity to view their own and others' productions, students can learn valuable lessons about clear communication of mathematical ideas.

Additional digital presentation tools can also help students to develop effective presentations that communicate mathematical ideas. Programs such as PowerPoint and HyperStudio allow students to integrate graphics, digital images and video, and text into their presentations. By using web sites, these digital presentations can be shared with learners and teachers around the country or around the world.

A few years ago, teachers correctly expressed concern that students producing multimedia presentations often spent an inordinate amount of time learning to use the presentation tools necessary for this work. As these tools have developed, however, the time required for learners (especially members of the "digital generation") to master these tools has decreased dramatically.

In his book entitled *Project-Based Learning: Using Information Technology*, David Moursund (2003) makes a strong case for using digital approaches in the creation and sharing of student projects and provides specific approaches for teachers.

CLASSROOM CONNECTIONS
Sharing a Good Plan for Solving a Problem

Earlier, I told you about Luke. That situation was a unique experience. So what do I do on a daily basis to challenge all my students? NCTM (2000) tells us how "procedural and conceptual understanding can be developed through problem solving, reasoning and argumentation" (p. 21). So my students keep a record of their problem solutions in math journals. After I look through their journals, I return them and ask certain students to share their strategies on a transparency. (Students are not forced to do this—it is always a choice.) I do this for several reasons. As I look through their journals, I can see who needs enrichment activities and who might benefit from more exposure to similar problems in order to grasp a concept. Most students love the opportunity to share on the overhead. In addition, I hope that some students will benefit from hearing about more advanced strategies than the one they used.

When answers are incorrect but strategies are still sound, I take the opportunity to talk about the importance of having a good *plan*. A good plan could have led to a correct solution, but something—probably something small—tripped the student. (Before I asked her to share an incorrect solution on a transparency, I asked for permission. I would never want a student to be embarrassed in front of her classmates.)

NcTm LEARNING

NcTm ASSESSMENT

IDEAS FOR STRUCTURING CLASS TIME:
Student Presentations and Assessment of the Presentation

Presentations do not always have to be made by the teacher. Students can give presentations about mathematics. If student presentations are to be somewhat formal, we should be certain to provide a clear explanation about the expected quality and give examples of presentations. Because we develop each unique student's knowledge (concepts and procedures) by carefully building on the knowledge and thinking of each student, there will be diversity in the level of mathematics in any given student presentation. Effectively designing lessons taking into account and building on students' unique knowledge can be based on projects that allow students to demonstrate knowledge growth. These projects can be designed to positively reflect diversity that will surely accompany any classroom. Tomlinson (2001) cautions that asking all students to present projects to the whole class may be "unduly time consuming—and even uninspiring, unless you've taught students how to be high-quality presenters" (p. 88). She recommends using exhibit booths, individual explanations to one or two adults, or even small-group (four or so students) presentations among classmates. In addition, such differentiation for product submission may meet unique needs of students in other ways, with respect to comfort level, interest, and expertise.

ADVICE FOR PROFESSIONAL DEVELOPMENT:
Any Activity You Choose Should Match Your District Goals

Not only does measurement bridge the concepts of *discrete* and *continuous*, it bridges geometry and number. So we have a lot of things

Try it! See it! Teach it!

Sharing a Good Plan

Step **One**: Try it!

Do the Math...

Eight people are going camping for three days and will carry their own water. They know that 12.5 liters are needed for five people for one day. Based on that information, what is the minimum amount of water the eight campers should carry in all? Explain your answer.

Step **Two**: See it!

Watch the Video...

Karen's fifth graders are trying to solve the problem above. Knowing more about the problem will help you make sense of the students' conversations about their strategies. The focus of this video is on sharing plans for solving the problem, not only sharing the answer. Please have your plan and solution ready before watching the video.

Things to Watch for...

- Get a sense of the importance of emphasizing "the plan" among students.
- Analyze the incorrect answer from James. What was he thinking at first?
- Recognize the steps that lead to students summarizing with their solutions (Phase 5 of the Phases of Instruction process).

Video Clip 5 *(time length: 5:10)*

Karen and James at the overhead.

Tanner at the overhead explaining his answer.

Step **Three**: Teach it!

Reflect on Your Own Teaching...

1. How did the familiarity with the metric system impact this solution? At what phase of instruction do you suppose Karen assured herself that her students knew about liters? How do you suppose she found out?

_____

_____

_____

2. What makes a problem-solving plan "good"? Look at the three solutions following question 4. Which plans are good? Which plans lead to incorrect solutions?

_____

_____

_____

3. How should you deal with incorrect solutions that come from good plans?

_____

_____

_____

4. What kinds of things did James say that demonstrate correct knowledge about measurement?

_____

_____

_____

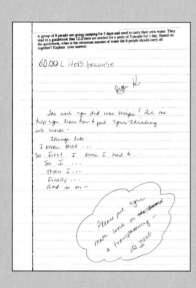

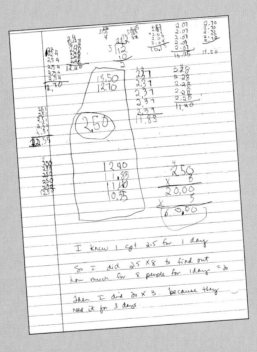

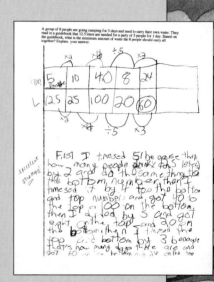

A Comment from Karen

When answers are incorrect, but strategies are still sound, I take the opportunity to talk about the importance of having a good *plan*. A good plan could have led to a correct solution, but something, probably small, tripped the student.

I remember a friend telling me she was amazed to see her daughter using an efficient, but unexpected, strategy for finding a percentage. When she questioned her daughter, the answer was, "Oh, Jason shared that the other day and it makes way more sense to figure it out that way." I like it when parents begin to understand that just because when they were young and shown *the* way to solve a problem, that this meant only the answer was considered, not the thinking.

GO BACK TO PAGE 190

MIDDLE SCHOOL CONNECTIONS

Have Fun and Create Wonder

NCTM TEACHING

Do you remember your favorite middle school teacher? He or she probably didn't lose control of the class in terms of behavior. But probably more than that, your teacher somehow knew how to have fun even in the midst of 25 fervent adolescents. The middle school years can be trying times (for adults *and* students) because students feel so physically and socially awkward. They appreciate it when we enjoy them, finding a way to strike balance between requiring adult behavior and sensing their need for us to endure silly moments. We can be fun-loving *and* let them know that we comprehend them and their awkwardness. When we wave our hands enthusiastically while describing some measurement idea and the chalk inadvertently flies into the trash can, we just laugh and say, "Wow!

Would you look at that? Even the chalk knows we can measure in centimeters or inches!" or "How could we find how far that piece of chalk flew? What would be the best unit?" It is important to have fun and laugh.

Once you remember how your favorite middle school teacher managed to alleviate your awkward feelings, you probably remember a simultaneous increase in your curiosity and wonder about the subject. How did your teacher create academic wonder in a room filled with awkward moments? The awkward moments were not allowed to consume the classroom environment. There was a genuine interest in the questions your teacher asked, and you found out that the world did not end with an awkward moment. Let your students know that adults too have those awkward moments but that we still bring them back to an interesting mathematical idea.

coming together under measurement. This might be one of the reasons students find it so difficult. We have mentioned several ways to create meaningful activities for students. However, we want to make it clear that guiding these decisions is the district curriculum of the students' schools. Each district asks teachers to deliver a specific curriculum to its students. Being accountable for delivering the content to students is dictated by the needs of the school board, parents, and even teachers in future grades. It is always important to monitor classroom activities to ensure compatibility with district goals. However, with instances in which students study numerous ideas simultaneously, one lesson often meets more than one district objective. You are encouraged to study your curriculum and find some new places where you could join ideas into one lesson.

ALGEBRA CONNECTIONS

Measurement

NCTM CURRICULUM

A Big Idea: Making Generalizations about Measurements

Algebraic ideas behind measurement rest in part in the development of formulas. Too often, formulas are simply given and memorized. This approach unnecessarily disallows students from developing and describing their own general formulas and creates unnecessary tension between formulas. By that, we mean that not only should students understand various formulas, but they should understand relationships that exist among the formulas. As students develop skill with generalizing situations with formulas (such as number patterns from Chapter 7), they become capable of recognizing and stating generalizations as measurement formulas. For example, finding distances, areas, and volumes by recognizing general trends in certain situations can lead students to develop formulas.

Algebraic Ideas for You to Explore: The Pythagorean Theorem

The ancients considered numerical (and hence algebraic) ideas through a geometric lens. When confronted with the idea of "four," they often visualized a square measuring two by two. It

ALGEBRA CONNECTIONS *(continued)*

was no different for their understanding of the familiar Pythagorean theorem, which you might remember as $a^2 + b^2 = c^2$. Even though you might recite this formula as a computation dealing with squaring numbers, we describe here how this formula is a generalization about the geometric relationship (a concept) within triangles. Because the Greeks at the time of Pythagoras did not have an algebraic way to describe this relationship, they thought about it by literally setting squares on each side of the triangle. Mathematicians at that time would have stated the theorem as *"setting* a square *on* the side," not as *"squaring* the side." Does it really make sense to square a side? Moreover, the concept can be extended to include all triangles, not just right triangles. As you complete Activity 10.1, think about the relationships between length of sides of the triangle and the largest angle (if one exists) in the triangle.

You should have found the following relationships:

1. When the angle across from the longest side is *obtuse,* the sum of the areas of the two squares setting on the two shorter sides of the triangle is less than the area of the square setting on the longest side.
2. When the angle across from the longest side is *acute,* the sum of the areas of the two squares setting on the two shorter sides of the triangle is greater than the area of the square setting on the longest side.

 *Activity* 10.1

MAKING TRIANGLES

1. Select any three squares from the bag.
2. Place the squares on the table. See whether you can form a triangle-shaped space by joining the vertices of the square.
3. Place the transparency over the squares to hold them in place.
4. Measure the angles of the interior triangular space and areas of the squares as requested on the record sheet. Record the information.

A What three squares were used? (List by #)	B Did the three squares form a triangle?	C Measure the angle across from triangle's longest side. (Use a protractor.)	D Is that angle obtuse, acute, or right?	E What is the area of the square on the triangle's longest side?	F What are the areas of the two squares on the other sides?	G Add those two values.	3 Compare the values of E and G. Is G greater, equal to, or less than E?

(continued)

<u>A L G E B R A   C O N N E C T I O N S</u> *(continued)*

3. When the angle across from the longest side is *right,* the sum of the areas of the two squares setting on the two shorter sides of the triangle is equal to the area of the square setting on the longest side.

How is your thinking different when you visualize the relationship as a concept about the triangle rather than as a procedure involving squaring numbers? Would you find it interesting to note that you could set any regular shape on the sides of the triangle and achieve the same results? Try setting a semicircle on each side. Recalculate the areas, and determine whether the ideas in relationships 1, 2, and 3 above hold. You will find that when the angle across from the longest side is obtuse, the sum of the areas of the two semicircles setting on the two shorter sides of the triangle is less than the area of the semicircle setting on the longest side. The Pythagorean theorem is about the relationships of the sides of the triangle, not about the shape setting on those sides. If you are still not convinced, try setting an equilateral triangle on each side.

Variable as a Generalization and an Unknown

Did you find a way to describe this situation using algebra? If you decided that $a^2 + b^2 = c^2$, you are using the variables a, b, and c as generalizations. If you try to find a value for c, once you know values for a and b, then you are using the variable c as standing for an unknown. The thinking is different, and it is critical to understand what you are asking a variable to *do* for you.

K–8 Algebra Connections: Relating the Area of a Triangle to Other Shapes

You know that the area of a triangle can be found by multiplying the altitude of the triangle by the base and then dividing that product by 2. Have you ever wondered how (or if) that formula is related to other measurement formulas? Students wonder the same things. We can help students make sense about measurement formulas when we develop these formulas from empirical measurements of the shape. Because algebraic ideas can result from making sense of arithmetic, this is a reasonable approach. We can use those same empirical measurements to help students develop ideas about relationships between the measurement formulas of related shapes. For example, what is the relationship between the area of a triangle and the area of a parallelogram? If you draw a parallelogram, could you find the triangle that is exactly half of its area?

Look again at Part Three opening activity (p. 143). There you developed a formula based on knowing the area of a triangle. Your class probably recognized more than one strategy for finding the areas of trapezoids. Some of you developed a process of cutting the trapezoid into parts and then adding the parts together. Some of you found a procedure for enclosing the trapezoid in a larger rectangle and deleting the parts you did not need. And some of you might even have used your knowledge about the area of parallelograms (base • altitude). Like you, students better understand ideas behind formulas and can remember them more clearly when they develop their own general ways to describe the area. You should be able to recognize how the formula for the area of a triangle can be created from experiences like this.

LET'S REVIEW

The role of the teacher in implementing effective measurement lessons is to plan for all learners to move through the five phases of teaching. Sometimes that means severely differentiating lessons to accommodate learners with special needs. But with the van Hiele theory at his or her disposal, a teacher can not only diagnose students' levels of thinking but also create meaningful tasks that allow all students to demonstrate their knowledge. Using a presentation model to build measurement lessons provides a nice forum for teachers to model well-known procedures and for learners to demonstrate newfound procedures. By observing several procedures, conceptual thinking also increases. For the measurement part of this book, we highlighted the presentation model of teaching. Remember that we have chosen to concentrate our lesson plan comments on one kind of model of teaching for each part of the book. Naturally, all models of teaching are appropriate for measurement lessons. Earlier, Ms. Hawthorne used a problem-solving format for measuring a bus. By the end of the book, we will have studied all five models of teaching as we consider the role of the teacher.

HOMEWORK

1. Select an elementary text-book and any measurement lesson from it. Create three different content differentiation lessons, tasks, or projects for high-ability students that you might make. Assume that you are certain that the student can already meet the expectations of the lesson. (Turn in a photocopy of the lesson with your answers.)

Table 10.1 **Homework Problem**

Problem: How would you measure a puddle?

PHASE	ROLE OF THE TEACHER	ROLE OF THE STUDENT
1		
2		
3		
4		
5		

2. Assume that you have a gifted student, Maggie, who quickly completed Problem 2 in Chapter 8. What might you ask of her to enrich this experience for her?
3. Use the puddle problem described earlier to demonstrate your understanding of the phases of learning. In Table 10.1, fill in each box. Briefly describe the role of the teacher during each phase. Next describe the role of the student.

SUGGESTED READINGS

Carpenter, T. P., & Lehrer, R. (1999). Teaching and learning mathematics with understanding. In E. Fennema & T. A. Romberg (Eds.), *Mathematics classrooms that promote understanding* (pp. 19–32). Mahwah, NJ: Lawrence Erlbaum.

McClain, K., Cobb, P., Gravemeijer, K., & Estes, B. (1999). Developing mathematical reasoning within the context of measurement. In L. V. Stiff & F. R. Curcio (Eds.), *Developing mathematical reasoning in grades K–12: 1999 NCTM yearbook* (pp. 93–106). Reston, VA: NCTM.

Sharp, J., & Hoiberg, K. B. (2001). And then there was Luke: The geometric thinking of a young mathematician. *Teaching Children Mathematics*, 7(7), 432–439.

Stephan, M., Cobb, P., Gravemeijer, K., & Estes, B. (2001). The role of tools in supporting students' development of measurement concepts. In A. A. Cuoco & F. R. Curcio (Eds.), *The roles of representation in school mathematics: 2001 NCTM yearbook* (pp. 63–76). Reston, VA: NCTM.

REFERENCES

Beisser, S. R. (1997). Differentiating the curriculum for the high-ability student. In L. Mann (Ed.), *ASCD curriculum handbook* (pp. 333–348). Reston, VA: Association for Supervision and Curriculum Development.

Moursund, D. (2003). *Project based learning: Using information technology* (2nd ed.). Eugene, OR: International Society for Technology in Education.

National Council of Teachers of Mathematics. (2000). *Principles and standards for school mathematics.* Reston, VA: NCTM.

Tomlinson, C. A. (2001). *How to differentiate instruction in mixed-ability classrooms.* Alexandria, VA: Association for Supervision and Curriculum Development.

Westley, J. (1994). *Puddle questions: Assessing mathematical thinking.* Bothell, WA: Creative Publications.

Now that you have finished reading about measurement ideas, it is time to synthesize the information from the previous three chapters. You are aware of the nature of measurement as requiring a joining of geometry and number. You are also aware of the nature of measurement as thinking as a continuous entity, which must be peeled away from the discrete materials that are often used in opening lessons. Students need to develop measurement knowledge with many experiences and coordinating concepts. As is typical, to help summarize the three chapters, we would like to engage you in a closing activity. We know how difficult it is to think about learning and teaching when you have spent most of your life as a learner, but we believe this activity will help you expand your thinking. To synthesize the information in a practical manner, imagine you are a second grade teacher who must develop a lesson to help learners meet the curriculum goal: *The student will be able to identify the starting point and ending point on a ruler and use the ruler to measure length.*

Closing Activity

WRITE A MEASUREMENT LESSON

This activity is an opportunity for you to put together all the information from Part III of the book. You are a second grade teacher who must create a presentation model lesson that will support the following measurement curriculum goal:

> The student will be able to identify the starting point and ending point on a ruler and use the ruler to measure length.

Because this is a curriculum requirement, it may take several weeks to achieve. Your task for this activity is to create a single lesson that will fall during those weeks. Remember that even though your ultimate goal is to help students achieve the more general curriculum goal, the lesson you create here should be completed in only one day. It serves as a small support toward the curriculum goal. We guide you through the lesson development task by asking you to complete the tasks outlined in 1–5.

1. **Think about the Mathematics.** First, think about the prerequisite knowledge in terms of measurement and the accompanying vocabulary that students would have and need in order to work toward this goal. Second, what is the difference between a concept and a procedure related to this goal? Third, write a focused narrow objective achievable through the presentation model of teaching. Be sure to focus on a small component of the curriculum goal. Fourth, please tell how this lesson will fit into the students' overall experience toward the curriculum goal.

2. **Think about How We Learn.** What are good experiences that foster measurement skills? Remember how we described the importance of coordinating several concepts? Recall the information about selecting teaching aids and create a list of materials you need to gather for the lesson.

3. **Think about the Role of the Teacher.** What does the teacher do in a presentation lesson? Recall that the teacher finds interesting ways to demonstrate procedures to the students. Take a moment to decide what sort of independent practice you think the students should complete. List at least two example demonstrations related to your objective.

4. **Think about How the Learning Theory Might Appear during Your Lesson.** Use your knowledge of the phases of instruction to present the information in a way that anticipates student comments. Prepare some follow-up questions (like you might need for phase 2–3) for answers you expect to hear.

5. **Finally, Think about Assessment.** How will you know when your students have met your objective? Write an evaluation in which you engage the students that indicates to you the objective has or has not been met.

As in the preceding lessons from Parts I and II, there are several correct answers for a measurement lesson. We remind you that the lessons you create for your own learners will depend on your district's curriculum and that you will have access to a textbook series that should help you write your lessons. However, we believe that there are correct types of lessons that might be created for this activity. We can imagine lessons based on measuring string, cake pans, or setting up playground boundaries. Sometimes it is helpful to work with a partner to create a lesson. Practicing teachers often work together when they are developing new lessons. When you have finished your lesson, you might compare it to the lesson we created, which can be found in the appendix. Please remember, our lesson is only one type of correct lesson.

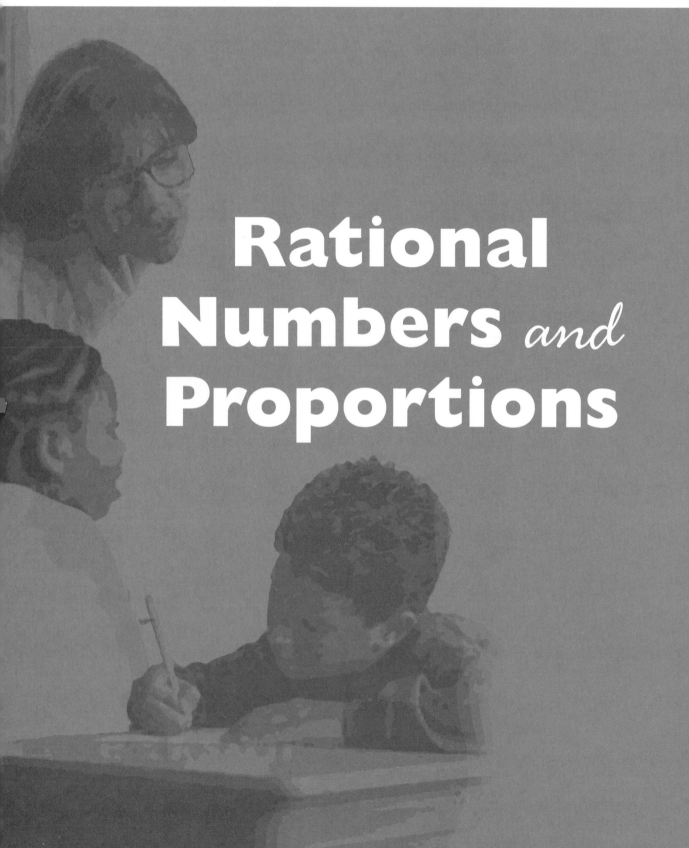

PART FOUR

Rational Numbers *and* Proportions

Read through the activity and answer the questions, paying attention to specific kinds of thinking you carried out to complete it. In particular, think about the most important information from the problem that is needed to answer each question.

Opening Activity

TEACHER RATIOS

In the Pine Bluff School district, four out of five teachers are women. The rest of the teachers are men. $\frac{2}{3}$ of all of the male teachers teach grades 7–12, and $\frac{2}{3}$ of all of the teachers teach grades K–6. Use the rectangle as one whole unit, and partition it to show this situation.

Use your picture to determine the following:

1. What fraction of all elementary (K–6) teachers are women?

2. What fraction of all women teachers are 7–12 teachers?

3. What fraction of all teachers are men who teach 7–12 grades?

4. What fraction of all teachers are men who teach K–6 grades?

● You probably had to carefully consider one whole unit for each question. Sometimes one whole unit was all of the teachers; other times it was only female teachers or elementary teachers. One thing to consider carefully in teaching and learning about fractions is to encourage learners to be aware of the whole unit or the unit of comparison.

Informally, fractions are thought to be parts out of a whole. More important, students must learn that fractions are a way to represent a comparison of two amounts.

C H A P T E R
11

Thinking about the
Mathematics of Rational Numbers and Proportions

UNDERSTANDING THE MATHEMATICS:
What Exactly Are Rational Numbers?

Rational numbers are defined as the set of numbers that can be written as a ratio of two integer values, where the integer of comparison (denominator) is not zero. Often, the rational number is written with a fraction bar separating the two values, $\frac{A}{B}$, with A as the numerator and B as the denominator, which cannot be 0. For example, $\frac{2}{3}$ is a fraction because 2 and 3 are integers and 3 is not zero. $\frac{\sqrt{14}}{3}$ is not rational because even though 3 is not zero, $\sqrt{14}$ is not an integer; it is irrational. Our fifth grade students explain how they think about fractions:

> *Min:* You can make a fraction with any number.
> *Lydia:* Fractions, percents and decimals all tell the part of something else.
> *Ryan:* I know that fractions can make a whole, and they are just parts of the whole.
> *Jamal:* In the fraction $\frac{5}{8}$, the line between the numbers means *compared to*.

We can use symbols to write about the comparison between two amounts, numerator A and denominator B, in several ways. A *ratio* is a way to compare any two amounts. We usually show this comparison with a ratio colon (:). We also compare a part to a whole (a common fraction) using a fraction bar (–) to separate the amounts. We compare a part to a whole that is a power of 10 using a decimal point (.). We indicate parts out of 100 with a percent sign (%). Use of the percent sign assumes that the reader knows the unit of comparison is 100. Table 11.1 shows examples of the four kinds of rational numbers.

Common fractions are typically encountered first in primary grades and are related to ratios because they compare some "part" out of some "whole." The familiar fraction bar (–) is often used exclusively. In the example of the

Table 11.1 **Different Kinds of Rational Numbers**

TYPE	SYMBOL	EXAMPLE	WRITE AS
Context: You have some small bags of mixed nuts. Each has 5 nuts, and 2 of them are cashews.			
Ratio	:	For every 2 cashews, there are 3 not cashews.	2:3
Common fraction	/	There are 2 cashews out of 5 nuts.	$\frac{2}{5}$
Decimal	.	There would be 4 cashews out of 10 nuts.	.4
Percentage	%	There are 40 cashews out of 100 nuts.	40%

bag of five mixed nuts, a common fraction would be that two out of five ($\frac{2}{5}$) are cashews.

Proportions are related to ratios because a proportion is a statement of equality between two ratios. We would use a proportion if the number of items being compared is changed, in a corresponding way and through multiplication. We could use a proportion to predict the number of cashews in a bag of 40 mixed nuts, writing 2:5 and ?:40. This allows us to predict (through multiplication) that there will be 16 cashews in the 40-nut bag.

A *percent* uses 100 as the unit of comparison. This translates to "If we had 100 pieces in our whole unit, what would we have in our part?" It is a way to standardize thinking about fractional amounts. We would say, "If our bag had 100 mixed nuts, we would expect 40 of them to be cashews."

Decimal representations are the subset of fractions expressed with denominators written as a power of ten. We would say that .4 of our bag is cashews. Interestingly, some decimal values terminate (such as .4, which is equivalent to $\frac{2}{5}$), while others repeat (such as $.\overline{3}$, which is .33333 . . . and equivalent to $\frac{1}{3}$). Whether terminating or repeating, values represented with decimal symbols are still rational numbers. For every common fraction, there exists a corresponding decimal representation. For every terminating or repeating decimal representation, there exists a corresponding fractional representation. The difference between a decimal and a common fraction is only one of representation: fraction bar (–) or decimal point (.). Although a universal symbol such as the fraction bar is necessary for purposes of communication, it can sometimes obscure the fact that fractions are deeply related to decimals, since decimals are nothing more than a standardized way to represent fractions. It is unfortunate that many students do not see the connection. Listen to these fifth graders talk about the different kinds of representations for fractions:

> ***Min:*** I know that $\frac{7}{25}$ is 28% because I can multiply both numbers by 4 to figure out problems like this.
>
> ***Lydia:*** A fraction can be made into a percent like $\frac{1}{4}$ is 25%, and you can turn a percent into a fraction. You can turn decimals into both!
>
> ***Ryan:*** Well, you can turn fractions into percents real easily if you take it out of 100, such as $\frac{3}{4}$ is 75 out of 100.
>
> ***Jamal:*** I know that the line between the numbers in $\frac{5}{8}$ also means *divide*, so that's how I change it to a decimal.

In this chapter, you study not only ideas related to rational numbers, but also the importance of representation (decimal, percent, fraction) that these students described. Too often, various kinds of ratios are cordoned off into groups. They may be treated as separate chapters and thus not appear connected to the ratio concept. Imagine how differently Lydia would think about ratios if her school experiences failed to connect ratio representations. We attempt to re-unite the groups so that you can think like Lydia. It is important to repeat that how the ratio is written is only a representation. Deciding on that representation can be a procedure as noted by Min or Jamal. Reasons for writing ratios in certain ways depend on the situation. Consider four students sitting in a small group, with two girls in the group. In this situation, we might need to compare "two out of four," or we might need to compare "two to two." Both situations are rational numbers that could be written as $\frac{2}{4}$, 50%, .5, or 2:2, respectively. As Ryan noted, percents tend to be associated more heavily with specific situations in which convenience of a standard denominator (100) makes sense. In Activity 11.1, use fleshed-out connection words and phrases that communicate relationships between ideas in the bubbles. For example, a ratio's numbers are always read in the same order as the context words used to describe the situation. Use this activity as an opportunity to add depth to your conceptual understanding of ratio.

Activity 11.1

INSPIRATION

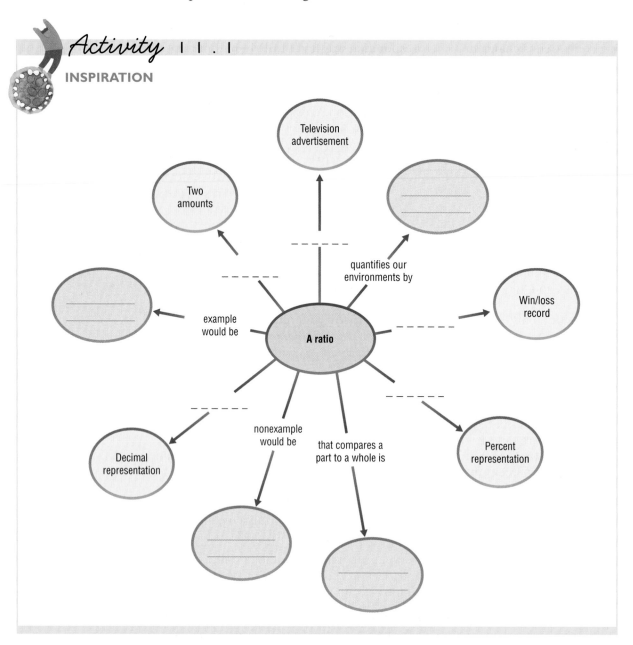

CONCENTRATING ON THE CONCEPTS:

Connections among Rational Number Genres

Sharing

Early concepts of fractions rely on children's awareness of sharing (Pothier & Sawada, 1983). As children learn to share, they come to understand that amounts can be partitioned and that those partitions are critical to the sharing process. Children can develop knowledge of a relationship between two amounts (say, parts of a cookie) if those parts must be shared. In so doing, they develop a basic knowledge of fraction ideas. As children establish an idea of sharing, they come to notice when parts to be shared are equal or not and can also begin to recognize any need to adjust. By comparing the two amounts to be shared, they establish the idea of a ratio as a relationship between two quantities. Take, for example, a *Sesame Street* skit involving the characters Ernie and Bert. Ernie wants to share a piece of licorice with Bert. First, he breaks the licorice into two pieces. Bert notices immediately that the two pieces are not equal. So Ernie eats a bit off of the larger piece in an effort to equalize the parts. But then that piece is smaller, so he eats a bit off of the other one. You can probably imagine the end result: Bert gets none of the licorice! But Ernie learned a lot about sharing and the ideas of equal-sized pieces. Listen to these third grade children describe strategies for rectifying a similar situation: *You and your older brother have just returned home from school. Your mom left a candy bar for you to share. Your brother breaks it into two pieces (clearly unequal). What would you do to fix the situation?*

> **Kylie:** Set the two pieces on top of each other and cut off the extra. Throw the extra away.
> **TJ:** I agree with Kylie. Set the two pieces on top of each other and cut off the extra. But I would also cut the extra in half and share it with my brother.
> **Zach:** I think I would cut each of those [rectangular] pieces in half again. I would make sure to cut corner to corner [he means along the diagonal] of each of them and then share out one piece from each.
> **Mindi:** Use the caramel to scrunch the two pieces back together and cut again. This time cut in the opposite [she means perpendicular] direction. Then give each person either the top or bottom.

These children have some sophisticated strategies for sharing. One thing they all have in common, though, is the idea of what stands for the whole unit: the entire candy bar. To push past the idea of simple sharing, children must be encouraged to become aware of situations by comparing several parts within a situation to the whole unit of the situation. For example, children who are comfortable comparing some number of orange segments (such as 6) to the number of segments in the entire orange (10) by counting the segments have developed some basic concept knowledge. This idea is important in part because it brings into question the concern of "What is the one whole unit?" or "What is the unit of comparison?" In our second example, the orange's 10 segments is the whole unit to which the 6 segments will be compared, for the fraction $\frac{6}{10}$.

Congruent Parts

Another concept demonstrated by the children who discussed sharing the candy bar is related to congruence. The importance of congruence cannot be overemphasized. For certain kinds of whole units, equal-sized pieces are paramount. Congruent pieces matter when the whole unit is something being cut into parts, to identify the fractional nature of the situation. This situation is usually associated with a whole unit that is continuous. For example, if you have a waffle for breakfast and you cut it into parts, then you would describe the fractional nature of the situation by comparing the sizes of the parts of the waffle. If you tell someone you ate $\frac{2}{3}$ of a waffle, that person could visualize how you might have cut the waffle into equal-sized pieces (thirds) and eaten two of those pieces.

But the box of waffles itself contains discrete waffles, and those waffles might or might not be congruent. Thinking about $\frac{2}{3}$ of a box of waffles conjures up images that are different from the image of cutting a waffle into parts. This is an example in which fractional parts do *not* need to be congruent. For example, in a new box of 16 crayons, all crayons are presumably congruent. However, in a used box of 16 crayons, the red crayon is *still* $\frac{1}{16}$ of the box but likely is no longer congruent to the other crayons. Knowing whether parts must be congruent or not in order to be represented with a ratio will play a large part in fraction knowledge. As you saw earlier, the children who wanted to share the candy bar were very concerned about the sizes of the pieces of the chocolate to be shared. That situation was continuous.

Equivalent Fractions

The relationship between various common fraction representations of equivalent amounts is also a concept. TJ, Zach, and Mindi each cut the candy bar (again) into four pieces to rectify the situation. They knew that there could have been more than two pieces and still have been a way for each to have half of the candy bar. Another example might help. If a child has one sandwich to share among three people (including herself), she could handle that situation by cutting the sandwich into thirds or sixths. In either case, each person could receive the same "amount," but in one case, a person gets one out of three ($\frac{1}{3}$) pieces, and in the other case a person gets two out of six ($\frac{2}{6}$) pieces. The relationship between representations for equivalent amounts is an example of a fraction concept.

Contextualized Situations

The sandwich and candy bar situations are real situations in which students might find themselves. Recognizing the fractional nature of personal situations such as this helps children to develop initial knowledge about fractions (Kieren, 1988). Fraction concepts also include understanding *relationships* among various rational number genres: ratio, decimal, common fraction, and percent discussed earlier. We work to establish concept knowledge so that students can connect these genres. We also know that procedures should be built on and layered with conceptual knowledge (Carpenter, 1986). Procedures for calculating symbolic representations that move back and forth between the different genres will be discussed in the next section. Groundwork for recognizing whether or not one of the genres is more useful than another one relies on students' awareness of the different genres as well as the extent to which one of them makes sense in a given situation. Before completing Activity 11.2, think about different ways to describe the same (fractional) amount and the importance of one whole unit in solving fraction problems.

The key to solving the dog problem is to recognize that the fractional amounts given do not make up the full (whole) amount of dogs in the park. On what sorts of misconceptions does that play, and in what sorts of thinking must the learner engage to successfully resolve this situation? The learner's

Activity 11.2

TRACY'S DOG

One day, Tracy took his dog for a walk in the park. He noticed that dogs were either on a green leash, on a red leash, on a blue leash, or running free. He did not see any other colors of leashes. Tracy's dog was on a **green** leash. He noticed that while he was walking in Dogland Park, 20% of the dogs were on a **red** leash, $\frac{1}{3}$ of the dogs were on a **blue** leash, and .25 of the dogs were **running free.** Tracy wondered, "What is the least number of dogs that were in the park at that time that day?"

(You might want to think about what portion of the dogs were on a **green leash!**)

mental answers to these questions also demonstrate connections among the rational number representations. It is important for a learner to make connections within and among various rational number representations because that gives the learner a steady concept base.

The Whole Unit

As has been noted, the importance of establishing the whole unit is critical for describing ratios as common fractions. Understanding that it is possible to move fluidly between differently sized whole units is a concept that needs to develop over time. There are two ideas to keep in mind when thinking about moving fluidly between whole units. One is the ability to move back and forth between *models* of the whole unit. In other words, can you visualize $\frac{2}{3}$ of a circular region (pie), a number line (licorice), a rectangular region (book cover), and a set of blocks (box of chocolates)? The other idea is the ability to recognize equivalent ratios without concern for the *number of parts* in the whole. That is, $\frac{2}{3}$ of a region might be shown with two out of three pieces, or it might be shown with 14 out of 21 pieces. So the whole unit might have been cut into some amount other than the denominator of the fraction. However $\frac{2}{3}$ is the same as $\frac{14}{21}$.

Activity 11.3 (p 208) is a game that will help you to think about different models for showing fractional amounts. Finding answers that are greater than 1 can be surprisingly difficult. If you have used pattern blocks before, you might have used the hexagon as the whole unit. This game includes situations in which the hexagon is the part. For example, look at whole unit E in the activity, and convince yourself that if the hexagon is the part, then it is the same as the fraction $1\frac{1}{2}$.

Activity 11.3

GET THREE IN A ROW!

Rules

Materials needed: four pattern blocks (one of each), markers for the game board (pennies work well), game board, whole unit board, spinners, and spinner board.

1. Spin a "whole unit."
2. Spin a "part" from the pattern block spinner.
3. Set the piece (from the second spin) on top of the shaded whole unit (from the first spin) and decide what part of the whole you have.
4. Once you decide what fraction of the whole unit you have, locate that value on the game board and place one of your markers on it.

Goal: Get three in a row, up and down, or diagonally.

Students may choose to play on a shared game board, thus introducing the idea of blocking opponents' progress.

After playing two rounds, answer these questions:

1. What is the mathematics to be learned from this game?
2. What sorts of disadvantages are there to using games in class?
3. What are the advantages to using games in class?
4. How could you modify this game to increase (or decrease) difficulty?

Game Board

$\frac{2}{3}$	$\frac{1}{12}$	$\frac{3}{4}$	$\frac{1}{8}$	1
1	$\frac{1}{3}$	3	$\frac{1}{2}$	$\frac{2}{9}$
$\frac{1}{4}$	$\frac{1}{9}$	$\frac{6}{8}$	1	$\frac{1}{6}$
2	$1\frac{1}{3}$	$\frac{1}{3}$	$\frac{1}{4}$	$\frac{3}{8}$
$\frac{1}{3}$	$\frac{1}{6}$	$\frac{1}{2}$	$1\frac{1}{2}$	$\frac{1}{18}$

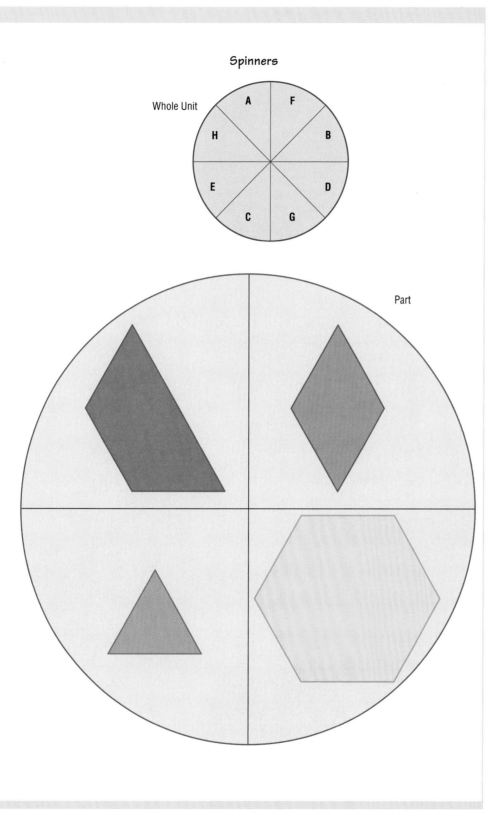

Spinners

Whole Unit

Part

(continued)

Whole Units

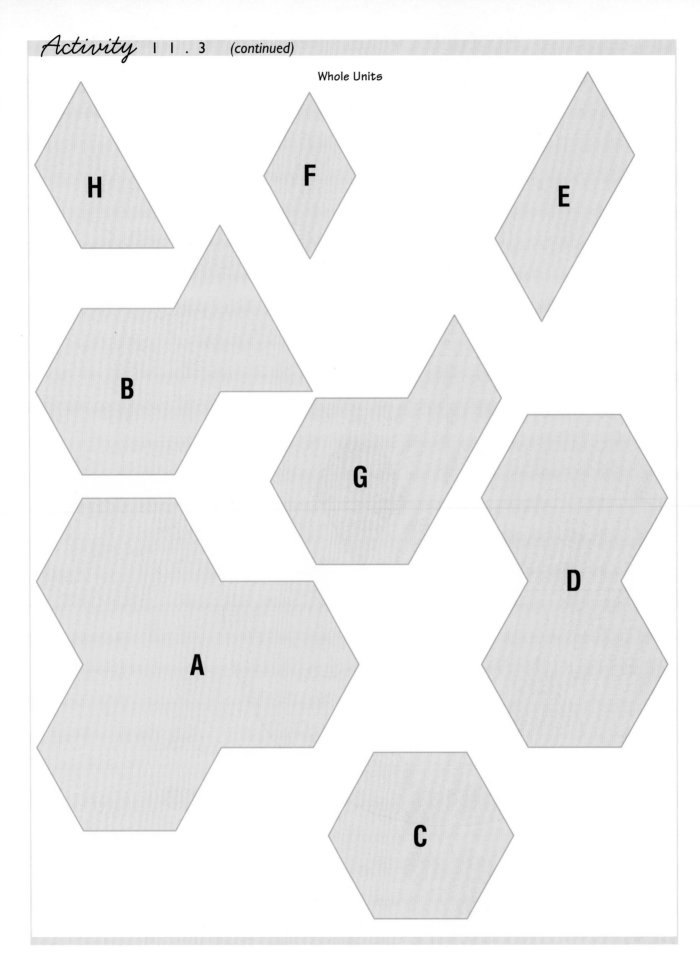

To illustrate the idea of equivalent ratios without concern for the number of parts, we asked a group of fifth grade students to solve the following problem: *Fred's basketball team is having a great season. His coach has separated all the players into the following five groups: $\frac{1}{2}$ are guards, $\frac{1}{6}$ are forwards, $\frac{1}{12}$ are centers, $\frac{1}{6}$ are specialty players, and 2 others are free-throw shooters. How many players are on Fred's team and how many are in each of the groups?*

Min: $1 - \frac{1}{2} = \frac{1}{2} - \frac{2}{6} = \frac{1}{6} - \frac{1}{12} = \frac{1}{12} =$ free-throw shooters, which is 2. So the centers, which is also $\frac{1}{12}$, was also 2. Then I found forwards and specialty players = 4 and guards = 8.

Lydia: I drew a picture and thought about what numbers went into each spot. The leftover slot had to be 2, and it was also $\frac{1}{12}$. Once I knew that there were two free-throw shooters (and that was the same as the centers), I just multiplied to get the number of the other kinds of players.

Ryan: I started out making a picture, but it didn't work. So I just thought about what numbers 2, 6, and 12 all go into and tested each of them until I got it.

Jamal: I knew that the two free-throw shooters would be $\frac{1}{12}$ of the team too, since $\frac{1}{2} + \frac{2}{6} + \frac{1}{12}$ only needed $\frac{1}{12}$ more to make the whole team. Then I just compared the rest of the fractions to the number of players needed to make up that fraction.

CLASSROOM CONNECTIONS

Illuminating Fraction Concepts

Imagine that I have invited a group of people to my home. Some are neighbors, some live in other parts of town, and some will be driving from neighboring towns. Gradually, the guests arrive. They don't all arrive at exactly the same time. Some guests have no problem getting to my home; others encountered various delays: roadblocks, construction, returning home for forgotten items, flat tires, and so on.

The same happens in my classroom. When my students begin a new concept in our mathematics classroom, some have no problems, while others encounter many detours and roadblocks on their way to understanding. The NCTM (2000) reminds me that "conceptual understanding is an essential component of the knowledge needed to deal with novel problems and settings" (p. 20). So when it is time to introduce a new kind of problem or topic, I need to make sure their concept knowledge is in place.

I also know that my students might not arrive at the same time or travel the same road to understanding, but gradually they all get there. Let's think about how this looks with fractions. I ask the students to begin our chapter on fractions by writing down what they know about fractions. Following are some actual statements:

"I don't know anything about fractions."
"We didn't learn them last year."
"I know that a fraction tells about part of one whole."
"Fractions are about sharing."
"I know that you write one number on top of another one."

After volunteers have shared their responses, I prod, "I'll bet some of you know more than you think you know. What if I said that half of our class would be asked to sing for an assembly. What would that mean?"

"We know that!"

"Okay, well what if I said that one-third of Anna's seating group is absent today?"

"Well, we know Jamal is absent, so that means one out of three is gone."

"See, you do know more than you think you know! Please write down some other examples."

It is clear to me that some students have a long way to go. As the facilitator, I must do all I can to provide opportunities for all to arrive. My students know that not all trips are smooth and easy and that's fine. With patience and hard work, we can travel safely and arrive at our destination. That doesn't mean that we'll remember each exact route, but we'll know more than we did when we began our journey.

As you think about students' solutions to the basketball problem, recognize how carefully they attended to all the information in the problem and were not daunted by the different number of parts described in the problem.

GRASPING THE PROCEDURES:
How to Operate and Move between Genres

Once concepts have been established, students should be encouraged to develop procedures operating with rational numbers. Skill in making calculations to move fluidly between genres is important. Whether moving back and forth between genres, finding strategies to ensure congruent parts, writing equivalent fractions, or completing operations, students should be inspired to invent their own strategies. As we saw in Chapter 6, children can invent meaningful procedures for dealing with operations with whole numbers. The same is true for operating with fractional amounts. The teacher must work toward helping students understand things that connect solidly to whole number knowledge and be ready to help students deal purposefully with the things that stretch that knowledge to new levels.

Whole Number Knowledge

There are a number of unique things you need to think about when you help students develop knowledge about fraction operations and procedures. Sometimes it seems that students are building fraction knowledge incorrectly on whole number knowledge. Some researchers refer to this problem as *whole number interference.* They are referring to situations in which students have tried to transfer whole number procedures to fractional situations. The problem is that although concepts transfer (e.g., addition is still combining two sets), procedures appear different (e.g., addition adds only numerators and not denominators as opposed to all values in a "place"). If students struggle with fraction knowledge about procedures, sometimes it is useful to assess whether they are trying to apply a whole number procedure rather than making sense of the situation and adjusting for different algorithms required for fraction values. Once you gauge how students are building up their knowledge, you can plan your instruction to accommodate your students.

Addition and Subtraction

Addition and subtraction require students to understand what role the whole unit plays in the operation. If the two values in the operation are being compared to a whole unit that has already been cut into same-sized pieces, then the answer is recorded with that same whole unit. In other words, $\frac{2}{5} + \frac{1}{5}$ is the same as 2 fifths + 1 fifth. Thinking in terms of fifths recognizes that the whole units are already cut into same-sized pieces and therefore the parts can merely be added and the answer compared to fifths. Knowing that the answer will be given in fifths informs the student of the need only to worry about 2 + 1. If the two numbers in the operation represent different cuttings of the whole unit, such as $\frac{2}{5} + \frac{1}{2}$, then the student must decide how the answer will have to look. To execute this procedure, the student must decide about the appearance of the final unit. Will it be fifths, sevenths, or perhaps something else? Pictures are of great help in this situation (see Figure 11.1). A context would be even better. Assume that we have a rectangular-shaped playground and $\frac{2}{5}$ of the playground is covered with basketball courts and $\frac{1}{2}$ of the playground has other play equipment on it. How much of the playground is covered?

It is immediately apparent that the addition problem should not result in sevenths, but neither halves nor fifths work either. To communicate the solution, the park must be cut into tenths. Many experiences using multiple representations (square regions, circular regions, city blocks) will lead students to develop procedures that include writing fractions with the same denominator (whole unit).

Selecting Contexts

Contexts determine the look and feel of the whole unit in the problem. Because of that, we typically find that computation experiences evolve more naturally and more efficiently from a continuous model of the whole unit than from a discrete model. Complete Activity 11.4 (p. 214) before continuing.

The context implies that we could use chips to represent the cookies in the situation, since it is a discrete context. For Rosalie, two-thirds of the chips are blue and for Ellie, three-fourths of her chips are blue. If we put the chips together, we would find that five-sevenths of the chips are blue. This is real-world accurate, but it does not lead to a sound procedure for addition of fractions because we are changing the one whole unit. With the discrete model, it is sometimes difficult for children to understand how to hold the whole unit steady. However, with the continuous model, they tend to have more success holding the whole unit steady, in part because the whole unit is an area being cut up and it is known before completion of the problem.

You probably remember that the procedure for adding fractions requires a common denominator. The essence of this procedure within the cookie context (discrete) would depend on understanding that it takes 12 cookies (or a multiple of 12 cookies) *to make a whole* set. So if Rosalie had $\frac{2}{3}$ frosted blue, she would frost 8 of 12 blue. Ellie would frost 9 of 12 blue. Put the blues together, and compare them back to the 12 cookie set. Now we understand that $\frac{2}{3} + \frac{3}{4}$ is the same as $\frac{8}{12} + \frac{9}{12} = 1$ and $\frac{5}{12}$, and 1 and $\frac{5}{12}$ is quite a bit different from five-sevenths. Thinking with discrete models requires proportional thinking, something that typically does not fully develop until around middle school.

The result of 1 and $\frac{5}{12}$ is more obvious with the area model (a specific type of a continuous model) because the size of the whole unit (12 cookies) is more obvious. Therefore, the context might be changed to connect to a continuous situation. A continuous model keeps the *empty* space obvious. In other words, $\frac{2}{3}$ in area is two parts (of the whole) filled and one part (of the whole) empty. Similarly, $\frac{3}{4}$ in area is three parts (of the whole) filled and one part (of the whole) empty. With the empty spaces clearly visualized, children can concentrate on the $\frac{2}{3}$ part that is filled, always knowing what it takes to make a whole. Showing $\frac{2}{3}$ with discrete manipulatives allows the child to use three chips, of which one is simply a different color, so what needs to be added might be unclear. See Figure 11.2 for an explanation.

Figure 11.1

Showing the Addition Task

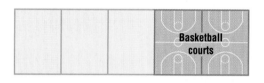

Activity 11.4

SUGAR COOKIES

Rosalie makes 3 sugar cookies and puts blue frosting on 2 of those cookies. She puts yellow frosting on the other one.

Ellie makes 4 sugar cookies and puts blue frosting on 3 of them. She puts yellow frosting on the other one.

Draw a picture of each girl's situation.

If the girls put all of their cookies together, they have 7 cookies, and 5 of those cookies have blue frosting.

The addition sentence looks like $\frac{2}{3} + \frac{3}{4} =$

The answer is $\frac{5}{7}$ cookies with blue sugar frosting.

But in school you probably learned that $\frac{2}{3} + \frac{3}{4}$ would become $\frac{8}{12} + \frac{9}{12} = \frac{17}{12}$ or 1 and $\frac{5}{12}$.

These fractions acted differently in the real world than they did in the school world!

This situation has to do with understanding two crucial ideas in developing fractional thinking. First, students must understand the role of the whole unit in fraction thinking. Second, teachers must understand the difference between a discrete model and a continuous model when showing fraction ideas to children.

Explain how the continuous model works to demonstrate addition of fractions.

Figure 11.2

The Complexity of Using Models to Show Addition

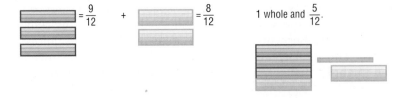

Set model:

Area model: = 1 (established first).

$= \frac{3}{4}$ + $= \frac{2}{3}$ Piled up, the blocks are hard to count.

So we get a common denominator and compare the sum to the whole unit.

$= \frac{9}{12}$ + $= \frac{8}{12}$ 1 whole and $\frac{5}{12}$.

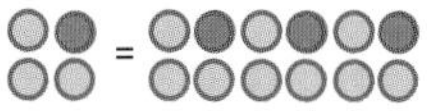

A key to generalizing procedures is establishing one whole unit, independently from the context. We used a slightly more complex example here with you than we would first use with children, so keep that in mind as you think through the situation. Although it might take a bit of cutting and pasting, possibly even some folding and a speck of measuring, you will become convinced that according to the whole unit we established, the result is 1 and $\frac{5}{12}$. However, had we used a set model, we would have had to sufficiently convince you that you would have had to first verify 12 cookies made a whole set, no matter how many cookies Rosalie actually frosted. And you would have had to understand that you would not be dealing with some of the pieces when it came time to add. With a continuous model, it appears to be more clear that the $\frac{3}{4}$ portions can be turned into $\frac{9}{12}$ and that the $\frac{2}{3}$ portions can be turned into $\frac{8}{12}$. It is also slightly more obvious that only the pieces you *have* are handled. (See Figure 11.3 for an example of the difficulties of showing $\frac{3}{4} = \frac{9}{12}$ with discrete objects.)

Figure 11.3

Using a Discrete Model to Show Equivalent Fractions

Multiplication

Multiplication of fractions presents special problems because suddenly, the idea that "multiplying makes things larger" does not necessarily hold, and students' whole number conceptions are challenged. However, the whole number definition still holds. We still make copies of one amount and then repeatedly add to find the total. It's just that the number of copies made may be fractional. For $1\frac{2}{3} \times \frac{3}{4}$, we have $\frac{3}{4}$ and make 1 copy of it and then $\frac{2}{3}$ of a copy of it. A visualization of this situation can feel difficult to conjure. Models can be helpful in connecting fraction multiplication to whole number multiplication.

The *area* model offers a visual of the exercise: $\frac{2}{3} \times \frac{3}{4}$ (see Figure 11.4). In this region, the lengths $\frac{2}{3}$ and $\frac{3}{4}$ are the two values being multiplied. Students see the numerator as the area created by 2×3, whereas the denominator is the area created by 3×4. You might see a familiar procedure (probably "multiply the numerators and multiply the denominators") displayed in this figure. The *set* model requires a slight modification, rather than using repeated addition language, such as two groups of three, the vernacular moves to $\frac{2}{3}$ of a group of $\frac{3}{4}$. A *number line* model can also be employed but is best left to situations in which one factor is a whole number. It also may be more useful for more experienced learners (Watanabe, 2002).

Division

Division presents special problems. First, the whole number idea that "division makes things smaller" does not necessarily maintain itself in fractional settings. For instance, $20\frac{1}{2} \div \frac{1}{4}$ results in 82. When students find the quotient larger than the dividend, the sheer size of the solution often interferes with their whole number knowledge.

Second, the *invert and multiply* algorithm requires understanding the property of multiplicative inverses in a fairly profound manner. This property is heavily associated with algebraic reasoning and typically appears in middle school. To understand invert and multiply, students must be aware of the role of reciprocals in fractional situations and be able to execute a multiplication procedure. Students must use the idea that $a/b \cdot b/a = 1$. An algebraic demonstration of the invert and multiply for $z/y \div a/b$ is as follows. First, $z/y \div a/b$ can be rewritten as $(z/y)/(a/b)$. This complex fraction is multiplied by another complex fraction representing 1—namely, $(b/a)/(b/a)$. Note the use of a multiplicative inverse. This results in $[(z/y) \cdot (b/a)]/[(a/b) \cdot (b/a)]$. Finally, the representation is simplified to $z/y \cdot b/a$. So $20\frac{1}{2} \div \frac{1}{4}$ is the same as $\frac{41}{2} \cdot \frac{4}{1}$. This results in $\frac{164}{2}$, or 82.

Figure 11.4

Using Models to Show Multiplication

(a) Area

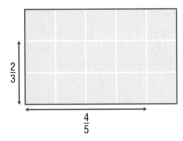

$\frac{2}{3}$

$\frac{4}{5}$

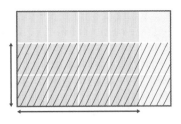

(b) Groups/sets

$\frac{4}{5}$ of a set

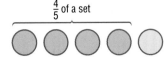

A whole unit is the complete set of circles. Imagine that it is a box of cookies.

Subdivide each circle into thirds, and denote two of the subdivisions.

Counting the sections (subdivisions) gives 8 sections. This model requires recognizing that there are now 15 sections in a set. Try not to confuse the "thirds" in the circle with $\frac{1}{3}$ of a whole unit. A whole unit in this problem is the entire box of cookies. So the whole unit is now composed of 15 sections, whereas previously it was composed of 5 circles.

(c) Number line

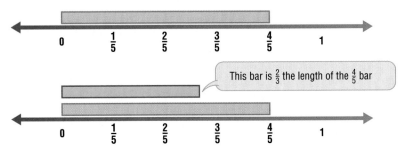

This bar is $\frac{2}{3}$ the length of the $\frac{4}{5}$ bar

The problem is thus "how long is the new purple bar compared to the whole unit?" This is difficult to tell. Each bar must be divided up using the same sized unit. In this case 15ths could be used to get the answer of $\frac{8}{15}$.

Third, an alternative algorithm, *least common denominator* (LCD), builds on whole number division thinking, using the repeated subtraction definition. However, it can be inefficient when applied to certain kinds of fractional values. In the LCD algorithm, students think of the situation as a succession of subtractions. So to divide requires subtracting fractions, which as you know, requires a common denominator—hence the name *LCD algorithm*. Rewrite $z/y \div a/b$ with denominator yb. This gives $zb/yb \div ay/by$. In repeated subtraction, count how many times ay can be subtracted from zb, which is simply $zb \div ay$. Using numbers, we have that $20\frac{1}{2} \div \frac{1}{4}$ is the same as $\frac{41}{2} \div \frac{1}{4}$. The LCD is 4, so the problem becomes $\frac{82}{4} \div \frac{1}{4}$ and in turn becomes $82 \div 1 = 82$. You will practice this algorithm later in the chapter. This process is probably unfamiliar to you, so we have shown another demonstration of it in Figure 11.5 for the division problem $9\frac{2}{3} \div \frac{2}{3}$.

Listen to these seventh graders explain division of fractions for $4\frac{4}{5} \div \frac{3}{5}$. Notice the variety of strategies. Each student used a different approach.

> **Fatima:** I rewrote it $\frac{24}{5} \times \frac{5}{3}$, and that's a multiplication problem. That's just 8.
>
> **Lucretia:** I rewrote it as $\frac{24}{5} \div \frac{3}{5}$, and that's 24 ÷ 3, which is 8.
>
> **Kaleb:** I kept adding up $\frac{3}{5}$ until I got to $4\frac{4}{5}$. So $\frac{3}{5} + \frac{3}{5} + \frac{3}{5} + \frac{3}{5} + \frac{3}{5} + \frac{3}{5} + \frac{3}{5} + \frac{3}{5}$. That took 8 sets.
>
> **Anthony:** I drew a picture of $4\frac{4}{5}$ wholes [similar to Figure 11.5] and split them each up into fifths. Then I subtracted out three-fifths over and over. The answer is 8.

Finding Equivalent Fractions

All four procedures require equivalent fractions either to execute or to reduce answers. Procedures for finding equivalent fractions depend on understanding the whole unit. For any two equivalent fractions, the mental image of the two whole units should be the same size cut into different numbers of parts. Procedures for finding equivalent fractions begin with the need to cut a whole unit up in at least two different ways. Often, early development of a procedure can be enhanced with language referring to equivalent fractions as being *the same as*. Issues with the algebraic concept of equivalence have been previously discussed, but they bear repeating here. In thinking about $\frac{2}{3}$ and $\frac{14}{21}$, it helps to say $\frac{2}{3}$ is the same as $\frac{14}{21}$ because students conjure up two images and can agree that these are the same. Describing the values as equal often suggests to students they need to do something to $\frac{2}{3}$ to change it to $\frac{14}{21}$.

A ratio table, also known as a pattern table (Cramer & Post, 1993; Middleton van den Heuvel-Panhuizen, 1995), is a good way for students to organize their thinking about equivalent ratios and fractions. It demonstrates how relationships between the ratios *change together*. That is, when those ratios are equivalent, the ratio table shows how multiplication acts on the numbers in the ratio. The table records the progress of the ratios, showing proportions, as students extend two number patterns simultaneously. The table keeps track of the multiplication being executed in the problem. With several meaningful experiences, students can develop an operation (shortcut) to move around in the table and thus move between equivalent ratios.

We asked our fifth grade students to solve the following problem: *We learned the school cafeteria orders 3 chocolate milks out of every 5 milks they order. We opened the cafeteria cooler and it had 25 milks in it. How many chocolate*

Figure 11.5

Using a Continuous Model to Show the LCD Division Process

Consider the exercise: $9\frac{2}{3} \div \frac{2}{3}$.

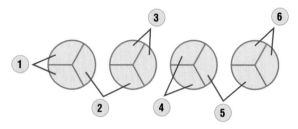
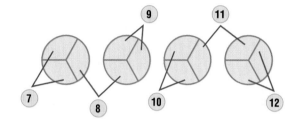
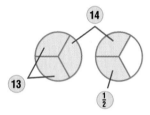

We can make 14 full groups of $\frac{2}{3}$ and $\frac{1}{2}$ of a group of $\frac{2}{3}$. So the answer is: 14 and $\frac{1}{2}$.

milks would you expect to see in the cooler? Use a ratio table to help answer the question.

Min's Table				
3	6	12	24	48
5	10	20	40	80

Lydia's Table (Same as Jamal's Table)				
3	6	9	12	15
5	10	15	20	25

Lydia described her procedure as skip-counting, and Jamal explained to the rest of the class that the place of the numbers was just that multiple of the first number. That is, 9 is in the third place from 3, so he would take 3 × 3 and 5 × 3 to fill in the table. Min described her procedure as doubling. But after she listened to Lydia, Min immediately said, "Oh my gosh, Lydia's table is so much better!"

In this case, Jamal's procedural explanation made sense to most students, including Ryan, and it became the class procedure. But Lydia and Min remained unconvinced of Jamal's procedure. Lydia's skip-counting procedure had produced the same information as in Jamal's table. Jamal's procedure was less meaningful for them than skip-counting. They wanted to be convinced but were just not there yet. After all, Min had just abandoned her procedure for Lydia's because she noticed that her table was missing some of Lydia's numbers, which she recognized should be in the table. Teaching in today's world, it is okay to hear, "I just don't get it." We can't all be ready at exactly the same moment. Moreover, an experience with an idea is not a one-time event in a given year. Throughout the year, ideas are revisited, probably in a different context, giving students many opportunities to *get it*.

Revisiting Procedures

Later in the year, these students returned to the task of using ratio tables, this time to find denominators of 100 for $\frac{3}{5}$. Conceptually, that task deals with percent, which means "If I had 100, instead of 5, what would this part (3) become?" Procedurally, our goal with the ratio table was to change the given representation to a representation with a denominator of 100. However, it is helpful to ask questions with a context. A good context for this objective might be "We have 3 candy bars *for every* 5 children. At that rate, how many candy bars would we need for 100 students?"

Moving back and forth between equivalent fractions can be accomplished by using a proportion, division, or a ratio table. You are probably familiar with the algebraic proportion: $\frac{3}{5} = \frac{x}{100}$. Using that approach requires algebraic thinking. Instead, Jamal revisited a familiar procedure dividing 3 ÷ 5, using a division algorithm he had presumably learned earlier. But students are often not proficient at that algorithm, even as late as fifth grade. Sometimes they turn the numbers around, not believing it to be an accurate task to divide 3 by 5. Or they simply claim that it is impossible to divide 3 by 5.

Sometimes procedures for making equivalent fractions, like the ratio table, work well for students. Lydia's procedure was to continue the pattern: $\frac{3}{5}, \frac{6}{10}, \frac{9}{15}$, and so on until reaching $\frac{60}{100}$. Jamal's ratio table procedure was to recognize that 20 × 5 gives 100, so 100 would be in the twentieth place. He knew that he should be able to multiply the numerator and denominator by 20. Thus, Jamal skipped to the important part of the table by multiplying by 20.

All three ratio table procedures require knowledge about concepts. Students must understand ideas of decimal representations and their relationship to denominators of 10, 100, 1,000, and so on. They must also understand that percent is always thought of as "What if I had 100?" Then procedures follow from those concepts. If procedural ideas are not related to concepts, then the learner is unaware of crucial relationships such as the relationship between *A/B* and *A* ÷ *B*. When procedures are learned in isolation from concepts, memorization is forced rather than allowing reasoning to prevail.

LET'S REVIEW

In thinking about the mathematics of rational numbers and proportions, we learned that both concepts and procedures are part of the mathematical knowledge base. The basic concept is that a rational number is a ratio, which describes a relationship between two amounts. The more familiar rational numbers are common fractions where the second amount (the unit of comparison) is a whole unit. A proportion is a statement of equality between two ratios. Perhaps sensibly, students often symbolize ratios backward. It is a natural event for youngsters to first determine the size of the unit of comparison (the whole unit) and then to tell how many parts. Writing the information in this order reverses the conventional manner of writing ratios in which we write a numerator (first amount) and a denominator (unit of comparison). Procedures for working with rational numbers requires awareness that although the operation is defined in exactly the same manner as with whole numbers, sometimes the operation appears to act differently with rational numbers. Sometimes we need a common denominator (addition and subtraction), and sometimes we do not need one (multiplication), whereas at other times (division), it depends on how the operation is understood to act.

HOMEWORK

1. Draw two pictures, one that shows $1\frac{2}{3} \cdot \frac{1}{2}$ and one that shows $1\frac{2}{3} \div \frac{1}{2}$. How are the two ideas the same and how are they different? When someone says, "Divide $1\frac{2}{3}$ in half," which process do they mean for you to execute? How might this wording lead to confusion?

2. A CD jewel case measures 13.8 cm by 12.4 cm. (a) What is the area of (the top of) a jewel case? (b) Draw a picture of the jewel case on a piece of graph paper in which each square centimeter is represented by one square on the graph paper. (c) Compare this multiplication problem to the multiplication of 138 and 124. In what ways might comparing these two processes explain the "move the decimal two places" part of the algorithm? (d) Recall the intermediate products approach to multiplication from Chapter 5. How would that process apply to 13.8 × 12.4?

3. What is the purpose of changing something from a fractional statement into a percentage statement?

4. Write a word problem for the computation: $\frac{2}{3} + \frac{5}{8}$.

SUGGESTED READINGS

Huinker, D. (1998). Letting fraction algorithms emerge through problem solving. In L. J. Morrow & M. J. Kenney (Eds.), *The teaching and learning of algorithms in school mathematics. 1998 yearbook for the National Council of Teachers of Mathematics* (pp. 170–181). Reston, VA: NCTM.

Sharp, J., Garofalo, J., & Adams, B. (2002). Children's development of meaningful fraction algorithms: A kid's cookies and a puppy's pills. In B. Litwiller & G. Bright (Eds.), *Making sense of fractions, ratios and proportions. 2002 Yearbook for the National Council of Teachers of Mathematics* (pp. 18–28). Reston, VA: NCTM.

REFERENCES

Carpenter, T. (1986). Conceptual knowledge as a foundation for procedural knowledge. In J. Hiebert (Ed.), *Conceptual and procedural knowledge: The case of mathematics* (pp. 113–132). Hillsdale, NJ: Lawrence Erlbaum.

Cramer, K., & Post, T. (1993). Making connections: A case for proportionality. *Arithmetic Teacher, 60*(6), 342–346.

Kieren, T. E. (1988). Personal knowledge of rational numbers: Its intuitive and formal development. In J. Hiebert and M. J. Behr (Eds.), *Number concepts and operations in the middle grades* (pp. 162–181). Hillsdale, NJ: Lawrence Erlbaum.

Middleton, James A., & van den Heuvel-Panhuizen, M. (1995). The ratio table. *Mathematics Teaching in the Middle School, 1*(4), 282–288.

National Council of Teachers of Mathematics. (2000). *Principles and standards for school mathematics.* Reston, VA: NCTM.

Pothier, Y., & Sawada, D. (1983). Partitioning: The emergence of rational number ideas in young children. *Journal for Research in Mathematics Education, 14*(5), 307–317.

Watanabe, T. (2002). Representations in teaching and learning fractions. *Teaching Children Mathematics, 8*(8), 457–463.

CHAPTER

12

How We Learn about

Rational Numbers and Proportions

Understanding Relevant Learning Theory

NCTM
LEARNING

To teach about fractions, we make several instructional decisions for dealing with students' knowledge about whole numbers and recognizing whether whole number knowledge is interfering with fractional knowledge or supporting it. We know quite a bit about how students learn fractions. In this chapter, we highlight three different but complementary, descriptions of learning. Moreover, the three theories are not mutually exclusive. Each has a different focus, and all are relevant here. Kieren (1988) describes how fractional knowledge begins with personal knowledge and grows to more technical knowledge. Pothier and Sawada (1983) highlight one particular area of fraction knowledge development: that the denominator amount, the unit of comparison, *matters* as students develop their knowledge. Whereas Kieren and Pothier and Sawada look at how fraction knowledge develops, Streefland (1991) proposes educational principles for the teacher that a child should experience en route to learning about fractions.

Personal Knowledge

Kieren (1988) theorizes that fraction knowledge develops in continual growth in all directions from a center of personal knowledge. An analogy helps in understanding Kieren's theory. Imagine a rock being thrown into a pond. The spot where the rock dropped is the core and is nothing but personal knowledge that is informal. This personal knowledge about fractions is deeply related to children's daily lives in their individual environments. At the rock, knowledge is uniquely personal and must be tapped by the teacher for students' knowledge to progress. Fractional knowledge begins to grow like a series of water ripples. As students learn more about the fractional nature of their personal experiences, they follow the ripples, moving outward in all directions beyond the personal core. As students move away from the core, they are ready to develop symbols and tools to represent their reality and their experiences.

Representations and Intuition

At this first ripple, students need help to build images and intuitions about how fractional ideas work. Here they consider pictures, intuition and images, and school–world fractional representations. They learn to describe situations with words, physical models, and pictures that the entire class shares. They also learn to manipulate the representations and draw conclusions based on the images. They begin to develop an intuition about magnitudes of fractional amounts, developing their mental images of fractions, and they can think about fractions with pictures. For instance, students learn to use a variety of pictures for a given fraction. They know that $\frac{3}{5}$ is sometimes based on a continuous model and sometimes based on a discrete model. Their number sense expands to include fractional relationships along with whole number quantities. They learn to describe various aspects of their environments using fractional thinking. Students also start to make connections to slightly more abstract ideas while continuing to ground their thinking in their real-world core of fraction knowledge.

Technical Symbols

At the next ripple, students use accurate conventional representations and technical symbols to represent fractional thinking. Here, we are on the lookout for students to write fractions in a way we would call "backward" even though, in some respects, it is quite sensible. Sometimes children want to record *first* the number of pieces in a whole unit and *then* the number of pieces they have. So for one-fourth, they might write $\frac{4}{1}$, meaning "It takes 4 to make a whole, and I have 1 piece." Of course, this is something we need to clear up so that our students record with symbols in ways that are consistent with conventional expectations.

The last (fourth) ripple is when students' knowledge expands to recognize that rational numbers form a *quotient field*, which is part of an advanced study of algebra and likely not relevant to K–8 classrooms.

Building Knowledge

At that first (core) level, children already possess knowledge about fractions. They just might not be aware of useful ways to communicate that knowledge. Or they might not have really noticed the situation from a ratio point of view. This central core requires that children see fractions in their personal lives. For example, one-half of their books might be on the top shelf of their bookcase, they might get $\frac{1}{4}$ of a bag of pretzels (particularly if there are four people sharing it), or they might save $\frac{1}{10}$ of their weekly allowance. Examples like these need to be consciously pointed out to students, showing them how to quantify their environment and make connections to ratio thinking. Instead of counting books, pretzels, or dollar bills, ask them to quantify by comparisons. As usual, the teacher's role is asking good questions. When a student gets out crayons, ask for half of the crayons to be red instead of asking for three to be red. This kind of comment brings ratio thinking into a context that is meaningful to children.

Moving toward the intuitive level requires lots of experiences with lots of representations. Students should become flexible in their selection of representations. Circular regions, square regions, graph paper, real pictures, and photographs should all be used to give students a full arsenal of intuitions and images for fractions. Care should also be taken to distinguish between discrete representations and continuous representations.

Then in the third level of knowledge development, students begin to use technically accurate symbols. They know how to write one-half as $\frac{1}{2}$, and they know exactly what the numerator and denominator mean. They might think of several different situations in which they have used or seen the symbols: $\frac{1}{2}$, but in the end, they are comfortable strictly using $\frac{1}{2}$ to represent this type of situation but can also work with $\frac{1}{2}$ independent of the context. They also understand a lot about how numerical representations can be manipulated. Removing themselves from the context allows them to manipulate $\frac{1}{2}$ without worrying about a real-world situation, without imagining pictures, and without depending on intuition. When students are at that third stage, we tend to believe that they are more ready to operate formally with fraction symbols. But it does not change the idea that these fraction ideas on which they formally operate still need to have evolved from experiences with their sense-making of real-world and school-world situations.

One other point Kieren is careful to make is that learners will move back and forth between levels as needed. If a student encounters a situation at a given level and does not understand the situation, the student will go back to a more comfortable level; for instance, one child might cut shapes into parts while a classmate works fully at the symbolic level. When a child encounters a situation at a symbolic level and is unfamiliar with that level, a return to a previous level is likely in an effort to make sense of the situation. Sometimes, students might even go back to the core of personal knowledge trying to make sense of the situation with their own unique life experiences. It becomes difficult to predict where students will go when they encounter a situation in which they need to move back. But students can work (with guidance) to move their thinking to the level at which the problem was originally given and expected to be handled. Similarly, teachers can ask questions that require students to fold back to a previous level and view the problem from a comfortable vantage point.

Designing Activities

Kieren described the process of learning. Streefland outlines a guide for designing activities and experiences learners need in order to learn about fractions. He describes how we can work to help children quantify their environments. Like Kieren, he does not prescribe an absolute order of learning and he is clear that children's realities must be part of early fraction experiences. Strong rational number knowledge must evolve from contexts. Development of symbols, schemes, and visual models are part of later learning experiences. With that in mind, Streefland's guide for the teacher guides effective instruction. Like Kieren, Streefland does not believe that once students succeed in one area, they never return. Streefland's theory is flexible and dynamic and is offered here as a guide.

Begin with Contexts

First, children need to encounter fractions in contexts, using both teacher-planned contexts as well as contexts that children develop. This need for relevance to the world recognizes Kieren's explanation for initial fraction knowledge. But Streefland's idea is not quite the same. Whereas Kieren emphasizes the intensely personal and unique nature of knowledge from a *learning* point of view, Streefland emphasizes how teachers can develop a common core of rich open contexts that the class can discuss from a *teaching* point of view. These ideas are certainly not mutually exclusive, but there is a subtle difference.

For example, imagine that a city planner is developing plans for a new city park. She wants $\frac{4}{5}$ of the park dedicated to play equipment and/or open grassy space for children. The other $\frac{1}{5}$ will be dedicated to benches, pathways, trees, or shrubs. A teacher might bring in a map and a rectangular sheet of construction paper to represent the land for the park and ask students to describe how they might help the city planner. How could you help students decide how the $\frac{1}{5}$ of the park might be viewed? What will they already know about this context? They will probably know that the $\frac{1}{5}$ of the land dedicated to pathways and shrubs will be scattered throughout park, not clumped together all on one side. But they will probably need help thinking about how they could build a model of the situation. Beginning with this type of a context and connecting it to a rectangular model or representation of $\frac{1}{5}$ helps students to represent their thinking with models. Streefland would suggest this approach because of the context surrounding it. Kieren would suggest this approach if the students know about parks personally and could understand a planner's attempt to divide the park. Activity 12.1 leads you through one strategy for thinking about this lesson.

Activity 12.1

THE NEW PARK

You have been asked to work on the park project with the city planner. She wants you to make a display of the park as you visualize how it might look. Remember that she is requiring $\frac{1}{5}$ of the land to be pathways, shrubs, and benches. The other $\frac{4}{5}$ of the land can be dedicated to playground equipment and open, grassy fields.

She has given you two sheets of construction paper. Save one for your final display of the park, and use the other one to do your thinking. You might even cut up the "thinking" piece and glue the parts into place on the final display piece. You should submit a sketch of your final park.

Do you think the construction paper can be used in more than one way to represent the land without changing the mathematics of the problem?

How did you think about $\frac{4}{5}$? Do you visualize the park or a model of the park? Are those different levels? What would Streefland or Kieren say about the use of the problem situation? How is a representation with construction paper different from the problem, and how is it the same?

Share Strategies

Second, the classroom is a forum for discussions, negotiations, and collaborations. Students can learn by discussing their constructions and deductions. This sort of learning process is highly interactive. Such interactivity requires popping back and forth between different types of fraction knowledge. Intertwining and interweaving types of fraction knowledge (decimals, percents, etc.) also require facility with a wide range of symbols diagrams and visual models. "Attention [must be] especially paid to the production of symbols, diagrams and visual models" (Streefland, 1991, p. 21).

After students' individual procedures are established, conventional algorithms can be introduced as learners compare their personal procedures. Typically, students will abandon less efficient procedures for more efficient procedures if they become convinced that the more efficient algorithm is useful and meaningful (Kamii, 2000). But the key points are that students must make the decision and that the new procedure must be meaningful to them. We do not insist that they abandon one procedure for another. Rather, we introduce one of these (presumably) more efficient procedures by carefully coordinating classroom discourse to give verbal space to students who invented the interesting and/or desired procedure(s). After several procedures have been discussed and shown to be accurate, the rest of the students often choose to use the most efficient and yet meaningful procedure as their algorithm for that particular operation. Sometimes a class procedure can be established if the teacher decides to highlight a certain child's approach.

Using Tools

Third, teachers should explicitly direct the students to develop tools for communicating their thinking and representing their contexts. Parks (hence, areas) will not always be rectangular; sometimes they may be circular or irregular. Students need to think about this as they develop a solution. Some tools will be pictures like our construction paper model of $\frac{1}{5}$, others will be manipulatives, and still others will be symbols. However, technical symbols should not be used first or exclusively. Students must be taught how to represent fractional ideas with several tools: symbols, diagrams, and visual models. A half of a pizza is not the same as a half of a sandwich, in the real world. But both situations could be represented with the same model or the same half-piece from the manipulative fraction circles. These tools are deeply conceptual and therefore require extensive experiences with the mathematical structures described in Chapter 7. Students will need to recognize and extend patterns that use fractions, to compare and contrast models of fractional amounts, to notice complementary characteristics between two or more fraction pictures and/or amounts, and to sort and classify fraction diagrams and values into several kinds of groupings.

Building Knowledge

Streefland (1991) suggests students' problems in understanding fractions stem from two basic causes: (1) There is an "extreme underestimation of the complexity of this area of learning for children," and (2) many classroom experiences take a "mechanistic approach to fractions, detaching [them] from reality and focusing on rigid application of rules" (p. 11). The fact of the matter is, if we want to help students understand fractions, we must help students to recognize that fractions are complicated and take time to learn, and we must encourage students to use and build knowledge on their personal and contextual knowledge. It is precisely during efforts to make sense of the real and school worlds that students explore how to use fractions to represent their thinking and to communicate their thinking. We must respect the rules students might invent as they learn how fractions work in a realistic situation.

For their explorations to foster this knowledge, we suggested earlier that students must be encouraged to discuss their thinking about the situations. Streefland urges us to recognize, respect, and nurture the students' chosen communication tools, for it is through communication that students learn the need to represent their thinking using mathematically accurate symbols. This approach fits nicely with our ideas that when students defend and explain their thinking, they learn from each other as well as from their own statements. So teachers have to structure activities that move the children from use of fractions in their personal worlds to use of fractions through images and intuition (school world) and culminate with fostering their use of technical symbols.

Streefland also suggests that students must encounter fractions, percents, decimals, ratios, and proportions together so that connections can form. Knowing the relationships between these genres (both conceptually and procedurally) will deepen the students' fractional knowledge.

Partitioning Whole Units

There is another theory of fraction knowledge development that concentrates exclusively on how children progress in abilities to work with specific fractional amounts. The first understanding a child must have in order to work with any fractional amount is the idea of *sharing*. "Share this candy bar with your brother" is a typical first step in fractional thinking. Children need to have sharing in mind to work with fractions because it is the foundation on which fraction ideas are built.

The next stage children should experience is to *repeatedly halve.* For example, children at this stage might imagine a pizza that they wanted to share with friends. They might cut it in half, then in half again (fourths), then in half again (eighths) until they are satisfied that the pizza could be shared. That means that the denominators of half, fourth, eighth, and so on (2^n) are accessible to children fairly early. If the teacher is unaware of this theory, it might be tempting to withhold large denominators such as eighths because the size seems daunting. But the reality is children can handle this denominator precisely because it is half of half of half. Think about how much more difficult such an activity would have been if they had been asked to cut the pizza into thirds.

Ms. Hawthorne Shares Cookies

Consider Ms. Hawthorne's first grade classroom. She challenged the children to share seven cookies among four children. She handed the children seven paper cookies to use for the problem, because breaking apart real cookies is difficult, even for adults. The children had absolutely no problems completing this task with paper cookies. First, they doled out the whole cookies. (Each child received one cookie.) Then they began to deal with the three cookies that were left. They cut all of the cookies in half (six halves) and doled out those halves to the children. (Each child received one half of a cookie.) Then they began to deal with the two halves remaining by simply cutting them in half again and doled out the pieces. (Each child received one-fourth of a cookie.) In sum, the children received 1 and $\frac{3}{4}$ cookies each, although some said 1 and $\frac{1}{2}$ and $\frac{1}{4}$, not realizing that it could be written as $1\frac{3}{4}$. The way Ms. Hawthorne's children handled the situation demonstrates both sharing ideas and halving ideas.

After halving, children can handle *evenness.* Even denominators are more accessible than odd denominators; for example, sixths are more accessible than thirds.

Revisiting Ms. Hawthorne

To clarify, let's revisit Ms. Hawthorne's first grade classroom as the children undertake their next problem. She challenged her children to share eight circular cookies among three children. First, the children doled out whole cookies as long as they could. (Each child received two whole cookies.) Then the children turned to the two remaining cookies. Their first strategy was to cut the cookies in half. This resulted in four halves. The children doled out these halves leaving themselves with one half with which to deal. After a moment, they decided that they did not like that situation, and they gathered back the halves. They asked for two new cookies (not cut into halves) with which to start over. A few more moments passed, and the children decided to cut the two cookies into sixths. Then they gave four sixths to each child. You might be surprised that the children did not cut the cookies into thirds, as you probably would have done. They chose to deal with sixths (an even number of diameters could be drawn across this circular cookie) rather than to try and figure out this business of thirds.

You may have seen many lessons including thirds (an odd denominator) fairly early in school. Thirds are often encountered well before sixths or eighths. There are two reasons for this situation. First, thirds are fairly typical in personal lives, so children who have experiences with them can handle them. Families might have three people who share a candy bar, a hockey game is broken into three periods, business letters are folded into thirds, and a typical (informal) place setting has three pieces of silverware. Pothier and Sawada might theoretically disagree with this sequencing, although they would likely give leeway to the idea that thirds connect to personal knowledge, something that Kieren might claim. Pothier and Sawada say that the stage at which learners can understand odd denominators, such as thirds, requires very different thinking than the thinking required by children dealing with even denominators. To illustrate, complete Activity 12.2.

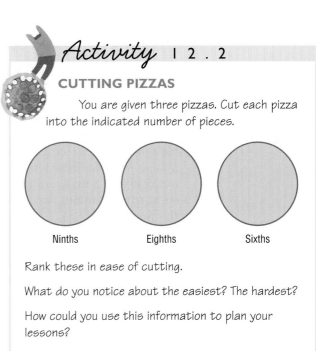

Activity 1 2 . 2

CUTTING PIZZAS

You are given three pizzas. Cut each pizza into the indicated number of pieces.

Ninths   Eighths   Sixths

Rank these in ease of cutting.

What do you notice about the easiest? The hardest?

How could you use this information to plan your lessons?

As you saw in the activity, the reality for students (and adults) is that diameters are simpler to draw than nondiameters. Diameters require that a circular area be cut into two equal pieces. Cutting with diameters will therefore always result in an even number of pieces. Sometimes students think of evenness as *matching partners*. Each piece of the pizza has a "partner" opposite of it. (The concept of "even" should be familiar to students.) In addition to dealing with diameters, Ms. Hawthorne's children demonstrated the necessity of understanding sharing, with the idea that the sharing had to result in equal amounts of cookies for each child. It is during such experiences at this third stage (evenness) that students also develop a keen sense and awareness for the necessity for equal-sized areas. It is success with this equal-sized awareness that allows learners to move into the fourth stage.

Oddness is the fourth stage when students can cut areas into any number of pieces. Students can deal with denominators of any size and can plan ahead for future cuts. They recognize that an odd denominator makes a diameter cut impossible. So when creating activities or assessments, we must be aware of the stage of the students' development in terms of the denominators used in the lesson. Knowing that there is a distinct sequence through which students pass as they acquire understanding of specific fractional amounts makes instructional planning a bit easier. It also helps a teacher to analyze students' responses meaningfully. When students miss a question, do they really not understand the information? Or was it the odd denominator (for example) that confused them?

You might be wondering whether students would experience the same process of development if they were asked to cut rectangular, square, or other noncircular areas into parts, since this could be accomplished without diameters. Even though the explanation would be slightly different, the fact remains that students can more easily think about even or matching pieces before being able to think about an odd number of pieces. This is in part because fraction thinking grows from the idea of sharing, and early ideas of sharing are between pairs of children.

USING RELEVANT PATTERNS:
Skip-Counting in Ratio Tables

It probably comes as no surprise to you that we revisit ratio tables in this section. Ratio tables are a tool that can help children to develop fractional thinking. By skip-counting along each row, the table keeps track of the multiplication being executed in the problem. The terms are changing together as in a *proportional* relationship. That is, just as we learned that skip-counting is a precursor to understanding multiplication, a ratio table serves as a precursor to understanding and finding equivalent fractions (proportions). Reconsider the pattern $\frac{3}{5}$, $\frac{6}{10}$, $\frac{9}{15}$, $\frac{12}{20}$, and so on. To move directly to $\frac{12}{20}$ from $\frac{3}{5}$, students eventually recognize that they could multiply both the 3 and 5 by 4 to land on $\frac{12}{20}$. The skips are merely multiplications. The difference in a ratio table (as opposed to skip-counting) is that we act on *two* numbers *in the same way*. To foster this thinking, it is important for students to think about values in the two rows of the ratio table as though they were acting together. That is, they would need to look for a way to relate the corresponding values.

It is important to recognize that students can describe the pattern of the numerators and the pattern of the denominators without really understanding the concept of equivalent fractions. The pattern is skip-counting by one amount in the numerator and (probably) by a different amount in the denominator. All the student needs to do is repeat this process to complete the table. Sometimes students complete the table by always doubling from the preceding value, as Min did earlier. It is important to help students see that they need to skip-count values in the ratio table, not just double them, and then to relate those values through multiplication ideas.

C U L T U R A L   C O N N E C T I O N S

Using and Making Unexpected Ratios

For our first example, we look to baseball, a sport that is deeply embedded in U.S. culture. In our second example, we discuss drum rhythms.

Counting Innings

Many cultures have some version of a stick and ball game. You have probably heard of the English game cricket. Since the Civil War, baseball has become the stick and ball game of the United States. Although there is some debate about the specifics of baseball's roots, we know that early teams were concentrated in the northeastern portion of the country. The first formally recorded contest took place in 1846 at the Elysian Fields, in Hoboken, New Jersey. Civil War soldiers are credited with carrying baseball from New Jersey across the country after the war. During the war, they played baseball to pass time and have fun while in camp. It was also an important means of escape, providing an opportunity to forget where they were for the moment (Millen, 2001). Eventually, small towns formed teams, and larger cities formed baseball clubs. Cities in the South and West wanted professional teams of their own.

In the United States, baseball has subtly influenced music (e.g., the song "Centerfield" by John Fogerty [1985]), literature (e.g., *A Connecticut Yankee in King Arthur's Court* by Mark Twain [1889] and *Leaves of Grass* by Walt Whitman [1855]), and countless films (e.g., *A League of Their Own* directed by Penny Marshall [Abbott et al., 1992]). Some laws are referred to as "Three strike laws." Baseball is even part of the cliché "as American as baseball and apple pie." Walt Whitman believed that the game of baseball would allow the nation to heal following the Civil War.

Even in the seventeenth century, equipment included a bat, a ball, and a base of some sort. Early versions have the ball sitting on a lever contraption on which the batter stepped, engaging the lever that thrust the ball into the air. The batter then hit the ball. However, you probably know that in today's game, a pitcher tosses the ball to the batter for him or her to hit. There are generally two camps in the culture of baseball: Is it a game of strategy or power? Strategy believers tout the importance of contact hitting, bunting at opportune times, and base stealing for offense. Power believers overwhelm defense with home runs and hits. Baseballs with a cork center were developed in the early twentieth century and changed the game. Batting records began to fall, the popularity of the game began to explode, and the "power" camp was born. Debate still lingers over the designated hitter rule, which further emphasizes the difference between the two approaches. In one league, there is a rule allowing coaches to swap one player in the batting lineup for one of the fielding players—thus *power*. In the other league, all fielding players are also batters—thus *strategy*. The baseball and softball cultures have staunch believers in each approach.

It is from the pitcher's role that we extract mathematics. Remember that mathematics must come from the culture and celebrate both mathematics and culture. If not for that particular culture, we would not know either the culture or the mathematics in the same way that we know it. The pitcher's statistic we consider is innings-pitched (IP). Check out any pitcher's baseball card, and you will find this category. Before you work through Activity 12.3 (p. 230), you need to meet Nolan Ryan, a pitcher for the Texas Rangers from 1989 through 1993. His innings-pitched statistics for that time period are given in Table 12.1. (No, the sum is not a misprint. Think about an inning and what the decimal part of an inning might represent.)

For baseball pitchers, their work is measured in innings. Innings are not measured by time like football's 15-minute quarters or basketball's 20-minute halves. Innings are measured by outs. So 239.1 innings is $239\frac{1}{3}$ innings. The decimal value is based on thirds (instead of the familiar tenths). Decimal values for innings pitched are in base-three.

Drumming Ratios

For our second example, we study how ratios connect to African and Afro-Cuban drumming rhythms. Our discussion of African and Afro-Cuban drumming history and its importance in culture is brief, and you are encouraged to read about and learn more about this rich history. For many centuries, drumming has been an important part of traditions in African villages. Some drumming

Table 12.1 **Some of Ryan's Statistics**

YEAR	INNINGS PITCHED
1989	239.1
1990	204.0
1991	173.0
1992	157.1
1993	66.1
Total (at Texas)	840.0

Activity 12.3

BASEBALL INNINGS PITCHED

Think about how base-ten blocks help you visualize decimals. The fraction 1.2 is shown below.

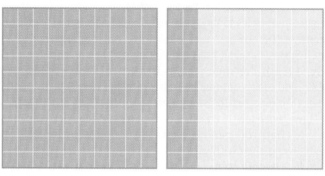

Do you notice how the square flat is one whole unit and the partitions separate the flat into hundredths? Where are the tenths on the flat?

In the space below, draw what you think a block picture for 1.2 innings pitched looks like. How do blocks help you think about that?

Next, think about the effect of the innings-pitched statistics if there were four outs in an inning. What would 1.2 innings pitched mean?

---

ceremonies to honor village leaders last an entire month. Others celebrate the birth of a child or to tell a history lesson. Historically, drummers were of noble origin. Moreover, drums were carefully prepared through a year-long process and were stored in a special hut designed specifically for their care. The drummer's role in celebrations and storytelling is to incorporate various rhythms into his or her music in ways that dramatically sway dancers. In addition, the polyrhythmic nature of the drummer's music adds to the listening pleasure of village elders and leaders. In polyrhythmic music, several rhythms are played simultaneously. Those individual rhythms are usually of different repetition length. That is, one rhythm in the song might be a three-beat repeating rhythm while a different rhythm in the song is an eight-beat repeating rhythm. A Western musician might think of these rhythm lengths as corresponding to beats in a measure. One purpose for this characteristic of the music is that the simultaneous rhythms create a strong desire for movement on the part of the dancers. As the dancers feel the different rhythms that make up the song, their body movements sway and create a dance that is in part a reaction to those different rhythms.

The mathematics underlying polyrhythmic music is the idea of ratio. Reacting to the mathematical ratios, the dancers' movements fluctuate. When two (or more) rhythms are played simultaneously, there will inevitably be moments when the music feels more in sync (both rhythms are on a count of 1 at the same time) than at other times in the song.

Figure 1 2 . 1

A Comparison of Two Drum Rhythms

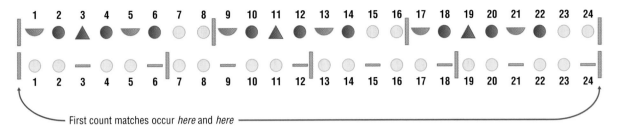

First count matches occur *here* and *here*

Look at Figure 12.1 for a picture of two rhythms. Different symbols mean that different types of hand strokes are being used that result in a different kind of sound from the drum. As dancers encounter beats close to the *simultaneous* counts of 1, dancing movements are more subdued; but at points with greater dissonance, say, around the sixteenth count, dancers are more compelled to move.

USING TEACHING AIDS APPROPRIATELY:
Discrete versus Continuous

Students must encounter fractional thinking in real-world contexts *and* be urged to move that thinking into the school world of manipulatives, pictures, and symbols. Some ideas for promoting that movement is outlined by Streefland, and some is outlined in the mathematical development from concrete to pictorial to symbolic only.

To establish tools that represent rational number ideas, teachers use both continuous models and discrete models to solidify fraction thinking. You learned previously that there are two basic models that can be used to represent whole numbers. These same two basic models of discrete and continuous are also used to represent fractional numbers.

Continuous

Continuous models represent fractions with measurement. Students have to understand basic concepts and procedures for measuring and congruence. A continuous model based on area requires sharing the whole unit (a closed plane region, such as a circle or square) into congruent parts. For instance, if a pie is one whole unit and it is cut into six congruent parts, then one piece is $\frac{1}{6}$ of the pie. The continuous model can be represented with a whole unit based on area, length (number line), or volume. For fractions, you are probably familiar with area regions (e.g., fraction circles or rectangles). But number lines have been found to be less helpful in *developing* fraction knowledge (Watanabe, 2002). It seems that number lines are more useful for students who wish to communicate something they *already understand* about fractions. Still, helping students to make meaningful connections among representations is important. Eventually, students should be able to use all three continuous ideas to show fractions such as $\frac{1}{3}$ and $\frac{3}{4}$. In all cases, the continuous whole unit is cut into congruent parts.

Discrete

Discrete models represent fractions with sets. A discrete model requires counting the number of elements in a set and seeing how many have a certain characteristic. For instance, in a box of 24 chocolates, seven have coconut filling. So $\frac{7}{24}$ of the box has coconut because seven out of 24 pieces have coconut. Individual pieces matter, and they do not have to be congruent. The discrete model does not rely on ideas from measurement, only on ideas from counting. But they have been found to be less helpful in developing operation knowledge. In Activity 12.4, use tangrams to model both discrete and continuous representations.

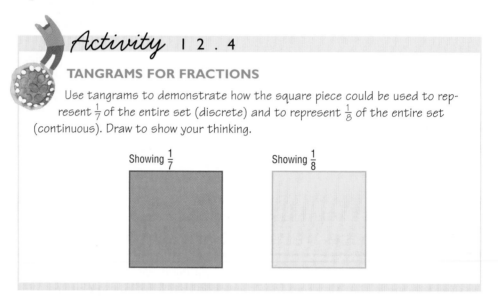

Activity 1 2 . 4

TANGRAMS FOR FRACTIONS

Use tangrams to demonstrate how the square piece could be used to represent $\frac{1}{7}$ of the entire set (discrete) and to represent $\frac{1}{8}$ of the entire set (continuous). Draw to show your thinking.

Showing $\frac{1}{7}$ Showing $\frac{1}{8}$

Role of Context

Students need to be able to communicate and think with both models. Teachers who use both models when they teach fraction ideas enable students to generalize the idea of fraction and foster a connection between models. The context will determine which model makes the most sense. Reconsider the two scenarios above. Imagine that in the pie scenario, only one piece is cut out of the pie (so there are two chunks: the $\frac{1}{6}$ slice and the rest of the uncut pie). Then that chunk represents $\frac{1}{6}$ based on the measurement model but $\frac{1}{2}$ based on the set model because it is one out of two chunks. In the chocolate box scenario, imagine that the entire box weighs 50 ounces. If, together, the seven coconut pieces weigh 10 ounces, then those seven pieces represent $\frac{10}{50}$ based on the continuous model, because it measures 10 of 50 ounces.

Types of Concrete Materials

Fraction Circles

Fraction circles are commercial manipulatives that teachers can use as a continuous model (in this case, area) of fractions. This manipulative uses a circular whole unit and usually includes halves, thirds, fourths, sixths, and eighths. Some sets also include tenths and twelfths. The materials are convenient because the whole unit is set up as the circular region. This has advantages and disadvantages. The advantage is the ease of communication, because all participants agree on the whole unit. The disadvantage is overgeneralizing that a whole unit must always be circular. However this usually occurs only if several different models are not used. It is important not to limit students to one concrete material.

Paper Folding

A good (and inexpensive) manipulative is paper folding. Students create their own set of fraction models. Initially, we recommend first experiences with a square region of paper. Thirds and sixths are somewhat challenging, but in the process of deciding how to fold for thirds, students develop their thinking about the continuous model of fractions. They must create congruent parts. In addition, equivalent fractions come to light when students recognize that sixths can be made from halves and thirds. Finally, a fun and challenging task is to fold for large odd denominators, such as sevenths. Jamal developed the procedure of tightly rolling a piece of paper and loosening it until he could see four layers on top and three layers on the bottom; then he squished the roll to create seven parts.

Chips

Teachers might also use chips as counters for students to establish the idea of the discrete model of fractional thinking. Students should also use familiar items, even items from inside their desks. In using a discrete model, it is paramount for students to agree on the whole unit.

Keep in mind these ideas about selecting continuous or discrete materials as you read Chapter 13. It will also be useful to think back to the notions discussed in the number and measurement chapters.

Base-Ten Blocks

When it comes time to study decimal representations, many teachers use base-ten blocks. Some teachers work with the flat as the whole unit, while other teachers work with a meter stick as the whole unit. Neither is more correct than the other one, but each will have implications for how students think about decimals. Do they imagine a number line or an area?

There are two concerns to keep in mind in using these manipulatives for decimal knowledge. First, using the flat to represent one whole unit requires that students have developed area thinking and that they can visualize the flat as being partitioned into 100 little square (or cube) sections or 10 long sections. The long is related to linear spatial thinking, the flat is related to area spatial thinking, and the small cube (as well as the large 1,000-cube) is related to volume spatial thinking. These blocks are set up in such a way that a child must be able to think in terms of length, area, and volume to use them effectively. Students who struggle with area may be unsuccessful. Cutting flats from construction paper can help students to clarify the decimal idea of hundredths because the students can literally cut the blocks apart, something that is impossible with the plastic commercial manipulative. As teachers, we should be acutely aware of difficulties a lack of understanding about area causes when using the base-ten blocks for decimal values. On the other hand, making a connection between one hundred, hundredths, and dealing with the faces of the blocks may be just the thing that solidifies the concept of plane thinking, so we should not be too quick to abandon the idea.

Second, the base-ten blocks are tightly linked to students' development of whole number place value and counting. Therefore, they may be able to convince us that they know decimal values when in reality they have merely achieved great facility with using the manipulative as related to whole numbers. For instance, consider the situation in which a child has shaded in 35 of the 100 squares on a pictorial representation of a flat. The child might say .35, and the teacher might applaud. But it is possible that the child has merely associated "what the teacher wants here" with "what the teacher wanted back when the topic of study was units." The child might not really understand 35-hundredths any differently from 35.

Using Metrics

Thinking in terms of tenths and hundredths might be more accessible to a child if the teacher uses the meter stick as a whole unit. Then the long (10 units long) and the unit cubes (one unit long) can be set directly on top of the meter stick and only require students to use the one-dimensional idea of length. Students do not have to convert their thinking between and among length and area, so they can concentrate on what fraction of the meter stick a certain number of the units cover. Moreover, this approach meshes nicely with the use of metric measurement the students will likely experience in other curricular areas. If decimal instruction follows fraction instruction, the meter stick is a good model, even though it models the number line. It is important to include useful contexts arising from measuring with the metric system, in which we easily use decimal values.

LITERATURE CONNECTIONS

Letting Characters Physically Illustrate Proportions

There are several books that require proportional thinking and encourage readers to quantify characters' environments with fractions. In *Half Magic* (Eager, 1999), children learn that their wishes are always granted at "half strength." So they learn how to adjust their wishes to compensate for this situation. In *The Indian in the Cupboard* (Banks, 1985) and *The Littles* (Peterson, 1967), readers meet characters who encounter situations in which they are physically out of proportion with the reader's real-world experiences. Reading these kinds of books allows students to expand their proportional thinking. Perhaps they should consider how to describe the small Indian figurine. He was about $\frac{1}{20}$ the size of an average adult. The Littles are one inch tall. What fraction of a typical cat's height was a Little family member?

A Giraffe and a Half is a playful story by Shel Silverstein (1975) about a giraffe who grows another half. He is quite silly and shares with the reader a variety of his antics, including tripping on a snake that is eating some cake. In the end, Silverstein suggests that reducing the giraffe and a half by a half would return the giraffe to his original size. The students should be encouraged to study this situation with mathematical eyes. Is the final solution correct? We know what Silverstein meant, but how does the specific language get interpreted through mathematical eyes? Would the giraffe not be three-fourths of his beginning size? It would be useful to revisit the concept of one whole unit with this delightful book.

LET'S REVIEW

To understand how we learn rational number knowledge and proportional thinking, Kieren (1988) and Pothier and Sawada (1983) suggest the importance of initial knowledge. Kieren is careful to discuss the importance of personal knowledge that is therefore meaningful to the learner, whereas Pothier and Sawada point out the different manners in which children think about subdividing a whole unit. As students experience meaningful contexts, they need to be encouraged to create tools and visual images such as pictures and eventually technical symbols to represent the information. It is important to help students recognize models that use both continuous thinking and discrete thinking. Continuous models (e.g., area) require facility with measurement but lead nicely to operations, whereas discrete models often result from personally relevant contexts. Students should use a wide variety of models (e.g., area pictures, paper folding, exact drawings, fraction circles) to come to see the ideas more generally.

Students must see fractions in highly personal contexts. It is important that children learn to quantify their (unique personal) environment using ratios rather than as mere counting. For example, asking, "What fraction of the books are red?" instead of "How many books are red?" is an example of quantifying environments using ratio thinking. Moving on to questions that involve proportions (e.g., "If for every three red books, I have five green books and I have 25 green books, how many red books do I own?") need to be carefully worded to communicate the idea of "for every."

HOMEWORK

1. Generate a list of five discrete contexts and five continuous contexts and (a) ask a counting or number question and (b) a fractional question about each of those contexts. Fill out the chart in Table 12.2 on page 236.
2. Explain the difference between a continuous model for fractional concepts and/or computations and the discrete model. Use the example of $\frac{3}{5}$.
3. Locate a primary (K–2), an intermediate (3–5), and a middle (6–8) textbook from the same publisher, and describe how they use discrete models and continuous models in their pictorial explanations of fraction lessons. Compare the levels of abstraction required of the middle school textbook in comparison to the other two. (Submit copies of the lessons.)
4. Find a textbook that begins discussion of fractional ideas with the concept of sharing. Describe whether or not the rest of that unit continues to sequentially develop the various denominators (halving, evenness, and oddness) as suggested by Pothier and Sawada. Defend your claim. (Submit a photocopy of the lesson.)

SUGGESTED READINGS

Huinker, D. (1998). Letting fraction algorithms emerge through problem solving. In L. J. Morrow & M. J. Kenney (Eds.), *The teaching and learning of algorithms in school mathematics: 1998 Yearbook* (pp. 170–181). Reston, VA: NCTM.

Lawton, C. A. (1993). Contextual factors affecting errors in proportional reasoning. *Journal for Research in Mathematics Education, 24*(5), 460–466.

Singer, J. A., & Resnick, L. B. (1992). Representations of proportional relationships: Are children part-part or part-whole reasoners. *Educational Studies in Mathematics, 23,* 231–246.

Sophian, C., & Wood, A. (1997). Proportional reasoning in young children: The parts and the whole of it. *Journal of Educational Psychology, 89*(2), 309–317.

Table 12.2 **Context Chart for Homework Problem 1**

DISCRETE CONTEXT	(a)	(b)
Silverware in a table setting	How many pieces are in a setting?	What portion of the pieces are spoons?
A box of waffles		

CONTINUOUS CONTEXT	(a)	(b)
A waffle		

REFERENCES

Abbott, E., & Greenhut, R. (Producers), & Marshall, P. (Director). (1992). *A league of their own* [Film]. Columbia/Tristar Studios.

Banks, L. R. (1985). *Indian in the Cupboard.* (Illustrated by Brock Cole.) New York: Doubleday.

Eager, E. (1999). *Half Magic.* (Illustrated by N. M. Bodecker.) Orlando, FL: Harcourt Brace.

Fogerty, J. (1985) Centerfield. On *Centerfield* [CD]. Burbank, CA: Warner Brothers.

Hickey, D. T., Moore, A. L., & Pellegrino, J. W. (2001). The motivational and academic consequences of elementary mathematics environments: Do constructivist innovations and reforms make a difference? *American Educational Research Journal, 38*(3), 611–652.

Kamii, C. (2000). *Number in preschool and kindergarten.* New York: National Association for the Education of Young Children.

Kieren, T. E. (1988). Personal knowledge of rational numbers: Its intuitive and formal development. In J. Hiebert & M. J. Behr (Eds.), *Number concepts and operations in the middle grades* (pp. 162–181). Hillsdale, NJ: Lawrence Erlbaum.

Millen, P. E. (2001). *From pastime to passion: Baseball and the Civil War.* Bowie, MD: Heritage Books.

Peterson, J. (1967). *The Littles.* New York: Scholastic.

Pothier, Y., & Sawada, D. (1983) Partitioning: The emergence of rational number ideas in young children. *Journal for Research in Mathematics Education, 14*(5), 307–317.

Silverstein, S. (1975). *A giraffe and a half.* New York: HarperCollins.

Streefland L. (1991). *Fractions in realistic mathematics education.* Dordrecht, The Netherlands: Kluwer Academic Publishers.

Twain, M. (1889). *A Connecticut yankee in King Arthur's court.* New York: Charles L. Webster.

Watanabe, T. (2002). Representations in teaching and learning fractions. *Teaching Children Mathematics, 8*(8), 457–463.

Whitman, W. (1855). *Leaves of grass.* New York: Modern Library [Reprint, 1993].

C H A P T E R

13

Role of the Teacher in
Rational Numbers and Proportions Lessons

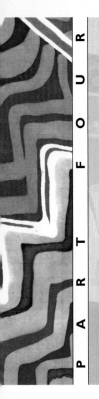

NCTM
TEACHING

ANALYZING ONE OF THE TEACHING MODELS:
Problem Solving (Discovery)

Problem solving is sometimes thought to be a content area in mathematics—that is, information that is consciously taught. And certainly, teachers do teach students strategies for handling problems in all content areas, such as science and language arts. Problem solving strategies, such as looking for a pattern, finding an equation, and working backward, are part of most mathematics curricula. However, in this chapter, problem solving will be analyzed as a teaching model. That is, problem solving is an avenue to teach something, not a content area to be taught. For a thorough treatment of problem-solving theory, read Schoenfeld's (1985) *Problem Solving*. Several of the ideas expressed in this portion of the chapter are based loosely on his work.

The problem-solving model of teaching starts with a very rich context that surrounds some existing personal or intuitive knowledge on which students can build new knowledge. Here, students encounter the problem from the context that is personal, engaging, and interesting. They must be inclined to wrestle with the situation. Worthwhile problems tend to put the learner in charge of the situations. Such problems begin with "You are a doctor" or "You have just come home from school" or "You just opened the refrigerator." Somewhere in the middle of the problem, something interesting happens that challenges the problem's original setup. Finally, the learner is urged and expected to resolve the situation.

Ms. Steffen's Experiment

Consider Ms. Steffen's fifth grade classroom, in which her students were preparing to study division of fractions. First, she prepared a collection of division of fraction problems based on contexts that would be relevant to the students.

Then she solved a few of the problems on her own time, taking care to note any prerequisite knowledge needed to solve them. She recognized that her students would need (1) tools for representing fractions (such as pictures), (2) ways to represent fractions as both improper and mixed numerals, (3) procedures for finding equivalent fractions, and (4) ways to think about division. She knew that her students had this bank of mental resources. Finally, she posed the problems to the students and guided students' discussion as they worked to understand and resolve the situations. To kick things off, she described the following situation (Sharp et al., 2002). You should solve it too, so that the explanation makes sense to you.

> When I got home last night, I found my dog not feeling very well. So I took her to the veterinarian. The veterinarian said to give the dog some medicine. Then she gave me 15 tablets. Because my dog is very large (100 pounds), my veterinarian said I would have to give the dog 1 and $\frac{2}{3}$ tablets each day. (One and a half tablets would not be enough, and 2 tablets would upset the dog's stomach.) I wondered for how many days this medicine would last.

That problem context set the stage for an engaging discussion about the students' efforts to resolve the situation. They were deeply interested in this situation and worked feverishly to resolve it. The ensuing discussion set up Ms. Steffen's problem-solving lesson. Her knowledge of how students learn about fractions outlined by Kieren (1988) guided her interactions with her students.

As the students worked, Ms. Steffen listened for cues about the *beliefs* different students brought to the situation. What they believed about the problem situation affected their ability to study it. For instance, some of the students did not believe that dog pills could (or should) be cut up. If left unchecked, these students could have begun to wonder whether the problem was a trick question or whether the solution even mattered. They might have gotten bogged down in this detail of the context and not moved forward with the mathematics. Ms. Steffen assured the class that she had often cut up pills for her own children when they were young. Several students remembered their parents doing the same thing.

Ms. Steffen listened for *strategies* her students used to help them think through the problem situation. Several students drew pictures and manipulated the drawings. Some pictures were very precise; others were basic representations. Ms. Steffen was learning a lot about her students' knowledge of fractions. She learned whether or not they could represent situations with any-shaped models or whether they needed to draw pictures more closely resembling the actual (circular) pills. Some students drew pictures of square regions and became concerned because they realized that the pills were circular. They scratched out those drawings and drew circular pills. (Or course, the square pills would have led to a solution, but these students abandoned that effort.)

Next, Ms. Steffen listened for opportunities to ask her students whether or not their *current efforts would lead to a solution*, should they be pursued. She asked, "And what would that tell you?" or "If you knew that, how would that change what you have written?"

Finally, she helped students to analyze their work independently, in pairs, and as a whole class. She knew that they needed to *see a pattern* to their work if they were to generalize a procedure. Her general objective for the unit was for the entire class to recognize division of fraction situations and to develop an algorithm. So they needed to analyze their work and check for trends. Ms. Steffen's individual students struggled with finding good ways to communicate their thinking in a way that made sense to the entire class. In some ways, this negotiation was nearly as difficult *and useful* as their mathematical sense-making. Sometimes

NcTm
ASSESSMENT

Ms. Steffen asked partners to decide who would be person A and who would be person B. Next she asked person A to explain his or her procedure to person B. After both students had a chance to clarify and discuss what A has said, she asked B to summarize what A had said. This is another example of partner-pair-share that Karen described earlier.

Listen to her fifth graders describe their thinking:

Min: I just kept on adding 1 and $\frac{2}{3}$ until I got to 15.

Even though the lesson was supposed to be about division, Min's addition did not daunt Ms. Steffen. She asked Min why adding helped her to handle this situation. Min was making sense of the situation and preferred to think of it as addition rather than subtraction. Students often prefer building up to tearing apart.

Lydia: I drew 15 pills and crossed off 1 and $\frac{2}{3}$ until I couldn't do it anymore. I did this nine times, so the medicine lasts 9 days.

Ms. Steffen was excited that Lydia repeatedly subtracted to complete her division. Lydia had no difficulty explaining her processes to the class. When asked, Lydia knew that division was another name for repeated subtraction.

Ryan: I started with a ratio table and saw that at three days we used five pills. Since I know that 3 × 5 is 15, then I knew the answer was 3 × 3, or 9.

Ms. Steffen showed Ryan's ratio table to the rest of the class so that his description made good sense to them.

Pills	$1\frac{2}{3}$	$3\frac{1}{3}$	5		15		
Days	1	2	3		9		

Jamal: I divided 15 by 1.66 and got 9. I knew it was a division problem, so I changed the fractions to decimals so I could divide.

Ms. Steffen asked Jamal how he knew the decimal way to show $1\frac{2}{3}$. Jamal said that he just knew it but that if he didn't know it, he would have divided 5 by 3 to get it.

Asking Good Questions

Sometimes it is tempting for the teacher to recite a rule, such as "invert and multiply" for the learners attempting to solve a division problem. Giving a rule to learners may give them a formalized way to deal with that particular situation. It would certainly give them an action to perform on the numerical information in the problem. But when instead the teacher opts to tag the emerging knowledge to students' existing knowledge, the students' knowledge becomes more formalized with roots in previous levels. With rooted knowledge, the learners can fold back at will whenever confronted with something they do not understand. How does a teacher do this? By using learning theory to diagnose the students' levels of thinking and then asking good questions. Good questions allow the learners to consciously connect information in the problem to similar or related information that is already known or good questions help learners formalize their thinking away from specific contexts. Pirie and Kieren (1994) suggest there are three kinds of questions a teacher can ask as part of a problem-solving lesson. First, a question can be designed to propel learners forward. Second, a question can be asked to guide students to fold back to previous kinds of thinking. Third, a question can merely be to offer validation to the teacher (and students) that the students' thinking is on track.

Min kept adding 1 and $\frac{2}{3}$ until she reached 15. Ms. Steffen recognized this result might mislead Min later since even though the solution to this problem could be found in this way, solutions to other problems (those with fractional answers) would not be easily found this way. So, she asked, "I see you added 1 and $\frac{2}{3}$ several times. Can you write that as a multiplication statement? Tell me how that information is related to the 15 in the problem." Ms. Steffen was hoping that Min would recognize the solution of 9 was not a number given in the problem and be propelled forward to recognizing that the situation was division, the inverse of multiplication. When Lydia drew pills and repeatedly subtracted off 1 and $\frac{2}{3}$, Ms. Steffen asked, "I thought subtraction always told me how much was left over. Why did subtraction work for you here?" This question runs slightly counter to Lydia's efforts. Ms. Steffen attempted to tempt Lydia to fold back into her existing understanding to help her solidify her new knowledge, but Lydia was not tempted. When Jamal changed 1 and $\frac{2}{3}$ to 1.66 before operating, Ms. Steffen asked, "What was it about this problem that made you decide to work with decimals?" Jamal explained that decimals are much simpler for him to operate with and that it did not matter what kind of problem he encountered. Ms. Steffen needed to assure herself that Jamal really knew about the numbers in the problem. In fact, Ms. Steffen used lots of theoretical information as she interacted with her students.

She used Kieren's (1988), Pothier and Sawada's (1983), and Streefland's (1991) theories to make decisions about how to guide these students and her other students. For instance, she recognized that when her students drew area pictures to show their work, they were comfortable with pictorial models. Other students wanted to know what the pills looked like so that they could draw exact replicas. When one of her students demonstrated an inability to cut a picture of a circular pill into thirds (oddness), she made an adjustment in her teaching, showing him some thirds and suggesting a rectangular region. Another of her students needed to see how pills could be cut into thirds. He wanted to touch the actual pills and manipulate those tools. Ms. Steffen was prepared. She had some precut circles for those students who were not ready to draw pictures or use symbols. She had colored pencils for students who needed to color-code their drawings. She knew that this problem asked her students to deal with thirds, a very high level, so she watched for instances of concern. With the wide range of sensible responses, Ms. Steffen knew that her students were ready to move through more division problems, such as those in Activity 13.1 (p. 242).

Solving Division Problems

Did you draw several pictures and record your work with symbols? As you look for a pattern in your work, notice that you were consistently trying to subtract a value over and over again. As Lydia noted, division is repeated subtraction. Attempting to *subtract* meant that you needed to have the values shown with a common denominator. This was your preparation to do the repeated subtraction (division) process. We hope that you recognize the LCD algorithm described earlier. After rewriting with a common denominator, just divide the numerators, using familiar, whole number knowledge.

You see that we started with contexts, built on existing knowledge of fractions and whole numbers, and encouraged you to use a variety of tools before expecting you to find a way to generalize your procedures with symbols only. Problems can ground algorithms, but problems do not do the teaching in and

Activity 13.1

DIVISION PROBLEMS TO CONSIDER

A. Here I have $2\frac{1}{4}$ cups of orange juice.

I take medicine each day, and my doctor wants me to limit the amount of orange juice I drink when I take my medicine.

I can have $\frac{3}{4}$ cups of orange juice each day with my breakfast.

For how many days can I have orange juice?

B. This container holds 24 cups of cat food.

My cat eats $\frac{3}{4}$ cup of food each day.

For how many days will this food last?

C. Last week, my dog had surgery to replace an injured knee ligament.

To ease her pain, our vet said to give our dog some medicine. She gave us 25 tablets.

She told us to give the dog $1\frac{3}{4}$ tablet each day!

For how many days will we give the dog a full dose?

What fraction of a dose would I have on that very last day?

Problem A is reprinted with kind permission from the *Journal of Educational Research*, Heldref Publications.

D. My mom made this teddy bear. She is thinking about making a whole bunch of them. She used ribbon for the bow.

This ribbon is 6 yards long.

She wants to use $1\frac{1}{2}$ yards of ribbon to make a bow for each stuffed animal.

To how many stuffed animals can she give a bow? Is there any ribbon left over?

E. This teddy bear is a lot smaller. My mom used special ribbon to make its bow.

This ribbon is only 11 feet long.

She used $1\frac{1}{2}$ feet of ribbon for each of these stuffed animals.

To how many stuffed animals can she give a bow?

What fraction of a bow could I make with the remaining part?

F. I had 2 pumpkin pies. My Dad ate 1 piece, so now I have $1\frac{5}{6}$ of a pumpkin pie. I want to take pie to my Grandmother's house. I am going to use some plastic carrying cases. But, only $\frac{1}{2}$ of a pumpkin pie fits inside my carrying case.

How many carrying cases are full?

How full is the last case?

G. This picture shows 1 batch of cookies.

$\frac{5}{12}$ of the cookies will be frozen in bags for distribution later.

How many bags will be needed to store the entire batch?

How many bags will be completely full?

How full will the last bag be?

Problem E is reprinted with kind permission from the *Journal of Educational Research*, Heldref Publications.

TECHNOLOGY CONNECTIONS
Using Digital Images to Make Mathematics Come Alive

The emergence of easy-to-use and affordable digital cameras for classrooms has provided an exciting new tool for mathematics teachers looking for real-world mathematics experiences for their students. Certainly, the idea of using images in the teaching of mathematics is not a new one. The Jasper Series, created by the Cognition and Technology Group at Vanderbilt University, has served has a valuable resource for mathematics teachers for more than a decade (Cognition and Technology Group at Vanderbilt, 1991, 1992, 1997). In the Jasper series, video is used to create complex, real-world problems for students to solve. The Jasper problems are interwoven in a 20-minute video drama that is entertaining as well as informative. Students become engrossed in the adventure story and find the emerging mathematics problem challenging and motivating. In the Jasper series, students follow the adventures of Jasper Woodbury as he confronts adventures and challenges that involve mathematics. In each video episode, an adventure unfolds, and the adventure ends with a question or challenge that students are asked to solve. In one such adventure, students are asked to determine a procedure for saving a wounded eagle; in another, students are asked to determine a plan for getting a boat back to dock before dark.

In essence, each Jasper adventure creates a rich and interesting problem environment for students. The context is real and motivating, and the problem is typically complex and multifaceted. Mathematics content is required for the solution of the problem, and the mathematics involved varies from simple arithmetic to geometry to simple algebra. To solve the challenge, students must do careful problem definition, data gathering, and data analysis, and they must communicate their ideas to other students and to the teacher. One of the interesting features of the Jasper series is that a good deal of mathematical data are included in each adventure that have nothing to do with the solution to the challenge. Thus, students are asked to develop strategies for determining which are the relevant data.

Research around learners' use of the Jasper series has yielded promising results. In addition to the positive effects from working in authentic environments, studies suggest the following outcomes (Barron et al., 1998; Cognition and Technology Group at Vanderbilt, 1992, 1993, 1997; Crews et al., 1997; Hickey,

et al., 2001; Van Haneghan et al., 1992; Young, et al., 1996):

- Students' abilities to identify their own mathematical questions, goals, and issues
- Students' abilities to work collaboratively in small groups to discuss mathematics and solve problems
- Students' abilities to differentiate relevant from irrelevant mathematical information
- Students' abilities in basic skill performance in math despite time taken away from drill practice

The success of the Jasper series and other similar projects provides a promising foundation for work in digital storytelling in mathematics. Although most teachers lack the funding necessary to create the types of problems exemplified in the Jasper series, many of the positive aspects of this project might be replicable through the use of digital cameras in classrooms.

The digital camera offers interesting new possibilities for mathematics story problems. At the simplest level, teachers can use digital cameras to create authentic story problems for students. After experiencing digital stories created by teachers, students can create and illustrate their own digital math story problems. Students equipped with cameras can begin to view the world around them as a potential mathematics problem. The statement "Math is everywhere" takes on a new meaning for a student with a digital camera and an interest in creating story problems for peers. At the higher levels, each student in a class studying fractions could create digital stories about a particular fraction. The story title "One-Fourth in My Home" suggests an intriguing challenge for learners.

For both teachers and students, digital stories can be created from everyday experience, and these stories will emphasize the importance of mathematics in everyday life. Like the episodes in the Jasper series, a typical mathematics digital story problem will contain irrelevant as well as relevant data. A good mathematics digital story will contain a plot of interest and will truly be a story as well as a mathematics problem. Parents and community members can also be involved in the mathematics digital story adventure.

of themselves. Students need prerequisite knowledge and many opportunities to compare their work with their classmates' work. Generalizing algorithms takes time but can be very rewarding. During discussions, students need guidance as they solve the problem. The point is that you do the teaching; the problem does not. Successful use of the problem-solving model requires teachers to hear the students and to build on the knowledge they display. The teacher follows and leads at the same time.

One simple note: Problems should be open-ended but not vague. In a vague problem, students have no launching point and might wander far from the day's objective. Problems should draw from the days' lesson objective, not merely represent some activity that sounds fun. Then, as students engage in solving the problem, we can watch and listen for clues about what each child knows. These clues are very important because they answer important questions: Was the day's objective met? How can students' conversations inform the questions that we ask?

MIDDLE SCHOOL CONNECTIONS

Problem Solving Can Ground Algorithms

Common algorithm procedures can emerge when students listen to classmates share diverse approaches to solving real problems. By pooling explanations from students' problem solutions, students can and do observe commonalties and construct meaningful algorithms. This approach to meaningful learning takes time and may result in our concerns about having time to prepare students adequately for their high school studies. To discuss this situation, we will think more about division of fractions. You might remember learning to divide fractions by being told to invert and multiply. You might have used that algorithm in your high school algebra studies. But now you know that the invert and multiply algorithm does not develop easily from concepts, procedures, or definitions for whole number division learned in elementary school. Nor does it match the way division of fractions is usually acted out in real-world contexts. Rather, "invert and multiply" is an algorithm designed to draw on the algebraic notion that multiplication and division is an inverse relationship. Hence, to teach the invert and multiply algorithm requires an immense leading of students through specific procedures, repeatedly pointing out that $3 \div \frac{1}{5}$, for example, gives the same result as 3×5. Streefland is clear that we should build fraction knowledge on realistic problem situations. But the invert and multiply algorithm might not develop when students are allowed to explore problems and build new knowledge on their own existing whole number knowledge. So what happens in middle school when students should layer their knowledge about division of fractions with *known* concepts and procedures when they do not typically *know* inverse relationships at an algebraic level?

First, we must respect the mathematical knowledge that students are actually ready to construct. However, we also must prepare middle school students for their upcoming high school mathematical experiences. The middle school experience can present a dilemma for these two reasons. All mathematical holes must be patched, and all foundational knowledge for algebra and geometry must be in place. Using problem solving to teach algorithms is rewarding and allows students the opportunity to grow in their own thinking, taking ownership of their knowledge. Still, if we recognize that students are not moving toward the algorithm *we* expected, we must respect their progress and maintain course. Telling them *the* algorithm they *should* have developed will sabotage any future attempts to use problem solving as a teaching tool. Students will wait for the shortcut! Instead, we revisit these same algorithms later in different contexts and watch for opportunities to call out prerequisite knowledge needed to develop the algorithm we need them to learn. So if we want students to invert and multiply, for example, we need to be certain they understand the property of multiplicative inverses. With this approach, we struggle less with the question "When students do not develop *the* algorithm, what do we do?"

NCTM CURRICULUM

ASSESSMENT:
To Monitor Progress toward a Goal

The first step in any assessment is determining which of the four reasons an assessment might be necessary. In this chapter, we discuss using assessment to monitor student progress toward a specific goal. A series of probing questions every three or four days or a pretest and a posttest are ways to assess improvement in knowledge about a particular topic. Looking at progress across a month or even a year can be monitored by using single questions or longer exams. As we noted earlier, many reform curricula allow students to revisit ideas later. This is consistent with assessment to monitor students' progress.

Because division of fractions is lightly introduced in fifth grade, Ms. Steffen wanted only to monitor students' progress in developing that knowledge. Using the process of assessment, she asked a series of probing questions. As she listened to students' responses to her probing questions about the problems, she interpreted those responses, watching for development of knowledge. As she looked back across the many problems students had solved that month, she determined that her students had gained much knowledge. She did not record achievement grades in her grade book; she merely checked for progress to the following unit objective: *Students will be able to recognize division of fractions situations, share strategies with meaningful communication, and generalize some sort of procedure for solving such situations.*

MIDDLE SCHOOL CONNECTIONS

Selecting Homework Thoughtfully

The middle school curriculum has become the home of many curriculum reform efforts, such as CMP (Lappan, et al., 2002), MiC (National Science Foundation, 1998), MATHematics (Billstein & Williamson, 1999), and EveryDay Math (University of Chicago School Mathematics Project, 2002). Sometimes, in works like these, the homework assignments do not look familiar to parents and guardians. We definitely *want* parents to know what their middle school students are doing at school. In fact, we recommend contacting each student's parent about every two to three weeks. If you have 150 students, that's approximately 10 phone calls each day. Yes, that sounds daunting; however, the energy and time spent are worth it when parents become teaching partners. One way to demonstrate your dedication to a partnership-oriented relationship is for the first phone call to relate a *positive* story about the student. That way, when you later want to use one of those unfamiliar homework projects as a way to communicate information to the parents, you have set the stage for a positive relationship. Selecting a page for homework that seems to be one that will engage parent and student should be based on potential for discussions and shared thinking.

Sometimes, though, if the student did not fully understand the concept related to the homework, he or she might show the homework to a parent in a frustrated way. Of course, parents are often happy to help with homework. Sometimes they read the assignment and get to work right away, showing the student exactly how to do it in the way the parent learned in school. But most recent middle school curricula ground thinking in concepts well before the formulation of an algorithm, so it is possible that on return to school, the middle school student would be even more frustrated. In addition to feeling confused by the concept in general, the student might very well now be confused by the parent's "help." It is critical to make sure to send home appropriate tasks. Of course, a continual challenge is dealing with the dilemma of selecting appropriate tasks on an individual basis. However, the more we know about our students, the better we are able to select tasks that match their needs for an assignment.

CLASSROOM CONNECTIONS

Assessing Problem Solutions with a Rubric

Do you remember story problems fondly? Many students express a strong dislike for them. At the beginning of the year, students might groan at the sight of a story problem. It is important to create a safe environment for students so that they will not feel afraid to try a particular strategy. And let's face it, some students have no idea, particularly at the beginning of the year, of how to get started.

I provide at least two problem-solving opportunities for my students each week. After a copy of the day's problem is distributed, we tape or glue it into our problem-solving notebooks. Then we read through the problem to make sure the students understand what they are being asked to answer. We read through a problem together before they get started because this isn't a reading test—I want to make sure they understand the task. We examine the data, going over what is already known and go from there. At the end of the day, the students turn in their problem-solving notebooks to me. In the evening, I write notes and suggestions in their books, such as "How did you decide to use this?" or "How do you know?" or "Tell me what this is?" By answering these questions, students have an opportunity to improve their scores. That evening, I also select some of the work and make transparencies of it so that we can present and discuss some interesting solutions to the class. (Before I make transparencies of anyone's work, I get that student's permission.) In particular, I look for an opportunity to talk about their problem-solving strategies. I want students to know that a plan that could lead to a correct solution is important. I use problem-solving tasks because assessment of them "convey[s] a message to students about what kinds of mathematical knowledge and performance are valued" (NCTM, 2000, p. 22). A good plan is important.

I like reading about students' thinking and assessing their needs. Reading over their work takes longer than correcting traditional computational types of work, but it is far more interesting and fun for me.

Part of my assessment also occurs when I listen to my students defend their viewpoints to their peers. On Wednesdays, I ask students to share their thinking, using the overhead projector. Year after year, justification is the most difficult thing for my students to do. "I just knew it" or "I multiplied" is often an adequate answer in their minds. This is where we talk about a courtroom. I stress the importance of explaining how they knew what to do. Listening to others' comments helps students to develop skills when it comes to explaining their own thinking. It also helps them when they are confronted with future problem-solving situations. They like listening to each other share strategies and justify their reasoning. I do my best to make sure each student has a turn to share. As students share, we discuss strategies and solutions. Students compare their work to the work being shared. This is such a valuable activity. Students often understand each other better than they understand an adult. They speak a common language. Some students stick with their way of doing things, while others pick up a more efficient strategy for working with a particular problem. One thing students quickly notice is that language that demonstrates reasoning is if–then thinking. Words and phrases they might use include *therefore, this means that, because, since, whenever,* and *this is like.* After they decide on a grade, we discuss what students could have done to receive a higher score. From this exercise, they know what I expect from them.

The first day's objective was as follows: *The students will be able to recognize the situation as division and successfully resolve the problem.* She hoped that any algorithms would eventually be at the symbolic-only level but was clearly more interested in students gaining knowledge and generalizing an accurate procedure. In the end, owing in part to this problem-solving approach, the students did not invent invert and multiply procedures. Rather, they invented an alternative strategy, closely resembling the least common denominator algorithm, which models the context and makes sense for division as repeated subtraction. This approach draws from whole number and fraction concept knowledge. Ms. Steffen's monitoring assessment verified that student's knowledge progressed toward the objective.

Go to "Try it! See it! Teach it!" on page 248.

Try it! See it! Teach it!

Grading Problem Solutions

Step **One**: Try it!

Do the Math . . .

Sandra is interested in buying party favors for the friends she is inviting to her birthday party. The price of the fancy straws she wants is 12 cents for 20 straws. The storekeeper is willing to split a bundle of straws for her. Sandra wants 35 straws. How much will they cost?

Step **Two**: See it!

Watch the Video . . .

These fifth graders in the video have been introduced to the rubric shown below. After discussing it, the students practice using it by scoring problem solutions from students in previous years. Next, they learn to self-assess by solving a problem themselves and scoring it.

Understanding the rubric helps you understand the conversation in the video. As you work through the problem, take care to spell out your plan, your solution, and a justification of your approach.

1. **The Solution.** Is it correct? Almost correct?

   ☐ 4 points   Correct solution with nothing missing
   ☐ 3 points   Almost correct (may be missing only minor information)
   ☐ 2 points   Partially correct (much more missing or incorrect information)
   ☐ 1 point   An atttempt was made
   ☐ 0 points   Impossible to score as no answer is given

2. **The Plan.** Is it workable? Could it lead to a correct solution? Is it almost correct? Flawed?

   ☐ 4 points   The plan is workable and could lead to a correct solution
   ☐ 3 points   The plan is almost correct, needs some minor adjustment
   ☐ 2 points   Flawed plan, incompletely developed
   ☐ 1 point   Plan would lead to an incorrect solution
   ☐ 0 points   No intelligible plan

3. **Justification of Reasoning.** Is the explanation clear and correct?

   ☐ 4 points   Clearly explains and defends reasoning correctly
   ☐ 3 points   Appears that correct reasoning was used, but justification is either incomplete or all decisions are not defended
   ☐ 2 points   Evidence can be found, but correctness of reasoning must be inferred by reader
   ☐ 1 point   Major errors in the reasoning (cited or inferred)
   ☐ 0 points   Completely faulty reasoning

Things to Watch for . . .

- Recognize how Karen uses the rubric as a tool to assess *and* as a tool to teach.
- Watch for a moment when a child learns something new from listening to classmates presenting their work.
- Pay particular attention to how Karen allows the students to use the rubric to evaluate themselves. Look at the two solutions shown below as you watch the video.

Video Clip 6 *(time length 4:22)*

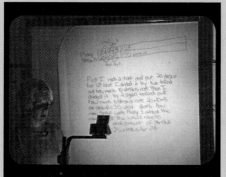

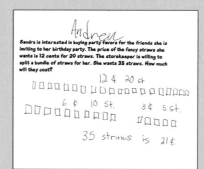

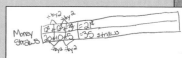

Student's solution is shown on overhead.

Step **Three**: Teach it!

Reflect on Your Own Teaching . . .

1. What kinds of things did Christian say that made you think he understood the solution?

2. "Next time you might do it a different way," said Evelyn. What do you think she meant by her comment? What does it tell you about the importance of a problem-solving plan?

3. How does the use of a rubric help you think about assessing the wide variety of solutions presented by the students?

4. Your turn to practice. Use the rubric to evaluate Evelyn's solution shown here. How did she know 15 straws cost 9 cents? Let's ask her. You'll notice my comment and then Evelyn's explanation. Does the score change as a result of her response? Do you know more about Evelyn's thinking now? What else would you ask Evelyn about her work?

A Comment from Karen

I find problem solving activities and use of a rubric are an opportunity for me to engage in dialogue with my students. It clarifies their thinking for me and for them. They know I need to know what they are thinking. It is important for students to recognize that the correct answer is not always the most important outcome. The rubric helps me learn about my students and what they need.

GO BACK TO PAGE 247

HIGHLIGHTS OF A LESSON PLAN COMPONENT:
Importance of Context (Lesson Setup)

Setting up the lesson in an engaging way, with an interesting context, is crucial to designing lessons that match how we learn about rational numbers. Kieren makes very clear the importance of personal knowledge, and Streefland requires the use of relevant contexts. For example, after a recent exploration with percents, we were interested that Min brought a yogurt container to school, proudly pointing out the percentages she found in her world. When problem solving relies on rich opening situations students are interested in solving the problems. Situations can be contrived and still be engaging and from the real world. It is not necessary to sit for hours looking for information from newspapers, television, or the Internet. The primary characteristic of a good context is that it is interesting and fun. Of course, *interesting* and *fun* are relative to the life experiences of each student. So several different kinds of contexts should be used to reach diverse groups of students. In Activity 13.2, you will read through some example problems to see whether they seem useful.

Another consideration in evaluating a context is striking a balance between continuous and discrete contexts. Teaching about operations begins with ensuring that the physical model does what the symbolic representation does. You know by now how important it is to appropriately select models (continuous or discrete), since they lay the foundation for fractional thinking. In some ways we have a catch-22 situation. Context is critical, and the discrete model

Activity 1 3 . 2

EVALUATING CONTEXTS

Read the contexts, **evaluate** the usefulness of the context, and **finish** the problem by asking a rational number question related to it.

"Let me tell you about my friend Lynn. Her family takes most of their trips on trains. She likes to know what part of the journey is left after each stop. Last summer, they took a 5-hour trip that had 6 stops. But the fourth stop came after only 3 hours on the train . . ."

"My father is a carpenter. Do you see that bookshelf in the back of the room? He built it. He often builds large cabinets and bookshelves. He built that bookshelf to fit exactly in that spot. That space is 43 and $\frac{1}{2}$ inches wide, and each board is $\frac{5}{8}$ inch thick. . . ."

"Fred plays basketball and is a good free-throw shooter. The scoreboard shows statistics throughout the game. He made a free-throw, and his percentage changed to 90%. Then he missed his next shot, and his percentage changed to 81%. What was his percentage before that first shot?"

seems to be common in the world. Continuous models lend themselves to establishing algorithms for operations, so they must be used. Because continuous models are slightly better for operations, we establish continuous models along with discrete models when fraction knowledge is first developed. To later establish algorithms, we show students how actions working on physical (or pictorial) models mirror operations and then help students to keep a corresponding symbolic record of the actions. Seeing consistencies in written records will lead students to their algorithms. So at least as many contexts need to be based on continuous ideas as discrete ideas.

SUGGESTIONS FOR DISCUSSION:
Listening for Benchmark Numbers $(0, \frac{1}{2}, 1)$

It is important to listen for and value students' comments that use benchmark numbers 0, $\frac{1}{2}$, and 1. Students begin to understand *benchmark fractions* from personal fraction knowledge. If a child quantifies her box of crayons with counting, she might say, "Oh, there are only 10 crayons in the box." If she quantifies that box of crayons with fractional thinking, she recognizes that ten-sixteenths of the box of crayons are present. But if she says, "Oh, that's just a little more than half a box," she is using a benchmark number. To generalize knowledge of benchmark values, a variety of situations and representations must be encountered.

Standard benchmark values help students to make accurate estimates and check their thinking. Students' use of these values can be encouraged by asking them to compare fractional values. It is eventually useful for students to be able to use a number line (mental or written) as they try to compare and order fractional amounts, which in turn helps with identifying proximity to benchmark numbers. However, as was noted earlier, the number line seems to be more useful after students already understand something about fractions, not while they are trying to develop basic fractional knowledge. A good example of using benchmark numbers might be when a child says, "I think one-third plus one-fourth is going to be a little more than a half." Another good example is when a child says, "I'm going to call it one, it's almost one."

Listen to these fifth grade students describe their thinking about the following questions even though we did not prompt them to use benchmark numbers:

1. Which is bigger: $\frac{2}{3}$ or $\frac{4}{7}$? How do you know? How could you prove it?

2. Put these values in order from smallest to largest: $\frac{2}{3}, \frac{1}{10}, \frac{1}{2}, \frac{1}{4}, \frac{1}{3}, \frac{4}{5}, \frac{1}{5}, \frac{3}{8}$.

> **Min:** Basically, if you know your fractions and you know where half of something is, you can do this.

Min easily located each of the amounts in order, in relation to the benchmark number of $\frac{1}{2}$.

> **Lydia:** $\frac{2}{3}$ is bigger than $\frac{4}{7}$ because $\frac{2}{3}$ is the same as $\frac{4}{6}$, and since sixths are bigger than sevenths, I know that four-sixths ($\frac{2}{3}$) is bigger than four-sevenths.

Lydia used her own number sense about fractions. She appears comfortable with sixths, and this is probably a personal benchmark number for her.

> ***Ryan:*** I put all those fractions on a number line. First, I divided the line into fifths so I could get the 5ths and 10ths on the line. Then I did the same thing to get the 3rds on the lines. Then I took half of half of half to get the halves, fourths, and eighths on the line.

Ryan used a series of benchmark numbers. He used multiplication and a number line. His marks for tenths did not confound his marks for thirds or eighths.

> ***Jamal:*** I changed everything to percents. In the first problem, I get 66% and 56%, so I know $\frac{2}{3}$ is bigger. Then, in the second problem, I just put the percent values in order.

Jamal coordinated his work around the benchmark number of hundredths (percent). He is using a common denominator to make sense of this task.

We also listen for some indication that students' answers are guesses and not uses of benchmark numbers. If students appear to be throwing out answers like "$\frac{2}{3}$," "$\frac{7}{8}$," or "1 and $\frac{3}{4}$," then the teacher should stop the conversation and ask clarifying questions or offer an opportunity for students to justify or explain their thinking. The suspect answers can be explored together to determine whether answers indicate number sense and use of benchmark number thinking. With whole numbers benchmarks began at 0 and focused on 5 and 10. Eventually, benchmarks grew to include multiples of those numbers. So, too, will reasonable benchmarks in fractions grow to include multiples of 0, $\frac{1}{2}$, and 1.

IDEAS FOR STRUCTURING CLASS TIME:
To Create Shared, Rich Experiences Using Proportions

Whether or not the problem-solving model of teaching is selected, the role of the teacher is to provide fractions in context first. Children will be unable to immediately pick up on symbolic representations of examples during early classroom discussions. Kieren claims that core fraction knowledge is intensely personal and that quantifying environments according to fractional ideas happens individually. Given the diversity of children's unique sets of experiences, it is a daunting task indeed to draw on each child's experiences to develop concepts and procedures associated with fractional thinking.

One strategy is to create new, rich problems that class members share in school, in other words, to create a set of common experiences related to fractional thinking that are unique to the class but that the teacher can control. Shared, rich experiences begin by having the potential to be realistic to each student. They cannot begin with traditional, unfamiliar word problems because those are often irrelevant to the students. Uniqueness within each child must be respected. One way to do this is to set up shared experiences in the classroom to establish a common collection of adventures.

Proportions are a useful area in which to set up common problem experiences. Proportions present a particularly difficult area to teach for two reasons. First, proportions are a difficult mathematical concept to grasp because two values are related in a consistent manner that is multiplicative in nature, rather than additive. Second, students can be heavily influenced by context. Given that each student enters a classroom with his or her own personal frac-

MIDDLE SCHOOL CONNECTIONS

Appropriate Tasks Build Proportional Thinking

NCTM CURRICULUM

How do you select an appropriate task for students so as to lead them toward general strategies? First, try to select according to whether or not the task is rich enough to cause discussion among the students. Sometimes you can use other curricular areas to extend mathematical concepts. In a typical middle school approach, students are in teams with the same core teachers. In this situation, you will be well acquainted with your students' language arts, science, and social studies teachers. Watch for opportunities to connect mathematics problems to those areas.

Second, students can get so caught up in a context that they do not or cannot focus on the mathematical task at hand. Because students need extensive experiences with the notion of variable in order to create generalizations, it is important to use tasks that allow students to ponder the generalization, not to worry about the context. Consider this context: *Every three times Lydia calls her grandmother, it costs her $2.* This is a good proportional situation from a mathematical

point of view. However, students who have extensive experiences with cell phones and calling plans might wonder about the relevance of this context. It would be easy for them to spend more time thinking about the plausibility of the situation than about the mathematics of it.

Third, be certain that the task focuses on your objective and builds on sound knowledge about variables. Proportional thinking is often intended to utilize a cross-multiplying procedure. This procedure usually requires manipulating a variable. The idea is that a variable standing for an unknown requires different sorts of thinking than a variable representing some sort of generalization. You might be so familiar with variables that you easily shift among the different ways of thinking about them, but it is important that you recognize that sometimes students' difficulties stem only from a wayward concern that they need to solve for the variable in question, when perhaps the objective of the activity was to generate a formula.

tion knowledge, it is important to expose students to a wide range of proportion problems. It is not uncommon at first for students to be unable to recognize that two different situations as identical mathematically if the contexts are different and vice versa. Look at these two problems:

1. The art teacher uses 2 boxes of crayons every 3 months. At the end of the 9-month school year, how many boxes will she use?
2. The gym teacher has 2 out of every 3 basketballs painted in the school colors. If she has 9 basketballs, how many are painted in the school colors?

In what ways do these problems use a proportion? Which one will generate discussion about proportions? With problems like these, students can develop a shared experience on which they can build rational number knowledge (in this case, proportions). Of course, you can now probably imagine how these efforts at shared experiences can meld with a teacher's use of problem solving as a teaching strategy.

ADVICE FOR PROFESSIONAL DEVELOPMENT:
Fraction Scavenger Hunt

Walk around your school building, and try to find 10 or so situations that make sense to use as contexts for fractional thinking. (See Homework Problem 3.) Count the coat hooks outside a classroom. Would it make sense to wonder "What fraction of the hooks have coats?" instead of "How many hooks have coats?" Generate a list of acceptable student responses to this question.

You might also want to produce a list of other questions you could ask about your classroom. Ask some of your colleagues for suggestions. What sorts of questions do they ask their students? What sort of fractional ideas make sense for students in your classroom?

Try doing one of the activities from this book with students. Listen for clues that illustrate Kieren or Pothier and Sawada's ideas. Concentrate on how to ask questions to move students to a new level. Make a mental note about what sorts of questions resulted in the most progress for students.

ALGEBRA CONNECTIONS
Rational Numbers and Proportional Thinking

A Big Idea: Proportional Thinking

Much conceptual and procedural knowledge lays the foundation for algebraic thinking. Proportional thinking plays a significant role in preparing students for algebra. You have seen throughout this chapter how students as young as fifth grade can use a ratio table to solve proportion problems. You should also think about instructional strategies perhaps related to asking good questions for moving students from a ratio table to the more efficient cross-multiplication algorithm. You might wonder why we don't show students how to solve problems by cross-multiplying first. We want them to build their own understanding first, and a ratio table does that in a very nice way. You will momentarily see students' solutions illustrating the ratio table approach and solutions that use multiplicative reasoning, another underpinning concept for proportional reasoning. Both strategies can lead to cross-multiplying.

Algebraic Ideas for You to Explore: Proportional Thinking

Proportional reasoning manifests itself in everything from percent problems to algebra-based variation (or *change*) problems. It is helpful to understand how proportional reasoning looks in the prealgebra classrooms. Before we discuss young students' strategies for dealing with proportional thinking situations, you should solve the problem in Activity 13.3.

What kinds of strategies did you use? Did you cross-multiply? Writing problems that require proportional reasoning should build on notions such as "for every" and "for each."

Activity 13.3

PULLING TAFFY

We have 22 students in our class. Millie has brought in a piece of taffy 40 inches long. Is that long enough if every two students are supposed to share $3\frac{1}{2}$ inches?

K–8 Algebra Connections: Recognizing General Strategies—The Case of Proportions

Because proportional reasoning is a critical component of success in algebraic thinking, we need to recognize how it looks for K–8 students. Our fifth graders solved the same problem.

Min: Yes, you will have enough. I know that I needed all 22 students to have some taffy but that every two students got $3\frac{1}{2}$. So I took $11 \times 3.5 = 38.5$. Since this is less than 40, I knew that Millie brought enough taffy.

Lydia: First, I found half of $3\frac{1}{2}$—that is $1\frac{3}{4}$. That way I know how much for one person. Then I had to multiply $1\frac{3}{4} \times 22$. I know $1 \times 22 = 22$. To find $\frac{3}{4} \times 22$, I wrote $\frac{3}{4}$, 22 times. The way I added all those $\frac{3}{4}$ was that a group of four made 3 whole

ALGEBRA CONNECTIONS *(continued)*

inches. I had five groups of 3 inches and then two more $\frac{3}{4}$ left over. So finally I added 22, 15, $\frac{3}{4}$, and $\frac{3}{4}$. This is $38\frac{1}{2}$. So 40 inches of taffy is enough.

Ryan: Yes, there is enough. I made a ratio table.

		double	double	double	add 7	add $3\frac{1}{2}$	
Taffy	$3\frac{1}{2}$	7	14	28	35	$38\frac{1}{2}$	
students	2	4	8	16	20	22	
		double	double	double	add 4	add 2	

Jamal: Yes there is enough taffy. I made a ratio table too! But it's not exactly like Ryan's table.

Taffy	$3\frac{1}{2}$	7	$10\frac{1}{2}$	14	$17\frac{1}{2}$	21	$24\frac{1}{2}$	28	$31\frac{1}{2}$	35	$38\frac{1}{2}$
students	2	4	6	8	10	12	14	16	18	20	22

The ratio table (Cramer & Post, 1993; Middleton & van den Heuvel-Panhuizen, 1995) sets a foundation for important proportional thinking that follows from it. We help students to recognize how to jump around on the table and apply multiplication ideas rather than arithmetic ideas to achieve the same result. Notice how Ryan knew that he could double along the top and bottom rows, but if he added, he had to add using the original ratio. That is, his proportional reasoning tells him that when he added $3\frac{1}{2}$ to the top row, he knew to add 2 to the bottom row. Knowing that students have solved proportion problems in the early grades can give the algebra teacher opportunities to ground proportional reasoning at an algebraic level. How could you build on Ryan's table to move him toward cross-multiplication?

Both Ryan's and Jamal's solutions used ratio tables, whereas Lydia's and Min's solutions illustrate multiplicative thinking. The problem was an appropriate task for these students. It was realistic and enjoyable, and it provided more opportunities to work with both fractions and proportions. When kindergarten children "generalize from observations about number and operations, they are forming the basis of algebraic thinking." (NCTM, 2000, p. 93). Generalizations about observations eventually lead children to concepts and to algorithms. Even young children can determine when their claims hold true or when they fail. Students need a variety of experiences and encouragement with this kind of thinking to generalize it appropriately.

 LET'S REVIEW

Before we summarize some of the big ideas for Part IV of the book about rational numbers and proportions with an activity, let's briefly summarize the information in this chapter. Using the works of Kieren (1988), Streefland (1991), and Pirie and Kieren (1994), the teacher can prepare sound lessons. The role of the teacher in developing fraction knowledge is to (1) introduce concepts and procedures related to faction knowledge through real-life problems and situations; (2) require students to develop related images growing toward more and more symbolic representations; (3) ask questions that guide students to fold backward or forward or to validate personal, intuitive, or technical levels of knowledge; and (4) facilitate students' eventual uses of symbols as exclusive representations of the situations. Like all representations, it is important to monitor students manipulation of the representations (whether concrete, pictorial, or symbolic) in a meaningful way.

HOMEWORK

1. If we accept the rule of thumb that it takes 12 inches of snowfall to equate to 1 inch of rain precipitation, how many inches of snowfall would it take to create $\frac{1}{2}$ of an inch of precipitation? 3 inches? $4\frac{1}{3}$ inches? Create a pattern table to show your thinking. Explain this situation using the words *for every*.

2. Rewrite the following statements (1) in ways that promotes the ideas of proportions (using language like *for every*) and (2) in ways that promote thinking about percents.

   (a) I have 35 M&Ms, and 7 of them are blue. You might finish this sentence: "If I had _____ how many of them would be _____?"
   (b) I saw 15 dogs in the park, and 8 of them were playing with sticks.
   (c) I was playing softball the other day, and out of 4 times at bat, I got a hit 3 times!

3. Four contexts are given in the figure. Your students are learning how to do an algorithm for addition of fractions. Of the choices, decide (a) which context would be best experienced first, (b) which would be last, and (c) which should probably not be used at all (for this addition algorithm). Note: Because there are four pictures, you may choose not to discuss one of them.

	This picture shows 1 batch of cookies.	I have $\frac{5}{6}$ of a batch, and Jill has $\frac{2}{6}$ of a batch. If we combine our cookies, how much of a batch would we have then?
	This picture shows 1 whole cake.	Jill has $\frac{2}{6}$ of a cake, and I have $\frac{5}{6}$ of a cake. If we combine our cake how much of a cake would we have then?
	This picture shows the sixth pieces of fraction circles.	I have $\frac{5}{6}$ of a pie, and Jill has $\frac{2}{6}$ of a pie. If we combine our pieces, how much of a pie do we have then?
	This picture shows pumpkin pies cut into sixth-sized pieces.	I have $\frac{5}{6}$ of a pumpkin pie, and Jill has $\frac{2}{6}$ of a pumpkin pie. If we combine our pie, how much of a pie do we have then?

4. Think about contexts that are meaningful to young learners. Select three of the following arithmetic statements and write word problems that use the given definitions for the operation. You may want to review the definitions from Chapter 5.

   a. $\frac{2}{3} + \frac{4}{5}$ (join)
   b. $1\frac{1}{2} - \frac{2}{3}$ (take-away)
   c. $1\frac{1}{2} - \frac{2}{3}$ (find-the-difference)
   d. multiplication $\frac{5}{6} \times 1\frac{3}{4}$ (repeated addition)

   e. $\frac{5}{6} \times 1\frac{3}{4}$ (rectangular array)
   f. $3\frac{1}{2} \div \frac{3}{4}$ (repeated subtraction)
   g. $4\frac{1}{3} \div 2$ (fair sharing)
   Challenge: $4\frac{1}{3} \div 2\frac{1}{2}$ (fair sharing)

SUGGESTED READINGS

Huinker, D. (1998). Letting fraction algorithms emerge through problem solving. In L. J. Morrow & M. J. Kenney (Eds.), *The teaching and learning of algorithms in school mathematics*. 1998 yearbook for the National Council of Teachers of Mathematics (pp. 170–181). Reston, VA: NCTM.

Warrington, M. A., & Kamii C. (1998). Multiplication with fractions: A Piagetian constructivist approach. *Teaching Children Mathematics, 3*(5), 339–343.

Warrington, M. A. (1997). How children think about division with fractions. *Mathematics Teaching in the Middle School, 2*(6), 390–394.

REFERENCES

Barron, B. J., Schwartz, D. L., Vye, N. J., Moore, A., Petrosino, A., Zech, L., Brandford, J. D., & Cognition and Technology Group at Vanderbilt. (1998). Doing with understanding: Lessons from research on problem and project-based learning. *Journal of Learning Sciences, 7* (3, 4), 271–312.

Billstein, R., & Williamson, J. (1999). *MathThematics*. Evanston, IL: McDougal Littell.

Cognition and Technology Group at Vanderbilt. (1991). *Assessing the outcomes of an innovative instructional program: The 1990–91 implementation of the "Adventures of Jasper Woodbury."* Tech. Report No. 91–1. Nashville, TN: Vanderbilt University, Learning Technology Center.

Cognition and Technology Group at Vanderbilt. (1992). The Jasper series as an example of anchored instruction: Theory, program description, and assessment data. *Educational Psychologist (27),* 291–315.

Cognition and Technology Group at Vanderbilt. (1997). *The Jasper Project: Lessons in Curriculum, Instruction, Assessment, and Professional Development.* Mahwah, NJ: Lawrence Erlbaum.

Cognition and Technology Group at Vanderbilt. (1993). The Jasper series: Theoretical foundations and data on problem solving and transfer. In L. A. Penner, G. M. Batsche, H. M. Knoff, & D. L. Nelson (Eds.), *The challenges in mathematics and science education: Psychology's response* (pp. 113–152). Washington, DC: American Psychological Association.

Crews, T. R., Biswas, G., Goldman, S. R., & Bransford, J. D. (1997). Anchored interactive learning environment. *International Journal of Artificial Intelligence in Education, 8,* 142–178.

Kieren, T. E. (1988). Personal knowledge of rational numbers: Its intuitive and formal development. In J. Hiebert & M. J. Behr (Eds.), *Number concepts and operations in the middle grades* (pp. 162–181). Hillsdale, NJ: Lawrence Erlbaum.

Lappan, G., Fey, J. T., Fitzgerald, W. M., Friel, S. N., & Phillips, E. D. (2002). *Connected Mathematics Project (CMP).* Glenview, IL: Prentice Hall.

Middleton, J. A., & van den Heuvel-Panhuizen, M. (1995). The ratio table. *Mathematics Teaching in the Middle School, 1*(4), 282–288.

National Council of Teachers of Mathematics. (2000). *Principles and standards for school mathematics.* Reston, VA: NCTM.

National Science Foundation. (1998). *Mathematics in Context (MiC).* Chicago, IL: Encyclopedia Britannica Educational Corporation.

Pothier, Y., & Sawada, D. (1983). Partitioning: The emergence of rational number ideas in young children. *Journal for Research in Mathematics Education, 14*(5), 307–317.

Schoenfeld, A. H. (1985). *Mathematical problem solving.* San Diego, CA: Academic Press.

Sharp, J., Garofalo, J., & Adams, B. (2002). *Children's development of meaningful fraction algorithms: A kid's cookies and a puppy's pills.* In B. Litwiller & G. Bright (Eds.), *Making sense of fractions, ratios and proportions: 2002 NCTM Yearbook* (pp. 18–28). Reston, VA: NCTM.

Streefland, L. (1991). *Fractions in realistic mathematics education.* Dordrecht, The Netherlands: Kluwer Academic Publishers.

University of Chicago School Mathematics Project. (2002). *Everyday mathematics.* Chicago, IL: Wright Group/McGraw-Hill.

Van Haneghan, J. P., Barron, L., Young, M. F., Williams, S. M., Vye, N. J., & Bransford, J. D. (1992). The Jasper series: An experiment with new ways to enhance mathematical thinking. In D. F. Halpern (Ed.), *Enhancing thinking skills in the sciences and mathematics* (pp. 15–38). Hillsdale, NJ: Lawrence Erlbaum.

Young, M. F., Nastasi, B. K., & Braunhardt, L. (1996). Implementing Jasper immersion: A case of conceptual change. In B. Wilson (Ed.), *Constructivist learning environments* (pp. 121–133). Englewood Cliffs, NJ: Educational Technology.

PART FOUR: Rational Numbers and Proportions

We know that by now, you are keenly aware of the interactive nature of a classroom. Teachers do not stand in front of the classroom and recite information for the duration of the mathematics time during the school day. Certainly there are key points that the teacher may choose to share directly with students, but those key points need to be embedded in the students' needs to know. Fractional ideas are among the most difficult topics for children to learn. However, helping students recognize a fractional interpretation of their surroundings is a good first step because not only do they recognize fractions in their worlds but they are also often propelled forward by their own need to know more about the information. Placing classroom learning in meaningful contexts and using students' ideas about how to solve problems in those contexts can guide learners toward your mathematical learning objective. We believe the best way to summarize this key point is to ask you to write a lesson as a closing activity for Part IV. We know it is difficult to write good problems. But since this is how teachers must approach fraction instruction, we ask you to engage in teacher behavior by completing the following activity at the end of this chapter, in which you plan a lesson to meet a sixth grade objective: *The student will be able to correctly compare and contrast ratios using meaningful combinations of proportions, percents, decimals, and/or fractions.*

Closing Activity: Summary Lesson

WRITE A FRACTION/RATIO/PROPORTION LESSON

This activity is an opportunity for you to put together all the information from Part IV of the book. You are a sixth grade teacher who must create a problem-solving model lesson that will support the following fraction/ratio/proportion curriculum goal:

> *The student will be able to correctly compare and contrast ratios using meaningful combinations of proportions, percents, decimals, and fractions.*

Remember that the curriculum goal may take several weeks to achieve. Your task for this activity is to create a single lesson that will fall sometime during those weeks. Remember that your ultimate goal is to help students achieve the more general curriculum goal. The lesson you create here should be completed in only one day, so it is a small component of the stu-

dents' overall learning experience. We guide you through the lesson development process, asking you to complete the tasks outlined in 1–5.

1. **Think about the Mathematics.** First, think about the prerequisite knowledge in terms of fraction/ratio/proportion and the accompanying vocabulary that students would have and need in order to work toward this goal. Second, what is the difference between a concept and a procedure related to this goal? Third, write a focused narrow objective achievable through the problem-solving model of teaching. Be sure to focus on a small component of the curriculum goal. Fourth, please tell how this lesson will fit into the students' overall experience toward the curriculum goal.

2. **Think about How We Learn.** What are good experiences that foster fraction knowledge? Remember how we described the importance of beginning with contexts? Recall the information about selecting teaching aids and create a list of materials you need to gather for the lesson.

3. **Think about the Role of the Teacher.** What does the teacher do in a problem-solving lesson? Recall that the teacher first creates a relevant, realistic context and second prepares to ask good questions. Questions might fold students back, propel them forward, or validate their thinking. The teacher must continually strive to move students toward symbolic representations of fractional ideas. List at least four example problems related to your objective.

4. **Think about How the Learning Theory Might Appear during Your Lesson.** Use your knowledge of development of fractional thinking to write your problems but also to anticipate questions you might need to ask.

5. **Finally, Think about Assessment.** How will you know when your students have met your objective? Write an evaluation in which you engage the students that indicates to you the objective has or has not been met.

As always, there are several correct lessons for this fraction/ratio/proportion curriculum goal. Depending on what you assume students know, those lessons might fall at different places during the school year. We remind you that the rational number lessons you create for your own learners will depend on your district's curriculum and you will have access to a textbook series that should help you write your lessons. In addition, once you become a teacher, you will become part of the classroom context, and the things you know about your students will inform your lesson development. However, we believe that there are correct types of answers for this activity. We can imagine lessons using contexts such as playground equipment, fish tanks, music, and trips to the grocery store. Before you check your lesson against the one we provide in the appendix, share your lesson with a classmate. Try to predict how our lesson will look. Then check your thoughts against our lesson in the appendix.

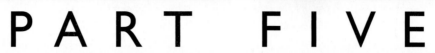

PART FIVE

Data
Analysis

To begin this part of the book, imagine a second grade class collecting data. They have organized the data as shown in the activity. Complete the activity before reading further.

Opening Activity

ORGANIZING DATA WITH A VENN DIAGRAM

Mr. Ross's second grade class collected this information one day. Each student put a sticker in the area of the picture that described him or her that day.

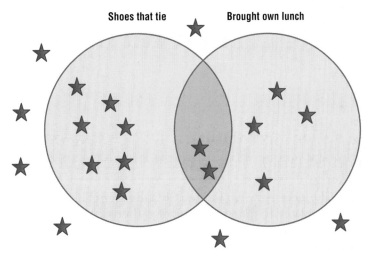

What can be said *in general* about Mr. Ross's second grade class? Defend your statement.

Later, Mr. Ross added his own sticker to the diagram. He brought his lunch and was wearing slip-on loafers. Where did he place his sticker?

Represent the information from the students and Mr. Ross in any other way.

Does the meaning change if you build a circle graph? A bar graph? A line graph?

● Looking at the class's data, were you able to describe any general characteristics about the students? If you could, then you analyzed the data to describe the existing situation with some sort of *statistical* statement. Did you decide that Mr. Ross's second graders were *mostly* wearing lace-up shoes? Perhaps you also found that his second graders were *mostly* wearing lace-up shoes *and* did not bring their own lunch. Checking for the most frequent event is a good way to get an *average* picture in many statistical instances. Did putting the data into a circle graph change your view about claims you could make about most students? Organizing data into a useful visual, such as a graph, is another way to *describe* the situation.

● Would you feel comfortable making an inference about the second grade class next door on the basis of these data? What if you met two students from Mr. Ross's class—what might you predict about their shoes on the basis of your general statements? Making a prediction based on data you gather and analyze involves an *experimental probability*. Making a prediction based on pure mathematical calculations involves *theoretical probability*. The next three chapters are dedicated to data analysis, which is composed of both statistics and probability.

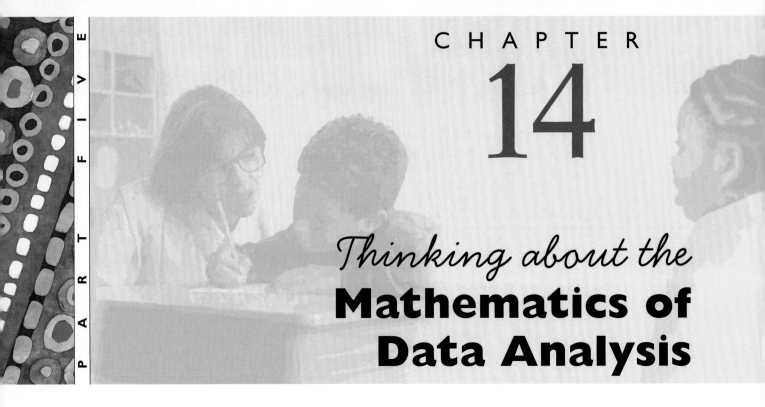

C H A P T E R

14

Thinking about the
Mathematics of
Data Analysis

NcTm

UNDERSTANDING THE MATHEMATICS:
Statistics and Probability

The need for *data analysis* results from asking an engaging question. Then data related to that question are gathered. Next, data are organized, studied, and possibly reorganized in order to find interesting tendencies, patterns, or trends. In the end, data analysis allows a generalization that answers or at least addresses the question in some way. Sometimes, that generalization will result in a *description* of the data using a statistic. Other times, the generalization will result in an *inference* about the situation. Still other times, that generalization will be a *prediction*, which usually incorporates some ideas about probability. So data analysis deciphers data to give some sort of generalized statistic, to make a prediction, or to infer something beyond the specific data collected. Because data analysis encompasses two types of mathematics, statistics and probability, we will think of *data analysis* as an umbrella under which we place both statistics and probability. However, statistics and probability are also different enough that we discuss them separately in this chapter.

Statistics

In part, we start here because statistical ideas are somewhat more accessible to younger children than probability ideas are. Children have some intuitive notions about statistics and can make sense of statistical ideas at a fairly young age. For instance, primary teachers often take hot lunch and milk counts at the beginning of each day. This task is a simple data analysis task. When learners find that more children drink milk at lunch than do not drink milk, they have found a statistic. Sometimes statistics are quantitative descriptions, such as "65% of all ice cream sold is vanilla." Other times, statistics are qualitative descriptions, such as "most students rode their bicycles to school that day."

Still other situations call for pictorial descriptions, such as bar graphs, pictographs, or line graphs. In any event, statistics are an organization of data to succinctly communicate one or more interesting tendencies or patterns in the data. Data under scrutiny are from a sample of the population.

Sample versus Population

A sample is a subset of a population. The idea here is that if you know something about the sample, then you know something about the population. For instance, your class is a sample of several populations. Earlier, you studied information about some second graders and their shoes. Those data come from a sample (that class) that is somewhat representative of larger populations or people who are (1) second graders, (2) living in that town, (3) going to that school, or even (4) acquainted with Mr. Ross. You probably have an intuitive sense of the potential problems with making a statement about all second graders on the basis of the information gathered from Mr. Ross's class. However, the idea of polling every single second grader is an equally daunting task. So we make a leap, assuming that if something is true in the sample, then it is *likely* also true in the population. The more randomly selected the sample (that is, if we could randomly study a few second grade students from all around the globe) and the larger the sample, the more confident we would be in our general statement about the entire population of second graders.

General Statements

A general statement is a sweeping assertion that can be (1) a description, (2) a prediction, or (3) an inference. A description literally describes the general nature of the data and assumes that the description applies to the population. A prediction suggests that a specific event will occur, based either on data or on mathematical calculations. An inference is a judgment about the population but is based on an *interpretation* of the data in the sample.

Types of Data

There are two kinds of numerical data: continuous and discrete. With *continuous* data, there could be values in between the values collected, and those values would make sense. Measurement of rainfall would be an example of continuous data. We might collect rainfall values of 1, 2, 2, 1.2, and 1.3 inches across five days. The number of cats in a child's home is *discrete* numerical data because it is impossible to have half of a cat. Ranking three movies with a 1, 2, and 3 is another example of discrete numerical data. Discrete data are also collected when ranking statements according to the extent to which you agree or disagree. *Categorical* data are discrete but are not numerical. Sometimes they are called nominal data. They are data on which we cannot operate with arithmetic because the data themselves are merely indicators of categories, such as wearing lace-up shoes or not wearing lace-up shoes. Categorical data include things like favorite ice cream flavors or movies. The type of data will in part determine the type of general statement that can reasonably be made about the situation.

Averages

An average is a *description* of the central tendency of data in the given situation, typically calculated as a mean, median, or mode. The mean and median can be calculated only with numerical data; the mode can be calculated with either numerical or nonnumerical data.

The *mean* is the arithmetic center of the data. That is, we add all the values and divide by the number of values added. The mean can be applied to situations in which it makes sense to lump data together and redistribute them evenly. The mean is not usually used for numerical data about rankings. The *median* is the literal center of the data. Line up the data from smallest to largest (or largest to smallest), and locate the middle point of the data. Median should be applied in situations in which there are extreme outliers or otherwise skewed data or in situations in which halves of data points would not make sense. Number of cats is a good example in that we cannot have a portion of a pet. The *mode* is the piece of data that occurs the most often. It is possible for data to have more than one mode. If 16 people select chocolate as their favorite ice cream flavor and that is the most often selected flavor, then we can say that in general people prefer chocolate. Here we are using the mode to describe the population. As you consider the questions in Activity 14.1, decide on the best way to describe the central tendency of the information.

Activity 1 4 . 1

TAKING A SURVEY OF YOUR CLASSMATES

Answer these questions and decide the best way to organize your entire class's information (if you had it) to report a central tendency.

1. What is your favorite season?
   a. Summer
   b. Fall
   c. Winter
   d. Spring

2. How many pets do you live with right now?

3. How tall are you (inches)?

4. How many credits are you taking this semester or quarter?

5. What is your favorite color?

Basic Variance

Variance is a way to describe the spread of data. *Range* gives the maximum and minimum values. Quartiles can be calculated after data have been ordered by being separated into four equal-sized groups (in contrast to the median described above, which essentially separates data into two groups). *Quartiles* are the points at which data are separated into the four groups. Often, statisticians are interested in the middle two quartiles. In addition, quartiles are used to build box-and-whisker plots.

Prediction versus Description

Think back to Activity 14.1. Assume that we have learned that the average favorite season was spring. Are we comfortable making a prediction about all

Doing Data Analysis with Physical Materials

How do you compute an average? It seems rather simple, doesn't it? Don't you just add up the numbers and divide? How do you build a circle graph? How can a student visualize what is being done in either of these situations? A lesson that shows the students the goals behind finding the mean or behind building the circle graph can be fruitful for discussion. That way, my students learn about the idea behind the statistics, and the procedures are more reasonable to them.

people's favorite season? We can certainly *describe* our group's preference. When we start to make *predictions* about other groups of people, we begin to run the risk of making unfounded claims because a prediction involves probability. How probable or likely is our generalization? If we look only at our group's answers, a prediction about a larger group of the population is uncertain. Listen to these fifth grade students explain their thinking about probability. You will notice how Ryan talks about a specific example that is relevant to his life. The students also use different words: *probably, chance,* and *prediction*.

Min: Probability is like "probably." You think something is probably going to happen.
Lydia: Probability means you want to know if something will happen.
Ryan: Probability is a prediction. It's like how you know if it's going to rain. A weather prediction of 20% rain means it's not very likely to rain.
Jamal: It's like a chance. You decide that something has a chance of happening, and you usually know how big of a chance.

In making a prediction, then, we move to probability. There are two kinds of probability. *Experimental probability* is calculated on gathered data and involves the law of large numbers. It is the number of successes that *did* happen divided by the total number of trials in the simulation or experiment. The law of large numbers means that "when the number of observations of an experiment repeated under identical conditions is sufficiently large, then . . . the proportion of some specific outcome will be close to the underlying probability of that outcome. . . . the greater the number of observations, the closer the agreement" (Gullberg, 1997, p. 967). *Theoretical probability* is calculated mathematically. Here, we mathematically calculate the number of successes that *should* happen divided by number of trials. Probabilities may be reported as percent, decimal, or fractional statements. Complete Activity 14.2 (p. 268).

Go to "Try it! See it! Teach it!" on page 266.

Prediction versus Inference

In making an inference generalization, we make a judgment statement about the population by *interpretation* of data in the sample. The difference between a prediction and an inference is in the nature of the statement. A prediction suggests that a *specific* event will occur, based either on data or on mathematical calculations. An inference is a judgment about the general nature of the population and is more general than a specific prediction. An inference is different from a description in that a description statement tells exactly what did happen and an inference uses that happening to make a judgment about the nature of the population.

Try it! See it! Teach it!

Making Statistics Physically

Step **One**: Try it!

Do the Math . . .

CJ is a good basketball player. She has scored points in her last six games: 2, 8, 6, 15, 7, 10. The local newspaper wants to report her scoring average, and they also want to use a circle graph to show her points in each game. Please decide on the best average, calculate it, and draw a circle graph to show the information.

Step **Two**: See it!

Watch the Video . . .

Karen's fifth graders are trying to solve the problem of showing how to manipulate data physically. In the first part of the video, students try to understand the concept behind the algorithm for calculating a mean. Think about finding the mean of 2, 8, 6, 15, 7, and 10. In the second part of the video, students try to understand the concept behind creating a circle graph.

Things to Watch for . . .

- Recognize how the algorithm for finding the mean of a set of data can be matched to physical manipulation.
- Appreciate the way a circle graph can be created without the traditional use of a protractor.
- See that there is a difference between changing some sort of final data analysis report back and forth among concrete, pictorial, and symbolic representations and the activity. In the activity here, we demonstrate a way to think about the actual *process* of data analysis (that is, during the actual analysis efforts) in a physical way. We do not simply change from one kind of *representation* to another.

Video Clip 7 *(time length: 7:43)*

Picture of the circle graph on the board.

Circle graph created with yarn on the floor.

Step Three: Teach it!

Reflect on Your Own Teaching...

1. What kinds of things did James say that demonstrate his knowledge about circle graphs?

_____

_____

2. How did the context of CJ scoring basketball points impact the data analysis?

_____

_____

3. What role did concept knowledge about data organization have in students' abilities to interact with the compensating task?

_____

_____

4. Look at the picture of the circle graph with the yarn and the picture of the drawing on the board. How did Karen deal with the fact that the physical circle graph and the drawing on the board were representations not in the exact same order? [This is with the yarn and tennis shoes worked from the top in clockwise rotation, but with the picture, Max drew the tennis shoes in a counter-clockwise rotation.]

_____

_____

5. Now, look at your height data. How could you deal with the data in a more physical sense?

_____

_____

6. What do the two video segments have in common?

_____

_____

7. Taking from one stack and adding it to another is called *compensating*. To practice the compensating technique, consider these test scores:

78   88   92   100   65

How could you use compensation to find the average of this student's scores?

_____

_____

A Comment from Karen

This visual, physical representation of evening out the data seems to help my students understand the ideas behind mean, as well as the procedure for calculating the mean. Traditionally drawn circle graphs require students to draw circles, as well as measure angles that are in proportion to the 360 degrees in a particular section of the circle and the same distribution of the data. This is a lot of information for children to coordinate. To lay the conceptual foundation for this kind of graph, I created the human circle graph, visually. This is helpful in later creating pie graphs on paper.

GO BACK TO PAGE 265

Activity 1 4 . 2

PROBABILITY WITH A SPINNER

The following activity has two parts. Use fraction ideas to mathematically calculate what you expect to happen if you spin 24 times. Write the information as a fraction or percent.

	Number	Fraction (or Percent)
Red		
Blue		
Green		
Purple		
Yellow		
Total	24	24/24

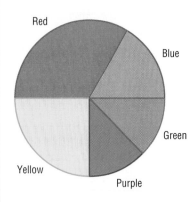

Spin 24 times, and record your findings.

	Your Group	Class Total	Fraction or Percent of Class Total
Red			
Blue			
Green			
Purple			
Yellow			
Total	24		

Khanemann, Slovic, and Tversky (1982) express a good way to think further of the differences. They describe statistics as a record of the past (description) and probability (prediction) as an attempt to predict the future. In general, then, prediction is based on study of likelihood and uncertainty. They suggest that everyday reasoning often confounds mathematical reasoning about predictions because students display a variety of misconceptions about the nature of probability. These misconceptions may involve any of the concepts to be described shortly. It is important to think about the importance of underlying concepts and the way incorrect understanding of the concepts might manifest themselves in students' work.

CONCENTRATING ON THE CONCEPTS:
What Generalizations Really Mean

Conceptually, data analysis should focus on answering the question "Why do we want to analyze these data?" or "What will we learn from studying the data?"

Statistics

In this section, we first elaborate on statistics concepts, some of which were mentioned earlier. The concepts described here (data, sample, organization, and generalization) are couched in the belief that there is some sort of *situation* we wish to better understand. The situation might be an event that is a one-time occurrence. One-time occurrences, for whatever reason, are difficult to repeatedly replicate, such as happening upon an intersection during a green light. The situation might be a phenomenon that is naturally occurring and therefore much more likely to have systematic repeated occurrences, such as weather or gravity. Or the situation might be related to a living population of beings and subject to changing conditions (such as changes in season or cultural mores and codes). Populations include any living being, such as people, bugs, or trees. In regard to the idea of situations, whether one-time events, phenomena, or populations, you should note that these three ideas are *conceptually* the same. However, in practice, the different contexts affect the terminology we use to make general statements about the situations.

Data

To learn something about situations, we first gather data. *Data* (or *datum* if singular) allow us to glimpse small pieces of a situation. As a concept, datum revolves around the very idea that there is a way to take some sort of representative bit of information about the situation. We gather data in an effort to understand the situation, even though the data themselves are not precisely the same as the situation. Recognizing that the data *represent* the situation and are *not the same thing* as the situation is critical for concept knowledge.

Sample

When a collection of data is taken, it is designated for analysis, then referred to as a *sample*. (A sample will also be described in the context of probability concepts in the next section.) In a statistical sense, an event from the situation occurred, and we gathered a sampling of data from that event. The more carefully we determine the sample to be studied, the more likely we are able to make certain assumptions about the sample. That is, if the sample is a well-thought-out gathering of the data, then the sample is expected to mimic the *situation*. As we consider the information in the sample, we find ways to organize and reorganize the data in a meaningful way.

Generalization

With a carefully selected sample, we can make a *generalization* about an event or phenomenon and how it acts in the entire situation of events because of information from the sample. Recall that we start with some situation we wish to better understand. There are three kinds of generalizations one can make about the situation. A *description* is a general statement that describes the currently existing situation on the basis of our information in the data. An *inference* is a sweeping statement about the situation, again based on our information in the data. If you move to forecast about an outcome that might occur, you have moved past the gathered data and on to making a *prediction.* In talking about predictions, we are teetering on the precipice of probability, which will be addressed shortly.

Activity 1 4 . 3

STATISTICS CONCEPTS

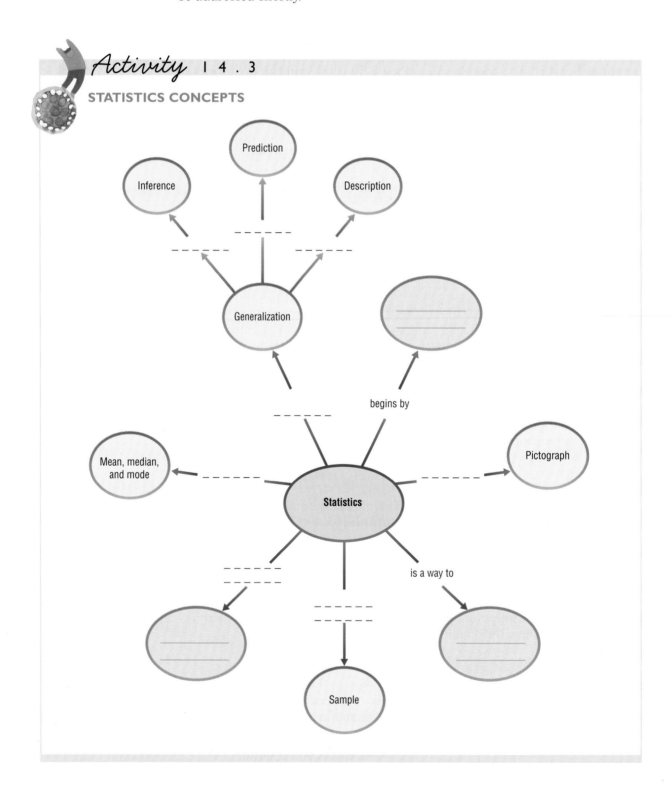

Table 14.1 **College Students Order Pizza Delivery**

CONCEPT/PROCEDURE	EXAMPLE	DEFINITION
Inference	Most college students prefer pepperoni pizza.	*A judgment* that is made about the population and is more reliable with a very large data set. Inferences are made by interpreting data in a sample.
Prediction	If students call in to order a pizza delivery, they will select pepperoni 75% of the time.	Some sort of statement about *what will happen* in a specific instance of a situation. If based on a sample, it uses an interpretation of the data. If based on mathematics, it uses theoretically derived probabilities.
Description	75% of college students surveyed indicated a preference for pepperoni pizza.	A statement that *characterizes* the population but is not a judgment. It is *not* based on an interpretation; it is something that is a fact about the data.
Generalization		A sweeping statement that can be a (1) description, (2) prediction, or (3) inference.
Conclusion	Pizza shops should stock plenty of pepperoni.	Some final statement about the situation based on the generalization *usually* involving a suggested course of action.
Organization	We sorted data and found that the mode is pepperoni.	A way of manipulating the data. Averages are a good example.
Interpretation	We think that mode is the best way to describe these data.	A statement about what we think the organization *means*. Here, you might make some leaps based on your analysis of the data.
Data analysis		The overall procedure of asking an engaging question; gathering data related to that question, studying data to find interesting tendencies, patterns, and directions; and finally making an interpretation in such a way as to then answer or at least address the question in some way.

The statistical concepts described above are a coherent collection of ideas that are at the same time separate ideas but also are coordinated in that they depend on one another. Because you know that a situation happens, you gather data about it, you analyze those data in an effort to know something new about the situation. If you take those data to make an overarching statement about the one-time occurrence, phenomenon, or population or to claim something you would not be able to (or simply did not happen to) observe but that you believe you can defend (based on your data), then you have made an inference. Complete Activity 14.3 to solidify your conceptual understanding of these ideas. You might want to look at Table 14.1 for a list of examples and descriptions of these ideas.

To make a prediction, you might ask, for example, whether it is likely that the next telephone call to a pizzeria will be a request for pepperoni. An inference is a more general statement, relying on the property of large numbers, which in turn relies on a very large sample. Only very large samples will be representative of the situation from which they are drawn. As an example, an inference is noting that most college town pizzerias stock lots of pepperoni. If you have several pizzerias from college towns with data to support this notion, you can be more confident that your inference is valid.

The Need for Probability

When you ask *exactly how likely* the telephone order will be for pepperoni pizza, then you have moved to probability. Probability concepts, described momentarily, are necessary to move to that step and make a specific prediction in terms of the *degree of likelihood* of the prediction. It is important to distinguish between an inference and a specific outcome prediction based on likelihood. The need to make these kinds of predictions leads us to probability concepts of likelihood (or chance), sample, difference between an experiment and theory, law of large numbers, and randomness.

Probability

Likelihood (or chance) is the idea that an outcome of a certain event might or might not happen. Adding some statement about the degree of likelihood about the certainty of that outcome is one way of noting what will probably happen—hence, probability. You should note that the concept of *impossible* is connected to this idea. If something is impossible, it is very likely that the event will *not* happen; that is, there is no chance of that event. Students can determine a list of items that are certain to happen, cannot happen, or just might or might not happen. What do you think fifth graders thought about the likelihood the next person to walk through their classroom door would be 6 feet 10 inches tall?

> **Min:** That is very unlikely because hardly anyone is that tall in real life.
> **Lydia:** Impossible! There are no kids that tall.
> **Ryan:** Well, I suppose it is possible since Angie [a member of the university women's basketball team] volunteers here. Wait a minute, I don't think she's that tall.
> **Jamal:** I agree with Min, it is not likely. I'd say it's about 1%.

It is interesting that at Jamal's school, there are 300 students and 42 teachers, staff, and volunteers. With the issuance of 1% as the likelihood, the mathematics says that 1 out of 100 people through the door will satisfy the 6 feet 10 inches requirement. Later in the school year, after we addressed percentages, we asked the question again.

> **Min:** I think the probability is much smaller than 1%.
> **Lydia:** I say it's zero percent. I think hardly anyone in this town is that tall.
> **Ryan:** It's not impossible. I do not agree that no one in town is that tall, though. I just think the next person through the door is most likely to be a kid. So, I'm going to *say* 0%.
> **Jamal:** It's not zero, but I think it's much smaller than 1%, maybe $\frac{1}{16}$% or something like that.

We earlier explained that a *sample* could be used to describe a situation. For Lydia, the population is everyone in town, so her sample could come from the whole town. Ryan is thinking that the sample is most likely coming from the students in the school, and he discounts the members of the town.

Experimental Probability

Sometimes a sample is the only way to give a probability of an event. When the sample is the only way of knowing, the probability statement is based solely on that sample. Here, the *law of large numbers* allows us to make our statement. The concept of *experimental probability* is that there is a way to know (although the level of confidence in that knowledge can vary) something about the situation based on trends in the sample. For the question of who might come through the door next, Lydia would probably want measurements of everyone in town, whereas Ryan would want measurements of everyone in the build-

ing. Both students would benefit from taking a sample of measurements of the next people through that doorway.

Curcio (1987) describes the differences between reading the data (pulling information from them), reading between the data (looking for relationships or trends in the data), and reading beyond the data (extending, predicting, and inferring). However, making these kinds of reads about gathered data is different from giving a probability. Probability means including the degree of likelihood that the prediction is accurate. Conceptually, then, we can use evidence from an existing situation to make some sort of prediction about the likelihood of an outcome from a future situation by describing what *did* happen. Consider the goal of determining the probability of one of Mr. Ross's second graders coming to school the next day in lace-up shoes. On the basis of the sample of his class, you would probably predict that almost half of the students would have lace-up shoes. A prediction based on a sample is an *experimental* probability.

Theoretical Probability

When we mathematically calculate the probability of an event, we use *theoretical probability*. Conceptually, theoretical probability can be thought of as what *should* happen across infinitely many trials of the situation. With a mathematically calculated prediction (theoretical probability) about the likelihood of an event, prediction is based on more than either a cursory or an in-depth read of data. Theoretical treatments of situations are used, in which the likelihood of a single event is known and used to make a prediction.

There are several supporting concepts in understanding theoretical probability. First, the possible events in the situation must be amenable to mathematical calculation. Second, a sample is composed of a finite number of trials, whereas theory is based on an infinite number of trials. Third, any predictions about the situation must take into consideration that unlikely things *do* happen. Fourth, the idea of *randomness* is involved in mathematical calculations. Randomness means that there is no way to be certain of an event unless there is only one possible outcome. Perhaps more important, randomness does not mean that results will necessarily be scrambled either. Randomness is the idea that there is no way to predict the *next* piece of data. Assuming that data will be scrambled is akin to predicting that the next piece of data will be somehow different from the previous piece of data. Underpinning concepts can be further understood by flipping a two-color counter. Complete Activity 14.4 (p. 274) before continuing with this section.

Likelihood

The *likelihood* (or chance) of flipping a red or a yellow on any given trial is equal. That is, these two outcomes to the situation are equally likely. However, in any given *sample* of flips, your data might or might not result in 50% reds and 50% yellows. No matter how large the sample in the experiment, it is always considered *small* because theory relies on infinitely many flips. So by comparison, any experiment will be a *small* collection of data. You should have mathematically concluded that the probability of red is 50% no matter what side was just flipped. The notion of *randomness* implies that for any given flip, the result is heedless of the last flip (or the next flip for that matter). You might or might not get what you expect—unless you expect that you cannot predict the next flip on the basis of the last flip. Even if you have just flipped ten reds in a row, this does not make yellow more likely on the eleventh flip. There is

Activity 1 4 . 4

TWO-COLOR COUNTER (COIN)

Use two-color counters. (We assume that the colors are red and yellow. Modify the notation if you use coins [heads and tails] or other colors.)

1. If you were to flip a counter exactly one time:

   • What is the likelihood of red?   • What is the likelihood of yellow?

   We calculate the theoretical probability, since the two sides are equally likely.

   $P(R) = .5$ $P(Y) = .5$

2. Maggie flipped her counter, and the red side showed up.

   • What is the probability that her next flip will be yellow?

3. Maggie flipped three more times and got red, red, red.

   • What now is the probability of the next flip resulting in a yellow?
   • What is the probability that her next flip will be red?

4. Extension: Simultaneously flip two counters. Run through 20 trials, flipping two counters at one time. Record the results with tallies.

2 reds	1 red and 1 yellow	2 yellow

   • If you had to make a prediction about likelihood based on this sample, what would you decide?
   • Did you notice anything interesting about the results?

5. Compare your data with those of the rest of the class.

   • Did one red and one yellow result occur more often than two reds and more often than two yellows? *You might think about how we so confidently ask that question.*

   Think theoretically, and use mathematics to fill in the table. Take into account that something interesting is happening for the one red and one yellow event.

2 reds	1 red and 1 yellow	2 yellow

   To determine the theoretical probability of finding probabilities, you need to understand that there are two different ways to achieve one red and one yellow but only one way to achieve two reds and only one way to achieve two yellows.

   $P(RR) = .25$ $P(RY \text{ or } YR) = .5$ $P(YY) = .25$

no "used up" theorem. The idea that yellow is *due* does not take into account the nature of randomness. Konold, Pollatsek, Well, Lohmeier, and Lipson (1993) refer to this ideas as the fact that "a coin has no memory" (p. 408). It is important to help students understand the concept that making successive flips of a counter (coin) will not *make* the data even out for them. It is equally important to help students understand that *theoretically*, a *very* large sample of flips *should* even out, getting closer to 50%.

GRASPING THE PROCEDURES:
Organizing Data and Finding Probabilities

Procedurally, data analysis answers the question "How can we analyze these data?" or "What sorts of calculations or organizations can we execute on them?"

Data Organization

The procedures that we outline are strategies for organizing and reorganizing data. However, the first course of action is to collect the data. Initially data will probably seem messy and disorganized. Students need to have many strategies available to them as they work with the data. Usually, a good first course of action is to arrange data into a frequency chart. We like to refer to a frequency chart as a preorganization technique since the number of times a datum appears is recorded, but no additional interpretation of the data takes place. For instance a frequency chart for the birthday information would literally list the number of birthdays in each month. But later when the data are studied in an effort to recognize or extend patterns, analysis might reveal a pattern of more birthdays in the summer months. Other early procedures for dealing with data organization need to include the conceptual tasks of *comparing and contrasting* different data, *noticing complementary characteristics* between two or more data points, and *sorting and classifying* collections of data into several meaningful kinds of groupings. Comparing and contrasting data includes ordering data to get a sense of a hierarchy in the data. Here we determine some sort of "more than" and "less than" aspect of the data and align them accordingly. Noticing complementary characteristics of data requires collecting exact pieces of data together. This kind of task is akin to sorting and classifying data, in which we manage to collect all the similar data together (instead of just noticing relationships between two data points) and then classify the collection according to some common tendency.

More sophisticated organization includes noting central tendencies of the data, such as mean, mode, and median. Procedures for organizing data can be helped with a variety of technological tools, including spreadsheet programs and graphing calculators. You should become familiar with any technology that is available to you and find the mode for the birth month data from Activity 14.5 (p. 276).

In Activity 14.1, you gathered data and discussed the nature of the data in terms of continuous and categorical data. Here, we return to that collection of data to give procedures for calculating averages. Activity 14.6 (p. 277) leads you through procedures for finding averages and basic variance.

Making Picture Representations

Picture representations allow quick communication of information gleaned from the data. A danger is that unwary readers of graphs can be misled by an incorrectly created graph (whether intentional or not). In the next section, we explain correct procedures for creating several different kinds of graphs.

To study different kinds of graphs and their commonalities, we ask you in Activity 14.7 (p. 278) to use technology to make three different graphs of the

Activity 14.5

ORGANIZING DATA

A group of fifth graders reported birth months.

January	January	December	March	April
June	June	June	August	December
March	March	February	December	August
August	June	June	July	September
January	March	June	October	June

Preorganize the information with a frequency chart.

Frequency Chart

Birth Month	Frequency
January	
February	
March	
April	
May	
June	
July	
August	
September	
October	
November	
December	

Then organize the information by:

Matching (notice complementary features)

Ordering (compare and contrast)

Sorting and classifying (find ways to classify that move beyond matching)

birth month data from Activity 14.5. Procedures for building graphs can be helped with a variety of technological tools, including spreadsheet programs and the graphing calculator. Instead of worrying about whether axes are drawn straight or the circle graph is drawn with accurate angles, we ask, "When I change from one kind of graph to another, what do I notice about the resulting representations?" In other words, what communication remains the same and what changes in different kinds of graphs? This is one advantage of technology. Questions can become more conceptual. We encourage you to become familiar with several types of technologies that support creation of graphs.

Bar graphs require sorting data into discrete groups and then using continuous bars to represent the number of items in each group. The bar graph is used if it is important to compare the number of items in the groups. *Pictographs* are similar to bar graphs. Data are sorted into discrete groups, and

Activity 14.6

FINDING THE MEAN

Gather the entire class's height data from Activity 14.1.

Distribute blocks to each person so that the number of blocks they have matches their height in inches.

Mean. To illustrate the procedures for *mean*, make a plan to redistribute the blocks so that each person in the room has the same number of blocks.

Median. To show the procedures for *median*, stand in line according to your heights, smallest to largest. Describe the importance of the person in the middle. How would the middle point be different if you stood largest to smallest. How will you deal with an even number of people? (There is no one literally standing in the middle.)

Mode. To show the procedures for *mode*, get in groups with classmates who have the same number of blocks. Which group is largest?

List a series of step-by-step instructions that gives a procedure for finding each type of average.

Mean	Median	Mode
1.	1.	1.
2.	2.	2.
3.	3.	3.
4.	4.	4.

1. Did the values for mean, median, and mode ever match? Should they match? What does it mean if they match?
2. Is it acceptable to have a half-of-an-inch value?
3. Is it possible that the median is a value that matches NO ONE?
4. If you needed to predict the height of your absent classmate, what would you predict?
5. If you needed to make an inference about all adults, what judgment would you make?
6. What is the range of the data? What does that mean?
7. Line up the data so they fall in four quartiles. What do you notice about the data in the second and third quartiles?

Quartile 1	Quartile 2	Quartile 3	Quartile 4

then discrete pictures are used rather than a continuous bar to represent the number of items in the groups, even though the discrete pictures are usually stacked in a row that looks somewhat like a bar. Usually, one picture in the stack matches one datum; however, older children should be expected to use one picture in the stack to represent more than one datum. *Line graphs* show a relationship between two characteristics (variables) of the data. They are best used to show trends across time, such as the height of a flower across the first month of its growth. Line graphs should be used only when data are continuous

CLASSROOM CONNECTIONS

Teaching Students to Move from Data to Representations of Data

NCTM CURRICULUM

An activity that is both fun and tasty for (and so is naturally loved by) students involves multicolored miniature marshmallows (or any candy or cereal). I give each student a small paper cup filled with the sweets or cereal. It is always important to know about allergies students have to any foods, culture-related food restrictions, or foods that they simply should not eat, as well as any district restrictions that prohibit food in the classroom. If food is not allowed, beads, blocks, or buttons can be used.

There are so many data analysis activities to do! Students can graph the items by color and compare their findings with the class, as well as compile the findings as a class. Students can even be asked to revisit earlier topics. They can count the total and express the various colors or sizes as a fraction, decimal, and percent. I agree with the NCTM (2000) that "a coherent curriculum effectively organizes and integrates important mathematical ideas so that students can see how the ideas build on, or connect with other ideas (p. 15)." I try to help students make connections between ideas.

I also love to watch my students' data analysis procedures become more and more sophisticated. They modify their organization choices, deciding whether a bar graph or a circle graph is the best way to display their cup of goodies. Their abilities to organize data in meaningful ways demonstrate to me that they are becoming more and more comfortable with a mere representation of the data. They no longer need to see the physical food. Their representations are often a picture of some sort, such as a line graph, *x-y* plot, bar graph, or pictograph. Knowing which kind of graph (or average) *best* represents the data depends on a variety of concepts and, of course, the situation we are trying to study. Nonetheless, we need skills in the procedures for creating graphs.

Activity 14.7

USING TECHNOLOGY TO ORGANIZE DATA

How could you use technology to help you analyze the birth month information (from Activity 14.5) with a picture (line, bar, circle, etc.)?

❏ Graphing calculator ❏ Computer spreadsheet ❏ Other program

(You might need to recode the month data as numbers.)

Which type of graph should you create?

❏ Scatterplot ❏ Line ❏ Picture/object ❏ Bar ❏ Pie/circle ❏ Box-and-whisker

Select three of the most useful representations, and create the graph. Sketch the results:

and points can therefore be connected. Use a *scatterplot* if numerical data are categorical or discrete and cannot be connected. Like line graphs, scatterplots also show a relationship between two characteristics (variables) but are usually discrete. *Pie/circle graphs* sort data into discrete groups and then use sections of the circle (reminiscent of fraction circles) to show the number of items in each group. The pie/circle graph is used if it is important to show parts of the sample compared to the whole sample. The representation is continuous. However, data might be categorical or continuous. Pie/circle graphs are similar to bar graphs, but the primary goal is different. Bar graphs compare the number in each group, whereas circle graphs compare the number in a group to the entire collection of data. *Box-and-whisker graphs* show all data across the entire range. The variance is more obvious in this representation, because data are segmented into four basic groups, the middle two groups being emphasized. See Figure 14.1 for examples of several of these graphs.

Picture/object graphs are accessible by young children because interpretation or manipulation of data is minimal. The pictures in the stack are discrete (as opposed to continuous). With a typical picture graph, children can literally represent information one picture to one data point. For advanced questioning and interpretation, we require one picture to represent two or more data points as shown for Xorinda in Figure 14.1. Sometimes pictures are lined up to quickly demonstrate the data occurring most often. Other times, we collect the pictures in a lump, like the opening problem that used a Venn diagram.

Ms. Hawthorne's Weather Data

Let's listen in as Ms. Hawthorne discusses the weather data her first graders have been gathering for three weeks. Each morning, as part of studying the month's pattern on the calendar, Ms. Hawthorne sent one child to the window to describe the sky. The child had four choices: completely cloudy (but not raining), some clouds, no clouds at all (sunny), or raining/snowing. When the child returned and reported the observation, Ms. Hawthorne selected a small (laminated) square-shaped card with a picture representing the report and used a water-based marker to record the date on the back of the card. The child then deposited the picture card into the basket with the previous days' cards about the sky.

Ms. Hawthorne knows how important it is to teach about data analysis using student-generated data, so she wanted three weeks' worth of their data before asking students to organize the information. "Can anyone think of a good way to sort these cards? It's hard to know what has happened for the past three weeks when they are all in a pile like this."

> **Akoya:** Just put all the cloudy pictures together and all the . . .
> **Stephanie:** Line up the pictures that are the same.
> **Tyler:** I think you should put the card on its date. That way, you know what day it rained and what day it was cloudy.

Notice how Tyler wants to order the data, whereas the other two children want to sort the data into like piles. Both kinds of data analyses are useful, and Ms. Hawthorne capitalized on these different approaches to data analysis. "How is Tyler's way different from Stephanie's way?" After a discussion among the children, Shera finally said, "You told us to *sort* the cards. I think Akoya and Stephanie's ways are what we're supposed to do."

Ms. Hawthorne continued, "What does it mean to sort?" Again, students discussed and decided that it meant to put all things together that were somehow the same. "Why would someone want to put the cards on their dates?"

Figure 1 4 . 1

The Number of Books Read by a Group of Fourth Grade Students

	First 9 weeks	Second 9 weeks	Third 9 weeks	Fourth 9 weeks
Allison	8	9	7	10
Hunter	7	8	6	8
Sori	4	4	3	5
Xorinda	12	11	13	10
Rashaun	9	9	7	10

Bar graph for Allison's quarterly reading

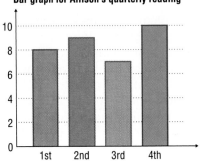

Pictograph for Xorinda's quarterly reading

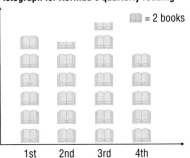

Line graph for Sori's accumulated reading

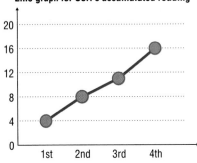

Pie graph for first 9 weeks

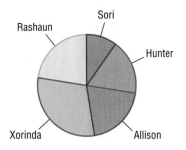

Box-and-whisker graph for first 9 weeks

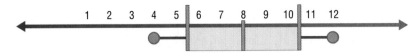

2nd quartile = 8 (Median of data: Allison)
1st quartile = 5.5 (Median of lower half: between Sori and Hunter)
3rd quartile = 10.5 (Median of upper half: between Rashaun and Xorinda)

After more discussion, they decided that would tell someone which day it rained. Shera, "It's like . . . if I needed to remember which day I wore my rain shoes, I could look at the calendar."

Helping children find meaningful ways to organize their own data is important. Ms. Hawthorne introduced the idea that data analysis would depend

CLASSROOM CONNECTIONS

Creating Picture Graphs with Physical Objects

I am constantly thinking about and contemplating tasks I could give my students. "Well-chosen tasks can pique students' curiosity and draw them into the mathematics. The tasks may be connected to the real-world experiences of students, or they may arise in contexts that are purely mathematical" (NCTM, 2000, p. 19). During our data analyses units, I use as many real-life situations as possible. One winter day, I noticed that the lost-and-found box at school was quite full. I had a brainstorm. The box was full of an assortment of mittens, gloves, scarves, hats, shirts, and so on. I sent two students to get the box. We dumped the contents on the floor and got busy sorting them by categories chosen by the students. When we had them sorted, we created a bar graph of the items on the floor.

Looking at the items on the floor gave me an opportunity to show the students the horizontal and vertical axes. We put masking tape on the floor and wrote on the tape to label the axes appropriately. Students de-

cided to title the graph "Lost and Found Items." We wrote that on a big index card and taped it above the graph.

Then we all noticed a problem. One sweater took up a lot more length of the sweater bar than one mitten took of the mitten bar. How would we be sure not to miscommunicate the information with our graph? I took this opportunity to extend this lesson by having the students recreate the graph on paper with the task of somehow making a correction for the mitten/sweater problem. Many students decided to use a mitten to represent *everything* and then labeled each bar according to whether the data were about sweaters, shoes, or hats. Other students created different pictures that were all the same size so that their sweater picture was as long as their mitten picture; then they used the pictures to create the bars in their graphs.

When we were finished, each student chose an item and drew it on a poster. We wrote "found" ads and displayed them in the hallways. The students were excited when other students were able to claim some lost items because of our graph and our advertisements.

on what one wanted to know as a result of analysis. Do we want to sort the data into groups, or do we want to know which day it rained? This conceptual foundation is important and grew from placing the burden of data organization on the students. Eventually, the children decided that they wanted to know what kind of weather happened most often. So they took Stephanie's advice and lined up the cards. (They built a pictograph.)

Go to "Try it! See it! Teach it!" on page 282.

Probability

To discuss procedures for calculating probabilities, play the game in Activity 14.8 (p. 284).

If you owned the game, about how much of the time would you expect to pay out on blue? On green? To answer these questions, calculate probabilities that Player B would spin those colors. The general procedure for calculating probability of an outcome is as follows: (1) Make a list of all possible outcomes, (2) find the number of favorable outcomes (the outcome for which you want to know the probability), and (3) state the probability as a fraction in which the favorable outcome is the numerator and the total number of outcomes is the denominator. As an example, calculate the probability of spinning blue. On any given spin, what is the likelihood that the spinner hand will point to blue?

First, build a list of all possible outcomes. A cursory review of the outcomes may lead to the list of four outcomes (blue, red, yellow, and green) with one blue. This information might help us to understand why students might think that the probability of blue is $\frac{1}{4}$, since blue is one of four possible color outcomes. A somewhat hidden idea in spinners is that the list of possible outcomes

Try it! See it! Teach it!

Organizing Messy Data

Step**One**: Try it!

Do the Math...

On pages 279–281, you will find a passage about Ms. Hawthorne's first graders creating a picture graph. Reading through that information may be helpful in thinking about the information in the video clip. Understanding the general problem of making pictographs helps you understand the conversation in the video.

Step**Two**: See it!

Watch the Video...

To prepare students for a science lesson on density, I asked students to gather data by checking whether fruits in an aquarium would sink or float. Students tried such fruits as grapes, pineapple, orange, banana, watermelon, kiwi, and many others. How could a physical object graph be made by lining up the fruit according to category: sink or float?

Things to Watch for...

- Recognize differences in how students think about reading data. Watch for moments when students appear to make judgments based on the data.
- Watch for a moment when Karen recognizes that a student is thinking only of the data at hand and how Karen urges the student to think between or beyond the data. Here she is using a theory about how children learn to phrase her questions.

Video Clip 8 (time length: 6:04)

Will the watermelon sink or float?

Karen lines up the fruit in a physical picture graph.

Step Three: Teach it!

Reflect on Your Own Teaching...

1. What kinds of things did Evelyn (the pineapple) say that demonstrate her knowledge about data analysis?

_____

_____

_____

2. How did Karen call out the problem with the sizes of the watermelon (float) and the grape (sink) as representations?

_____

_____

_____

3. To read between the data, students had to represent the information correctly. What sorts of questions did Karen ask to get students to do this?

_____

_____

_____

4. Did you notice any moments when it seemed important for the students to have gathered their own data before they could do some data analysis? Are you surprised that Evelyn's pictograph used pineapples? See figure.

_____

_____

_____

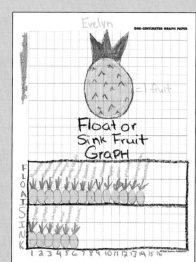

5. After three straight fruits floated, two students predicted that all fruits would float. What does that say about their statistical maturity?

_____

_____

_____

A Comment from Karen

Sometimes students do not say exactly what I want, and I have to resist the urge to say it for them. Okay, the sinkers were small, what did that do to your thinking? It might be a way to move the conversation into a different direction.

　　We extended the question to "Does a can of cola sink or float? How about a can of diet soda?" There was general agreement that both would sink. Hmmm. Imagine the surprise when the diet soda floated!

GO BACK TO PAGE 281

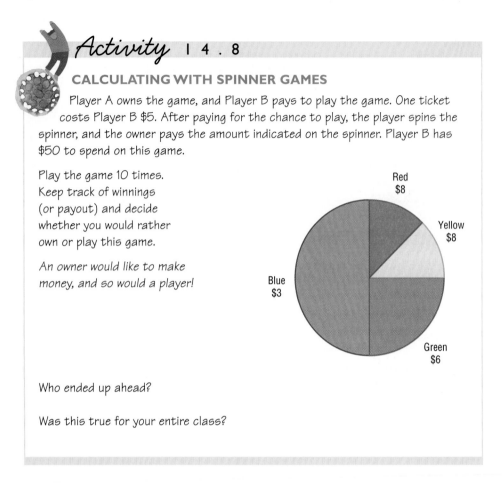

Activity 1 4 . 8

CALCULATING WITH SPINNER GAMES

Player A owns the game, and Player B pays to play the game. One ticket costs Player B $5. After paying for the chance to play, the player spins the spinner, and the owner pays the amount indicated on the spinner. Player B has $50 to spend on this game.

Play the game 10 times. Keep track of winnings (or payout) and decide whether you would rather own or play this game.

An owner would like to make money, and so would a player!

Who ended up ahead?

Was this true for your entire class?

Red $8

Yellow $8

Blue $3

Green $6

is actually the 360 degrees around the center of the spinner. The spinner hand may land on any of those degrees. (We assume that the spinner hand is free to spin and could land after a random number of degrees have passed.) So for spinners, we list degrees to build our list of outcomes. Second, select favorable outcomes from that list. The blue space could take any one of the 180 available degrees. Third, state the probability as a fraction with the number of blue degrees as the numerator and the total number of degrees as the denominator. Therefore, the probability of spinning blue is $\frac{180}{360}$, or $\frac{1}{2}$. We invite you to return to the game and calculate the probabilities of red, yellow, and green.

Fairness

What else did you notice about the game? As you included class data, you may have been able to infer that the game was completely *fair*, even though the likelihood of each color was not equal. A fair game is one in which the player and the owner have equal chances of winning *over the long term*. Fairness of a game is calculated by looking at individual probabilities in the game to calculate the expected value of the game. Before we demonstrate that procedure, first you might be interested to hear fifth graders describe the notion of fair. Students often have a practical view of fair and a mathematical view of fair.

> ***Min:*** Fair means everyone has an equal chance of winning.
> ***Lydia:*** Fair is a way of making sure that each person has the same chance of winning.
> ***Ryan:*** Fair means equally shared.
> ***Jamal:*** Fair is something split out into equal portions.

Ironically, sometimes students do not believe that a game is fair if it is structured in such a way that it does not appear to give anyone an advantage. We are sure that you can imagine a young child saying, "That's not fair!" when confronted with a practical situation in which there is no way to ensure a win. Listen to these second graders explain the idea of a fair game.

Sydney: In a fair game, there has to be a way to win.
Victoria: A game is not fair if no one wins.
Macy: I think it's fair when people go in turn and we all get a turn.
Dustin: A game is not fair if most of the time, you lose.

As you can see, it is critical to develop a common understanding of *mathematical* fairness. Mathematically, a fair game is one that is structured so that each player (and the owner) has an equal chance of winning. We note Dustin's comment in particular. Mathematically, it would not be possible to have a fair game when most of the time someone wins. However, he sees losing most of the time as an indication that a game is rigged in some way. We have much to overcome when we think about students' conceptions of fair.

Expected Value

We think further about the issue of a fair game by studying the spinner in more detail. To determine whether a game is fair, we calculate its *expected value.* An expected value is the amount a game, such as the spinner game, is expected to *pay out* over the long term. The procedure for this calculation is as follows: (1) Determine the probability of each outcome, (2) multiply each probability by the amount paid out for that color, (3) add those values, and (4) compare that value to the cost to play the game. If the cost to play is more than the expected value, it is unlikely that you (as the player) will win money *in the long run.* If the cost is less than the expected value, it is likely you will win money *in the long run* (as the player.) If the cost is equal to the expected value, then the game is fair. No one has a theoretical advantage. For practice, you might choose to calculate the expected values for Activity 14.8.

In the spinner game, we thought carefully about whether or not the different color outcomes were equally likely and used those calculations to determine fairness. On the spinner, we found that blue was more likely than other colors because the outcome list was really about degrees in an angle, not number of colors. In Activity 14.9 (p. 286), we ask you to think carefully about calculating probabilities for *flipping counters.* Here, we consider possible ways in which any given counter can land. Each of the four individual counters could land either red or yellow for any given collection of reds and yellows. Table 14.2 shows a good way to think about the different ways the counters could land. You might want to use it as you complete the activity and calculate the probabilities of each kind of outcome.

You might be surprised to find the probability of four reds and the probability of three reds and one yellow were not equally likely. Why is that? Interesting experiences such as this can motivate students to think carefully about probability issues.

Odds

Another procedure warranting discussion is calculating odds. Odds are closely related to probabilities. To calculate odds, (1) determine the list of possible outcomes, (2) select the number of favorable outcomes from the list, (3) write a ratio comparing the number of favorable outcomes to the number

Activity 14.9

HOW TO COUNT OUTCOMES

In this game, you need four players (A, B, C, and D) and four two-color counters. We assume that the colors are yellow and red. Each player has one two-color counter, and all four counters are flipped at the same time. Award points according to how the counters land.

Points are awarded as follows:
Player A = exactly 4 reds
Player B = exactly 3 reds
Player C = exactly 2 reds
Player D = exactly 1 reds
No one wins if no reds are showing.

Play the game for 30 simultaneous flips. Record the results in a table and determine experimental probabilities.

Next, we calculate theoretical probabilities.

(1) We built a list of possible outcomes:

4 reds, 3 reds and 1 yellow; 2 reds and 2 yellows; 1 red and 3 yellows; and 4 yellows. **(Are there *really* five outcomes?)**

(2) Collect the number of favorable outcomes for each collection.

(3) Record the theoretical probability of each outcome.

	Number of Favorable	Probability
4 reds	1	1/
3 reds and 1 yellow	4	4/
2 reds and 2 yellows		
1 red and 3 yellows		
4 yellows		

Table 14.2 Organizing Four Coins Information

WAYS		COUNTER A	COUNTER B	COUNTER C	COUNTER D
1	4 reds	Red	Red	Red	Red
4	3 reds and 1 yellow	Red	Red	Red	Yellow
		Red	Red	Yellow	Red
		Red	Yellow	Red	Red
		Yellow	Red	Red	Red
	2 reds and 2 yellows				
	3 yellows and 1 red				
	4 yellows				

Total number of outcomes possible when four counters are flipped at once: _____

of unfavorable outcomes, and (4) state the odds first in words and then as a number ratio.

Odds are often used when it is important to compare one idea against another. You might have heard commercials in which doctors recommend something 2 to 1 or the odds of winning the lottery are said to be around 1:80,000,000. The work in Activity 14.10 helps to elucidate the fact that eighty million is a very large number.

With 80,000,000 unfavorable outcomes and only one favorable one, the likelihood of anyone selecting the correct second is remote. Experiences with such activities are helpful in developing large number sense as well as knowledge about data analysis. It is important to understand procedures for calculating odds as well as concepts behind the idea of odds. As you can see, data analysis is composed of a great many concepts and procedures that must be coordinated meaningfully.

Activity 1 4 . 1 0

GUESSING THE SECOND

This game requires four players and each player (A, B, C, and D) starts with $10.

The objective of the game is to finish with all the money.

Play constitutes taking turns selecting 1 second of time in Player A's life out of the last 80,000,000 seconds of his or her life.

How to Play
Player A: Select 1 second of time in the last 80,000,000 seconds of your life.

Players B, C, and D: Take turns buying chances ($1/chance) to also select the second that matches player A's life selection until someone has all the money.

Player A: Pays $10 to anyone who guesses the correct second.

Worksheet for Player A:

Today's date: _____

Calculate the date 80,000,000 seconds ago: _____

Randomly select one second of your life from the last 80,000,000 seconds, and secretly write it down.

It usually helps to write out all six values.

Year /month /day /hour /minute /second
___ /_____ /___ /____ /_____ /____

LET'S REVIEW

In thinking about the mathematics of data analysis, we learned that concepts and procedures for both statistics and probability are part of the mathematical knowledge base. Statistics is a matter of representing real events with some sort of more symbolic description, such as a mean or a graph. Several concepts related to statistics are important to understand in order to work with statistics. Students must understand that a data point represents an event, a sample represents the situation, a generalization is a statement about the situation, and data can be organized to help make the generalization. Probability is a matter of knowing the likelihood of an event. Several probability concepts ground thinking in this way. Like statistics, the concept of a sample as a representation of a situation is important—this time, in developing experimental probabilities. There is a difference between an experimental probability and a theoretical one in that the theoretical probability is strictly calculated from mathematical principles. But they are also related in that the law of large numbers tells us that over a long time, the experiment will match the theory. The concept of randomness is nicely summed up in the statement, "A coin has no memory" (Konold et al., 1993, p. 408). That is, there is no *certainty* about an upcoming event, there is only *probability* about it.

There are several procedures to analyze data. One such procedure is building a bar graph in order to describe a population: (1) Collect data, (2) build a frequency chart, (3) transfer numerical information to a bar graph (make bars the same length as the size of the frequency), and (4) compare lengths of the bars. This process allows a quick glimpse into the overall tendencies apparently at work in the population.

HOMEWORK

1. Create a circus game in which the probability of drawing a green marble is 50%. Test this game on your classmates. Use your algebraic thinking to design a dice or spinner simulation for drawing marbles from a bag that upholds your probabilities.
2. Complete the concept chart on page 289 for probability shown.

SUGGESTED READINGS

Falk, R., & Konold, C. (1994). Random means hard to digest. *Focus on Learning Problems in Mathematics, 16*(1), 2–12.

Jones, G. A., Langrall, C. W., & Thornton, C. A. (1996). Using data to make decisions about chance. *Teaching Children Mathematics, 2*(6), 346–350.

Konold, C. (1989). Informal conceptions of probability. *Cognition and Instruction, 6*, 59–98.

Konold, C., & Pollatsek, A. (2002). Data analysis as the search for signals in noisy processes. *Journal for Research in Mathematics Education, 33*(4), 259–289.

REFERENCES

Curcio, F. R. (1987). Comprehension of mathematical relationships expressed in graphs. *Journal for Research in Mathematics Education, 18*(5), 382–393.

Gullberg, J. (1997). *Mathematics: From the birth of numbers.* New York: W. W. Norton.

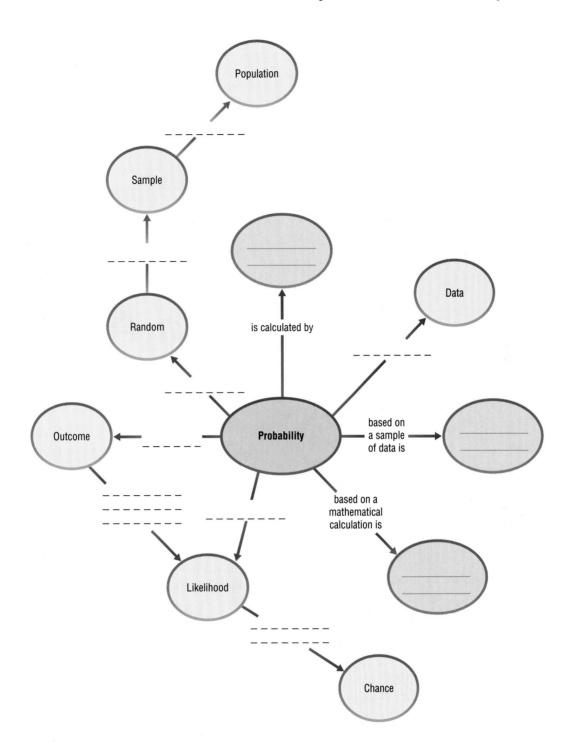

Kahnemann, D., Slovic, P., & Tversky, A. (1982). *Judgment under uncertainty: Heuristics and biases.* New York: Cambridge University Press.

Konold, C., Pollatsek, A., Well, A. D., Lohmeier, J., & Lipson, A. (1993). Inconsistencies in students' reasoning about probability. *Journal for Research in Mathematics Education, 24*(5), 392–414.

National Council of Teachers of Mathematics. (2000). *Principles and standards for school mathematics.* Reston, VA: NCTM.

15

How We Learn about
Data Analysis

NCTM LEARNING

UNDERSTANDING RELEVANT LEARNING FRAMEWORKS:
Friel, Curcio, and Bright (Statistics) and Jones, Langrall, Thornton, and Mogill (Probability)

In general, less is probably known about how learners develop data analysis knowledge than about the other areas we have described. Our understanding about how students learn data analysis is continually growing because we are coming to better understand exactly what young children can and should do with data. Because this is a developing field, current researchers opt to identify their findings as a *framework* rather than a *theory*. Before 1990, very few experiences with data analysis were included in typical primary curricula. So you will enter a classroom with expectations of your students that are very different from expectations of students in the twentieth century. We encourage you to do your best to stay current with research and literature as they become available to you as a practicing teacher, particularly in this area.

Underlying Facts

That said, there is some general agreement with regard to six underlying facts about the learning and teaching of data analysis. First, a problem-solving approach to teaching is consistent with how learners develop data analysis knowledge (Lajoie, Jacobs, & Lavigne, 1995). Second, concept knowledge must be developed before developing procedural or conventional knowledge. Then procedural knowledge can grow from problem-solving experiences, which build *more* concept knowledge and build *on* concept knowledge. For example, students should understand the concept of a sample before using a simulation to understand a problem situation (Horvath & Lehrer, 1998). Third, concepts and procedures are heavily interdependent (Konold & Higgins, 2003). Students should use concept and procedural knowledge to invent procedures for organizing data, as well as methods for representing those organizations (Konold, 2002). Fourth, statistical representations can become more and more sophisticated as students have more experiences dealing with data (Friel et al., 2001) and as their knowledge of probability ideas such as likelihood become more sophisticated (Horvath & Lehrer, 1998). Fifth, data organization can be greatly aided by appropriate use of technology (Konold, 2002; Lehrer & Romberg, 1996). Sixth and last, there are certain early experiences that lay the foundations for the more sophisticated ideas behind data analysis (statistics and/or probability). That is, we must sequence our instruction so that students examine certain kinds of situations before other kinds, and we must be cognizant of the students' existing knowledge before creating the task. A good example of that idea is our belief that students should study situations in which all outcomes are equally likely before studying situations in which all outcomes are not equally likely (Horvath & Lehrer, 1998; Konold et al., 1993). Students should study categorical data (grouping) before studying continuous data, which usually requires some sort of measurement, and students should almost always study data with which they are familiar.

The Importance of Student-Generated Data

Learners must roll up their sleeves and work with their own data. You probably noticed that we suggested that you gather your own data for most of the activities in the previous sections. A starting point for early learning experiences with data analysis is the opportunity to work with data that make sense to the learner. Initially, the data that make sense are data about the learners themselves. Such data are not published; they are gathered in the classroom.

Moreover, it is critical here (as it was with previous topics) that students be encouraged to and allowed the time to engage in explorations with an eye toward making sense of the data—hence, data analysis. Good questions are paramount in tasks that drive students toward more expert data analysis. When we think about a mathematical fact such as 16 + 27, we know that in base 10, it is always equal to 43. However, when we think about gathering a data sample from a population, such consistency is not the case. Each sample will probably be different and be different enough to require a slightly different approach to analysis. Memorizing steps and always finding the same representation are simply not options. Students must see how relationships exist between data pieces and understand for themselves what is going on. The very content is in some ways unpredictable, so students must truly understand the concepts before thinking about applying procedures. Therefore, this is information that simply cannot be rotely memorized.

Statistics Framework

The general framework behind developing data analysis knowledge within the realm of statistics is described by Friel, Curcio, and Bright (2001). Students progress through three kinds of analysis: (1) extracting information *from* data, (2) finding relationships *in* data, (3) moving *beyond* data to make claims. Students must serially progress through these stages. Students' organization of data can grow progressively sophisticated as students work in each of the three stages of analysis. But students must first learn to extract information from the data before organizing data to find relationships. Simply making some sort of sense of specific data collections is one way students extract information

Table 15.1 **"Looks Like, Sounds Like" Table for Statistics**

Refer to the question "What kind of shoes do Mr. Ross's students wear?"

STATISTICS

	Looks Like	Sounds Like
Reading the data	Points to the largest collection of data.	"More students are in the lace-up shoes group than any other group."
Reading between the data	Groups data in a new way. Looks at students who *did not have* lace-up shoes. Essentially recreating the information into only two groups—lace-up and not lace-up—rather than as four separate groups.	"Most students do not have lace-up shoes."
Reading beyond the data	Plots the information on circle graph to show portions: Lace-up shoes (9) Not lace-up (11)	"I bet Ms. Chandler's second graders have about half lace-up shoes too. Can we go ask?"

directly from the data. See Table 15.1 for the familiar "looks like, sounds like" information for the question of Mr. Ross's students' shoes.

Organizing Concepts

Students must first understand the concept of *data* before extracting information from them. Data are literally examples, and the collection of data constitutes a sample. That sounds kind of obvious. But it is surprisingly difficult to understand. Students must know that situations can be described by data from the situation before students are ready to make subsequent organizations of data. Extracting some sort of information from specific data is dependent on these data.

Konold and Higgins (2003) describe how the *process* of turning observations of events into data involves simplification and abstraction of the event. The process includes recognizing the event and recording corresponding data. *Data* as a simplification and abstraction of a situation is an underlying concept for the concept of a *sample*. The process of turning those observations into data is a procedure for building a sample that requires understanding of the concept of data in the first place.

As students work with their own data, they should be prompted to think about different ways to *organize* and reorganize the data in the sample. By creating and studying several different organizations, students are more able to see relationships within and between data. Students might note that one kind of value occurred more often than another. They might organize information into two or more groupings rather than looking at individual pieces of data. By rearranging data, they develop the capacity to see relationships. The concept here is that data can be reorganized, sometimes in unanticipated ways. Finally, students know enough about the data that they can describe the situation and answer a question about the situation. When they are ready to communicate certain ideas that they have seen in the data, they are finding relationships. We cannot make an exhaustive list of the many representations students might use when they describe relationships. In part, this is true because there are so many kinds of representations. But mostly, this is true because we want to open your mind to the fact that students will invent different kinds of organizations than you might expect, and those organizations are often quite sensible, no matter how unexpected (Konold, 2002). Furthermore, we might or might not have the intuitions that our students have simply because we have been programmed to think of representations learned from school and society (bar graphs, mean, mode, etc.).

After they solidify understanding of organization and making representations, students can interpret data by making *generalizations*. Students move beyond the data to make these generalizations and know that their generalizations are indicative of the situation under investigation. Knowing that their sample is not the same thing as the population is still critical. However, understanding this notion can prove very difficult. When students are ready to make some sort of claim beyond data, it is because they believe that a claim can be substantiated or inferred from their data. Usually, this claim is provided along with a representation, which probably grew from their decisions about how to organize the data.

Making Interpretations Based on a Sample

Let's visit our fifth graders' class, where the ratio of boys to girls is unusual this year with 17 boys and six girls. We asked students to organize and show that information with a graph. The *boy* bar was much longer than the *girl* bar. Then we asked whether they thought all classrooms were made up of 17 boys and six girls. Of course, students know that this is not the case.

> **Min:** I think our class is unusual. I know other classes are closer to half and half.
> **Lydia:** I can see how someone might think our school had more boys, though.
> **Ryan:** Maybe it means another class has more girls than boys.
> **Jamal:** I don't think we can say anything about other classes. They should be 50–50, shouldn't they?

The students have a sense that they should not make any rigid claims about the boy:girl ratios in other fifth grade classrooms. They recognize that their class is unusual in some way. Their conceptual knowledge about making generalizations about this situation appears to be grounded. This situation sets the stage for discussing the importance of gathering enough information before making an interpretation. When we asked students how many classes they thought they would need to survey before making a statement about the ratio of fifth grade boys to girls, they excitedly accepted this challenge. Min said, "I know someone at Glenville Elementary. I could ask him how many are in his class." Lydia offered, "I could email my cousin in Florida." Ryan said, "My uncle lives in Canada. I could call my cousin—he's in fifth grade too." These are further examples of how making mathematics real to the students creates an opportunity for developing data analysis reasoning.

Probability Framework

The general framework behind sequential development of data analysis knowledge within the realm of probability is described by Jones, Langrall, Thornton, and Mogill (1999). They found students progress through four levels of thinking: (1) subjective, (2) transitional, (3) informal quantitative, and (4) numerical.

Horvath and Lehrer (1998) provide further guidance about students' development of probability knowledge. They describe how students begin with a basic understanding of concepts, move toward developing connections between and among concepts, and then finally are able to attach numerical statements to their concept ideas. In the next section, we delineate Jones and colleagues' framework for probability thinking and use Horvath and Lehrer's work to further substantiate your thinking about learners' levels of sophistication.

Subjective students (level 1) tend to think "narrowly and inconsistently" (Jones et al., 1999, p. 490) about the information under investigation. When spinning a four-color spinner, students might be swayed by their favorite color rather than by the information gathered about their class. Transitional students (level 2) seem to recognize some usefulness to quantifying or organizing information to make a general statement. But often they are not sure enough or experienced enough to justify their claims, and they can still be convinced of subjective claims. Informal quantitative students (level 3) use quantitative reasoning. They make sense of multistep problems and organize information in a structured manner. They are less swayed by subjective claims and can concentrate on several aspects of a single event. Numerical students (level 4) make abstract connections and precise calculations about the nature of the probability situation. See Table 15.2 for a "looks like, sounds like" table about probability.

Recognizing Development through Likelihood

The concept of *likelihood* is described as the level of certainty of an event. The subjective (level 1) understanding of the concept of *certain* as opposed to *impossible* is the launching point for probability. At level 2, students grow to include notions of *most likely* or *least likely* in thinking about probability. By level 3, students develop more sophisticated thinking, attaching notions of *more likely*

Table 15.2 **"Looks Like, Sounds Like" Table for Probability**

Refer to question "What is the likelihood the next person walking in the room is 6 feet 10 inches tall?"

PROBABILITY

	Looks Like	Sounds Like
(1) Subjective	Does not really ponder the situation, just thinks about own personal experiences.	"Impossible. I don't know anyone that tall." Or "James's dad is that tall, so it's very likely because sometimes he comes to visit."
(2) Transitional	Gathers data only from within the school.	"It is not likely, no one at this school is that tall."
(3) Informal quantitative	Gathers data from classmates about parents' and older siblings' heights.	"It is around 1% because one of our 103 parents and siblings is that tall."
(4) Numerical	Checks science book and finds the "mean height" of human males to be 5 feet 11 inches with a standard deviation of 2.7 inches.	"It is much less than 1% because 99% of the population is within 3 standard deviations of the mean, so 99% of the population is less than 6 feet 8 inches."

or *less likely* as opposed to notions of *most likely* or *least likely*. Here, they also become more comfortable justifying their thinking with some sort of quantitative statements. At a final stage (level 4), students learn to attach a numerical estimation (probability) to the degree of likelihood of an event.

Recognizing Development through Randomness

Being able to calculate the degree of likelihood of an event requires awareness of the concept of *randomness*. In an experiment, students learn that data represent the situation, and they begin to use samples to calculate probabilities. Level 1 learners think solely about their own experiences and are unaware of the mathematical notion of randomness in data. Randomness (the extent to which there is or could be bias in the data) appears as level 2 learners put more faith in small samples but still do not take the mathematical nature of randomness into full account. Level 3 learners begin to recognize the role a larger sample could have in capturing the essence of random events. Level 4 learners believe in and make calculations to determine degrees of randomness.

According to Horvath and Lehrer (1998), understanding the general nature of gathered data in an experimental trial, as a viable representation of the situation, must be consciously developed. At first, children might not understand the differences between their small sample and the entire set of possibilities in the situation. Subjective learners think about possible outcomes from a situation by listing only familiar outcomes. At level 2, learners begin to list complete sets of outcomes and can begin to understand and make sense of situations that may have two steps. Level 3 students list outcomes from a situation, no matter how complicated. By level 4, learners are able to generate strategies for listing the outcome set rather than mechanically writing down all possible outcomes.

Comparing Probabilities

As students engage in experiences that help them to develop awareness of randomness and likelihood while thinking about the difference between a sample and the whole situation, they coordinate their concepts to understand the relationship between their small sample and the whole situation. Here, they use knowledge about what Horvath and Lehrer (1998) call the "structure of events." Students apply procedures to organize information (in a way that means they understand the structure of the population) and calculate corresponding values to make numerical predictions about the situation.

When the data information is a collection of experimental data, the data can be used to find an *experimental probability*. An experimental probability is necessary when the true likelihood of individual events is impossible to know. For instance, when forecasting weather, the statement "There is a 30% chance of rain" means that meteorologists have gathered much data and that in the past, conditions similar to today's conditions have produced rain 30% of the time. When instead, the information is mathematically derived, it results in a *theoretical probability*. A theoretical probability is calculated when likelihoods of individual events are known. For instance, the likelihood of pulling B7 out of the bingo cage on the first draw is exactly 1/75, since there are 75 spots and each is equally likely to be drawn.

Recognizing Development through Sampling

Interestingly, the sample, though gatherable, is not predictable, whereas the situation, which can never be fully gathered, *is* predictable. On the surface, this is counterintuitive. However, experiences in developing knowledge about how to use samples and the law of large numbers to give *generalizations* develop this knowledge.

Students at level 1 are generally unconcerned with data gathered from random samples and maintain their statements about probability based on subjective assessments. Students remain unconvinced of the usefulness of anything beyond their own subjective reasoning for making a theoretical claim about probability. Level 2 students are comfortable with very small sample sizes in making their claims and are able to predict *likely* and *unlikely* events based on theory. However, there are still moments when these students may be swayed by subjective claims. At level 3, students begin to recognize the importance of a larger sample size in predicting *likely* and *unlikely* (as in level 2) events. Finally, level 4 students collect adequate amounts of data and collect it appropriately. They can recognize when a situation must be articulated with an experimental probability as opposed to a theoretical probability. These students assign numerical probabilities to theoretical events.

Confronting Enigmas

Horvath and Lehrer (1998) describe the importance of learners understanding what to do with data when those data do not seem to fit an understanding of the situation. In early experiences, when students are merely considering data that are either certain or impossible, the introduction of an instance that is neither certain nor impossible allows students to extend their knowledge about the nature of data. As they move to situations that produce data that are not all equally likely (as in the case of the spinner in Activity 14.8), students can use these seeming nonexamples to develop concept knowledge. The need to reconcile the relationship between a known likelihood and an instance in which

---

CLASSROOM CONNECTIONS

Guiding Students' Uses of Vocabulary

NCTM CURRICULUM

Incorporating probability vocabulary can be fun! Words such as *probably, most likely, unlikely, never,* and *always* are words that students are familiar with. Remember the game of hunting for a hidden item? Those watching you hunt would yell out that you were getting hot, or warm, or cool, or cold. I use the game to develop probability vocabulary. I know that students need to "describe events as likely, unlikely and discuss the degree of likelihood using such words as *certain, equally likely,* and *impossible*" (NCTM, 2000, p. 176, emphasis in original). I try to find ways to make the curriculum meaningful for my students.

If you were in my class, I would ask you to write down something that will happen in your life in the next week. It could be as simple as "I will eat breakfast" to "My mom is going to have a baby." Now imagine that you have been chosen to stand on the middle of an imaginary line that runs across our classroom. If you move toward the right, you are heading to being positive it will happen; moving to the left indicates a very low chance of something happening. Students now take turns reading what they have written. Suppose someone reads, "I will celebrate my birthday next week." Your task is to consider that comment for yourself. Where will you go? If it is not going to be your birthday, you would head clear to the left end of the line, explaining to the class that there is no chance of that happening to you. Suppose someone else reads, "I will go to the grocery store with my mom." Hmmm. Now that seems likely in your life. You head toward the right, perhaps stopping at about 75%. You explain, "Yes, it is likely that I will go to the store with my mom this week." The students enjoy this activity, especially trying to think of comments their classmates will like. In the process, they learn probability vocabulary.

an unlikely event occurred often propels learners forward. Finally, as they learn to calculate theoretical probabilities mathematically, they are able to argue thoughtfully about the nature of any *outliers* they may have gathered in an experiment. As you can see, concepts must be coordinated in a deep and meaningful fashion.

USING RELEVANT PATTERNS:
Organized Counting (Pascal's Triangle)

Issues of probability can be studied within the context of patterns found in Pascal's triangle. Complete Activity 15.1 (p. 298), in which you count possibilities in a variety of situations.

Pascal's triangle is a useful tool when it is necessary to count possible outcomes in a variety of situations so you can calculate probabilities and make a prediction. For instance, if we wondered about the probability that a woman decided on a perm and a cut, we could start our work with the numerical information in the triangle. Because the perm/cut choice is one of sixteen options, the probability is $\frac{1}{16}$. Recognizing when realistic situations will mimic the numerical patterns that appear in Pascal's triangle occurs when learners are capable of numerical thinking, level 4. Familiarity with the specific numbers in Pascal's triangle and how the triangle is constructed is also helpful. You might note that subjective (level 1) students would have decided whether a woman would choose a perm and a cut based solely on their own unique experiences in beauty salons. By comparison, those more experienced students use more numerically based strategies for reporting probabilities. Moreover, checking for patterns in data, regardless of whether the pattern is in Pascal's triangle, requires having previously been able to extract information from and within this kind of data in the first place. So you can start to see the interconnectedness between probability and statistics thinking.

After one gathers experimental data, organizes them, and searches for a pattern or trend (relationship) in the data, then it is time to move beyond the data and make a prediction. To demonstrate moving beyond the data, our fifth graders decided to write about visiting a funny grocery store after they completed a lesson about Pascal's triangle. The students' funny store had exactly seven cans of soup on the shelf. The fifth graders asked, "What is the probability that a person buys one can of tomato soup and one can of potato soup (and nothing else)?" They used Pascal's triangle to find all the ways a person might make (or not make) a purchase in this funny store. In this way, students used Pascal's triangle to demonstrate their numerical probabilistic understandings and to move beyond data, writing their own problem.

CULTURAL CONNECTIONS
Organizing Data and Simulating Game Situations

**NCTM
EQUITY**

Statistics and probability knowledge have long been major contributors to understanding leisure activities and even important historical events. You are encouraged to think about situations that require statistical and probabilistic thinking, such as reporting about

Activity 15.1

BUILDING PASCAL'S TRIANGLE

In each scenario, count the number of possibilities. Count all options. Write the values in the chart on page 2. *The fourth one has been completed for you.*

1. You serve chips at a picnic. You have supplied one kind of dip. How many different ways could your guests have chips? (Don't forget plain.)

2. You serve coffee at a breakfast. You have supplied two kinds of taste enhancements: **cream and sugar.** How many different ways could your guests have coffee? (Don't forget black.)

3. You select a pizza. Three different toppings are available: **olives, mushrooms, and pepperoni.** In how many different ways could you have a pizza? (Don't forget plain; think of this as the cheese pizza.)

4. You are at a hair salon, standing in line behind a woman who is deciding about her hair. The salon offers four types of service: **permanent, coloring, simple cut, and styling.** In how many different ways might she decide to proceed? (Don't forget that she can refuse to have anything done at all.)

   No service (she walks back out)
   One option: (1) perm, (2) color, (3) cut, or (4) style
   Two options: (1) perm and color, (2) perm and cut, (3) perm and style, (4) color and cut,
     (5) color and style, (6) cut and style
   Three options: (1) perm, color, and cut; (2) perm, color, and style; (3) perm, cut, and style;
     (4) color, cut, and style
   All four of the options: perm, color, cut, and style

5. You decide you might buy some new pets for your classroom. There are currently five different pets in the store—**bird, gecko, gerbil, fish, and mouse**—but only one of each. In how many different ways might you make your purchase? (Don't forget that you can refuse to buy any pets at all.)

6. You work in a fast-food restaurant that specializes in burgers. You have six toppings available for patrons: **ketchup, mustard, cheese, onions, pickles, and mayonnaise.** In how many ways might a person build a burger?

sporting events or deciding who will be president. For our first example, we study the statistical information that was published in an almanac around the time of the Declaration of Independence in the United States. For our second example, we discuss the probabilities of an interesting game played by women of the Native North American Cheyenne people.

Organizing Astronomical Information

Benjamin Banneker is a famous statistician who wrote the first American almanac exclusively dedicated to farmers. He published the first of his six astronomically based almanacs in 1792, at the age of 61. Benjamin was born in Maryland in 1731. He was the son of Robert, a freed man, born enslaved (Robert's father was born in Africa), and Mary, a free woman of mixed heritage (Mary's father was a freed slave, and her mother was an English maid in England and an indentured servant in America). Mary was free in part because she was born after her mother (Benjamin's grandmother) completed her servitude.

Record the information for each situation:

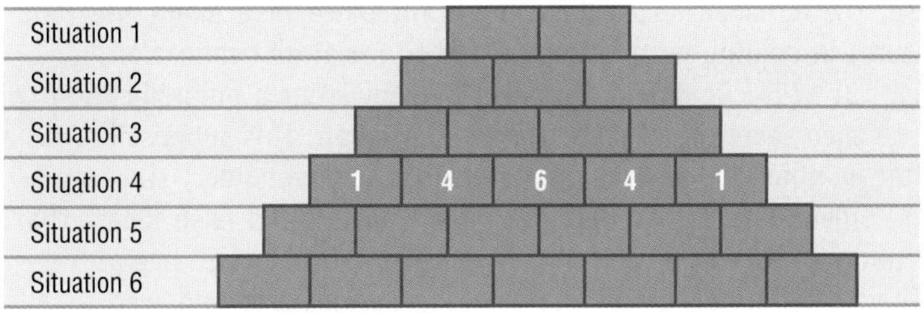

Situation 1				1		1			
Situation 2			1		2		1		
Situation 3		1		3		3		1	
Situation 4	1		4		6		4		1
Situation 5									
Situation 6									

You are building something called Pascal's triangle. Look for a pattern from one row to the next. On the basis of this number pattern, fill in the numbers for the next four rows.

Row 7 _____

Row 8 _____

Row 9 _____

Row 10 _____

Pascal's triangle is useful in many ways. Relevant to this chapter is its use in quickly counting the number of options for a certain scenario to help calculate a probability.

Write a scenario for the information found in the seventh row of Pascal's triangle.

_____

_____

_____

_____

Robert was later free because Mary bought his freedom. Benjamin was considered born free, even though his father, Robert, had been born enslaved. This put Benjamin in the first-generation of his family *born free* with the name of a parent (his father) who was *born enslaved* because of his skin color. Benjamin's African heritage was regarded by many in the power base of the American culture as a reason to dismiss him. Yet amidst a culture of discrimination, he used his skill with statistical information to prepare information for six almanacs and worked as part of the survey team for the then-new urban area now known as Washington, D.C.

One reason he dedicated his almanac to farmers was because of his own background. He grew up on a farm and was aware of the importance of tricking nature and understanding how weather affects successful crops. His father irrigated with ditches and dams during times of drought that destroyed other farms. Benjamin's interest in weather together with his statistical skill laid the foundation for his almanac. After Benjamin's parents died, he rented out the farmland and built a small cabin complete with a skylight so that he could study celestial bodies and record his calculations instead of doing farming chores. With his calculations, Benjamin successfully established an accurate planting and harvesting cycle. His almanacs were celebrated by farmers, sailors, gardeners, and other people whose work depended on weather prediction. But perhaps more important in his particular case, the almanac became an important piece of a man's life (and of North American culture) in dealing with issues related to racial discrimination.

On August 19, 1791, Benjamin Banneker brazenly sent a prepublication copy of his first almanac to then secretary of state Thomas Jefferson. This submission was accompanied by a letter in which he questioned Jefferson's (a slaveholder) sincerity as a "friend to liberty" and urged Jefferson to help get rid of "absurd and false ideas" that one race is superior to another. He wished Jefferson's sentiments to be the same as his—that "one Universal Father . . . afforded us all the same sensations and endowed us all with the same faculties." He offered his almanac as clear evidence. Jefferson responded with praise for Banneker's work.

Almanacs are statistical archives that communicate general information based on statistical analyses of data. Almanac authors collect data, organize data, and make inferences (a generalization) about data. Many kinds of data have been recorded and preserved in almanacs throughout time on all inhabited continents. Almanacs can be political in nature, religious, medicine-oriented, or historical, as well as astronomical. Almanacs reflect the targeted culture and are usually designed to give good guidance. In early Rome, almanacs were literally pounded into stone with chisels. From 1733 through 1752, Benjamin Franklin published *Poor Richard's Almanac,* an almanac dedicated to historical information. The kind of almanac Benjamin Banneker wrote was designed to provide calculations about the earth's rhythms and the universe's celestial events. The amateur astronomers whose occupations required weather-related information welcomed Banneker's expertise.

Clearly, Banneker collected enough data to comfortably and accurately make predictions about weather. He published those predictions with confidence, and he achieved acclaim, even in the eyes of a future U.S. president. Banneker successfully forecast a 1789 solar eclipse, and his estimate was the best in the country at the time. Banneker understood statistics and data well and used them to make inferences. Note that Banneker's dedication resulted in six almanacs.

As an example of the mathematics similar to Banneker's work, we encourage you to complete Activity 15.2.

Analyzing Dice Games

Games play an importance in solidifying group identity in most societal groups, whether playing cards by the fireplace on a cold winter night or U.S. Civil War troops playing baseball to maintain morale between battles. Group identity unites group members of a culture (Cheska, 1979), and as such, games themselves become an important part of a culture.

Women of the Native North American Cheyenne people often gathered to play a game (Mon Shi Mo Ut) that used five disks, a basket, and eight small sticks (eight for each player) that served as currency for the game. The game provided an opportunity for a social gathering, during which small bets were placed along with "constant chatter and joking" (Bell, 1969, p. 79). The game required an even number of women. The women formed two teams. However, each woman on one team would also have a small side bet with one woman on the other team. When they seated themselves to play the game, they sat directly across from the woman (on the opposing team) with whom their side bet was placed. So there was a team outcome and an individual outcome as well.

The contest required some equipment. Each woman started with eight sticks. The sticks served as currency for the game. The game also required five specially crafted disks and a basket. Usually the disks were made of stone or bone and were painstakingly painted or burned as shown in Figure 15.1 (Bell, 1969). The coiled basket was usually woven from

A TWO-WEEK ALMANAC

Collect daily temperature data from your region (state, city, neighborhood, etc.) over the next two weeks.

Day														
Temperature														

Organize the data in some meaningful way:

Represent the data in some meaningful way:

What predications can you make? Use probabilities if possible.

1. Year-round temperatures?

2. Monthly temperatures?

3. Temperatures six months from now?

4. Seasonal temperatures?

5. Temperatures for the fifteenth day?

coarse grass. The disks were placed into the small basket, which was handed to the first player, and play commenced. The first player lifted the basket and brought it down on the ground with a smack. The little disks were expected to jump into the air and land back into the basket in some sort of arrangement. If a disk flew out of the basket, the toss was considered spoiled, and the player lost her turn. In this case, the disk was replaced into the basket, and the basket was passed to the next player on her team.

The three disks on the left are referred to as *maidens,* and the two on the right are *bears.* Different combinations of throws resulted in acquisition or loss of a certain amount of currency (sticks) and are listed in Activity 15.3 (p. 302). After the first player finished her turn, she handed the basket of stones to the teammate who was seated on her right. The basket was passed similarly down the line until the entire team was finished. Then, finally, the basket was passed directly across to the woman on the opposing team. The first woman

Figure 15.1

The 5 disks for Mon Shi Mo Ut

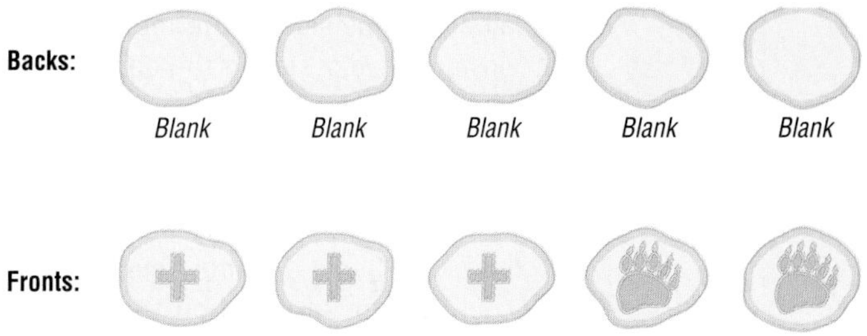

Backs:

Blank   Blank   Blank   Blank   Blank

Fronts:

Activity 15.3

PLAY THE CHEYENNE WOMEN'S DICE GAME

In two teams of 3 or 4, play the game to get a feel for the data. Keep track of the way the disks land. Then determine the experimental and theoretical probabilities for each outcome.

Rules for the contest

Players separate into two equal-sized teams. Every player begins with 8 sticks. The game's 5 disks are placed into a basket and play begins.

The first player on one team tosses the disks. Awards and penalties for various tosses are shown below. Awards and penalties are given to or received from the opposing player seated across from the player who tossed the disks.

Toss	Award (and gets another turn)
5 blanks	Receive 1 stick for each player on the team
3 blanks and 2 bears	Receive 1 stick
1 blank, 2 bears, and 2 maidens	Receive 1 stick
2 blanks and 3 maidens	Receive 3 sticks
2 bears and 3 maidens	Receive 8 sticks and the game is over

Toss	Penalty (still gets another turn)
2 blanks, 2 bears, and 1 maiden	Lose 1 stick from each player on the team
4 blanks and 1 bear	Lose 1 stick

ANYTHING ELSE	Player's turn ends for that round.

When the first player's turn is over, pass the basket to the next teammate. After every player on one team has played, then the basket is passed to the opposing team. Play continues until one team possesses all the sticks and is thus declared the winner.

Calculate the experimental probabilities for each of your outcomes noted above.

Now create a theoretical table. List all possible outcomes with the disks and determine the theoretical likelihood of each outcome.

tossed the stones, received her stick currency, and on finishing her turn, passed the basket to the teammate who was seated on her right. In that way, the basket made its way all along one side before returning back to the beginning by traveling all along the opposing players' side in the opposite direction. Play continued in this way until one team had no sticks left. The women won or lost as a team. But on conclusion of the game, the agreed-upon side bets were settled individually between the two women who had placed the wager.

After you play the game in Activity 15.3, think about how you could use the probabilities to build a spinner model (simulation) of the Cheyenne women's game. A spinner could be set up based on the theoretical probabilities so that with one spin, the score (number of sticks) could be known. Of course, you should uphold the probabilities of the game in your spinner model. Just as you experienced this approach to an unfamiliar problem, so too can your students gather data, just as you did, to help them build a good model for any situation.

Now listen to Katie describe her use of a distance-time graph.

Great-grandmother's Long Walk

A century ago, my great-grandmother, Jolanta, and her family lived just inside Poland on the Polish/German border. The community was tightly knit and somewhat self-sufficient. That is, most shops and grocers were within the town. Jolanta's father owned the blacksmith shop, where he made all sorts of iron tools for his customers. All that began to change, though, in 1933, when Adolf Hitler and the Nazis took power of Germany. After that, life would never be the same for my great-grandmother's village. Over the next few years, the countryside and especially the town became a scary place for anyone to live. Concentration camps sprang up in the country, and buildings in the village were used as targets in Hitler's artillery ranges. As more and more people left Poland, Hitler fully developed those artillery ranges and concentration camps, which eventually became death camps.

Full war in Poland came to pass in late 1939. Luckily, in 1938, my great-grandmother's family moved to Berlin, away from the unprotected country areas of Poland, even though this meant leaving the village where they had lived for generations. They knew that transformation from small-town workers to big-city workers would prove a difficult adjustment. But they packed up their belongings and began the long trek to Berlin anyhow. They walked the entire distance, stopping along the side of the road only for short rests from time to time and to camp for the night. The path they walked from the northern Polish border to Berlin is 96 miles long. Within days, my great-great-grandfather sent Jolanta to America to live with a German family. She arrived in New York City on her twenty-third birthday.

I gained a new appreciation for distance (and measurement) by thinking about miles through my great-grandmother's eyes. I wondered what it felt like to walk 96 miles in constant fear. I wondered how long it took them to walk that far. It started to dawn on me that 96 miles would be a long walk! When I go on my daily walk, I set a pace of four miles per hour. At that pace, it would take me 24 hours to walk 96 miles. But if I were carrying my most precious belongings with me, I know I would walk more slowly. My great-grandmother's family made the journey in five days. They walked almost 20 miles each day for 10 hours each day. That distance is nearly a marathon. Walking 20 miles each day scared, cold, and tired would surely seem like a very long distance taking a very long time.

Katie decided to organize the numerical information in a time-distance line graph shown in Figure 15.2 to visually compare Jolanta's walk, a typical marathon, and her power walk. An average marathon runner, makes the 26-mile race in around four to five hours, which is 17 hours for the 96-mile walk. Of course, neither Katie (on her power walk) nor

Figure 1 5 . 2

Katie's Great-grandmother's Distance-Time Graph

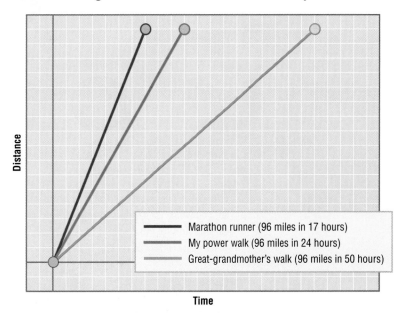

Distance / Time

— Marathon runner (96 miles in 17 hours)
— My power walk (96 miles in 24 hours)
— Great-grandmother's walk (96 miles in 50 hours)

L I T E R A T U R E   C O N N E C T I O N S

Using Stories about Chance and Organized Counting

The characters in the story *Cloudy with a Chance of Meatballs* (Barrett, 1978) received daily weather that corresponded with their need for three meals per day. After reading the story, think about the likelihood of meatballs falling from the sky (owing to weather patterns formed in the atmosphere) on our world. Of course, you realize that the likelihood is impossible. But for the characters in the story, meatballs were as likely as spaghetti! Reading this kind of story is a good way to develop the concepts of likelihood (possible, impossible, and certain.) Complete Activity 15.4. As you work through the activity, think about writing an almanac to help the good people of Chewandswallow predict their next meal. What sorts of data would you gather, and how would you try to display and communicate those data?

Activity 15.4

THE WEATHER IN CHEWANDSWALLOW

The following weather predictions were made in Chewandswallow.

Monday	Meatballs: 30%	Tuesday	Bread rolls: 75%
Wednesday	Pancakes: 45%	Thursday	Chocolate cake: 5%
Friday	Pepperoni pizza: 80%	Saturday	Breadsticks: 95%

Decide what the weather forecaster means when reporting a chance of a particular type of weather. Draw spinners that could be used to simulate the weather for each of these six days.

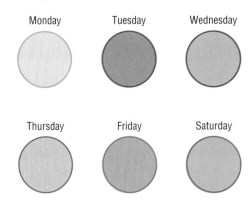

Select one day: _____

Simulate the weather for a season of the day you selected by spinning that day of the week 13 times (to mimic a season). State the results of your season-long simulation in the form of a sentence using the word *probability* and either the word *experimental* or the word *theoretical*.

The story *One Grain of Rice* (Demi, 1997) is an ancient folktale about a clever young peasant girl, Rani, who uses mathematics to trick the raja into being fair to his people. She receives favor with the raja because during a time of great famine, she ingeniously saved several grains of rice from spoiling. The raja had been saving the rice for himself, rather than using it to feed the starving people of his land. For payment, Rani asked to receive a grain of rice (on the first day) and then an amount of rice doubled (from the previous day) for each day after that for a month. Look at Activity 15.5 for a description of the mathematics. Like the raja, calculate the amount of rice leaving his stores each day. You should, like the raja, develop a growing awareness of the magnitude of Rani's request.

Activity 15.5

ONE GRAIN OF RICE CALENDAR

Complete the calculations for the grains of rice Rani will have received at the end of the 30-day month.

1	2	3	4	5	6	7
8	9	10	11	12	13	14
15	16	17	18	19	20	21
22	23	24	25	26	27	28
29	30					

Do you notice a pattern in these numbers?

Compare your numbers on each of the first eight days to the first eight rows of Pascal's triangle (from Activity 15.1).

Do you think the raja is going to run out of rice?

Why or why not?

the marathon runner would keep pace for 50 hours. Katie's graphs show only the time spent actually walking or running, not the time spent resting.

Throughout the course of this book, you have heard several students talk about mathematical connections to their own cultures. We encourage you to find the mathematics of your culture, but also to explore mathematics in others' cultures.

USING TEACHING AIDS APPROPRIATELY:
Using Student-Generated Data

When we teach about data analysis, it is critical to use student-generated data. The data may be about students themselves, from a situation that is meaningful. But in any case, the task must require students to keep track of the information. Teaching aids can help. For instance, when gathering data about students' favorite seasons, it may be helpful to prepare square cards, one showing a sun, a snowflake, an autumn leaf, or a budding flower. Then, after students decide on their favorite season, we can give them a corresponding picture. (We recommend not asking young children to select the picture first, as many of them may decide to select the picture they like the best, independent of the season it represents.) As we learned earlier, helping children find useful ways to organize their own data is important. Easing the burden of *record keeping* can be beneficial to students as they think about ways to organize the information.

We also discuss materials that help students to gather data that are not about themselves. These data-gathering devices simulate the situation, in terms of likelihoods of events. In Chapter 6, you learned that materials, such as base-ten blocks, model the number system. A simulation is a way to model the probabilities of a situation when something is known about the likelihoods in the situation. Modeling situations gives students a chance to understand how mathematics can be made to imitate real-world phenomena. The results of the simulation then become data for further analysis. First and foremost, in selecting data-gathering devices, the device must truly mimic the likelihood of instances from the population. Second, the devices should be simple to use and familiar to the children. Most children have experiences with spinners or dice from playing board games. Finally, we bring up an issue related to classroom management. During data-gathering sessions, you might want to consider the noise level of the classroom. Sometimes it can be difficult for you to concentrate on listening to students' discourse when words are fighting for verbal space with the clanking sounds of rolling dice. For flipping coins and rolling dice, we recommend lining old shoebox lids with felt and directing students to flip or roll the materials onto the quiet felt lining.

Types of Concrete Materials

Two-Color Counters

There are numerous ways to make two-color counters. Affixing colored stickers to plastic poker chips and spray-painting lima beans are both fairly inexpensive ways to make these counters. Commercial counters are also available.

Dice

Dice are basic random-number generators. Inherent in the construction of a die (*die* is the singular of *dice*) is the notion that each face of any given polyhedron die is equally likely to land up. Depending on the number of sides (faces) on the die, we calculate the likelihood of a face arriving in the up position. The most common die is a cube, with six faces. However, interesting mathematical ideas behind probabilities can be generalized by using dice with different numbers of faces. For instance, for a 12-sided die, it is interesting to find the likelihood of an even number, prime number, or a multiple of 3.

Spinners

Like counters and dice, spinners are constructed to demonstrate likelihoods. The advantage of spinners is the ease with which we can create biased spinners. That is, spinners can be constructed so that certain regions are more likely than other regions. Remembering that probability with spinners is related to the angle through which the spinner hand must spin, we can develop a spinner to simulate likelihoods from a variety of situations. We simply translate the event in the situation to a fraction with a denominator of 360. An inexpensive spinner can be constructed with a pencil and a paper clip. Placing the pencil point inside the paper clip and then giving the paper clip a good spin causes it to travel nicely around the pencil point as illustrated in Figure 15.3. To use this type of spinner, the pencil point should be placed at the point around which the degrees are calculated.

Figure 1 5 . 3

A Home-Made Spinner

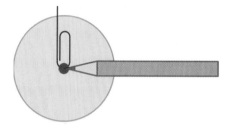

An interesting question, posed by Welchman-Tischler (1992), is whether or not the coincident vertices of the spinner's separate spaces must be placed at the exact center of the circle. Thinking about how spinner probabilities are calculated can help you to determine the answer to her challenge. (This problem is left as a homework exercise.)

Different materials may have hidden ways to calculate their probabilities. We have considered various activities throughout this chapter that demonstrate the probabilities behind the materials. It is important to keep those ideas clearly in mind in selecting materials for data analysis lessons and activities.

LET'S REVIEW

To help us understand how we learn data analysis, two frameworks have been created. For statistics, Friel, Curcio, and Bright (2001) suggest that we may progress through a series of three stages: (1) Learners learn to extract information from the data, (2) learners recognize and find relationships within the data, and (3) learners move beyond the data and make claims about the population based on their findings. It is important to recognize that learners are often swayed by the data themselves and that it takes many experiences to find relationships. For probability, Jones, Langrall, Thornton, and Mogill (1999) have developed a four-stage framework that seems to explain the learning process. Learners begin at the subjective level, at which they are easily swayed by personal experiences when making probabilistic statements. At the second level, transitional, learners begin to recognize the importance of organizing information rather than simply relying on personal experience. Third, learners are informal quantitative thinkers. They can be convinced of a probability by a numerical argument. Finally, learners work at the fourth, purely numerical, level, understanding the nuances of a numerical argument and using sophisticated procedures to determine numerical facts.

For students to fully comprehend data analysis, all frameworks agree that students should generate their own data. They should work with simulations that model real situations. Simulation apparatus include dice, spinners, two-color counters, and coins. As students gather their own data, they need to be consciously aware of any graphical representations they might choose to use, recognizing that there are differences between discrete situations and continuous situations. Finally, technology is a highly useful tool to help students make sense of data analysis tasks.

 # HOMEWORK

1. Consider Welchman-Tischler's (1992) question. How are the probabilities in the following two spinners related? Use your protractor and determine the probabilities of red, yellow, and blue in each spinner situation.

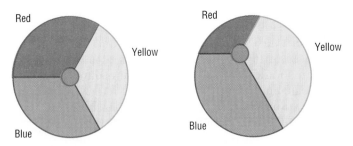

2. Create a "looks like, sounds like" table for Friel, Curcio, and Bright's ideas described in their framework for statistical thinking for the questions you answered in Activity 15.2. Then use the same information to create a "looks like, sounds like" table for Jones and colleagues' ideas described in their framework for the probability thinking.
3. Locate a primary (K–2), an intermediate (3–5), and a middle (6–8) textbook, and describe how they use spinners to discuss probability. Compare the levels of algebraic thinking required at each level.

 # SUGGESTED READINGS

Jones, G. A., Thornton, C. A., Langrall, C. W., & Tarr, J. E. (1999). Understanding students' probabilistic reasoning. In L. V. Stiff & F. R. Curcio (Eds.), *Learning mathematics for a new century: NCTM Yearbook* (pp. 146–155). Reston, VA: NCTM.

Lajoie, S. P. (1998). *Reflections on statistics: Learning, teaching and assessment in grades K–12.* Mahwah, NJ: Lawrence Erlbaum.

Lehrer, R., & Schauble, L. (2000). Inventing data structures for representational purposes: Elementary grade students' classification models. *Mathematical Thinking and Learning, 2*(1, 2), 51–74.

Lehrer, R., & Schauble, L. (2000). Developing model-based reasoning in mathematics and science. *Journal of Applied Developmental Psychology, 21*(1), 39–48.

Metz, K. E. (1998). Emergent ideas of chance and probability in primary-grade children. In S. P. Lajoie (Ed.), *Reflections on statistics: Learning, teaching, and assessment in grades K–12* (pp. 149–174). Mahwah, NJ: Lawrence Erlbaum.

Table 15.3 **Blank "Looks Like, Sounds Like" Tables**

STATISTICS

	Looks Like	Sounds Like
Reading the data		
Between the data		
Beyond the data		

PROBABILITY

	Looks Like	Sounds Like
Subjective		
Transitional		
Informal Quantitative		
Numerical		

REFERENCES

Barrett, J. (1978). *Cloudy with a chance of meatballs.* New York: Scholastic.

Bell, R. C. (1969). *Board and table games from many civilizations* (vol. II). New York: Dover.

Cheska, A. T. (1979). Native American Games as Strategies of Societal Maintenance. In E. Norbeck & C. Farrer (Eds.), *Forms of play of Native North Americans* (pp. 227–247). St Paul, MN: West.

Demi (1997). *One grain of rice.* New York: Scholastic.

Friel, S. N., Curcio, F. R., & Bright, G. W. (2001). Making sense of graphs: Critical factors influencing comprehension and instructional implications. *Journal for Research in Mathematics Education, 32*(2), 124–158.

Horvath, J. K., & Lehrer, R. (1998). A model-based perspective on the development of children's understanding of chance and uncertainty. In S. P. Lajoie (Ed.), *Reflections on statistics: Learning, teaching, and assessment in grades K–12* (pp. 121–148). Mahwah, NJ: Lawrence Erlbaum.

Jones, G. A., Langrall, C. W., Thornton, C. A., & Mogill, A. T. (1999). Students' probabilistic thinking in instruction. *Journal for Research in Mathematics Education, 30*(5), 487–519.

Konold, C. (2002). Teaching concepts rather than conventions. *New England Journal of Mathematics, 34*(2), 69–81.

Konold, C., & Higgins, T. (2003). Reasoning about data. In J. Kilpatrick, W. G. Martin, & D. E. Schifter (Eds.), *A research companion to principles and standards for school mathematics* (pp. 193–215). Reston, VA: NCTM.

Konold, C., Pollatsek, A., Well, A. D., Lohmeier, J., & Lipson, A. (1993). Inconsistencies in students' reasoning about probability. *Journal for Research in Mathematics Education, 24*(5), 392–414.

Lajoie, S. P., Jacobs, V. R., & Lavigne, N. C. (1995). Empowering children in the use of statistics. *Journal of Mathematical Behavior, 14*(4), pp. 401–425.

Lehrer, R., & Romberg, T. (1996). Exploring children's data modeling. *Cognition and Instruction, 14*(1), 69–108.

National Council of Teachers of Mathematics. (2000). *Principles and standards for school mathematics.* Reston, VA: NCTM.

Welchman-Tischler, R. (1992). *Mathematical tool box.* White Plains, NY: Cuisenaire Company of America.

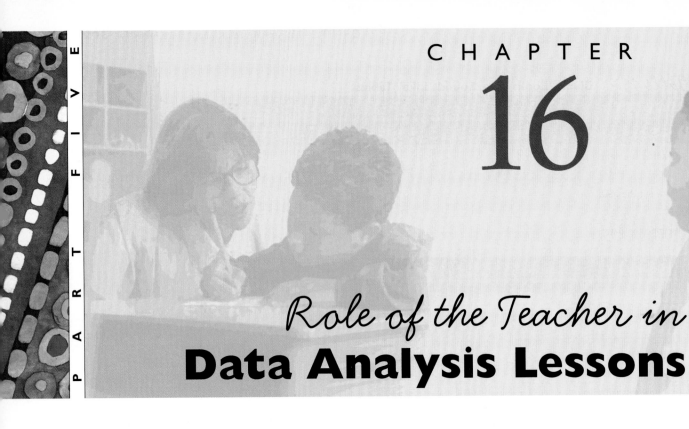

16

Role of the Teacher in Data Analysis Lessons

ANALYZING THE TEACHING MODELS:
Presentation, Problem Solving, Partnered Learning, Discussion, and Concept Attainment

For this final discussion of the teaching models, we describe a method of instruction that utilizes all five models of instruction described in Chapter 1 and explained in previous chapters. For data analysis, Lajoie, Jacobs, and Lavigne (1995) outline a comprehensive method for statistics instruction. Their work follows a sequence, though we suspect that they would not recommend that these steps be done serially or be thought of as having definite ending and starting points. The work of the teacher shifts back and forth as you have seen in all of the applications of learning theories you have studied in this book, and taken together, the steps in this method of instruction employ more than one teaching model.

Lajoie and colleagues suggest that the role of the teacher begin by providing students with an interesting situation (a component of the *discovery/inquiry/problem solving* model). In addressing the situation, the teacher models expert skills (as in the *presentation* model) and *coaches* students by providing hints about what they might do next. As students recognize trends and patterns to the coaching, they develop concept knowledge, so the coaching lays the groundwork for *concept attainment.* Then the teacher slowly fades into the background as his or her students become proficient in discussing their ways of dealing with data (*discussion* model).

Modeling, coaching, and fading are followed by articulation and reflection. The goal is to "help students gain conscious access to and control of their own problem solving process" (Lajoie et al., 1995, p. 420). Here, the teacher continues to carefully select meaningful activities. These meaningful activities generate further examples and nonexamples so students continue to develop *concept* knowledge. The selection of meaningful activities allows and encourages students to "become their own critics by learning to summarize, clarify and question themselves" (Lajoie et al., 1995, p. 420). When the data and situation are both meaningful, students are more likely to understand the data well enough to follow their own ideas about how to organize the data. The ultimate

TECHNOLOGY CONNECTIONS

The Power of the Spreadsheet

In the model of rote learning, material is treated as meaningless; it is a dissociated model. Some of our difficulties in teaching a more culturally integral mathematics have been due to an objective problem: Before we had computers, there were very few good points of contact between what is most fundamental and engaging in mathematics and anything firmly planted in everyday life. But the computer—a mathematics-speaking being in the midst of the everyday home, school, and workplace—is able to provide such links. The challenge to education is to find ways to exploit them (Papert, 1980, p. 47).

All of the "Technology Connections" sections in this book have emphasized what Papert calls points of contact between mathematics and everyday life. As a tool that allows students and teachers to explore issues of "what if" as they work with data, the spreadsheet can be a powerful point of contact for mathematics teachers and students.

The spreadsheet was one of the first software applications designed for microcomputers in the late 1970s, and contemporary spreadsheet programs have changed little from the early software. The spreadsheet was based on the simple observation that people tend to organize mathematical data in rows and columns before they manipulate the data. The spreadsheet, although powerful in its possible applications, is basically a means to organize and then manipulate data.

"What if" thinking involves testing different hypothetical situations. "What if my rent goes up $50 per month?" is a simple example of this type of exercise. "What if we doubled our inventory?" is a type of question that might be useful to small business operators. If the template for the spreadsheet is correctly designed, every item that depends on the changed value will be automatically changed.

"What if" thinking gives students this chance to play with data and build important estimation and in-

tuitive mathematics skills. The spreadsheet can create a mathematical environment in which students are free to play, guess, and experiment. It can help to develop the intuitive sense for numbers and numerical relationships that many students lack. Building this intuitive sense for numbers can also help students to develop mathematical and numerical self-confidence, an important asset in almost any field in today's world.

A simple example of a spreadsheet for "what if" thinking uses a student-constructed spreadsheet designed to record income and expenses for a student play production. Using this template, students could then play with some of their options to maximize their profits. They could begin by trying out various options with respect to the sale of food and drinks. They might contrast buying more drinks and candy and selling them for a lower profit to buying less and selling them for a higher profit. They can ask, "What if we don't sell all the candy or drinks?" Similarly, students can experiment with different ticket prices for adults and students and immediately observe the effect on profits.

Students might wish to aim for a particular profit and adjust both ticket prices and food sales in an optimum manner to project this profit. A good spreadsheet template eliminates the need for much tedious calculation. In doing this, the spreadsheet provides an environment in which students can escape from some of the details of calculation into the formation of mathematical generalizations and concepts.

From upper elementary school through college, the spreadsheet can be used as a tool to create dynamic mathematical environments for learners. The type of mathematical experimentation modeled in the simple play profit example can be replicated in situations throughout the mathematics curriculum. More ideas for using spreadsheets can be found in Spreadsheet Magic (Lewis, 2001).

goal here is for students to *articulate* the information they have studied. For the students to articulate the information, they should be familiar with one another's work. Sometimes a large data set is necessary. Hence, *partnered learning* is appropriate. The teacher's role is to supply clearly appropriate vocabulary for the discussion and discourse. The impact of the students' discussion is enhanced by implementing components of the *discussion* model of teaching. For instance, appropriate use of the terms *mean, median,* and *mode* could be articulated. To encourage students to reflect, they should be asked to compare their work to other students' data analyses as well as to the teachers' samples of analyses.

After experiences with this sort of classroom activity, students are able to engage in *exploration*. Here, students are autonomous in their data analysis efforts, able to carry out the learning processes in a variety of situations.

HIGHLIGHTS OF A LESSON PLAN COMPONENT:
Matching Materials to Objective

Matching the materials to the mathematics objective is critical in the data analysis section because you need to think about whether students are studying statistics or probability. Do you want students to do statistical analyses of data or calculate some of the data's probabilities? Look at your objective, and refer back to the information on teaching aids to select materials that most carefully mimic the situation under investigation.

Creating the Situation

When preparing either kind of data analysis lesson, first plan a situation (that matches the objective) for investigation by the students. Analyzing data from this situation should lead students to a better understanding of the mathematics behind the situation. So the materials selected must simulate the situation in question in such a way that the materials mimic the intended mathematics of your objective. A simulation provides a classroom activity that enables students to gather experimental data that somehow match how the data would naturally occur in the situation. For example, for an objective related to unequal likelihoods, you might think about asking students to flip a pair of two-color counters or spin an unequally distributed spinner. The materials must reflect the actual mathematics within the objective. Recall that in the activity of flipping two coins the probability of red and yellow is found to be twice as likely as the probability of red and red and twice as likely as the probability of yellow and yellow. (The probability of red and red is equal to the probability of yellow and yellow.) So these materials appear to demonstrate unequal likelihoods. For an objective related to predicting weather patterns, you might well choose to create a spinner that matches actual data collected. Complete Activity 16.1.

Selecting Supportive Materials

Selecting materials that appropriately match data analysis lesson objectives also includes deciding about the appropriate use of technology. Technology can be a powerful aid to the students in record keeping, freeing them to do serious thinking. The graphing calculator or spreadsheet can store a list of numbers and quickly sort them in order, for example. Such technological aids can also execute calcu-

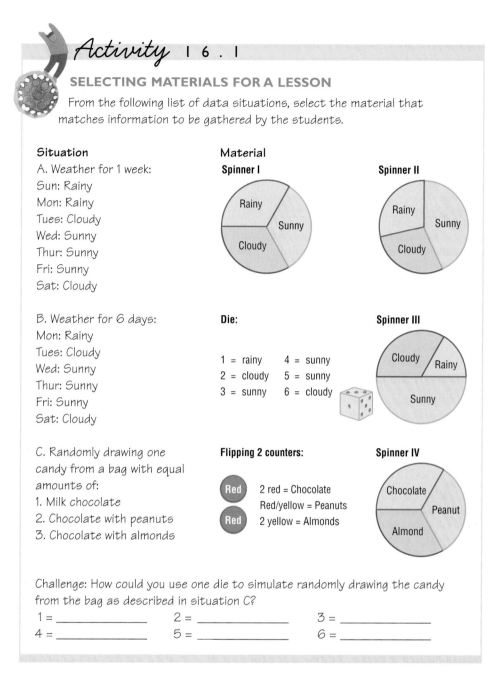

Activity 1 6 . 1

SELECTING MATERIALS FOR A LESSON

From the following list of data situations, select the material that matches information to be gathered by the students.

Situation

A. Weather for 1 week:
Sun: Rainy
Mon: Rainy
Tues: Cloudy
Wed: Sunny
Thur: Sunny
Fri: Sunny
Sat: Cloudy

Material

Spinner I

Spinner II

B. Weather for 6 days:
Mon: Rainy
Tues: Cloudy
Wed: Sunny
Thur: Sunny
Fri: Sunny
Sat: Cloudy

Die:

1 = rainy   4 = sunny
2 = cloudy   5 = sunny
3 = sunny   6 = cloudy

Spinner III

C. Randomly drawing one candy from a bag with equal amounts of:
1. Milk chocolate
2. Chocolate with peanuts
3. Chocolate with almonds

Flipping 2 counters:

2 red = Chocolate
Red/yellow = Peanuts
2 yellow = Almonds

Spinner IV

Challenge: How could you use one die to simulate randomly drawing the candy from the bag as described in situation C?

1 = _____   2 = _____   3 = _____
4 = _____   5 = _____   6 = _____

lations (e.g., mean) quickly. When choosing whether or not to utilize technology, it is a simple task of checking your objective. Is your objective for students to practice calculating means or practice building graphs? Perhaps this situation calls for traditional pencil-and-paper calculation. But if your objective calls for students to interpret a mean, find several different kinds of averages and select the best average, or compare a variety of graphical representations of data, then the calculator (or other technology) is appropriate.

Guiding the Data Analysis

Efficent data analysis can be facilitated by a strong bit of number sense if the data are numerical. Students must be able to study numerical information and look for trends, relationships, or patterns. The ability to complete these tasks mentally requires facility with number relationships and hence number sense. Konold (2002) found that students were much more able to thoughtfully study data when they used technology that helped them to organize and reorganize information first. We caution teachers to make reasonable use of technology to provide students with the opportunity to engage their mental number sense and reasoning.

ASSESSMENT:
To Guide Instructional Decisions

During the course of *coaching* and subsequent *articulation* and *reflection*, instructional decisions will likely be based on minute-by-minute assessments as well as on some final demonstration by the student. As you carefully select meaningful activities, you are making instructional decisions based on your assessment of the situation. Listening to students articulate and reflect on their reasoning will enable you to understand whether students are reading the data (first level of statistics knowledge) or subjectively reasoning (first level of probability knowledge) about their situation. As you listen, you will more ably decide on a next course of action. As you read the next section, think about the instructional decisions you would make to support students' thinking.

SUGGESTIONS FOR ESTABLISHING DISCOURSE:
Using Student Comments to Analyze Teaching

Friel, Curcio, and Bright (2001) suggest the importance of giving students a graph and asking about perceptions of it. First, ask them specific targeted questions about the graph. Then ask them to *judge* the graph. In reading the graph for judgment purposes, they look at the graph and sort of search for some general sense they can make regarding the graph. This gives insight into their thinking about the information. When they are able to interpret the graph within the contextual setting they should be able to make a generalization about the situation.

As students make claims about the graph, whether single-data-point answers, judgments, or interpretations, teachers gain helpful information to analyze how to move forward. Are students basing their claims on subjective feelings and knowledge? Are they making a somewhat counterintuitive claim while using the information? We cannot overemphasize the importance of listening to the students' reasoning as a way to analyze your teaching. Look at the graph shown in Figure 16.1, and think of a story that could be represented by this graph before you listen to our fifth graders make sense of the graph.

> *Min:* I think it's the stock market. I labeled the left point 9 A.M. and the right point 4 P.M. I labeled the vertical "number of trades." It seems like there would be times during the day when the trading leveled off.

> *Lydia:* I think it's the number of kids who go to the mall on a summer day. At 8 A.M., there is no one at the mall, and then around noon, there are

Figure 16.1

Write a Story That Could Be Shown with This Graph

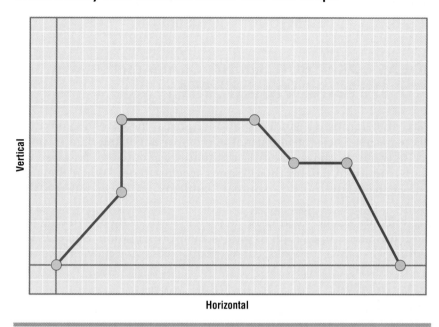

lots of people. Then, by night time, no one is there. I labeled the horizontal 8 A.M. to 10 P.M. and the vertical "number of kids."

Ryan: I think it's the number of kids running in the halls. I put the time along the horizontal of my graph so recess (10:50) matches the highest point. I know I always run a little bit when I'm going to recess.

Jamal: I labeled the horizontal with six pizza stores. Then, I figured the dot represented how many slices of pizza they sold each day.

We asked Ryan to tell us the label on his vertical axis. He said, "That's the number of kids running." So we asked, "What time of day is no one running?" He thought for a moment, "Before school and after school." Then he looked at the graph, "I guess this says someone is always running in the halls." He laughed and continued. "Oh I see now, I thought the level parts [of the graph] meant no one was running." As we listen to students explain their reasoning, we can grow in our abilities to make sense of their answers. Time-distance graphs can illuminate students' interpretations of graphical representations. Sometimes the picture made by the graph conjures up a direct image of an event, such as Ryan's leveling-off ideas, but the reality of the graph's construction requires a reanalysis of the picture. Here, Ryan was able to recognize his erroneous explanation of the graph.

We know how helpful it can be for students to hear their classmates explain their thinking when we want to make a point. Before discussing Jamal's answer, we first asked Lydia to point to a spot "in between" two points and to explain what that point meant. She said, "That looks like it's about 2:40, and I think some kids would leave to go to the 3:00 movie." We asked Jamal the same question. He selected a point, paused, and said, "It doesn't really mean anything." We waited patiently. He then said, "I think this should have been a bar graph." We remind you that we do not bring out Ryan or Jamal's original incorrect analyses and interpretation of the graph for you to judge them. Our only intention is to hear their thinking and describe how we handled the situation.

NcTm
EQUITY

IDEAS FOR STRUCTURING CLASS TIME:
To Defend Viewpoints

Part of listening to students also requires them to defend their viewpoints to peers. The ever-important activity of analyzing data to make some sort of general claim about the situation should be followed up with an opportunity to defend those claims to classmates. When their defenses will be heard by outside sources, students are even more highly motivated.

During students' studies of graphs, they should gather their own data and report that information in a graph as part of their presentation. Students like to discuss things like favorite books, candy, pizza, colors, and movies. They en-

CLASSROOM CONNECTIONS

Using Sports to Create Interest

In our community, students are great fans of basketball. They follow our university's men's and women's teams closely. So we use basketball-related tasks to reinforce some ideas from statistics and probability. You might think that some students would experience difficulties with sports-related tasks if they don't know enough about basketball. But in my experience, students become excited about the tasks, and they quickly want to learn. And, of course, we take the time to make certain that they know basketball facts and information. (I also make sure that my students understand abbreviations for categories listed in statistics: *FG/FGA* being "field goals made/field goals attempted," etc.)

Quite often, I bring in basketball statistics from the newspaper, enlarge them, and create a transparency. I show the transparency to the students and ask them to look at our team's statistics. I ask many questions, such as the following:

"Who had a good night shooting?" Of course, this can be reported in terms of points or in terms of shooting percentage. My students have learned to make a fraction of FG/GFA. They have learned how to turn that fraction into a percentage. By the end of the season, they are pretty good at estimating percentages. (They are free to use a calculator for this activity.)

"Who should have sat on the bench?"

"Why do you think Willey kept shooting if he was only a 23% shooter last night? Why did the coach keep him in so long?"

"Who needs to spend more time practicing free throws?"

"Why did Smith spend so many minutes playing? Gosh, she doesn't take very many shots."

I have made the following assignment: *"You are the coach of the next team we will play. Look at these statistics, and make a game plan. Who do you need to guard? Why?"* (And so on.) I encourage you to try the same thing because I have found that using interesting contexts such as sports helps to reinforce our study of data analysis and revisits fractions, decimals, and percents in a meaningful way. I like how the problem is open but still manages to address students' abilities to analyze data. Whenever I develop my own questions, I try to keep them open. If I ask a question that is too pointed, then I have done all the mathematics for the students. It is important for me to ask questions that challenge my students and that "support students without taking over the process of thinking for them and thus eliminating the challenge" (NCTM, 2000, p. 19).

NcTm
TEACHING

MIDDLE SCHOOL CONNECTIONS

Wise Consumers of Statistical Knowledge

NCTM CURRICULUM

You should not underestimate the amount of money adolescents spend or ask their parents or guardians to spend. Businesses surely do not. This characteristic of adolescence can also be a rich ground for situating statistical explorations. Does one kind of juice drink really taste better than another? Do students really come running home for a certain kind of meal? How much music does the average student possess? Do some kinds of batteries really last longer in a portable music player? Why does the newest animated movie have songs with short rhyming phrases? Why does the newest teen angst movie have a 13-year-old in the lead role? Can a 12-year-old really stop invasion by a foreign power?

Setting up situations that are interesting to middle school students and requiring them to gather data to better understand the situation can lead them to recognize slants or spins in product advertisements. It is important that students become not only sophisticated data analysts, looking beyond gathered data and being able to reason about probability numerically, but also wise consumers of someone else's data analysis claims. "The curriculum should emphasize the mathematics processes and skills that support the quantitative literacy of students" (NCTM, 2000, p. 16). Students in the middle grades are emotionally charged, and using interesting, relevant, data-driven tasks can be quite engaging for these adolescents.

joy comparing birthday months, types of pets at home, lucky numbers, or numbers of students in the classroom. Before they write survey questions, it is important to discuss appropriate techniques for writing proper questions. Sometimes it is a good idea to approve their questions; other times, it is worth the time to let them understand the importance of good question writing. In any event, allowing 10 minutes or so for students to collect data (ask classmates questions) and organize the data is well worth the time. Once they have organized the data, they can create an appropriate graph. Finally, students should present the information to their classmates and defend their organization as well as their selected form of graph. (They often take pride in making the graphs visually appealing. But sometimes visually appealing graphs end up showing misleading representations.)

Writing appropriate questions is not as simple as it sounds. Open-ended questions may result in answers that students have great difficulty organizing because of the diverse nature of the answers. Imagine organizing the answers to "Who is your favorite person?" Multiple-choice questions force the respondent into a category. "Of the following, which person is your favorite?" The dilemma of not liking anyone on the list can be resolved by having a "none of the above" option. However, that means that everyone in the "none of the above" category is somehow the same, which might or might not be appropriate. Questions that elicit numerical answers need to be carefully organized and analyzed. Recall that some numbers should not be halved, as might happen in the calculation of mean.

After they have put their data into graph form and presented the information to the class, you might think students are ready to submit their graphs for further assessment. But we like to ask students to report the information using at least one other type of graph. For instance, one student might report favorite types of soft drink on a bar graph and also on a pie graph. This tells us whether students purposely selected a style of graph that matched the information they wanted to convey.

Advice for Professional Development

A school district usually has some sort of support agency for teachers, one of whom should be able to find technology for use in the classroom. When used appropriately (that is, to *support* learning, not *in place of* learning), technology can make a strong impact in the classroom. Technology can enhance data analysis instruction because it can offer students the opportunity to make sense of the information rather than to spend their energy crunching numbers. Of course, we expect students to be able to crunch the numbers; however, we also recognize there are times, such as during concept development, when number crunching can and should take a back seat to concept development. Your local support agency should have a comprehensive list of available computer programs and web sites. We strongly encourage you to utilize this agency, since the effort involved in finding high-quality web sites can impose a time drain on your own instructional planning time.

ALGEBRA CONNECTIONS

Data Analysis

NCTM CURRICULUM

A Big Idea: Using Models to Represent Quantitative Relationships

One big algebra idea is that data-driven models can represent relationships in the real world and that those models can be analyzed to make some decisions about real-world phenomena (NCTM, 2000). When the models grow from analysis of their own data, students often make sensible decisions about the situation. Real-world data are often messy, and it is with algebraic thinking that students develop the skills necessary to make sense of such data. Finding a strategy to determine an experimental probability is an example of building a model that helps students to represent relationships found in real-world situations. We encourage you to watch for opportunities to nurture students' efforts to build models as a way to quantify their environments. In so doing, you are developing their algebraic thinking.

Algebraic Ideas for You to Explore: Linear Regression

To complete this section, we first ask you to complete Activity 16.2. This activity results in making data-driven predictions.

Looking at data, were you able to describe any general characteristics of the number of syllables in people's names? If you could, then you analyzed the data to describe the existing situation with some sort of *statistical* statement. Would you feel comfortable making an inference about the number of syllables in people's names for your entire school, town, state, or country on the basis of these data? What if you met two people: Dr. Maconnehay and Dr. Bly. What might you predict about the length of their first names on the basis of your general statements? Which person is more likely to have named their child Victoria? Making a prediction based on data you gather and analyze involves an *experimental probability*.

Making a prediction based on pure mathematical calculations involves knowing *theoretical probabilities* of individual events within the situation. Because our situation is based solely on data collected from a sample, we do not know any theoretical probabilities. However, we can move *beyond the data* rather than looking for relationships *within the data*. Create a scatterplot of your data. When you checked for a trend in the

<u>A L G E B R A   C O N N E C T I O N S</u> *(continued)*

Activity 1 6 . 2

CHECKING THE SYLLABLE COUNT ON CHOSEN NAMES

We have selected 15 names from literature.	Write your name and the names of 14 other people you know. (Use birth names, not married names.)
Peter Pan	
Jo March	
Luke Skywalker	
Joe Hardy	
Harry Potter	
Laura Ingalls	
Nancy Drew	
Sam Gribley	
Oliver Twist	
Willie Wonka	
Amber Brown	
Amelia Bedelia	
Salamanca Tree Hiddle	
Cinderella	
Captain Hook	

Count the syllables in first and last names.

Record the information as ordered pairs (last name, first name) for all 30 people.

Plot the data on the grid below.

1. Do you see a general trend in the data?
2. What general statement(s) could you make about how names are selected by authors or parents?

• Write an algebraic statement that describes the sum of the number of syllables in first name and syllables in last name?

• Rewrite that statement as a $y = mx + b$ form linear equation.

(continued)

MIDDLE SCHOOL CONNECTIONS

Algebra as Social Justice

NCTM
EQUITY

Moses and Cobb (2001) claim that because so many life opportunities hinge on algebraic thinking, algebra must be considered a civil right for all people. Algebra seems to be a particularly important key to mathematics literacy and therefore economic success. Social justice provides the same opportunity for everyone, not just a select few. Moses and Cobb remind us that our goal is for *all* students to be ready for the college math prep sequence by the end of middle school. But they also ask, "How do we empassion students with a desire to learn mathematics in ways similar to those blazing civil rights speeches and gatherings of the previous century?" (p. 5).

First, we have to believe that all students can learn algebra.

In the middle school years, teachers can mesh data analysis and algebra in ways that make both areas of the curriculum exciting and engaging for all students. Analysis of data and patterns should use statistical and probabilistic thinking, as opposed to the more subjective thinking of younger students. Students should begin to incorporate more symbols and use more abstract reasoning. As students gain a collection of experiences, building on previous knowledge, they will be better able to fluidly work with linear expressions representing certain situations.

Second, it is vital to remember that as teachers, we cannot learn the information for our students. We already know the mathematics.

"High expectations are necessary, but they are not sufficient" (NCTM, 2000, p. 13). In addition to high expectations, we must provide access to a range of worthwhile mathematical opportunities for all students. They need to think about relationships among data with a variety of representations, pictorial *and* symbolic. They need to connect data analyses representations to algebraic reasoning, such as slope, coordinate graphs, and continuous versus discrete. When students make connections, they are more likely to enter high school ready for a college prep program. For equal opportunity to become a reality, algebraic literacy must be achieved *by the student*.

Third, we cannot teach as though we have a secret that the diligent student (those select few) will discover.

We cannot assume that mental connections will be automatic for all students at the same moment in time following a specific activity. Moreover, we have to recognize the mathematical thinking we *do* see, even if it does not look like mathematics to us. Remember, though we already know the mathematics, we do not have the luxury of a singular understanding of mathematics. We have to know and communicate freely a multitude of mathematics ideas to entice *all* students to connect knowledge in ways that prepare them to reach for opportunity when it appears.

For example, students have elementary school experiences with coordinate graphing, and as middle school students, they *can* learn to fit lines to data plotted on an *x-y* grid. But they might think of the *x-y* grid as the collection of streets downtown, a collection of county roads, or even a chess board. We have to recognize these contexts and draw the mathematics from them, encouraging students to analyze patterns and data using algebraic thinking, independent of the context of their *x-y* grid. Coherent connected understandings allow algebra to take the lead toward the lofty goal of social justice.

ALGEBRA CONNECTIONS *(continued)*

information earlier, did you notice any sort of generalization? First, look at the information and eyeball the data to see whether you can come up with an equation for finding the sum of the syllables in a typical first and last name. Eyeballing the data is a good starting point for describing general trends in information. What was the average sum for your data? (Names come from cultures. So the cultural makeup of your class will probably affect this sum.) You might even talk to your parents and ask them why they selected the name for you that they did. You might find that they spent some time saying potential names over and over again in order to find a name that had a nice ring to it.

With the technology that is available today, there are other powerful ways to develop an equation for information like this. Use available technology to complete Activity 16.3. The regression equation will give a way to predict the height of a person if you know that person's arm span.

Activity 16.3

RUNNING A REGRESSION TO FIND A LINE OF FIT

Question: Is there a relationship between the length of your arm span and your height?

Gather these two pieces of data from at least 10 people you know.

Enter the data into either your graphing calculator or spreadsheet. Be sure to include any duplicate sets of ordered pairs as many times as they occur in your data. Then use the technology to run a linear regression (line of best fit) on the information.

Before you enter the data, decide **which variable should be the independent variable and which should be the dependent variable?** That is, what is a given and what would be a consequence? Why?

- After you run the regression, you should be able to write an equation as $y = ax + b$, using the values found by your calculator.

What does this equation mean?

Algebra in Unusual Places

Driscoll (1999) suggests finding algebraic relationships in unusual places. You should recognize that studying the number of syllables in a pair of names is not a typical place in which one might think to look for an algebraic relationship. However, with a little ingenuity, we are able to develop an algebra-based question that is relevant to us. And we used ideas from data analysis to move beyond the data. We used real data, relevant to students, to pose the problem. When we find algebraic relationships in unusual situations, we have to be certain that the formula makes sense for the data the relationships describe.

K–8 Algebra Connections: One Grain of Rice

Sometimes algebraic relationships in unusual situations are not linear. At first, this can appear to limit the level of abstraction students are able to develop. We turn our attention now to two earlier activities (Activities 15.1 and 15.5). You calculated the values of Pascal's triangle. One of the ideas in the triangle is that the sum of values in each row of the triangle can be found by raising 2 to the power of that row. After reading *One Grain of Rice* (Demi, 1997), think about how this story offers an unusual place for algebra and also about how this story is related to the information in Pascal's triangle. Children are often interested in the pattern 1, 2, 4, 8, 16, ... However, this pattern as an algebraic expression is seemingly elaborate, requiring abstract exponent notation, 2^n. Yet even young children can work with this kind of problem because it builds on their knowledge of doubles, which, as you will recall from Chapters 6 and 7, is an important component of number knowledge. It also allows children to work with large numbers in a meaningful situation.

(continued)

ALGEBRA CONNECTIONS *(continued)*

But the algebraic expression for the information is complicated, and the graphical representation of the information flies off of the graph paper fairly quickly. However, you should not be daunted by the knowledge you have of algebraic representations when the problem itself is still accessible to younger children, even if at a slightly less symbolic level.

LET'S REVIEW

The role of the teacher in providing meaningful and productive data analysis tasks is to coordinate the learning experience through problem solving. The learning experience must begin with an interesting question. A rich situation allows for discussion that prompts articulation, reflection, and summarization from the students. Partnered learning is particularly useful in the data analysis lesson, particularly owing to the need to gather data and conduct simulations.

HOMEWORK

1. Find a textbook that encourages the use of technology in students' early experiences with data analysis ideas. Determine the appropriateness of the technology usage.
2. One of your students earned the following scores on the chapter homework: $\frac{3}{4}$, $\frac{4}{8}$, $\frac{10}{12}$, and $\frac{5}{6}$. Then, the student earned $\frac{23}{25}$ on the chapter exam. Assume that you work with a grading scale of 90–100 = A, 80–89 = B, and so on. What grade would you give this student? Compare your answer to other students' answers. You should find that some of you gave a B and others gave a C. Determine how that happened and which approach is the mathematically sound approach to calculating a student's grade.

SUGGESTED READINGS

Konold, C. (1991). Understanding students' beliefs about probability. In E. von Glasersfeld (Ed.), *Radical constructivism in mathematics education* (pp. 139–156). Amsterdam: Kluwer.

Lajoie, S. P. (1998). *Reflections on statistics: Learning, teaching and assessment in grades K–12.* Mahwah, NJ: Lawrence Erlbaum.

McClain, K., Cobb, P., & Gravemeijer, K. (2000). Supporting students' ways of reasoning about data. In L. V. Stiff & F. R. Curcio (Eds.), *Learning mathematics for a new century: NCTM Yearbook* (pp. 93–106). Reston, VA: NCTM.

REFERENCES

Demi. (1997). *One grain of rice.* New York: Scholastic.

Driscoll, M. (1999). *Fostering algebraic thinking: A guide for teachers grades 6–10.* Portsmouth, NH: Heinemann.

Friel, S. N., Curcio, F. R., & Bright, G. W. (2001). Making sense of graphs: Critical factors influencing comprehension and instructional implications. *Journal for Research in Mathematics Education, 32*(2), 124–158.

Konold, C. (2002). Teaching concepts rather than conventions. *New England Journal of Mathematics, 34*(2), 69–81.

Lajoie, S. P., Jacobs, V. R., & Lavigne, N. C. (1995). Empowering children in the use of statistics. *Journal of Mathematical Behavior, 14*(4), 401–425.

Lewis, P. (2001). *Spreadsheet magic: Forty lessons using spreadsheet to teach curriculum in K–8 classrooms.* Eugene, OR: ISTE.

Moses, R., & Cobb, R. (2001). *Radical equations.* Boston: Beacon Press.

National Council of Teachers of Mathematics. (2000). *Principles and standards for school mathematics.* Reston, VA: NCTM.

Papert, S. (1980). *Mindstorms: Children, computers and powerful ideas.* New York: Basic Books.

Throughout all five parts of this book, we endeavored to provide a summary of important pieces of each chapter. The summary for the data analysis part is once again an invitation to write a lesson. In the activity at the end of this chapter, you will work with a first grade curriculum goal: *The student will be able to ask a good question about the whole class, gather information, and correctly construct a meaningful graph to represent the entire class.*

Closing Activity: Summary Lesson

WRITE A DATA ANALYSIS LESSON

This activity is an opportunity for you to put together all the information from Part V of the book. You are a first grade teacher who must create a combination model lesson (using problem solving, presentation, concept-attainment, and discussion) that will support the following data analysis curriculum goal:

> The student will be able to ask a good question about the whole class, gather information, and correctly construct a meaningful graph to represent the entire class.

Remember that curriculum goals may take several weeks to achieve. Your task for this activity is to create a single lesson that would fall sometime during those weeks. Your lesson should be planned to last approximately one day. But you should keep the more general curriculum goal in the back of your mind as you structure the lesson. Remember, it should allow students the opportunity to learn one small component of the more general curriculum goal. We guide you through the lesson development by asking you to complete the tasks outlined in 1–5.

1. **Think about the Mathematics.** First, think about the prerequisite knowledge in terms of data analysis and the accompanying vocabulary that students would have and/or need to work toward this goal. Second, what is the difference between a concept and a procedure related to this goal?

Third, write a focused narrow objective achievable through a combination model of teaching. Be sure to focus on a small component of the curriculum goal. Fourth, please tell how this lesson will fit into the students' overall experience toward the curriculum goal.

2. **Think about How We Learn.** What are good experiences that foster data analysis knowledge? Remember how we described the importance of beginning with a good question? Recall the information about allowing children to gather and then work with their own data? What are the materials that will model the task correctly?

3. **Think about the Role of the Teacher.** What does the teacher do in data analysis lessons? Recall that the teacher first describes an interesting situation and asks something about that situation that requires data analysis. Explain the expected process of your lesson, keeping in mind that you may draw from all models of teaching.

4. **Think about How the Learning Theory Might Appear during Your Lesson.** Use your knowledge of development of data analysis thinking to think about stumbling blocks students might meet.

5. **Finally, Think about Assessment.** How will you know when your students have met your objective? Write an evaluation in which you would engage the students that would indicate to you the objective has or has not been met.

As always, there are several correct answers for a data analysis lesson like this. We remind you that the lessons you create for your own learners will depend on your district's curriculum and you will have access to a textbook series that should help you write your lessons. However, we believe that there are correct types of answers for this activity. We can imagine lessons using contexts such as favorite fruits, temperature and climate, and books read. When you are ready to check your lesson, feel free to consult our sample lesson found in the appendix.

Appendix

Answers to Part-Closing Activities

Part One: Write a Geometry and Spatial Thinking Lesson   **72**
Part Two: Write a Number and Operation Lesson   **140**
Part Three: Write a Measurement Lesson   **198**
Part Four: Write a Fraction/Ratio/Proportion Lesson   **258**
Part Five: Write a Data Analysis Lesson   **324**

PART ONE: Write a Geometry and Spatial Thinking Lesson

1. We assume the children have had a little experience visualizing different solid shapes. We assume this lesson will help them learn to analyze similarities between shapes, based on the shape of the faces.

   Focused narrow objective achievable through the discussion model of teaching:

   As a result of categorizing several solid shapes cut from various thicknesses of paper, foam, and wood, students will be able to create groupings of the solid shapes based on whether the solids have the same planar faces.

2. List of materials you need to gather for the lesson.

   Each pair of students should have several sizes of triangular prisms and pyramids, rectangular prisms and pyramids, pentagonal prisms and pyramids, cylinders, and cones made from four thicknesses: paper, posterboard, foam, and wood. Be sure several of the solids have faces of the same-shaped plane faces. Have hoops or string loops to lay on the floor, so students can place the materials in sets.

3. Discussion questions related to your objective:

   Susie and Nirvan, could you share how you decided to group the objects?

   Select two related shapes, such as a triangular prism and a triangular pyramid. "How are these solids the same and how are they different? What if we stretched or twisted the foam solid, what different plane faces could we make?" Set up a visual demonstration. Use a toy steam roller and a solid figure. "If a giant steam roller squashed these solids, what might happen? Would the shapes change? How would they change? What are you thinking?"

   What would happen if I tried to make a solid shape using many copies of the same plane face? Here are several copies of the same shape. "Gather a collection of triangles, as an example. How could you use them to create another shape?"

4. Anticipate student answers and prepare follow-up questions for each kind of answer.

   "They look the same; they have points at the top." Children's answers would probably use very simple language, depending on their vocabulary and prior knowledge. Words such as *prism*, *face*, and *plane* would need to be in place if students are expected to use them.

   Teacher: Please point to the parts that make the faces look the same.
   Student: These faces are all triangles.
   Teacher: What makes a face a triangle?
   Student: Since all pyramids have triangular faces, all pyramids will be in the same pile.
   Teacher: What other solid shapes always have triangular faces?

5. Evaluation

   Give students several solid shapes and ask them to match them to an appropriate group and to explain why each belongs to that group.

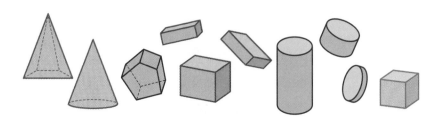

PART TWO: Write a Number and Operation Lesson

1. We assume the learners already know their multiplication and division facts. We assume this lesson will help them recognize that multiplication and division facts are related.

   Focused narrow objective achievable with the concept-attainment model of teaching:

   As a result of sorting and classifying several multiplication and division problems, students will be able to use the relationship between multiplication and division to supply missing facts in fact families.

2. List of materials you need to gather for the lesson.

   Prepare a large T-chart. One column is titled Yes; the other is titled No.

   Show children a card (like one of the ones shown below) and classify it into either the No category or the Yes category. Be sure to give them enough time to look over the card and think about where it is placed. After demonstrating this procedure with several examples, ask "Who thinks they know why some fit here (Yes side) and some fit here (No side)?" Share several more examples to solidify students' thinking. Then ask children to classify all remaining cards. Continue asking, "Where shall I put this one? Avanthi is correct, this one is a Yes (or No)." After all cards have been classified, ask the children to write down their thoughts and then share them with a neighbor. Finally, ask each of them to come up with one Yes/No example.

   A collection of cards each showing sets of facts.

   Make at least five examples, five best examples, and five nonexamples. A few such cards are shown.

3. What kind of concept lesson:

   The lesson is indirect and uses sorting and classifying activities. The teacher will show each card to the students and sort them into Yes/No piles, depending on whether the card shows a multiplication and division fact from one fact family. Students' efforts to explain the teacher's grouping should help lead them toward an understanding of an inverse relationship between multiplication and division.

4. Anticipate student answers and prepare follow-up questions for each kind of answer.

   Student: The Yes examples all have numbers that match

   Teacher: Could you come up and show us what you mean?

   Student: The No examples have just division problems or just multiplication problems.

   Teacher: Show us which ones you are talking about. Pick one of them. How could you make it become a member of the Yes pile?

   Student: The Yes examples have both multiplication and division problems.

   Teacher: Work with your partner and make a Yes example.

5. Evaluation

   Some paint has spilled on these cards. Decide whether each card would have been in the Yes pile or the No pile. For cards in the Yes pile, write the information that is under the paint.

   Expected answers:

   Students correctly identify the cards that show members from the same fact family. They use fact-family membership to report the missing information.

Yes

$3 \times 8 = 24$ $24 \div 3 = 8$	$3 \times 4 = 12$ $12 \div 4 = 3$
$18 \div 3 = 6$ $6 \times 3 = 18$	$2 \times 3 = 6$ $3 \times 2 = 6$ $6 \div 3 = 2$

No

$3 \times 5 = 15$ $3 \times 6 = 18$ $3 \times 7 = 21$	$20 \div 5 = 4$ $2 \times 10 = 20$
$48 \div 6 = 8$ $48 \div 4 = 12$ $6 \times 4 = 24$	$16 \div 2 = 8$ $8 \div 2 = 4$ $4 \div 2 = 2$

$3 \times 5 = 15$ / $15 \div 5 = $ ● $\times 3 = 21$ / $21 \div 7 = 3$ $9 \times$ ● $= 27$ / $24 \div 8 = $ ●   ● $\times 5 = 35$ / $35 \div 7 = $ ● $9 \times$ ● $= 18$ / $18 \div 6 = $ ●

$6 \times 4 = $ ● / $6 \times$ ● $= 30$ / $6 \times 6 = $ ● $7 \times 5 = $ ● / $5 \times$ ● $= 35$ / $35 \div 7 = $ ● $20 \div 4 = $ ● / $20 \div $ ● $= 4$ / ● $\times 4 = 20$ $42 \div $ ● $= 6$ / $6 \times 8 = $ ●   ● $\div 2 = 4$ / $4 \times$ ● $= 8$ / $8 \div 2 = $ ●

PART THREE: Write a Measurement Lesson

1. We assume students already have a sense that objects have size and that the sizes can be compared. We assume this lesson will help students practice identifying beginning points on a ruler.

   Focused narrow objective achievable with the presentation model of teaching:

   As a result of several teacher-led demonstrations measuring length, the students will be able to correctly demonstrate the measurement process appropriately noting the beginning point on the ruler.

2. List of materials you need to gather for the lesson.

   Two enlarged rulers (one with numbers rubbed off and one with paint drops) to demonstrate the measuring tasks. Enlarged rulers will be demonstration tools like the regular rulers given to the students

   Several regular rulers with numbers rubbed off

   Several regular rulers with paint spilled over some of the numbers

   Several books to measure, including several that are the same size in length

   Several broken rulers (be sure to be careful that the rough edges are not dangerous) and a collection of objects for students to measure in their evaluation (pencils, pens, CD cases, chopsticks, ceramic tiles, greeting cards, tissue boxes, photographs, picture frames)

3. Two examples to demonstrate.

   First, use the enlarged ruler to demonstrate how to measure the length of the books using the enlarged ruler that has had the first few numbers rubbed off. Be sure to begin the measuring process from a number that is not rubbed off. Ask for student volunteers to measure the lengths of several different pencils, so the results will be different. Be prepared for different answers.

   Second, demonstrate how to measure the lengths of the books using the enlarged paint-spotted ruler. Then measure the lengths of several same-sized books, making the error of not accounting for the paint-covered zero indicator. Ask for student volunteers to measure the lengths of some pencils and the edges of the tissue boxes.

4. This is a Phase 2 lesson. In Phase 1, we would have determined that students are familiar with standard units and the concept that objects have length. But the following questions help us navigate toward and possibly into Phase 3.

   Anticipate student answers and prepare follow-up questions for each kind of answer.

   Student: These books look the same but did not end up at the same number with the two rulers.
   Teacher: Could you point to the ending number? What is the beginning number each time?
   Student: These books all had the same length because they match up.
   Teacher: How do they match according to the ruler?
   Student: Since all these books are 6 inches long, they will take up 6 inches on the ruler, no matter where you start.
   Teacher: How could you know that for certain?

5. Evaluation

   Hand out the broken rulers. Double check that none of the edges are dangerously rough. "Use these rulers to find the length measures of the books."

   Expected answers:

   Students correctly use the rulers and recognize the beginning point of the measurement with broken rulers is not at zero.

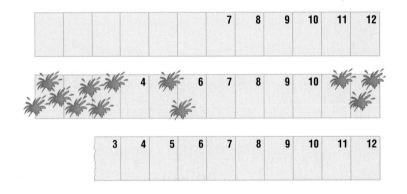

PART FOUR: Write a Fraction/Ratio/Proportion Lesson

1. We assume students have experience finding equivalent fractions. We assume this lesson will help them practice finding equivalent fractions with a denominator of 100 (percents).

   Focused narrow objective achievable with the problem-solving model of teaching:

   After students solve several problems that provide information in fraction format, the students will be able to correctly match percent representations to common fraction representations in another context.

2. List of materials you need to gather for the lesson.
   Problems, graph paper, 100-grids

3. Examples of problems.

   > Derek's newest CD has 15 songs. He likes 12 of them because those 12 each have a drum solo. The CD jacket says 80% of the songs have a drum solo. Is this correct?

   > Before last night, John usually made 65% of his free throws. Last night he made 3 out of 7 free throws. Is that better or worse than before?

   > CJ plays soccer and scores 2 points out of every 13 points her team scores. What percentage of the points are hers?

   > Tabitha's sport drink says it contains 110 calories. If she needs 1800 calories that day, what percentage of her calories is her sport drink?

   > Erica writes about 2/3 of a page in her diary each evening. She always continues from where she finished the night before, rather than start a new page. Her diary has 50 pages in it. What percent of her diary is filled after 18 days?

4. Lesson begins with contexts that make sense to the students. We have assumed these contexts are meaningful to the students. Here are some anticipated student comments that may arise, where students need to be (1) propelled forward, (2) tempted back, or (3) validated.

   Student: Ten out of twelve seems a lot more than 80 percent.

   Teacher: (1) If there were 100 songs, how many would have drum solos? [expecting answer of 80] How can you compare 80/100 to 10/12?

   Student: Three-sevenths is less than half, and 65 percent is more than half.

   Teacher: (2) How many sevenths would have been the same as 65 percent? How many sevenths would be 50 percent?

   Student: I think 18 days means I take 18 times 2/3. That's 12. But I'm not sure what to do next.

   Teacher: (3) Where is it you are trying to get? What does it mean to find a percent?

5. Evaluation

   Jenni volunteers at the Spotted Puppy animal shelter. She helps dogs get daily exercise walking them in the nearby park. She knows that at the Spotted Puppy, 5/7 of the dogs are large dogs. Emily volunteers at the Fuzzy Puppy animal shelter and walks dogs too. Emily read that 7/10 of the dogs at her shelter are large. Which shelter has a higher percentage of large dogs?

   Extension:

   Make up a problem similar to the ones above that can be answered by your classmates.

PART FIVE: Write a Data Analysis Lesson

1. We assume the children are somewhat familiar with data gathering processes, such as taking lunch counts or gathering daily data about the weather. We assume this lesson will help students understand the importance of gathering whole class information.

   Focused narrow objective achievable by combining the four models of teaching:

   After students are shown plans for a new playground, they will organize their preferences (the data) for different pieces of playground equipment and be able to explain to the building contractor why they suggest certain playground equipment.

2. List of materials you need to gather for the lesson.

   Picture of a grassy playground area, some official-looking school letterhead, blank index cards, sticky notes.

3. Process of lesson.

   Give the students a picture of the playground area. Show them the contractor's equipment suggestions and ask them if they think anything is missing. After we make our list, put the name of each piece of equipment (from our complete list) on one index card and pile them on the floor. (Of course, it is important to remember that some types of traditional playground equipment, with which some children may be familiar, are no longer allowed on school grounds. Things like teeter totters, slides and merry-go-rounds are not allowed.) Then tell them the contractor can only include four pieces of equipment.

Teacher: What pieces of equipment are the most wanted? How could we decide on the important equipment? What is a good way to make the most kids happy?

Encourage children to order the data.

Find an opportunity to suggest asking other classes for their preferences (increase sample size).

4. This situation should be meaningful to the children. Student comments and teacher questions that may arise, where students need support:

   Student: I don't like to swing. I don't think we need them.
   Teacher: I wonder why so many parks have swings? Do you know anyone who likes to swing?
   Student: Let's put all the equipment that needs other stuff, like basketballs, together.
   Teacher: Interesting idea. After we do that, let's see if there are any other ways to group cards together.
   Student: I can't decide. I like to play on more than one thing.
   Teacher: Write your name on some sticky notes and put one on each of your favorites. If everyone in the class does that, what will we know?

5. Evaluation

   As a class, students will dictate a letter to me for the building contractor. Students will correctly use some sort of grouping organization (perhaps a bar graph) to defend their suggestions for limiting the playground to four pieces of equipment.

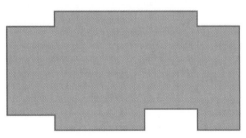

Equipment suggestions:

Swings, pitcher's mound, hard ground or concrete for skipping rope, basketball hoop, wood structure for climbing, benches, etc.

Index

Abbott, E., 229
Acceleration, enrichment versus, 185–187
Activities
  Adding Four Numbers, 98
  Applying van Hiele, 160
  Baseball Innings Pitched, 230
  Basic Patterns, 44
  Building Pascal's Triangle, 298
  Building Perspectives, 53
  Building Polyhedra, 33
  Calculating with Spinner Games, 284
  Checking the Syllable Count on Chosen
    Names, 319
  Color in the Numbers of These Patterns, 111
  Cutting Pizzas, 227
  Danny Dixon's Problem, 7
  Decorative Tiles, 17
  Des Cartes, 69
  Describe the Pattern in Each Month, 110
  Division Problems to Consider, 242–243
  Draw in the Next Block Pile, 134–135
  Evaluating Contexts, 250
  Finding Angle Measurements without
    a Protractor, 164
  Finding More Angle Measures, 165
  Finding the Mean, 277
  Generalize the Area for a Trapezoid, 143
  Get Three in a Row!, 208–210
  Grading Problem Solutions, 248–249
  Guessing the Second, 287
  How Many Ways Can You Score 42 Points?, 81
  How to Count Outcomes, 286
  Inspiration, 23, 204
  Louise's Block Quilt, 175
  Making Photocopies, 169
  Making Statistics Physically, 266–267
  Making Triangles, 195
  The New Park, 224
  Notorious Locker Problem, 75
  One Grain of Rice Calendar, 305
  Orchestrating Sharing Strategies, 128–129
  Organizing Data, 276
  Organizing Data with a Venn Diagram, 261
  Organizing Messy Data, 282–283
  Picturing Addition, 83
  Picturing Division, 89
  Picturing Multiplication, 87
  Picturing Subtraction, 84
  Planning a Volleyball Tournament, 113
  Play the Cheyenne Women's Dice Game, 302
  Probability with a Spinner, 268
  Pulling 2-D Ideas from a 3-D Model, 19
  Pulling Taffy, 254
  Rigid Motions and Symmetry in Algebra, 70
  Running a Regression Line of Fit, 321
  Selecting Materials for a Lesson, 313
  Sharing a Good Plan, 192–193
  Something More about Triangular
    Numbers, 167
  Statistics Concepts, 270
  Subdividing a Region, 149
  Sugar Cookies, 214
  Symbolizing Someone Else's Thinking, 100
  Taking a Survey of Your Classmates, 264
  Tangrams, 40–41
  Tangrams for Fractions, 232
  Teacher Ratios, 201
  Thinking About 1 Million, 80
  Tool List, 146
  Topological Alphabet, 30–31
  Tracy's Dog, 207
  Two-Color Counter (Coin), 274
  Two-Week Almanac, 301
  Understanding Hopi Moon Cycles, 172–173
  Understanding Number Relationships, 96–97
  Understanding van Hiele on the Geoboard, 161
  Using Discrete Materials to Measure, 180
  Using Technology to Organize Data, 278
  Using van Hiele Theory to Guide
    Instruction, 64–65
  The Weather in Chewandswallow, 304
  What Could Be the Shape?, 62
  Write a Data Analysis Lesson, 324–325
  Write a Fraction/Ratio/Proportion Lesson,
    258–259
  Write a Geometry and Spatial Thinking Lesson,
    72–73
  Write a Measurement Lesson, 198–199
  Write a Number and Operation Lesson, 140–141
  Writing More Word Problems, 108
  Writing Word Problems, 105
  Your Culture and Mathematics, 51
Adams, B., 239
Addition
  algorithms for, 78–79, 82–83
  classifying problems in, 101–102
  of fractions, 212–213
  learning, 104–105
  "Looks Like, Sounds Like" table for, 100, 101
  nature of, 77
  problem solving with, 99–102, 104–105
Algebra Connections
  for data analysis, 318–322
  described, 3
  for geometry and spatial thinking, 67–70
  linear regression, 318–321
  for measurement, 194–196
  patterns in, 133–136
  properties in, 133
  rational numbers and proportional thinking,
    254–255
  variables in, 136–137

Algorithms, 82–90
  for addition, 78–79, 82–83
  for division, 78–79, 86–89
  generalizing, 88, 245
  for multiplication, 77–78, 84–86
  problem solving to ground, 245
  for subtraction, 77, 83–84, 102–104, 106
Analysis. *See* Data analysis
  in Van Hiele theory, 39
Anghileri, J., 112
Angles, measuring, 163–164, 165
Area grids, 78
Area model of multiplication, 215, 216
Arrays, 78, 85, 86
Articulation, 314
Assessment principle (NCTM)
  evaluating achievement, 126–127
  forms of assessment, 13, 14
  guiding instructional decisions, 314
  making instructional decisions, 61–62
  matching evaluation with objective, 125–126
  monitoring progress toward goal, 246–249
  problem solving and, 239
  statement of, 5
  student presentations and assessment of
    presentations, 191
  thinking carefully about assessment, 63
Averages, 263–264

Banks, L. R., 234
Bar graphs, 276, 279, 280
Barrett, J., 304
Barron, B. J., 244
Barron, L., 244
Base-ten blocks, 119–120, 233–234
Battista, M. T., 43
Beishuizen, M., 82
Beisser, S. R., 185, 186
Bell, R. C., 300
Benchmark numbers, listening for, 251–252
Bennett, C. I., 49
Billstein, R., 246
Biswas, G., 244
Bogart, J. E., 117
Boulton-Lewis, G., 69, 136
Box-and-whisker graphs, 279
Bransford, J. D., 244
Braunhardt, L., 244
Bright, G. W., 291, 307, 308, 314
Bruchac, J., 177
Bruner, J. S., 45
Burns, M., 177, 179
Bushnell, D., 158

Calendar approach to skip-counting, 108–109, 110
Carpenter, T. P., 84, 92, 125–130, 132, 206
Carroll, W. M., 107
Categorical data, 263
Cauley, K. M., 84
Center for Highly Interactive Computing in
  Education, 130
Cheska, A. T., 300
Chips, 120–121, 233

Chunking, 94
Circles, 20–22
  analyzing, 21
  cylinders versus, 21–22
  defined, 21
  as mathematical idea, 20
Clark, F. B., 107, 154, 156, 157
Classroom Connections
  assessing problem solutions
    with rubric, 247, 248–249
  clarifying fraction concepts, 211
  creating picture graphs with physical
    objects, 281, 282–283
  data analysis with physical materials, 265, 266–267
  dealing with incorrect comments, 126
  described, 7
  enriching gifted student learning, 188
  forms of assessment, 14
  guiding student use of vocabulary, 296
  high-ability students, 187, 188
  literature in, 178, 179
  magnified inch, 152
  moving from data to presentations of data, 278
  number relationships, 94, 95–97
  providing interactive instruction, 12
  reacting to cognitively guided
    instruction (CGI), 132
  sharing of strategies, 127, 128–129
  sharing plan for solving problem, 191, 192–193
  thinking carefully about assessment, 63
  understanding how children learn math, 8
  using sports to create interest, 316
  van Hiele theory to guide instruction, 63, 64–65
Clement, R., 178
Cloudy with a Chance of Meatballs (Barrett), 304
CMP, 246
Coaching, 314
Cobb, P., 156, 178
Cobb, Robert, 3, 320
Cockcraft, W. H., 20
Coerr, E., 117
Cognition and Technology Group, Vanderbilt
  University, 244
Cognitively guided instruction (CGI), 92,
  104, 121, 127
  comparing across grades, 131–133
  listening to guide thinking, 127–131
  reacting to, 132
Common fractions, defined, 202–203
Commutative property, 106–107
Compacted curriculum, 186
Comparison approach
  to measurement, 148, 156, 168
  to subtraction, 77, 84, 102–104
Concept attainment, 9, 124–125, 310
Concepts
  building algorithms from, 82–90
  clarifying fraction, 211
  in concept attainment model of teaching, 9
  connections among rational number
    genres, 205–212
  coordinating counting, operation, and number
    sense, 79–81

in data analysis, 269–275
defined, 22
examples in, 22–24, 26–27
idea of "size," 147–152
nonexamples in, 22–24, 26–27
procedures versus, 126–127
relationships among shapes, 22–29
Concrete materials, 46–53
assessing use of, 48–49
selecting supportive, 312–313
types of, 47–48, 119–121, 179–181, 232–234,
306–307
visualization and, 46–47
Concrete representations
discrete versus continuous materials and, 118
nature of, 45–46
other types of representation and, 47
skip-counting and, 109–111
Congruence
Hopi calendar and, 170–174
importance of, 205–206
in measurement, 168, 170–176
rational numbers and, 205–206
Conservation, in measurement process, 148, 150
Context
in lesson plans, 250–251
with rational numbers, 206–207, 213–215,
223–224, 232
Continuousness
of data, 263
of materials, 118–121, 231
in measurement, 145
with rational numbers, 231
Coordination, in measurement process, 151–152
Corners, 29, 32
Cossey, R., 152
Counting, 79–81. *See also* Skip-counting
principles of, 95
of spaces, 153
Counting on Frank (Clement), 178
Counting strategies for subtraction, 103, 104
Coverage, in measurement process, 150–151
Cramer, K., 217
Crawford, J., 53
Crews, T. R., 244
Crowley, M. L., 38, 160–161
Cubes, 47, 179–181
Cuisenaire rods, 120
Cultural Connections
analyzing dice games, 300–303
in data analysis, 297–306
great-grandmother's long walk, 303–306
Hopi calendar, 170–174
measuring bushels, 176
mosaics in, 49–52
numeration systems in, 114–117
organizing astronomical information, 298–300
quilting and congruence, 174–176
using and making ratios, 228–231
Curcio, F. R., 273, 291, 307, 308, 314
Curriculum principle (NCTM)
algebra connections to data analysis, 318–322
algebra connections to geometry, 67–70

algebra connections to measurement, 194–196
algebra connections to number
and operation, 133–137
consumers of statistical knowledge, 317
developing mathematical imagery, 54
figurating numbers, 112–114
geometry in measurement, 144–147
interactive instruction, 12
literature and problems, 178
mental ideas versus physical models in, 18
moving from data to presentations of data, 278
nature of rational numbers, 202–204
number and operation, 76–79
number in measurement, 144–147
problem solving to ground algorithms, 245
rational numbers and proportional
thinking, 254–255
relevant patterns in measurement, 166–176
statement of, 5
student use of vocabulary, 296
symmetry in nature, 28
tasks to build proportional thinking, 253
understanding mathematics of statistics and
probability, 262–268
updating, 13–14
using magnified inch, 152
worthwhile tasks and, 66
Cylinders, circles versus, 21–22

Daily routines, with numbers, 131, 132
Data
defined, 269, 292
organization of, 275, 276
Data analysis, 260–325
algebra and, 318–322
concepts of, 269–275
procedures in, 275–287
relevant learning frameworks for, 290–297
relevant patterns in, 297–306
teaching aids for, 306–307
understanding mathematics of, 262–268
Decimals, defined, 203
Deduction
deductive lesson plans, 125
informal, 36, 37, 39
Deep structure, pattern structures and, 44
Demi, 117, 305, 321–322
Demonstrations, 90
Descriptions, predictions versus, 264–265
DeVries, R., 98
Diameter, 227
Dice, 300–303, 307
Digital cameras, 244
Directed orientation, as phase of learning, 162
Direct modeling strategies for subtraction,
103, 104
Discourse strategies
in geometry, 56
importance of knowing mathematics, 58–61
listening for benchmark numbers, 251–252
listening to students, 127–131
sharing thinking, 187–190
Discreteness, of materials, 118–121, 232

Discussion model of teaching, 9, 56, 310. *See also* Discourse strategies
Distance-time graph, 303–306
Division
    algorithms for, 78–79, 86–89
    as fair sharing, 79, 89
    of fractions, 215–217, 246
    nature of, 78–79
    problem solving with, 107, 241–245
    as repeated subtraction, 78–79, 86–89
Driscoll, M., 68, 321

Eager, E., 234
Ellis, F. H., 170, 171
Empson, S. B., 92, 127–130, 132
Enigmas, confronting, 296–297
Enrichment
    acceleration versus, 185–187
    of gifted student learning, 188
Equity principle (NCTM)
    acceleration versus enrichment, 185–187
    algebra as social justice, 320
    dealing with high-ability students, 187, 188
    dealing with incorrect comments, 126
    defending viewpoints, 316–317
    Hopi calendar, 170–174
    measuring bushels, 176
    numeration systems and, 114–117
    in organizing data and simulating game situations, 297–306
    questioning and, 12–13, 58
    quilting and congruence, 174–176
    statement of, 5
    students writing own problems, 185
    using and making ratios, 228–231
Equivalent fractions, 206, 217–218
Estes, B., 156, 178
Evaluation. *See also* Assessment principle (NCTM)
    of achievement, 126–127
    matching with objective, 125–126
EveryDay Math, 246
Examples, 22–24, 26–27, 28
Expected value, 285
Experimental probability, 265, 272–273, 295, 318–321
Explication, as phase of learning, 162
Exploration model of teaching, 312

Facts, underlying, in data analysis, 290–291
Fairness, 284–285
Fair sharing, division as, 79, 89
Family Math (Stenmark), 152
Features, in learning process, 3
Fennema, E., 92, 127–130, 132
Fey, J. T., 246
Fibonacci, 114
Find-the-difference approach, to subtraction, 106
Fitzgerald, W. M., 246
Flipping counters, 285
Fogarty, John, 229
Footprints, 20
Formal deduction, in Van Hiele theory, 36, 37, 39

Formulas
    in measurement process, 154
    as relevant patterns, 166
Fraction circles, 232–233
Fractions
    common fractions, defined, 202–203
    contextualized situations with, 206–207, 213–215
    division of, 215–217, 246
    equivalent, 206, 217–218
    listening for benchmark, 251–252
    operations with, 212–218
    partitioning whole units, 226–228
    scavenger hunt based on, 253–254
    sharing concept and, 205
Franke, M. L., 92, 127–130, 132
Free orientation, as phase of learning, 162–163
Freewrite, 130
Friel, S. N., 246, 291, 307, 308, 314
Fuson, K. C., 93
Fuys, D., 24, 35, 54, 158

Garofalo, J., 239
Geddes, D., 35, 54, 158
Generalizations
    algorithms and, 88, 245
    of area of trapezoid, 143
    making, 293
    measurements and, 194
    nature of, 269–271
    of ratios for similar shapes, 168
    variables as, 136, 196
General statements, 263
Geoboards, 159, 161, 181
Geometer's Sketchpad, 57
Geometry, 2, 16–73
    algebra and, 67–70
    assessment in, 61–62
    building shapes in, 29–33
    concrete materials in, 46–53
    concrete representation in, 45–46, 47
    creating good questions in, 58, 61
    discussion in, 56
    importance of knowing mathematics and, 58–61, 66–67
    making instructional decisions in, 61–62
    in measurement, 144–147
    mental ideas versus physical models in, 18–22
    pattern starters in, 43–44
    pictorial representation in, 46, 47
    professional development and, 66–67
    reflection time in, 66
    relationships among shapes in, 22–29
    symbolic representation in, 46, 47
    symmetry in, 25–27, 28
    technology in, 57
    Van Hiele theory, 35–43, 46–47, 63, 64–65
George, P., 158
Gifted students. *See* High-ability students
Giraffe and a Half, A (Silverstein), 234
Goldman, S. R., 244
Gravemeijer, K., 156, 178
Greenberg, M. J., 144

Greenhut, R., 229
Guided exploration, 186–187
Gullberg, J., 265

Half Magic (Eager), 234
Hall, J. W., 93
Handheld computers (PDAs), 130
Hearson, R., 53
Hendry, A., 163
Hiebert, J., 99, 130, 148, 152
Higgins, T., 291, 292
High-ability students
    acceleration versus enrichment for, 185–187
    dealing with, 187
    enriching learning of, 188
Himler, R., 117
Homework, selecting, 246
Horvath, J. K., 290, 291, 293–296
How Big Is a Foot? (Myller & McGrath),
    148–149
Hubalek, L. K., 177
Hunting, R. P., 94–95

Indian in the Cupboard, The (Banks), 234
Individual education plan (IEP), 185
Inductive lesson plans, 125
Inferences, 262
    defined, 270
    predictions versus, 265–268
Informal deduction, in Van Hiele theory,
    36, 37, 39
Inquiry/information, as phase of learning,
    161–162
Integration, as phase of learning, 163
Interactive instruction, 12
International Society of Technology in Education
    (ISTE), 6
Interpretation of data, 265
Intuition, representations and, 222
Iteration, in measurement process, 147, 150

Jacobs, V. R., 290, 310–311
Jacobson, C., 144, 157, 178
James, S. E., 171
Jasper Series, 244
Jenkins, M., 159, 162, 178
Jones, G. A., 293–294, 307

Kahnemann, D., 268
Kamii, Constance, 92–96, 98–100, 104, 107, 118,
    121, 131, 152, 154, 156, 157, 181, 225
Kato, Y., 104
Keats, E. J., 117
Kemeny, V., 144, 157
Key Curriculum Press, 57
Kieren, T. E., 206, 221, 223, 224, 227, 235, 239,
    241, 250, 255
Klein, A. S., 82
Knowledge
    levels of, 222–223
    rational numbers and, 221–223, 225–226
    of whole numbers, 212
Konold, C., 274–275, 288, 291–293, 313–314

Lajoie, S. P., 290, 310–311
Langrall, C. W., 293–294, 307
Langton, J., 53
Language of number words, 93–94
Lappan, G., 246
Lavigne, N. C., 290, 310–311
Lawrence, G., 158
LCD algorithm, 216–217, 241–245
Learning principle (NCTM)
    clarifying fraction concepts, 211
    concept of "size," 147
    connecting K-8 arithmetic to algebra, 137
    connections among rational number
        genres, 205–212
    learning frameworks for data analysis, 290–297
    manipulatives in middle school, 48
    for measurement, 156–158
    mental ideas versus physical models in, 18–20
    methods of learning math, 8
    prediction versus description, 264–265
    probability and, 272–273
    for rational numbers, 221–228
    rhombus lesson, 59
    sharing plan for solving problem, 191, 192–193
    statement of, 5
Learning theory
    for geometry and spatial thinking, 35–43
    for measurement, 156–165
    for number and operation, 93–107
    number as mental relationship and, 93–98
    procedures from solving problems, 99–107
    for rational numbers, 221–228
    Van Hiele theory, 35–43, 46–47, 63–65, 159–165
Least common denominator (LCD), 216–217
Lee, L., 137
Lehrer, R., 144, 157, 159, 162, 178, 181,
    290, 291, 293–296
Lesson plans
    acceleration versus enrichment in content
        differentiation, 185–187
    components of, 11–12
    concept attainment, 124–125
    context in, 250–251
    creating good questions, 58, 61, 240–241
    deductive, 125
    inductive, 125
    matching evaluation with objective, 125–126
    matching material to objective, 312–314
    Write a Data Analysis Lesson (activity), 324–325
    Write a Fraction/Ratio/Proportion Lesson
        (activity), 258–259
    Write a Geometry and Spatial Thinking Lesson
        (activity), 72–73
    Write a Measurement Lesson (activity), 198–199
    Write a Number and Operation Lesson
        (activity), 140–141
Levi, L., 92, 127–130, 132
Lewis, P., 311
Liebov, A. K., 24
Likelihood. *See also* Probability
    nature of, 272, 273–275
    recognizing development through, 294–295
Linear regression, 318–321

Line graphs, 277–279, 280
Line segments, 18
Lipson, A., 274–275, 288, 291
Literature Connections
    comparing counting books to literary
        works, 117
    mathematical imagery, 53
    proportions represented by characters, 234
    understanding cultures and solving
        problems, 177, 178, 179
    using stories about chance and organized
        counting, 304–305
Littles, The (Peterson), 234
Logowriter, 57
Lohmeier, J., 274–275, 288, 291
London, J., 177
Long, K., 152, 157

Manipulatives
    middle school use of, 48
    nature of, 45
    types of, 47–49, 119–121, 179–181, 232–234,
        306–307
Marshall, J., 20
Marshall, P., 229
MATHematics, 246
Mathematics in Context (MiC), 132
McClain, K., 156, 178
McCrath, S., 148–149
McGrath, B. B., 117
Mean, 263–264
Measurement, 142–199
    algebra and, 194–196
    comparison in, 148, 156, 168
    congruence in, 168, 170–176
    conservation in, 148, 150
    continuousness in, 145
    coordinating concepts in, 151–152
    coverage in, 150–151
    geometry in, 144–147
    idea of "size" in, 147–152
    iteration of units in, 147, 150
    learning theory in, 156–165
    nature of, 144
    nonstandard units in, 147
    number in, 144–147
    part-whole relations in, 151
    of shapes, 152–154
    standard units in, 145–147, 148–150
    summative concept in, 148
    tiling in, 151
Measuring devices, 164
Median, 263–264
Metrics, 234
Mexican subtraction, 115–116
MiC, 246
MicroWorlds, 57
Middle School Connections
    algebra as social justice, 320
    consumers of statistical knowledge, 317
    creating wonder, 194
    daily routines and, 132

demonstrations and, 90
described, 4
encounters with integers, 119
fact families for integers, 113
generalizing algorithms, 88
knowing math well enough to ask questions, 61
manipulative use, 48
measurements from the real world, 158
net of solid shape, 32
problem solving to ground algorithms, 245
selecting homework, 246
students writing own problems, 185
to subtraction, 106
tasks to build proportional thinking, 253
Middleton, James A., 217, 255
Millen, P. E., 229
Mindstorms (Papert), 57
Missing-addend approach, to subtraction, 77, 106
Mitchelmore, M. C., 158, 180–181
Mixing units, in measurement process, 157
M&M's Brand Counting, The (McGrath), 117
Mode, 263–264
Models of teaching, 7–9, 56, 124–125, 184,
        238–245, 310
Mogill, A. T., 293–294, 307
Moore, A., 244
Moses, Robert, 3, 320
Moursund, David, 190
Multiplication
    algorithms for, 77–78, 84–86
    with fractions, 215, 216
    nature of, 77–78
    problem solving with, 105–107
    as repeated addition, 78, 84–86
Myller, R., 148–149

Nagahiro, M., 104
Nastasi, B. K., 244
National Council of Teachers of Mathematics
        (NCTM)
    assessment principle. *See* Assessment principle
        (NCTM)
    content standards, 4–5
    curriculum principle. *See* Curriculum principle
        (NCTM)
    equity principle. *See* Equity principle (NCTM)
    learning principle. *See* Learning principle (NCTM)
    mission of, 4–5
    original curriculum standards, 5–6
    teaching principle. *See* Teaching principle (NCTM)
    technology principle. *See* Technology principle
        (NCTM)
National Research Council, 144, 161
National Science Foundation, 132, 246
Nieto, S., 49
Nonexamples, 22–24, 26–27, 28
Nonstandard units, 147
Number ideas, levels for, 93
Number in Preschool and Kindergarten (Kamii), 92,
        94–98
Number line model of multiplication, 215, 216
Number lines, 111

Numbers. *See* Rational numbers; Whole numbers
Number sense, 81, 98
Number words, 93–94
Numeration systems, 114–117

Oberle, C., 52
Oddness, rational numbers and, 227–228
Odds, 285–287
One Grain of Rice (Demi), 117, 305, 321–322
Open-ended questions, 317
Operations, 82–90. *See also* Addition; Division;
    Multiplication; Subtraction
  concept of, 81
  connecting skip-counting to, 111–112
  with fractions, 212–218
  number and, 76–79
  types of, 77–79
Ordering
  in measurement process, 156
  whole numbers and, 77
Osana, H., 159, 162, 178
Outhred, L. M., 158, 180–181
Over in the Meadow (Keats), 117
Oxenbury, H., 53
Ozaki, K., 104

Paper folding, 233
Papert, Seymour, 57, 311
Parallelograms, examples and nonexamples of, 26
Parker, R. A., 53
Partnered learning model of teaching, 9, 184, 312
Part-whole relationships, in measurement
    process, 151
Pascal's triangle, 297, 298
Pattern blocks, nature of, 47–48
Patterns. *See* Relevant patterns
Pattern starters, 43–44
  deep structure and, 44
  extending, 43–44
Pepper, C., 94–95
Percents, defined, 203
Peterson, J., 234
Petrosino, A., 244
Phases of learning, 159–163
Phillips, E. D., 246
Physical models
  effective use of, 20
  pulling plane knowledge from solid shapes, 20
Piaget, Jean, 92, 98, 131
Pictographs, 276–277, 280
Pictorial representations
  discrete versus continuous materials and, 118–119
  nature of, 46
  other types of representation and, 47
Picture/object graphs, 279, 281, 282–283
Picture representations, 275–279
Pie/circle graphs, 279, 280
Pillay, H., 69, 136
Plane shapes, 18–20
  building, 29–32
  measuring, 152–154
Points, 18

Pollatsek, A., 274–275, 288, 291
Polygons, measuring area of, 159
Populations, samples versus, 263
Porter, D., 107
Post, T., 217
Pothier, Y., 205, 221, 227, 235, 241
Predictions, 262, 271
  descriptions versus, 264–265
  inferences versus, 265–268
Presentation model of teaching, 9, 184, 310.
    See also Student presentations
Principles and Standards for School Mathematics
    (NCTM), 13–14
Probability
  comparing probabilities, 295
  experimental, 265, 272–273, 295, 318–321
  "Looks Like, Sounds Like" table for, 294
  nature of, 272
  need for, 271–272
  procedures in, 281–287
  relevant framework for, 293–297
  theoretical, 265, 273, 295, 318–321
  understanding, 271–275
Problem solving, 99–107
  with addition, 99–102, 104–105
  assessing solutions with rubric, 247, 248–249
  with division, 107, 241–245
  to ground algorithms, 245
  as model of teaching, 9, 10, 238–245, 310
  with multiplication, 105–107
  sharing of plan for, 191, 192–193
  with subtraction, 102–105
  understanding cultures and, 177, 178, 179
Problem Solving (Schoenfeld), 238
Procedures
  building algorithms from concepts, 82–90
  building from problem solving, 99–107
  concepts versus, 126–127
  in data analysis, 275–287
  how to build shapes, 29–33
  how to measure shapes, 152–154
  how to operate and move between rational
    number genres, 212–219
  in probability, 281–287
  revisiting, 218–219
Professional development
  comparison across grade levels, 131–133
  in data analysis, 318–322
  fraction scavenger hunt, 253–254
  in geometry, 66–67
  knowing mathematics in different ways, 66–67
  matching district goals, 191–194
Project-Based Learning (Moursund), 190
Properties, in algebra, 133
Proportions, 228
  algebra and, 254–255
  characters in representation of, 234
  creating shared, rich experiences with, 252–253
  defined, 203
  rational numbers and proportional thinking,
    254–255
  tasks to build proportional thinking, 253

Pyramids, examples and nonexamples of, 27
Pythagorean theorem, 181, 194–196

Quadrilaterals
    comparing, 60–61
    defining, 42
    hierarchical diagram for, 24
    Venn diagram for, 25
Quantification, in teaching numbers, 94–98
Quartiles, 264
Questioning
    creating good questions, 58, 61, 240–241
    importance of, 12–13

Randomness, 273–275, 295
Range, 264
Rational numbers, 200–259. *See also* Fractions;
    Proportions; Ratios
    algebra and, 254–255
    congruence and, 205–206
    connections among types of, 205–212
    context with, 206–207, 213–215, 223–224, 232
    defined, 202
    partitioning whole units, 226–228
    procedures for working with, 212–219
    relevant learning theory for, 221–228
    relevant patterns with, 228
    teaching aids for, 231–234
    types of, 202–204
Ratios
    counting baseball innings, 228–229
    defined, 202
    drumming, 229–231
    generalizing for similar shapes, 168
    skip-counting in ratio tables, 228
Ratio table, 228, 255
Rectangles
    defining, 42
    examples and nonexamples of, 26
    lesson on, 60
Reflection symmetry, 25–26
Reflection time, 66, 314
Relationships
    in measurement process, 151
    among shapes, 22–29
    in teaching numbers, 94, 95–97
Relevant patterns
    in algebra, 133–136
    in data analysis, 297–306
    extending pattern starters, 43–44
    figurating numbers, 112–117
    formulas, 166
    generalizing ratios of similar shapes, 168
    in measurement, 166–176
    Pascal's triangle, 297, 298
    rational numbers and, 228
    skip-counting, 107–112, 166–168
Repeated addition, multiplication as, 78, 84–86
Repeated subtraction, division as, 78–79, 86–89
Research-based learning theories, 2
Reynolds, A., 144, 150, 157
Rhombus, lesson on, 59, 61–62, 66–67

Rigid motions
    in algebra, 68, 70
    in geometry, 24–25
Rigor, in Van Hiele theory, 37
Roat, E., 171
Roman numerals, 116–117
Romberg, T., 291
Rotational symmetry, 26
Rowling, M., 51
Rubrics, assessing problem solutions with, 247, 248–249
Rulers, 178–179

Sadako and the Thousand Paper Cranes (Coen & Himler), 117
Samples and sampling
    defined, 269
    making interpretations based on, 293
    populations versus, 263
    recognizing development through, 295–296
Sawada, D., 205, 221, 227, 235, 241
Scaffolding, 87, 89
Scatterplots, 279
Schauble, L., 181
Schoenfeld, A. H., 238
Schwartz, D. L., 244
Scieszka, J., 53
Secakuku, A. H., 170, 171
Senk, S., 37
Set model of multiplication, 215, 216
Shapes. *See* Plane shapes; Solid shapes
Sharing
    creating shared, rich experiences with proportions, 252–253
    division as fair, 79, 89
    fractions and, 205
    of plan for solving problem, 191, 192–193
    of strategies, 127, 128–129, 224–225
    of thinking in discourse strategies, 187–190
Sharp, J., 239
Silverstein, Shel, 234
Sketchy, 130
Skip-counting, 105–112
    calendar as context for, 108–109, 110
    concrete representations and, 109–111
    connecting to operations, 111–112
    fact families for integers and, 113
    in figurating numbers, 112–114
    in measurement process, 166–168
    number line and, 111
    patterns of, 107–112, 166–168
    in ratio tables, 228
Slesnick, T., 107
Slovic, P., 268
Social interaction, in teaching numbers, 98
Solid shapes, 18–20
    building, 32, 33
    measuring, 152–154
    net of, 32
Soloway, Elliot, 130
Sowder, J., 98
Spaces, counting, 153

Spaghetti and Meatballs for All! (Burns & Tilley), 177, 179
Spatial visualization, 27–29
Specific events, 265
Spinners, 268, 284, 307
Spreadsheets, 311
Squares
  defining, 42
  drawing, 29–32
Square tiles, 179–181
Standard units
  describing part of, 153–154
  nature of, 145–147, 148–150
Statistics
  generalizations in, 269
  "Looks Like, Sounds Like" table for, 292
  procedures in, 275–287
  relevant framework for, 291–293
  understanding, 262–271
Stenmark, J. K., 152
Stigler, J. W., 99, 130
Stratton, J. L., 174
Streefland, L., 221, 223–226, 241, 250, 255
Strom, D., 144, 157
Structure of events, 295
Student comments
  to analyze teaching, 314–316
  dealing with incorrect, 126
Student-generated data
  in data analysis, 291, 306
  importance of, 291, 306
  as teaching aid, 306
Student presentations
  assessment of presentations and, 191
  moving from data to presentations of data, 278
  presentation tools, 190
Subtraction
  algorithms for, 77, 83–84, 102–104, 106
  of fractions, 212–213
  learning, 104–105
  "Looks Like, Sounds Like" table for, 103
  nature of, 77
  problem solving with, 102–105
  strategies for, 102, 103, 104, 106
Summativeness, 148
Symbolic representations
  in algebra, 68
  in geometry, 46, 47
  nature of, 46
  numerals as, 76
  other types of representation and, 47
  rational numbers and, 222, 250–251
Symmetry
  in algebra, 68, 70
  examples and nonexamples of, 28
  finding in nature, 28
  in geometry, 25–27, 28
  nature of, 25–27
  in operations with integers, 119

Take-away approach, to subtraction, 77, 84, 106
Tangrams, 40–41, 48, 232

Teachers. *See also* Lesson plans; Professional development; Teaching principle (NCTM)
  in data analysis, 310–325
  in geometry and spatial thinking lessons, 56–73
  importance of knowing mathematics, 58–61, 66–67
  in measurement lessons, 184–197
  in number and operation lessons, 124–139
  role of, 3, 56–73, 124–139, 184–197, 238–259
Teaching aids. *See also* Manipulatives
  in data analysis, 306–307
  discrete versus continuous materials, 118–121, 231–232
  in geometry, 45–53
  in measurement, 177–181
  with rational numbers, 231–234
  student-generated data as, 306
  types of, 306–307
Teaching models. *See* Models of teaching
Teaching principle (NCTM)
  concept attainment, 124–125
  conservation and, 148
  context with fractions, 213–215
  creating picture graphs with physical objects, 281
  creating wonder in middle school, 194
  dealing with incorrect comments, 126
  demonstrations in middle school, 90
  development through likelihood, 294–295
  enriching learning of gifted students, 188
  homework selection, 246
  knowing math well enough to ask questions, 61
  lesson plan components, 9–12
  measuring devices and manipulatives, 177–179
  mental ideas versus physical models in, 20
  models of teaching, 10–11, 56, 184, 310–312
  organizing concepts for data analysis, 292–293
  partnered work, 184
  phases of learning and, 159–163
  problem solving, 99–107, 238–245
  procedures in data analysis, 279–281
  rational numbers and, 222–224
  reflection and, 66
  revisiting procedures, 218–219
  statement of, 5
  teaching aid use, 45–47, 118–121, 231–234, 306–307
  for teaching numbers, 94–98
  using sports to create interest, 316
  using student comments to analyzing teaching, 314–316
Technical symbols, rational numbers and, 222
Technology Connections
  communication tools, 130
  described, 5–6
  digital images, 244
  digital technologies as geometry discussion platforms, 57
  power of spreadsheet, 311
  presentation tools, 190

Technology principle (NCTM)
communication tools, 130
digital technologies as geometry discussion
platforms, 57
power of spreadsheet, 311
presentation tools, 190
statement of, 5
10 for Dinner (Bogart), 117
Teppo, A., 37
Theoretical probability, 265, 273, 295, 318–321
Theories, in learning process, 2–3
Thirteen Moons on Turtle's Back (Bruchac &
London), 177
Thompson, P., 118
Thompson, V., 152
Thornton, C. A., 293–294, 307
Tiered assignments, 186
Tiling, in measurement process, 151
Tilley, D., 177
Time management
creating shared, rich experiences with
proportions, 252–253
daily routines in, 131
defending viewpoints, 316–317
reflection time and, 66
student presentations and assessment of
presentations, 191
Tischler, R., 35, 54, 158
Tomlinson, C. A., 185, 191
Tompert, A., 53
Trail of Thread (Hubalek), 177
Transitivity, in measurement process, 156–157
Translation symmetry, 25
Trapezoids, generalizing area for, 143
Treffers, A., 82
Triangles
drawing, 32
examples and nonexamples of, 27
Pythagorean theorem, 181, 194–196
relating area of triangle to other shapes, 196
Trivizas, E., 53
Tversky, A., 268
Twain, Mark, 229
Two-color counters, 306

Usiskin, Z., 37

Van den Heuvel-Panhuizen, M., 217, 255
Van Haneghan, J. P., 244
Van Hiele, P., 35–43
Van Hiele theory, 35–43, 159–165
characteristics of, 37–42
to guide instruction, 63, 64–65
levels of, 35–37, 39, 46–47, 159
in measurement process, 159–165
phases of learning and, 159–163
in promoting development, 38–41
Variables
as functional, 68–69, 136
as generalizations, 136, 196
K-8 concept of, 69–70
as standing for unknown to be found, 136–137

Variance, 264
Venn diagrams, 261
nature of, 22–23
for quadrilaterals, 25
Visualization
concrete materials and, 46–47
issues in, 42–43
in measurement process, 158
spatial, 27–29
in Van Hiele theory, 36, 39, 42–43
Vocabulary, guiding student use of, 296
Vye, N. J., 244

Watanabe, T., 231
Welchmann-Tischler, R., 307, 308
Well, A. D., 274–275, 288, 291
Westley, J., 189
"What if" thinking, 311
Wheatley, Grayson H., 144, 150, 157
Wheeler, D., 137
Whitman, Walt, 229
Whole number interference, 212
Whole numbers, 74–141
algorithms for, 82–90
assessment and, 125–127
concept attainment and, 124–125
counting, 79–81
daily routines with, 131, 132
figurating numbers, 112–117
knowledge of, 212
levels of number ideas, 93
in measurement, 144–147
and number as mental relationship, 93–98
numbers as amounts, 76
number sense and, 81, 98
number words and, 93–94
numerals as symbols, 76
operations for, 77–79, 81, 82–90
order and, 77
principles of teaching number, 94–98
problem solving with, 99–107
skip-counting and, 107–112
teaching aids for, 118–121
Whole units, nature of, 207–212
Williams, S. M., 244
Williamson, J., 246
Wilss, L., 69, 136
Word processors, 130
Worthwhile tasks, 66
Wright, B., 171

Yakimanskaya, I. S., 46
Young, M. F., 244
Young Children Reinvent Arithmetic (Kamii), 92

Zech, L., 244
Zero point, 152–153